CAIRO
a practical guide

Deborah Cowley   Aleya Serour

CAIRO
a practical guide

Sixth Edition

Compiled and Edited by

Cassandra Vivian

The American University in Cairo Press

First Edition 1975
Second Edition 1977
Third Edition 1981
Fourth Edition 1984
Fifth Edition 1986

Sixth Edition © 1988 by
The American University in Cairo Press
113, Kasr el Aini
Cairo, Egypt

Desktop publishing by Sheira & Sheira, Management, Computer and Publishing Consultants

Dar el Kutub No. 2753/88
ISBN 977 424 190 8

Printed in Egypt at Arab World Printing House

CONTENTS

CONTENTS   vii

ACKNOWLEDGMENTS

We gratefully acknowledge the help of the following:

At The American University in Cairo: Ali El Arabi and the Support Services; Buildings & Grounds; Chief Engineer's Office; Clinic; Mail Office; Purchasing; Public Relations Office; Telephone Operators; Travel Office; and all Press Office personnel: Abd El Latif Aly; Atef El Hoteiby; Aleya Serour; Brigitte Shidrawi; Hala el Ganayni; Laila Ghali; Nabila Akl; Nadia Dessouki; Nadia Salah; R. Neil Hewison; Samir Bishay; Samira H. Ammar; Susanna Shankland; Tahany El Shammaa.

American Chamber of Commerce; American Cultural Center; Cairo Zoo; Commonwealth Graves Commission; Egyptian government offices; Foreign Press Association; International Language Institute; United Kingdom Embassy; United States of America Embassy; U.S Fish and Wildlife Service.

Abd El Rahman El Shafei; Adel Taher; Ahmed Hassanein; Ahmed Mohamed Riad; Alicia Sams; Anne A. Meyer; Ahmed Sami; Aziza Rashad Lotayef; Barbara Eysselinck; Deborah Wickering; Deborah Wilson; Ed Suvanto; Ghada El Kady; Gloria Karnouk; Harold K. Monson; Hassan El Geretly; Indji Ahmed Ali; Jamie Weissman; Jayme Spencer; Jeanne Sullivan; Kamar Abdou; Karam Metawe; Kathy Hansen; Laila El Hamamsy; Liliane Karnouk; Margot Hoerrner; Mark Kennedy; Mazen Ali Shaat; Michael Frease; Mohamed Ibrahim; Mohamed Salmawi; Mohamed Shebl; Morsi Saad El Din; Mohei El Din Abu Shadi; Naim Atef; Priscilla Blakemore; Rania El Sherif; Raouf Zaidan; Reda Mohamed Tewfik; Sabri Nashet; Samir Halim Makram; Sandra Gamal; Sherine El Mofty; Soha Abdel Kader; Sue Khalifa; Tim Sullivan; Virginia Stevens.

INTRODUCTION

Those of us who live in Cairo today are living in a city whose nooks and crannies are filled with more than a thousand years of history.

One hears wonderful stories of Cairo in the 1930s and 1950s when she was a chic, elegant, grand lady, and one reads even more intriguing tales of splendor from the khedival era, when what we call Modern Cairo was being created. Eulogized for centuries with such epithets as Mother of the World, this city, which was one of the major commercial centers of the medieval Arab world and once the capital of a huge empire, justly deserves such praise. She is, and always has been, an exciting place to live.

One wonders about the foreigners who lived in Cairo those many years ago: how did the medieval Venetian merchants find their way around such a city? Who gave them a guide to Cairo? What kind of visas did they need? Who told them how to find living space, what to expect from domestic help and where to buy the basic essentials? Was there a medieval equivalent to **Cairo: A Practical Guide**?

Such a guide would confirm that for all the change in Cairo, much remains the same. Today's city is not what it was a hundred, fifty, or even ten years ago. It is bursting at the seams with too many cars and too many people; but medieval Cairo also had housing shortages and crowded streets. Our Cairo has new suburbs, enormous building projects, diversified business establishments and a cultural explosion of restoration, innovation and creativity; but one could also be talking about Fatimid or Mamluk Cairo. Today the city of the caliphs, rich in history, patience and diversity, is merely beginning yet another of its many transformations.

The first edition of **Cairo: A Practical Guide** was published in 1975 when the Open Door Policy was in its infancy and the incredible transition that has marked Cairo in the past decade was just beginning to occur. This edition, like its predecessors, aims to keep the English-speaking community up to date on the where and how of living and working in Cairo; but it offers its readers Cairo of the 1980s, a megacity in perpetual motion.

There is an added bonus, a rich dividend, in the pages of this book. While making one's way through types of cheeses and varieties of coffee, buying a car and renting an apartment, visiting khedival palaces, the medieval city and the Cairo Zoo, something else emerges. One touches the people. One feels the rich culture of Cairo. Through learning how to cope, how to shop, how to run a home and fill leisure time, one grows and changes and is touched by this city, a city that has left its mark on the world.

Cassandra Vivian
Editor

READER'S GUIDE

Abbreviations

The following abbreviations occur throughout the text. If in an address a Cairo district is not given, the location is Central Cairo:

AG	Agouza	**S**	Sunday	**p**	piaster
DO	Dokki	**M**	Monday	**LE**	Egyptian pounds
GC	Garden City	**T**	Tuesday	**E**	Egyptian
GI	Giza	**W**	Wednesday	**F**	foreigner
HE	Heliopolis	**Th**	Thursday	**km**	kilometer
MA	Maadi	**F**	Friday	**ex**	extension
MN	Madinet Nasr	**Sa**	Saturday		
MO	Mohandiseen				
ZA	Zamalek				

All other abbreviations are defined in the text as they occur.

Telephone Numbers

The telephone system in Cairo has been undergoing major renovation for the past six years. All the telephone numbers in this book have been confirmed and were in operating order as of June 1988.

In Central Cairo some 74 and 75 numbers are in the process of being changed. This edition incorporates the changes up to June 1988; for any changes after that time, substitute **392** for 74 and **393** for 75.

When two telephone numbers are listed in the text with the same prefix or set of numbers, the prefix or numbers are not repeated in the second instance. Thus

      353-0000 and 353-9999 are listed as 353-0000/9999
and   353-0000 and 353-0009 are listed as 353-0000/9

When calling government offices, public sector companies, services, utilities, the police, etc, you can expect an Arabic speaker to answer.

Finally, note that the telephone system is still overloaded and telephoning can sometimes be a frustrating experience. Our suggestion is try, and try again.

Transliteration

Transliteration is always a problem when rendering Arabic names into English. No set system has been used throughout this book. The Vocabulary section transcribes words to help with pronunciation. For the names of companies and individuals, we have retained personal preferences, but the text is uniform in regard to street and public names.

The maps (and their index) follow the spelling conventions of the **Cairo A-Z**. If you cannot find the street name you are looking for in the index, try an alternative spelling; in particular, note that **Q** may be substituted for **K**, and that **Al-** may be prefixed to the name. Also note that squares are listed under **Midan**, and that Maadi roads designated by numbers appear in numerical order at the end of the index. See page 229 for the pronunciation of numbers in Arabic.

Help With the Next Edition

The next revision of **Cairo: A Practical Guide** will soon be underway. We consider our readers a valuable resource, and appreciate any help they can provide in updating or adding to the information in the book. Also, if you appear in the guide and there are changes or corrections to your entry, or if you are a new business and want us to consider including you in the next edition, let us know.

Every effort has been made to ensure the accuracy of the information presented in this guide at the time of going to press. However, readers should be aware that Cairo is a city of rapid and unpredictable changes, and in particular that prices are prone to inflation.

CAIRO
a practical guide

EGYPT

Official name: Arab Republic of Egypt (ARE)
Official religion: Islam
Official language: Arabic
Capital city: Cairo
Flag: three horizontal stripes, red, white, and black, with a gold eagle on the white stripe.
Anthem: Beladi, Beladi, Beladi
Population: 50.5 million (1986); 49% in urban areas; 3% growth rate per annum. Estimated population by 1990: 56.7 million; by 2000, 70 million. Population of Cairo: 12 million.
Area: 1,001,450 sq. km. (386,661 sq. mi.)
Climate: Summers (April to October) hot and dry in the desert, while humid in Cairo. Winters (December to February) mild, with cold desert nights, balmy days, desert fogs and occasional rains. Subject to spring winds from April through May called Khamaseen (meaning fifty) which blow hot air and sand out of the southwest and can be dangerous to persons traveling in the desert. Rainfall: 28mm (1.1 inches)/year in Cairo. Weather report telephone number: 862020
Temperature Conversion Table:

Centigrade	10	20	30	40
Fahrenheit	50	68	86	104

Principal cities and towns (by size): Cairo, Alexandria, Giza, Al Mahalla al Kubra, Tanta, Port Said, Mansoura, Assiut, Zagazig, Suez, Damanhour, Fayoum, Minya, Ismailia, Aswan, Beni Suef.

GOVERNMENT OF EGYPT

Officially, Egypt is a democratic, socialist republic with executive, legislative and judicial branches of government and a multi-party system.

Executive branch: President: Mohammed Hosni Mubarak, Commander-in-Chief of the Army, Leader of the National Defense Council, and Leader of the National Party. The president must be over 40, nominated by at least one third of the members of the People's Assembly, approved by at least two thirds, and elected by popular referendum. This occurs every 6 years (last held in 1987). The president appoints the vice-president, the ministers and the governors. At present (1988), Egypt does not have a vice-president.

Legislative branch: The **People's Assembly**, maglis ish-sha'b (Sharia Maglis al Shaab, GC 354-3130/0690), has 458 members with 5-year terms. Four hundred are elected on a party list system; 48 may be independent; and 10 are appointed by the President. Elections are held

3

according to a party list system, in which a party must receive at least 8% of the national vote in order to be represented. Also, one seat in each governorate is elected at large, and for these seats independent candidates may seek office. One half of the Assembly members must be workers and farmers. The People's Assembly is responsible for ratifying all laws and approving the national budget. It may be dissolved by referendum. The **Shura Council**, maglis ish-shuura (Sharia Maglis al Shaab, GC 354-3000/5000/3116), which oversees the media and the government, was inaugurated in 1980 to preserve the principles of the revolution. It is composed of 210 members with 6-year terms, of which 140 are elected and 70 are appointed by the president.

Major political parties

National Democratic Party (il-Hazb il-waTani il-dimuqraaTi), 113 Corniche al Nil 758535 772755 770285. The ruling party of Egypt, established by Anwar Sadat. Publishes **Mayo** newspaper.

New Wafd Party (il-wafd il-gidiid), 39 al Sheikh Ali Youssef, al Mounira 348-8903 355-4440/ 5233/5522. Considered the traditional party of Egypt; publishes **al Wafd** newspaper.

Socialist Labor Party (Hazb il-'amal il-ishtiraaki), 313 Port Said, Sayeda Zeinab 926761 928012 358-5816. The official opposition party in the present parliament; publishes **al Shaab** newspaper.

National Progressive Unionist Party (il-Hazb il-ahli il-taqaddumi), 1 Karim Al Dawla; or 23 Abdel Khalek Sarwat 759011/114 742306/408. Left-wing; publishes **al Ahali** newspaper.

Liberal Socialist Party (Hazb il-aHraar), 19 al Gumhuria 910422 340-9706 909045/744. Founded in 1976; advocates the open-door policy and private enterprise; publishes **al Ahrar** newspaper.

National Party (Hazb il-umma), 73 Helwan, Sayeda Zeinab 984793. An Islamic religious party.

Judicial branch: The Supreme Judicial Council which oversees all courts is under the chairmanship of the President. The highest court is the Supreme Constitutional Court. The two main judicial branches are the civil and the criminal courts; there are also a military court and courts of public security, ethics, and personal status. Court sessions are usually open to the public.

Military: 460,000 personnel. 68.5% army, 7.2% navy, 24.3% air force (1984). (The **Border Patrol**, a special branch of the military, is composed primarily of Nubians with expert desert survival, tracking, and camel-riding skills. Responsible for patrolling all borders, escorting border forces and tracking smugglers, the border patrol is dependent on skills disappearing in the modern world and the numbers of qualified men are diminishing.)

Police: The General Security Department of the Ministry of the Interior is responsible for police services and criminal investigation. **Tourist Police**, identified by a green armband, are on duty at the major tourist sites and hotels and usually know at least 2 languages. **Head Office:** 5 Adli 912644. **Airport Office:** Cairo Airport 965239. **Khan al Khalili:** Midan al Husein 904827. **Main Railroad Station:** Midan Ramsis 753555. **Pyramids:** Pyramids Road near Mena House Hotel 850259. **Traffic Police** wear black and white in winter and white in summer and can be found on most major street corners directing traffic, helping in case of an accident, and issuing tickets for traffic or parking violations. The **Central Security** policemen wear all black and are special security forces who guard embassies, hotels, and public buildings. **Water Police** control the Nile and the High Dam Lake; they are responsible for traffic flow and safety. The Nile headquarters is on the Corniche al Nil, MA 350-3882/3844/3766. **Vice Squad** (Boliis al Adaab) are primarily responsible for controlling prostitution. They have the right to enter a home at any time and investigate the occupants. Usually they do not disturb foreigners. **Municipal Police** handle all crimes. They wear black and white in winter and white in summer.

Police stations are found in all districts. Stations are open 24 hours a day, and fully staffed from 10am to 2pm and again from 8pm to 10pm. Although many policemen speak English, you may not find an English speaker via the telephone. **Abdin** al Gumhuria at Abdel Aziz, behind Cairo firefighting department, Midan Ataba 391-4657/6604/9847; **Agouza** 5 Nawal 715588 712129 341-3102 710102; **Bab al Shaaria** al Geish, Abbassia, 936133 937748 920325; **Bulak** Wekalet al Karnoub 751933 741426 770539; **Darb al Ahmar** Midan al Helmia 911247; **Dokki** Midan al Galaa, in front of Cairo Sheraton, Giza 348-5501; **Ezbekia** al Galaa 740356; **Gamalia** Midan Beit al Qadi 905965; **Garden City** Abdel Rahman Fahmy 354-0686; **Giza** al Bahr al Aazam 723428; **al Elaam** Abu al Moaty, behind Balloon Theatre 346-6850; **Heliopolis** al Roda, Midan al Gama 627381 432305; **Kasr al Nil** 11 Aisha al Taymuria GC 766229; **Maadi** 70 Road 13 350-3958/2584; **Mohandiseen** Shehab 347-9216; **Muski** 918116; **Madinet Nasr** al Nasr 601999/600522; **Nuzha** Midan Saint Fatima HE 244-5981; **Old Cairo** Midan al Mamaleek, Roda Island 841328; **Pyramids** Pyramids Road (Sharia Al Ahram) 853955; **Zamalek** 2 Hasan Sabri 340-1719.

TRAVEL AND TRANSPORTATION

PASSPORTS, VISAS AND PERMITS

Passports
You must have one of the following to enter Egypt: a passport valid six months beyond your stay in Egypt; a Laissez-Passer issued by the United Nations to Palestinians, refugees and stateless persons; or a seaman book (excluding Taiwan). **Exclusions** include seaman books issued by Taiwan, or not valid for Egypt; nationals of South Africa (excluding students attending Egyptian Universities); and nationals of Libya, unless married to an Egyptian.

Passport renewal
Americans may renew their passports at the American Consulate, 4 Latin America, GC. You will need your old passport or other proof of identity and two photos. Costs are $20 or LE40 for under 18 years of age and $35 or LE70 for adults. Hours 8-3.   British nationals may renew their passports at the British Embassy, 7 Ahmed Ragheb GC, 340-0850. Other foreign nationals should consult their embassies. **Lost or stolen passports** should be reported to the nearest police station as soon as possible. You will receive a slip of paper indicating the police report file number. Take this and two photographs with any personal identification to your consulate to apply for a new passport, then, take your new passport, along with the police report, to room 90 of the Mogamaa (see visas and permits below). Verification of your entry will be noted in your passport. This is necessary for exit formalities. You will need the appropriate visa and residence permits for your new passport.

Passport photographs: BKY Photo Lab & Studio 68 Road 9 MA 351-2919 24hr service; **Commercial Photographers Inc (CPI)** 34 Yehia Ibrahim ZA 340-6504, Studio: 23B Ismail Mohammed ZA 340-1604; **Egypt 2000 Co.** 6 Alfi 743914 756463 instant b/w and color in 48hrs; **Instant Passport Photo Kiosk** Midan Sphinx, next to Cinema Sphinx, MO; **Kodak** 3 Harun al Rashid 290-8265 HE, and Road 9 MA; **Nile Hilton Photo** Corniche al Nil 750666 740777; **Nour al Tasweer** 22 Talaat Harb instant b/w; **Tudor** 57 Road 9 MA, instant service via polaroid.

Visas and Permits
All official documents needed by foreigners are available at the **Mogamaa**, Government Office Building, Midan Tahrir. across from The American University in Cairo. Hours 8-1, closed Fridays.

Room Numbers 1-11 for **non- Arab** countries; 12-13 for **re-entry visa** (tourist); 16-21   **Arab** Countries; 22-27 for **tourist residence** visa (no work permit); 28-29 for **three years residence** when married to Egyptian; 30-37 for **Palestinians;** 38 for **special residence** (foreign born); 39-40 **cashier** (buy forms and stamps); 41-42 for **five-year residence** .

Visas

To enter Egypt, **visas** are required by all persons except the following: nationals of Egypt; citizens of Arab countries maintaining diplomatic relations with Egypt; holders of diplomatic passports accredited to Egypt; holders of a re-entry permit; employees of the UNO; and transits. A **single entry visa** is good for one entry into the country and is valid for one month. A **multiple entry visa** is issued to persons expecting to exit and re-enter Egypt within a short period of time. These visas are obtained from Egyptian consulates abroad. Take or mail the following documents: a valid passport, one passport photo and a fee of $12 or equivalent. Personal application at a consulate will entail a short wait. Applications by mail may take up to two weeks. Be sure to send a self-addressed stamped envelope. You may obtain an **emergency tourist visa** valid for one month at **Cairo International Airport,** the **Port of Alexandria** and all other air and sea arrival ports. Visas are not issued at land crossings. It is no longer necessary to exchange foreign currency at the port to receive an emergency tourist visa. To obtain this type of visa you must go to the passports area at the port of arrival. You will need the arrival card which is available on your plane or boat and at the arrival terminals. The visa fee is LE17.

Some Egyptian Consulates: Canada 3754 Cote de Nieges, Montreal; 454 Laurier Avenue M.E. Ottawa. **France** 56 Avenue d'Iena, Paris; **Germany** Taunusstrasse 35, Frankfurt; **Great Britain** 19 Kensington Place Gardens, London W8: **Greece:** 3 Vassilissis Sophias Avenue, Athens; **Italy** 19 Via Bissolati, Rome; **Spain:** Alcala 21, Madrid 14; **Switzerland:** 11 Rue de Chantepoulet, Geneva; **United States** 2310 Decatur Place, N.W. Washington, D.C. 20008; 1110 Second Avenue, New York, NY 10022; 3001 Pacific Avenue, San Francisco, CA 94115; 505 N. Lakeshore Dr., 4902, Chicago, IL 60611; 2000 West Loop So., Houston, TX 77027.

Student visas are issued to persons studying at an Egyptian University. Students must enter the country on a tourist visa, as student visas will not be issued until the student has proof of registration at a university. Some universities help students obtain their visas, other do not. To obtain a student visa fill out a student visa application, available at the Mogamaa (rooms 1-11 for non-Arabs; rooms 16-21 for Arabs; rooms 30-37 for Palestinians). The following documents are required: a passport, two passport photos, a statement in Arabic from the university/school confirming student status, and a fee of LE8-12. The visa is valid for two months, then renewable for the current school year at an additional cost of LE30. You must apply for renewal at least ten days before the first visa expires.

Business visas are required for all persons planning to do business in Egypt. In the United States, information on Business visas can be obtained from the **Egyptian Commercial Office** at 2715 Connecticut Avenue, N.W. Washington, D.C. Companies usually handle visa requirements for employees. See the Business section for more information.

Tourist residence visa A foreigner ineligible to work in Egypt, but anticipating an extended stay, may apply for a tourist residence visa. This is issued against the exchange of $180 or equivalent in foreign currency each month. Up to 6 months may be paid at a time, provided the appropriate amount of foreign currency is exchanged. Tourist residence visas are obtained at the Mogamaa, rooms 28-29.

Re-entry visas are required only if persons holding a tourist visa plan to exit and re-enter Egypt during the time their visa is valid. Foreigners working in Cairo on a non-tourist visa are not required to get a re-entry visa as long as they intend to return to Egypt within six months.

Visa extension There is a 15 day grace period for renewal of all expired visas. A fine of LE56.50 is imposed for non-compliance. A letter of apology from your embassy within two months of the official expiration date can exempt you from paying this fine. To obtain a visa extension go to the Passport Department of the Mogamaa, first floor, Room 16. You will need a valid passport, one passport photo, and residence forms purchased from the cashier at the Mogamaa, rooms 39-40 (LE7).

Work permits
In order to work in Egypt foreigners must have a work permit issued to their place of business by the Ministry of Manpower. A work permit cannot be issued unless the company is eligible, under Egyptian law, to employ foreign staff. Companies usually handle this matter. See the Business section for more information.

Residence permits
A **special residence permit** valid for ten years is issued to foreigners born in Egypt before 1952 or in residence since 1932. An **ordinary residence permit** valid for five years is issued to foreigners residing in Egypt since 1937. A **three year residence** visa is issued to all foreigners married to Egyptians. A **temporary residence permit** is issued for all foreigners working in Egypt, their spouses and family members. It is valid for one year. Usually companies handle this matter. You will need a letter of application from your company stating that you work for them, a copy of your work permit, your passport, 2 photos, and family members' passports and photos. Cost is about LE42 per passport.

Continuous residence stamp
Persons who can verify residence of 5 consecutive years may apply for a continuous residence stamp for their passport. This stamp allows the holder to pay hotel bills and airline, train, and boat tickets in Egyptian pounds. Application is made at the Mogamaa, rooms 41-42. The necessary documents are a passport, proof of 5 years continuous residence, and LE2.50-3 (price of forms and fiscal stamps).

The **International Student Identity Card** is acknowledged in Egypt. Applications can be made in the US to the Council on International Educational Exchange (C.I.E.E.) 205 East 42nd Street, New York, NY 10017, (212) 661-1450. C.I.E.E. also has offices in San Francisco, Los Angeles, Berkeley, San Diego, Seattle, and Boston. In England, students with school or university identification cards may try World Student Travel off Tottenham Court Road, or Student Travel Centre, Euston Road, both in London. All cards expire on December 31 of each year. In Egypt, you may obtain a card at Cairo University Faculty of Engineering Office of Student Exchange IAESTE; or from Cairo University Faculty of Medicine, Manial. You will need one passport photo, identification (passport), and proof of current student status. Fee is LE6 (subject to LE/ $ rate). Validity is one year.

TRAVEL TO EGYPT

Arrival

Air
There are now 4 terminals at **Cairo International Airport. Terminal 1 (old airport)** has three halls: **One** for Egypt Air international flights: **Two** for Egypt Air flights to Arab countries; **Three** for Egypt Air domestic flights. **Terminal 2 (new airport)** has two halls, both for international airline flights. **Terminal 3** is for Saudia airline. **Terminal 4** is the international cargo terminal. For English language information on all airline offices and other airport authorities call 291-4255/ 2266.

Lost luggage is claimed through the airline office at the airport. If closed, contact the customs office and, as soon as you get to your destination, the airline.

Ground transportation from the airport includes **Misr Limousine,** dark blue Mercedes taxis, 259-9813/9814, and regular taxi service, both available at curbside. Limousine **bus** service to downtown is available in the parking lot of Terminal 1, hall 1. (Service will soon start at Terminal 2.) Tickets are available from a brown kiosk in the parking lot with a sign saying **Misr Travel Airport Bus Service.** Open 24hr and leaving when the bus is full, the run includes Midan Tahrir, Mohandessin and Sharia Ahram. For English language information call 291-4255. Regular **city buses** leaving from Terminal 1 (near Hall 1) include the 400 to Tahrir and the 410 to Ataba; **minibus** line 27 also goes to Tahrir.

Sea/Nile
Private vehicles may enter Egypt via all borders except the Libyan and Israeli borders. Entry from the Mediterranean is via Alexandria or Port Said. Entry from the Red Sea is via Nuweiba and Suez. Entry from the Sudan is via a twice-weekly steamer from Wadi Halfa. For detailed entry information from the Sudan see the end of this chapter.

Alexandria Port Authority 66 Hurria, Alexandria 483-1640; **Port Said Port Authority** Cabin 24, Tarh Maamouret al Bahr, Port Said 754072; **Suez Port Authority** al Ershad Building, Ismailia 748350; in Cairo: 6 Lazoghli GC 354-0746/9; **Red Sea Port Authority** Suez and Port Tawfik 765121 763536; **General Authority for the Development of the High Dam Lake and Aswan Dam** PO High Dam Aswan 322810 323000.

Shipping lines
Adriatic Lines Castro and Company, 12 Talaat Harb 743213/144 (passengers and shipping); **DFDS Seaway,** 14 Talaat Harb 740864/955; **The Egyptian Navigation Company** 26 Sherif 393-8278; 1 al Hurria, Alexandria 472-0824; **Favia Shipping Lines** 18 Adli 393-8983; **Federal Arab Maritime** 27 Gezira al Wosta ZA 341-5823 340-6351; **The International Agency for Tourism, Navigation and Trading Services** 13 Midan Tahrir 762892 779452; **International Transport & Maritime Service Co.** 26A Asma Fahmi, Kulliet al Banat, HE 661783; **Misr Edco Shipping Company** Menatours 14 Talaat Harb 776951; **North African Tourist Shipping** 171 Mohamed Farid 391-3081/4682, or al Takkadom, Madinet Nasr 608417 (only from Port Said to Cyprus and Haifa).

All arrivals

Health regulations
The only immunization requirements for Egypt are **Yellow Fever** and **Cholera.** Even these requirements are limited to persons who have passed through (within the past six days), or are

arriving from, areas known to be infected. In these instances persons who do not have a current inoculation record are subject to a 36 hour quarantine and immunization at the port of entry. The **International Certificate of Vaccination, WHO card,** issued by the World Health Organization is the only recognized immunization record. It is available from authorized doctors in all countries. In Egypt, WHO cards are available from the World Health Organization 341-2156. Immunization shots are available from: the **British Community Association Medical Service** at the Anglo American Hospital, Zohria ZA 341-8630 from 9-12 daily and 9-11 on Friday, Saturday and Sunday. If you are not a member of this medical scheme there will be a consultation fee of LE40 in addition to the inoculation fee; **Public Health Unit** Midan al Taawon at crossroads of Road 12 and Road 71 beside Mohamed Farid School MA 350-3381, 9-1 and 4-6 except Friday; **Public Health Unit,** Continental Savoy Hotel, Midan Opera 10-1 and 5-7. In all instances you will need your passport, WHO card, and stamps (damgha). These stamps are in small denominations and available from any post office (it is wise when dealing with any official business in Egypt to purchase a large quantity). These Units use disposable syringes.

Customs The last procedure at the ports is to go through customs. You may bring into Egypt 200 cigarettes, 25 cigars or 200gr of tobacco, one liter of alcohol, and personal possessions. There are **duty free shops,** among the most inexpensive in the world, upon arrival at all passenger terminals at Cairo International Airport. Payment must be in hard currency or VISA/ American Express Cards (with some restrictions). Items are subject to Egyptian customs. Customs officials check carefully for any electronic equipment including videos, tape recorders, etc. Upon entering Egypt, visitors may have their valuable equipment endorsed on their passports rather than pay the duty. The endorsement ensures the items will be exported when the individual leaves the country. If the items are lost the owner can expect to pay full customs duty. Residents do not have this privilege and may be taxed at a rate of 10%-110% on dutiable goods.

Registration
The Ministry of Interior requires all non-Egyptians to **register** within seven days of arrival. Each time a non-Egyptian leaves Egypt this registration is automatically canceled and must be renewed on returning. Failure to register upon your return to Egypt may subject you to severe penalties. When traveling in Egypt, you must register within 48 hours at each temporary residence. If you are staying in a hotel, the management will take care of this. Also, you must register within 24 hours of a change of address. Registration is a simple matter and usually takes a few minutes. You will need your passport. Go to your neighborhood police station or the Mogamaa Government Building, Midan Tahrir, second floor, 8-1 or 5-8. All foreign nationals should also register at their embassy.

Shipping
To Egypt
Contact any international airline or shipping line for information. Plan carefully and leave heirlooms and non-essentials home. Jewelry, furs, silverware or fragile accessories will not be covered by insurance. Use sturdy trunks and suitcases. Lock all containers. Use banding for extra protection. An itemized list of the contents of each container is required for insurance and for passage through point of departure and Egyptian customs. The list should be in two parts:

one marked **durable goods** and another marked **consumable.** Lists should include quantity, description and current value of each item. List books, tapes, and records individually (consumables). If there is more than one container in the shipment, on each label mark "Piece No.___of___" (the former space being for the number of the specific piece and the latter space being the total number of pieces in the shipment; number the pieces consecutively). Identify all electric and electronic appliances by brand and model number. Make six copies of the inventory to be used by the various officials during transit. Take the shipment to an airline cargo office. On the airway bill, address the shipment to yourself, c/o your company. Insure the shipment on the airway bill for its full value. Dispatch the shipment at a time that will ensure its arrival in Cairo after you arrive to avoid storage charges in Customs. Keep a copy of the airway bill and know the date and flight that your shipment is scheduled to arrive in Cairo. Without your airway bill you will not be able to trace your shipment if it is lost.

Pets You must think seriously before deciding to ship your animals to Egypt. Transferring a pet to Cairo involves considerably more than travel procedures and expenses. Boarding facilities in Cairo are extremely limited, and any animal tends to be an obstacle to travel. Pet foods are limited and expensive. Pets cannot be allowed to run loose. Animal diseases, especially rabies, are prevalent. However, airlines and veterinarians will have information about carrying cases, costs of shipping, preparing the animal for a transatlantic flight, inoculations and travel documents. Carry an official record of the pet's inoculations and a veterinarian's statement, preferably dated within a few weeks of departure, that the animal is in good health. Airlines allow only one small animal to travel in the passenger cabin at a time, and that privilege must be reserved in advance along with the owner's reservation. It is dangerous to tranquilize an animal. Many airlines will refuse to ship an animal that has been given any sort of sedative. If the pet arrives at a different time than the owner, the pet could suffer the consequences since the ports of Egypt have minimal facilities for animal care. When transporting animals from Egypt to another destination arrangements must be made with the airline prior to departure. Payment is made at the airport at the time of departure. Payment may be made by credit card or in Egyptian pounds, with proof of exchange. Five year residents with a stamp in their passport do not need the bank receipt.

Air freight cargo will be delivered to Terminal 4 at the airport. You cannot expect delivery at the same time the airplane arrives. **Sea freight** may be collected from the ports of Alexandria, Suez or Port Said. Allow at least one month from the US and two weeks from Europe. Customs clearance may take several days.

Receiving your shipment Be prepared to take all day and more. It is advisable to contact a Customs Clearing Agency (see below). You will receive a delivery order from the airline/ship concerned and must take it and a bill of shipment (received when articles were taken to a shipping agency at point of departure) to the Customs area. The customs area at Cairo International Airport is at Terminal 4.

Permission to enter the airport customs area is obtained at the cargo village at Terminal 4. Upon entering, you will receive a number and must wait until you are called. The shipment will be assigned two customs officers, one to identify claimed objects and a second to reestimate price value. Both will speak English. Forms must be filled and registered at the same terminal where the shipment is located. Personal receipts of prices are not helpful as Customs have their own pricing system depending on size and items. The officer will decide on duty to be paid (maybe up to 110% of the value). Be prepared for an item by item inspection. Defend your costs.

You must make arrangements to move the shipment from the airport. Medium sized trucks are available just outside the Customs gate. You can bargain for fares but do not expect to pay less than LE20 per trip. Be prepared to tip workers for locating, moving and loading your shipment. There are no refreshments in the Customs area so bring your own, especially water. Usually companies handle shipping and customs clearance for their employees.

Companies obtain permission for **temporary admission** of employee's belongings by issuing a letter of guarantee to the Egyptian Customs Authority covering the total value of the employee's shipment. This letter contains assurance that the employee will re-export all property upon termination of his/her contract in Egypt; however upon entry the shipment must still undergo the customs inspection described above.

From Egypt
The individual's airline ticket, passport, and personal effects forms received at entry are required for clearance from customs. Foreigners with at least 12 months residency in Egypt are entitled to take out of the country LE200 worth of Egyptian goods. If the value of your shipment exceeds this amount an export license or bank exchange receipts for the total value of the merchandise are required.

When **buying crafts and artifacts** in Egypt, it should be remembered that an individual is permitted to export only a limited amount of these goods. Some of the more valuable crafts can only be exported upon proof that they were purchased with Egyptian pounds bought at the official exchange rate from an Egyptian bank. Some goods such as gold and precious jewelry; antiques, including cars older than 10 years; carpets (mostly Persian and not local kilims); and paintings of great painters, local and foreign, may not be exported under any circumstances because they are regarded as national treasures. Books purchased in Egypt are also subject to export restrictions because they represent an outlay of hard currency by the Egyptian book dealer or publisher. The Egyptian Antiquities Department and any clearing agent will be able to inform you of the status of precious items or have an item verified. Items that have not been declared upon entry into the country require an export license.

Export licenses are obtained from the **Ministry of Economy and Foreign Trade** 8 Adli 919661/278. You will need your work permit and a photocopy of same, certificates from the Tax Department that you do not have outstanding tax payments, a letter from your employer/company certified by your embassy stating the date and duration of work in the country, proof of salary and tax status, list of items to be exported, and passport number. If a car is to be shipped along with other personal items the following papers are also required: original and photocopy of purchase contract of the car, original and photocopy of car permit, and a letter from the Traffic Department stating there are no traffic violations on the car.

Clearing agents: A. Gadalla 36 Sherif 747411; **Alpha Trade Center** 2 al Zafaraan GI 861988; **Badr Express** 226 Ahram GI 863954; **Expo Services International** 15 al Basra MO 349-0065; **Express International Company** 60 Tahrir DO 705378; **Favia International Transport** 18 Adli 772612; **Global Transportation Services Group** 44 Mohamed Mazhar ZA 340-6064; **Hamsa Transport Co** 8 Talaat Harb 759918; **International Agency Group** 8 Abdel Rahman Fahmi GC 355-3010, all over the world, packing, clearing, forwarding, door to door, import/export; **Quick Cargo** 5 Tehran DO 706932; **Sedra Services & Trading Co** 140 Sudan MO 707179.

TRAVEL IN CAIRO

By Train

Underground

Cairo has the first underground railway in Africa and the Arab world. The first phase of the first line, from Helwan in the south of Cairo to Ramsis, a distance of 29 kilometers, was completed and opened to the public in October 1987. The second phase of this line will soon extend a further 14 kilometers from Ramsis to al Marg in the north of Cairo. Two other lines are planned for the future: Shubra al Kheima to Bulaq al Dakrur (via Ramsis, Ataba, and Tahrir); Imbaba to Darrasa (via Zamalek, Ataba, and al Azhar).

Passengers have been using the Helwan-Ramsis phase since 1987. A big red **M** for Metro marks the entrance of the underground stations. Tickets are purchased at the ticket booth in each station. Price ranges from 25p-50p depending on the distance. Not holding a ticket in the train may result in a LE2.50 fine. Trains run every few minutes in either direction from 5:30am-

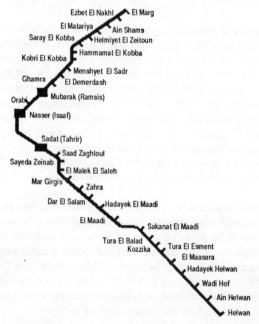

1am. Peak hours are 7-10 and 2-4. The system is clean, easy to use, and fast: Ramsis to Tahrir, 5 minutes; Tahrir to Maadi, 20 minutes. Yearly, quarterly, monthly, or weekly passes issued by the Egyptian Metro Authority are available at main stations. These passes are available in two forms, **1/2 distance** and **full distance**. The former allows passage over a limited area of the line. The latter permits travel all over the line. There are discount rates for public sector workers and students.

Fares (quarterly)	1/2 distance	full distance
regular fare	25.70	36.00
public sector	7.50	15.70 (15.15 to renew)
students	5.05	8.10

Heliopolis Metro

The Heliopolis tram system is also, confusingly, known as the Metro. Three lines run, on the same track, from Midan Abd al Monim Riad (behind the Egyptian Museum) via Ramsis to Roxi, at which point they diverge to serve different parts of Heliopolis: the **Abd al Aziz Fahmi** line (green direction board) runs via Merryland, Mahkama, and the Heliopolis Hospital to the Shams Club; the **Nuzha** line (red direction board) runs via the Heliopolis Sporting Club, Salah al Din,

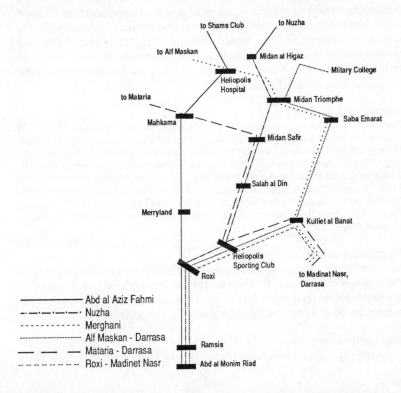

and Midan al Higaz to Nuzha; the **Merghani** line (yellow direction board) runs via Sharia al Merghani, Saba Emarat, and Midan Triomphe to the Military College on the airport road.

Three other lines, not color-coded and therefore only distinguishable by their Arabic direction boards, run as follows: from **Roxi** to **Madinet Nasr** via Sharia al Merghani and Kulliet al Banat; from **Alf Maskan** to **Darrasa** (junction of Azhar and Salah Salem) via Midan Triomphe, Kulliet al Banat, and Madinet Nasr; and from **Mataria** to **Darrasa** via Mahkama, Midan Safir, Kulliet al Banat, and Madinat Nasr.

The Heliopolis Metro is maintained by the Heliopolis Company for Housing 28 Ibrahim al Lakkani HE.

By Bus

Egypt has one of the cheapest public bus transportation systems in the world. In Cairo red-and-white and blue-and-white large buses as well as orange-and-white minibuses move through the city on regular routes. Major public bus stations are in Midan Tahrir, in front of the Mogamaa (minibuses) and in front of the Egyptian Museum (regular buses); in Midan Ramsis; in Midan Ataba; in Midan Roxi in Heliopolis; and behind the Maadi Hotel in Maadi. Rush hours 7-10 and 2-4.

Public bus routes

Bus stops for the large red and white or blue and white buses are designated by prefabricated metal sheds. Buses usually stop briefly, if at all, and one must move quickly to get aboard. You will often find people catching these buses on the run or clinging to the side of the door. They are often overcrowded and uncomfortable. Fares are 10p a journey, or LE6 for a one month pass and LE16 for three months. Invalids and war veterans ride for free. Numbers appear in Arabic on the front, side and back of all buses.

Some major bus routes:

From Tahrir: 8 and 900 Pyramids, Mena House; 16 Midan Dokki, Agouza; 50/ Dimishq, Heliopolis; 99 Midan Sudan, Midan Libnan; 160 Sayeda Zeinab, Basateen; 167 Shehab, Midan Libnan; 170 Manial, Mamalik; 300 Kobba, Ain Shams; 400 Roxi, Airport (a 24hr bus service on the hour); 420 Kubba Palace, Airport; 401 Mukkattam; 174 Sayeda Zeinab, Citadel; 600 Zamalek, Madinet Nasr. **From the Pyramids:** 3 Abu al Hol, Talebia, Midan Giza; 8 Pyramids, Kasr al Aini, Tahrir. **From Zamalek:** 13 Zamalek, Gezira, Falaki; 13/ Zamalek, Corniche, Falaki. **From Heliopolis:** 50 Dimishk, Ataba; 95/ Ramsis, Manial, Mamalik; 335 Roxi, Oruba, Airport; 67 Madinet Nasr, Roxi, Masalla. **From Mohandiseen:** 99/ Midan Libnan, Sudan, Ataba. **From Maadi:** 704 Khan al Khalili, Maadi; 901 Pyramids, Maadi; 405 Maadi Gedida, Basateen, Citadel.

Minibuses

Minibuses (orange and white) connect most areas of the city. There is a major station in Midan Tahrir (in front of the Mogamaa). Unlike the red and white city buses, the minibuses are comfortable and are never crowded, as standing is not allowed. They also come to a full halt at bus stops. Fares are flat rate, and range from 25-50p depending on the route.

Some minibus routes:

From Tahrir: 24 Ramsis, Abbassia, Roxi; 27 Ramsis, Abbassia, Airport; 35 Ramsis, Nuzha; 82 Malik al

Saleh, Pyramids. **From Giza: 26** Tahrir, Ramsis, Abbassia, Roxi. **From Heliopolis: 20** Shams Club, Roxi, Ataba; **25** Roxi, Ataba; **34** Madinet Nasr, Abbassia, Ataba. **From Maadi: 52** Saqr Qureish (New Maadi), Maadi, Tahrir. **From Mohandiseen: 72** Midan Libnan, Zamalek, Ramsis. **From Zamalek: 48** 26th July, Ataba.

River buses
These boats, part of the public transport system, make frequent runs between Maspero Station on the Corniche opposite the Radio and Television Building (north of the Ramsis Hilton), south to Old Cairo with stops at the mosque near Swiss Air Restaurant, Manial, Roda, and Giza. Boats also leave from Maspero Station
north to the Nile barrages 7-5 daily.

Service taxis
Usually vans (called microbuses) or seven-seater Peugeots, these are an excellent and inexpensive alternative to buses and taxis. They follow set runs to destinations throughout the city. They can be flagged down, just like taxis. The fare is 25-50p depending on destination.

Some service taxi routes: From Tahrir near Omar Makram Mosque: Salah Salem, Roxi, Heliopolis via Nuzha metro line; Salah Salem, Roxi, Heliopolis via Abd al Aziz Fahmi metro line; Midan Giza, Pyramid Road. **From Heliopolis at Midan Ismailia or Roxi:** Salah Salem, Bab al Louk, Tahrir; Salah Salem, Opera, Sherif, Tahrir. **From Maadi under the overpass:** to all parts of the city. **From Mohandiseen at Midan Libnan:** to all parts of the city. **From Ataba:** via Zamalek to Imbaba. **From Ramsis:** Midan Giza, Pyramid Road.

By Taxi
Taxis are usually black and white Fiats or Peugeot station wagons. All taxis have an insignia and vehicle number on the driver's door and an orange license plate. Many drivers do not speak English, so if you know no Arabic get your directions written in Arabic in advance. Due to the shortage of taxis in the city people often share taxis, so you can stop a taxi already carrying passengers. To catch a taxi, stand out in the road as far as is safe, put out your hand, and shout out your destination. Check with a local person as to roughly how much to pay for a given journey. The meter should register the fare starting from 25p. Some taxi drivers do not turn on the meter, but you have the right to ask for it to be turned on.

Some taxi fares
Zamalek to Agouza 75p-LE1.00; **Dokki to Midan Tahrir** LE1.00; **Downtown to Khan al Khalili** LE1.00; **Downtown to Heliopolis** LE2.00-3.00; **Downtown to the Pyramids** LE4.00-5.00; **Downtown to the airport** LE6.00-10.00; **Downtown to Maadi** LE3.00-5.00.

Taxi stands
Dokki 710018; **Finney** 710019; **Maadi** 90 Rd 9, 350-1118; **Tahrir** 765259; **Sabaa Emarat** 676873.

Limousines
Efficent limousine service is available on a destination, hourly or daily basis. **Bita Limousine Service** Gezira Sheraton 341-1333/1555, Marriott Hotel 340-8888; **Budget Limousine Service** Semiramis Intercontinental Hotel 355-7171 x8991; **Limousine Misr (24hr)** 7 Aziz Bil-Lah, Zeitoun, 259-9813/14; **Egyptrav (24hr)** Nile Hilton 755029 766548 393-2644.

By Car

The biggest problem in car travel in the city is parking. There are automated multi-storey car parks at Midan Ataba; Midan Opera; off Gumhuria near Alfi; and behind the Ramsis Hilton. Street parking is bumper to bumper. It is customary to leave the hand brake off and the wheels aligned with the curb so parking attendants can push the cars to make parking spaces. These attendants must be tipped approximately 25p a day.

TRAVEL WITHIN EGYPT

Tourist Information is available from any travel agency and the following government agencies: Ministry of Tourism Information 110 Kasr al Aini, 354-6295 355-2600; Tourist Information Offices: Main Office 5 Adli 913454; Pyramids Office, Pyramid Road, 950259; Cairo Airport, Main Terminal, 667475; Emergency phone 126. Tourist police are available at all major tourist sites and usually speak several languages.

By Air

Egypt is served by the government owned EgyptAir and Air Sinai airlines and the newly inaugurated private sector Zas Passenger Service. EgyptAir Offices: 6 Adli 390-2444; 9 Talaat Harb 392-2835 393-2836; Nile Hilton 759806/703; Cairo Sheraton 348-8600; 22 Ibrahim al Lakkani HE 664305; Abbassia 830888. EgyptAir offices exist in all major tourist areas. EgyptAir flies to Alexandria, Luxor, Aswan, Abu Simbel and Hurghada. Air Sinai Offices: Kasr al Nil 750600; Nile Hilton 760948. Air Sinai flies regularly to Hurghada, Saint Catherine's, Sharm al Sheikh and al Tor. Zas Passenger Service Office: Novotel Cairo International Airport Road 291-8032. Zas flies daily except Thursday to Luxor, Aswan, Hurghada and St. Catherine's. It also offers domestic and international charters. Aircraft charter is also available from Nile Delta Air Service 1 Midan Talaat Harb 746197.

Tickets for all domestic flights are paid in Egyptian pounds, but there are two rates: Egyptians and foreign residents with a 5-year residence certificate pay approximately half the tourist fare. With Zas you can get a reduction with a work permit and/or a residence visa. Tickets must be reconfirmed for return to Cairo.

By Boat

There are over 75 excursion boats currently in service on the Nile. Any travel agent will be able to tell you about the many Nile cruises. For overnight felucca travel from Luxor to Aswan arrangements must be made in either city via local boatmen.

By Train

The Egyptian State Railway, founded in 1851, maintains over 5,000 km of rail, and offers inexpensive, comfortable travel throughout the Nile Valley and Delta. Holders of International Student Identity Cards receive a 50% reduction on all Egyptian State Railway trains. Service includes first, second and third class. Tickets can be purchased at the Cairo Railway Station (Ramsis Station) at Midan Ramsis 147 753555, from various windows via segregated lines:

women in one, men in the other, alternately moving toward the window. The train number is posted at the window so be sure you are in the right line. To book a sleeper ticket you will need a valid passport for each member traveling. Train bookings can be made up to seven days in advance. Your car (carriage), seat number and date of departure should be written on your ticket. You cannot book a return ticket from your point of departure; however, if you cannot book a ticket when you wish to return, you may board any Cairo-bound train without one and take the chance of finding a seat. You will pay on board. A railroad pass issued by the Railway Authority can be obtained from any main station. Anyone may purchase a railroad pass. Cost will vary depending on distance required.

Some railway passes

Distance	Valid	1st Class	2nd Class
2,000km	3 months	LE25.25	LE 8.60
3,000km	3 months	LE28.10	LE11.10
5,000km	6 months	LE41.20	LE15.98

Cairo To Alexandria (daily)

Stations	Train # 903	905	907	911	913	915	917	919	705
Cairo	0655	0800	0930	1120	1220	1310	1400	1405	1410
Benha	0735	-	1006	1156	-	1348	-	-	1453
Tanta	0815	-	1046	1230	1329	1433	-	-	1530
Damanhur	0908	-	1130	1316	-	1522	-	-	-
Sidi Gaber	0952	1028	1213	1358	1453	1607	1628	1643	1702
Alexandria	1000	1035	1220	1405	1500	1615	1635	1650	1710

	923	925	25	31	927	933
Cairo	1550	1750	1810	1830	1900	2130
Benha	1626	1826	1852	1908	-	2206
Tanta	1700	1901	1925	1944	2009	2241
Damanhur	1746	1948	2015	2030	-	2327
Sidi Gaber	1828	2028	2058	2113	2133	0008
Alexandria	1835	2035	2105	2120	2140	0015

Alexandria to Cairo (daily)

Stations	Train # 902	904	906	910	912	914	916	922	924
Alexandria	0610	0750	0920	1030	1140	1240	1415	1530	1710
Sidi Gaber	0621	0800	0930	1040	1150	1251	1425	1540	1720
Damanhur	0707	-	1013	1122	-	1340	-	1622	1802
Tanta	0803	-	1057	1207	1313	1426	-	1707	1847
Benha	0845	-	1132	1247	-	1504	-	1742	1922
Cairo	0920	1025	1205	1320	1420	1540	1650	1810	1955

	26	32	926	928	926	796
Alexandria	1745	1800	1825	1910	1925	1945
Sidi Gaber	1755	1810	1835	1920	1935	1957
Damanhur	1840	1855	-	2005	2017	-
Tanta	1926	1941	1958	2055	2107	2132
Benha	2003	2017	-	2130	2142	2209
Cairo	2040	2050	2105	2205	2215	2245

Cairo to Aswan (daily)
Stations   Train

	980	984	982	160	990	84	86	88	868
Cairo	0730	1000	1200	1225	1610	1900	1935	2000	2030
Giza	0747	1017	1221	1245	1627	-	-	2021	2050
Beni Suef	0924	1115	1359	1428	1804	-	-	2205	2234
Minya	1050	1339	1538	1600	1939	-	-	2348	0018
Assiut	1229	1525	1723	1745	2129	-	-	0144	0212
Sohag	1413	-	1840	1925	2310	-	-	0320	0343
Qena	1705	-	2203	2341	-	-	0606	0637	0755
Luxor	1530	-	-	0120	-	0606	0830	0855	0930
Aswan	2320	-	-	-	-	1000	1235	1330	1427

Aswan to Cairo (daily)
Stations   Train

	981	85	89	87	991	869	159	983	999
Aswan	0515	1445	1650	1745	-	2008	-	-	-
Luxor	1014	0930	2124	2222	-	0102	0415	0515	-
Qena	1126	-	2246	2336	-	0237	0605	0704	-
Sohag	1424	-	0310	-	0430	0721	0937	1022	-
Assiut	1545	-	0342	-	0608	0853	1205	1134	1825
Minya	1728	-	0535	-	0804	1046	1348	1311	2016
Beni Suef	1303	-	0722	-	0939	1231	1525	1446	2210
Giza	2041	-	0906	-	1116	1416	1716	1621	2346
Cairo	2055	0640	0920	0950	1130	1430	1730	1635	2400

Wagon Lits trains
These are privately owned sleeper trains offering first, second and third class compartments. They leave daily from Ramsis Station for Luxor and Aswan. You must book one week in advance either through a travel agent or Compagnie Internationale des Wagons Lits Egypte, 9 Menes HE 290-8802/4; 48 Giza GI 348-7354 349-2365. The number of the train is marked on the train windows. Fares for Egyptians and foreigners are the same. There are no reductions for residents or students.

From Cairo

Train #	Cairo	Luxor	Aswan
84	1900	0500	0925
68	1920	0530	0955

From Aswan

Train #	Aswan	Luxor	Cairo
84	1545	1935	0630
68	1830	2240	0920

Al Takamul train, a newly inaugurated service in conjunction with the Sudan, offers inexpensive travel exclusively for Egyptians and Sudanese. Return ticket to Aswan LE25. No advance booking.

By Bus

Air-conditioned buses make regular runs between Cairo and the major towns. Reserved seat tickets can usually be bought up to two days in advance. Additional routes, in non-air-conditioned buses, run to all parts of the country including Sinai and the Oases. Bus times are subject to change without notice; however, departures to major destinations are so frequent that schedule changes are not a major problem for travelers.

To Alexandria
West Delta Bus Company 15 Midan Tahrir 759751; 5 Murad GI 721121; Midan Ismailia HE 676720. Bus leaves from behind the Nile Hilton in front of the Arab League building in Midan Tahrir and Midan Ismailia, Heliopolis. Departure times: in winter every one to one and a half hours from 5:30am-6:30pm daily; in summer to 9pm daily. Fares range from LE3.50-5.50.
Super Jet: Luxury air-conditioned buses with refreshments, WC, and video. From the airport; Midan Ismailia, Heliopolis; behind the Hilton, Midan Tahrir; and Midan Giza. Departure roughly every hour from 6am-1am. Journey time 3 hrs. Fare LE11 from Airport; LE7 from Heliopolis, Tahrir, Giza. 6 Mokhtar Hussein, al Hegaz, HE 672262.
Federal Arab Land Transport Company: (prefab behind Nile Hilton) Midan Tahrir 772663. Departure every hour from 6:30-6:30. Journey time 3 1/2 hrs.

To Marsa Matruh
West Delta Bus Company from behind the Nile Hilton. Departure times 7:30am daily in winter and 7:30am, 8:30am, 9:30am and 11pm daily in summer. Fares range from LE7.50- LE17.00.

To Siwa Oasis
Buses to Siwa Oasis leave daily at 10am from Midan al Gumhuria Railroad Station in Alexandria. Fare LE8. Foreigners must stop in Mersa Matruh for permission to enter Siwa (see Restricted and Difficult Travel at the end of this chapter).

To the Delta Towns
East Delta Bus Company Offices at 4 Tayaran MN 261-1882/3/5/6. Terminals at al Kulali (by the underpass to Shubra).

Destination	Departure	Fare
Mansura	0600-1800 every 15 minutes	LE2.00
Mataria	0715-1815 every 15 minutes	LE3.50
Damietta	0600-1700 every hour	LE3.00
Ras al Barr (summer only)	0715, 0915, 1315, 1500, 1700	LE3.50

Benha	0600-2100 every 1/2hr	LE0.75
Gamasa	0800-1500	LE3.50
Zagazig	0530-1700 every 15 minutes	LE1.25
	1700-2100 every hour	
Faqus	0830-1800 every 1/2hr	LE1.50
Kafr Sagr	0530-2100	LE1.45

To Upper Egypt and the Oases

Upper Egyptian Bus Company Offices at 4 Yussef Abbas, MN 260-9304/9297/9298. Bus terminals at 45 al Azhar (at Sharia Port Said) 390-8635 and Midan Ahmed Helmi, north of Ramsis Station 746658. There are two standards of bus travel to Upper Egypt. To assure travel on the best available transport, buy your ticket at the kiosk at the appropriate terminus, and not on the bus. The "deluxe" bus is advertised as having a toilet, air-conditioning, and sometimes a video, but this is not always the case.

To the Oases: Daily from al Azhar station. Bus travel to the oases in the western desert, though scheduled to run at the times listed below, is a bit erratic, for a variety of reasons. Normally, no single route links all four oases; however connections can be made at each major village. Once in the oases it is best to consult the tourist information offices. For more information on oases travel see the Restricted and Difficult Travel section of this chapter.

Destination	Departure	Fare
Dakhla via Baharia/Farafra	0600	LE13.00
Dakhla via Kharga	0700	LE12.00
Kharga via Assiut	1000	LE6.50
Baharia/Farafra	0900	LE5.00/8.00
Kharga via Assiut	1800, 2000	LE9.00

To Upper Egypt and the Fayoum: Daily from Ahmed Helmi terminal.

Destination	Departure	Fare
al Saff	0600 every 1/4hr	LE0.75
	1730-1830 every 1/4hr	LE1.00
Fayoum	0615-1645 every 1/4hr	LE1.25
	1700-1845 every 1/4hr	LE1.50
Beni Suef	0600, 0700, 0815, 1015, 1115,	
	1215, 1315, 1430, 1630	LE1.75
	0915, 1030, 1730, 1900	LE2.00
Samalut	1615	LE3.25
Minya	0630, 0930, 1015, 1230, 1330	LE3.50
	1100, 1130, 1430, 1530	LE3.25
	1700, 1830	LE4.00
Abu Kurkas	1400, 1500	LE3.25
	1745	LE4.50
Mallawi	0715, 1930	LE4.00
	1300, 1315, 1600	LE3.50
Dairut	1515	LE3.75
Assiut	0800, 1015, 1200, 1400	LE4.00
	1700, 1830, 2000, 2130	LE5.50

Sohag	0630, 0730, 1030	LE5.50
	1800, 1915, 2045	LE7.50
Naga Hamadi	0600, 0645, 0745	LE6.50
	1800, 1945, 2115	LE8.50
Luxor	0545, 0700	LE8.00
	2030, 2200	LE11.00
Kena	0615	LE7.50
	1830, 2000, 2100	LE10.00
Esna	0700	LE9.00
Aswan	1730	LE14.00

To Canal Towns (Port Said, Ismailia and Suez)
East Delta Bus Company Offices at 4 Tayaran, MN 261-1882/3/5/6. Terminal at al Kulali (by the underpass to Shubra) 750570.

Destination	Departure	Fare
Fayed	0700, 1000, 1400, 1630	LE2.00
Ismailia	0630-1800 every hour	LE2.25
Port Said	0600-1800 every hour	LE3.50-4
Suez	0600-1730 every 1/2 hour	LE2.00

To the Red Sea
Travco Shark al Delta Offices at Midan Ahmed Helmi. Bus departure from Abbassia to Hurghada, daily at 9am, except Friday.
Upper Egyptian Bus Company Daily from Ahmed Helmi.

Destination	Departure	Fare
Hurghada	0730, 2100	LE8.00
	2130	LE12.00
	0900	LE5.00

To Sinai
East Delta Bus Company Offices at 4 Tayaran, MN 261-1882/3/5/6. Departure from Sinai Terminal, Abbassia.

Destination	Departure	Return	Fare
Arish	0700, 0800, 1500	0700, 0800, 1500	LE10.50
Dahab	0700	2030	LE12.50
Nuweiba	2400	varies	LE15.50
St.Cath/Dahab	1030	1400	LE15.50
Sharm al Sheikh	1000, 1300, 2330	0700, 1000, 1300, 2330, 2400	LE9.50/ 12.50
Sharm/Dahab	2400	2400	LE12.50
Taba	0700, 1630	1000	LE20.50

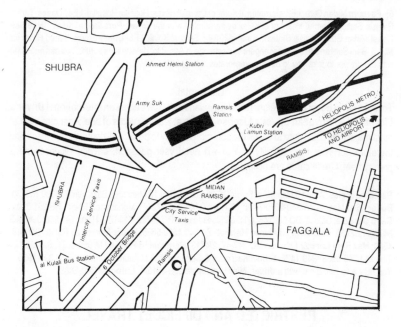

Buses to Tel Aviv via Rafah
East Delta Bus Company Offices 4 Tayaran MN 824753 839589. Departure from Sinai Terminal, Abbassia S, M, W, Th at 7:30am. One way LE40, Round trip LE78. **Isis Travel** 48 Sharia Giza GI 348-7761. Th, S only, at 4:00am, from Midan Tahrir. One way LE50, round trip LE75. **Travco** 112 26th July; 13 Mahmoud Azmi ZA 340-4308/4064. Daily 5am in front of Cairo Sheraton. One way LE52, round trip LE81.

Bus rental
Bus rental, with driver, can be arranged through travel agents. **American Express of Egypt Ltd.**17 Mahmoud Bassiouni 750444; **Cairo Transport and Touring Company** 28 Talaat Harb 756015; **Orouba Tourist Transport** 59 Midan Gumhuria 939750; **Tour Egypt** 347 Pyramids GI 856947; **al Rehab** 10 al Shahid Helmi al Masri, Almaza, HE 662362; **Oonas Tours** 32 Baron HE 668747; **Sharaby For Tourist Transport** 5 al Shahid Helmi Goma, Ard al Golf, HE 872990; **Bestours** 85 Mustafa Kamel MA 350-1834/7976; **Badr Tourism Transport** 46 Bahgat Ali ZA 340-5530.

By Service Taxi
Peugeot service taxis leave regularly from various parts of the city to destinations throughout Egypt. They operate on a first come first served basis and carry 7 passengers. You may buy the seat next to you for more comfort. You may also rent the vehicle for private use. They travel very fast.

Peugeot stations for inter-city travel from Cairo
Alexandria al Kulali; **Beni Suef** Midan Giza, LE3; **Delta** Ahmed Helmi LE4 winter season, summer LE5-

6; **Fayoum** Midan Giza, LE2; **Ismailia** al Kulali or Darrasa next to Hussein Hospital, LE4; **Oases** Tahrir, Ramsis Station, Ahmed Helmi or al Kulali by agreement with the driver; **Port Said** al Kulali; **Red Sea Coast** Midan Giza; Ramsis Station; **Sinai** al Kulali; **Suez** al Kulali, LE6; **Upper Egypt** Ahmed Helmi for Minya, Beni Suef and Assiut; passengers must change in Assiut for destinations south. You can negotiate with the drivers to take you to other governorates.

Car Rental

To rent a car in Egypt both foreigners and Egyptians must have either an **International Driver's License** or an **Egyptian Driver's License,** and be at least 25 years of age. Agencies exist at most major hotels. Be sure to check the contract carefully to be sure all dents, etc are listed and therefore not your responsibility.   You will need your passport, driver's license and a prepayment. Credit cards are accepted.

Rental agencies: Avis 16 Maamel al Sukar GC 354-8698; **Bita** 15 Mahmoud Bassiouni 774330 753130; **Budget** 5 al Maqrizi ZA 340-0070/9474; 85 Road 9 MA 350-2724; 1 Mohammed Ebeid HE 291-8244; **Cairo Car** 6B al Salouli DO 988146; **GTS** 84 Musaddaq DO 719729 714676; **Hertz** 195 26th July, AG 347-4172/2238; **Inter Rent** 33 Ahmed Hishmat ZA 340-1508/5885; **Kadry Motors** 29 Refaa DO 348-4530; **Max Rent Cars** 27 Lebanon MO 347-4712/4713; **Merghani** 85 Road 6 MA 366-6027; **Sahara** 141 Tiba MO 348-8958 349-1472; **Sunshine Tours & Services** 106 Mohamed Farid 760559 393-1955. You may also rent a car with a **driver. Misr Limousine** 259-9813/4; **Europcar** 340-8888.

RESTRICTED AND DIFFICULT TRAVEL

Certain areas of Egypt, particularly the Red Sea Coast and some wadis in Sinai, are still mined in parts, and great care should be taken in selecting beaches for camping and swimming. On no account should barbed wire fences, fallen down or not, be crossed to reach the beach, attractive as it may seem. It is inadvisable to walk on beaches in Egypt after sunset. Most beaches are patrolled by police or military personnel who do not expect to find anyone around at night. Anyone walking on the beach after dark is liable to be challenged and shots may be fired.

Oases

There are no restrictions for travel to 4 of the major oases in the western desert: **Kharga, Dakhla, Farafra,** and **Baharia**; but you must have permission to visit **Siwa Oasis.** The first four form a loop connected by a well-paved ring road that can be joined from Cairo or Assiut. If you intend to visit all 4 by car you must allow a minimum of 7 days. Siwa is a separate trip requiring at least 5-6 days. For all the oases bring camping gear, including water, sunglasses, food, a gerry can for petrol, your car papers (be sure they are up to date) and your passport. You might want to bring candy or ball-point pens for the children, and tea for the hosts. The best time to visit any of the oases is late autumn or early spring when the heat is not too intense and the light is spectacular. Winter nights can chill to the bone, while summer heat creates a haze on the horizon and the escarpment, the high cliff that runs along the edge of the depression, which is often barely visible. On any day, if a sandstorm is brewing, stay put. **Do not venture into the desert in a sandstorm. Stay in one of the towns or at your campsite.** Be sure your car is in good condition and you know how many kilometers or miles you get to a liter of gas. If you break down in summer it is a bigger problem than in winter because of the heat. Don't panic. Someone will pass by and it would be extremely rare if they did not stop to help. Do not leave your vehicle and strike out on your own unless you are off the road and feel no one will find you.

If you do get lost, you can make your own compass by using either a long straight stick or your watch. The **shadow stick method** of determining true north can be used at any time of day as long as there is sunshine. Place the stick upright into the ground on a flat area. Mark the end of its shadow with a pebble. In the Northern Hemisphere (Egypt is in the Northern Hemisphere) this is true west. Wait at least 15 minutes and mark the shadow again with another pebble. This is true east. Join the two. North-south will be at right angles to this line. The **watch method** of determining true north in the Northern Hemisphere is done by holding the watch horizontal and pointing the hour hand at the sun. Half the distance between the hour hand and 12 o'clock points to true north. In other words if the sun is at 4 o'clock the direction of true north is at 2 o'clock. This system works only if the watch is set to true local time and not daylight savings time.

You are required to register with the Tourist Information Office and the police at each oasis. There is a governorate tax of LE4.50 per person, usually payable at Dakhla. You must keep the receipt to show at the other oases so you will not be charged a second time.

Kharga Oasis (233km from Assiut, no petrol en route) The road to Kharga leaves the Nile valley on the northern outskirts of the city of Assiut. There is a petrol station 100 meters south of the Kharga road, and it is best to top your tank before heading into the desert. The first interesting site you come to is the **Valley of the Melons**, a field of unusually round stones scattered on the desert floor on both sides of the road. It is a good place to picnic. Occasionally you may find the carcass of a slaughtered camel, probably left behind by the herders who travel from the Sudan to Daraw and Cairo to sell their herds. There is a small resthouse and checkpoint half way to Kharga city. (For detailed information on checkpoints throughout the country see Owning Your Own Car section.) The escarpment is 65 kilometers before Kharga city. If you haven't been counting your kilometers you will know the escarpment (or scarp), is approaching when radio towers appear to the north of the road. Just before the scarp there is a checkpoint. You will need your car papers. There are two roads leading down the scarp, the one to the right is newer and more scenic. Try to arrive in late afternoon when the light reflects off the scarp. There is one more checkpoint just before Kharga city. You will need your car papers and the passports of all passengers.

This oasis is dotted with small gardens. The main population center is Kharga city equipped with two good hotels and several small ones. It is a small community and everything is easy to find. Things to see include **Bagawat**, a medieval Christian cemetery; **Temple of Hibis** a late Pharaonic temple; and modern pottery by the internationally known potter **Mabrouk**. The gas station is in the center of town, but it closes early and opens late so make a petrol stop a priority. Kharga city has modernized and is a disappointment for those expecting a true oasis atmosphere; however, there are many places to explore. Immediately outside the city, on the road to Dakhla are 20 kilometers of sand dunes. High and crescent shaped, they continually encroach upon the road, which must continually be rebuilt around them. You will have plenty of time to get to Dakhla, so stop to explore them. The best way to climb a sand dune is to walk

along the crest.   Tourist Information office at Hamed Alla Hotel, Sharia al Nada 900638.
Agent: Mr. Adam.

Dakhla Oasis (187km west of Kharga city; no petrol en route.) You travel over a scenic route
between pyramid-like hills for most of the way to Dakhla. There are many places to stop to picnic
or explore. Dakhla has many cultivated areas and 14 small villages. Each has a small hospital,
post office and electricity. There are three secondary schools. The people are friendly and
hospitable. Before arriving at Mut, the capital, the village of Bashandi, signposted on the right
hand side of the road, is worth visiting. One can find a few old traditional dresses and some
jewelry and, perhaps, be invited into a home for tea. The village is very clean. There is a new
school for rug weaving, which has unusual designs including the artists' impressions of tourists.

At the entrance to Mut one finds the only gas station in this oasis. Nearby, before the main
square, is a tire shop. Things to see in Mut include an ethnographic museum, which will be
opened upon request. The banks will exchange foreign currency, but will not accept traveler's
checks. Not only can you telephone Cairo at the local exchange, but you can also reach Europe
and the US. Taxis may be hired to take you around the oasis. One has a good feeling in Mut;
it is a town which is modernizing without losing sight of its traditions. Tourist Information
Agent: Omar Ahmed Mahmoud. Telephone 407. Next door is a first-aid station.

A tourist hot spring exists at Tourism Wells between Mut and Kasr. It is here that the people
of this oasis have created a hospitable area for tourists. There is a campsite, a restaurant, and
a resthouse with 26 beds. It is best to make arrangements early in the day, order your lunch,
then go sightseeing. All will be ready when you return. The main attraction at Tourism Wells
is the hot sulfur spring, one of many you will encounter in the oases. Unfortunately it has been
carefully enclosed so as to provide privacy and the wonderful primitive atmosphere is lost. If you
swim, and it is recommended that you do, wear an old bathing suit because the sulfur stains.
No nude bathing please. It must be noted here, that one reason the hot springs throughout the
oases have been sheltered is because tourists have not always used discretion when
swimming. Although one is far removed from city life, one is still governed by its mores. Egypt
is a conservative country and tourists should act accordingly.

Kasr is a medieval fortress village situated on a strategic hill with old Ayyubid, Fatimid and
Turkish buildings. It is a pleasant village to explore for, in addition to the historic buildings, there
are potters and basket weavers. As you leave Kasr their are two checkpoints, one for the Border
Police, who will ask for passports and car registration and a second, for the local police, who
will ask for car registration only. If you filled your gas tank at Mut, be sure to allow for the
kilometers you traveled in this oasis. It is a long haul to Farafra and Baharia. You must travel
nearly 500km to the next gas station.

Farafra Oasis (311km from Dakhla, no petrol en route or in the oasis.) You will encounter few
vehicles between Dakhla and Farafra Oases. Traveling through vast, empty land not far from
the Great Sand Sea, the solitude of the desert descends upon you. All your senses sharpen.
You hear better, see better and your sense of smell is enhanced. Flat yellow sand gives way
to the distant pink and white of the escarpment and the light blue of the sky makes the scene

complete. All is pastel. You will turn east at the checkpoint at Abu Minqar, a mere 100km west of Libya and about 230km out of Dakhla. Then you will begin your climb out of the depression. This is spectacular scenery. As you move toward the Farafra depression the white chalk that is the predominant feature of Farafra begins to come into view. There are sand dunes and small oases all the way to Kasr Farafra, the only village in this oasis. Once you arrive, there is a clean government resthouse, but with no privacy. The camping facilities are near Bir Setta (Well Six), and consist of thatched huts enclosed by a rush wall. They are recommended, especially at night when you can bathe in the hot springs while looking at the Milky Way. This spring retains its former atmosphere. Farafra city is a true oasis town with gentle, hospitable people and an interesting old fortress with covered pathways. This village has changed very little in recent years, and although new buildings exist near the main road, the town square offers a wonderful atmosphere. In return for the hospitality you receive it is customary to offer tea, sweets and the like. It is impolite to offer money. There is one small restaurant on the main road. It is best to bring your own food. **Tourist Information Agent: Mr. Awis Mohamed. There is no petrol in Farafra.**

Eighteen kilometers after you leave Kasr Farafra on the road to Baharia you enter the **White Desert**, one of the truly outstanding places on earth. It is a good place to camp. It is clean and unspoiled, so please keep it that way. The white chalk outcroppings which dot the desert floor and give it its name are accessible via regular vehicles. Stop by all means, if only to have a cup of tea. (You will have to make it yourself for this is pure wilderness.) At a checkpoint half way to the Baharia escarpment, a paved road turns west to Ain Della, believed to be the last known location of the lost army of Cambyses. The road travels 120km across the desert floor and through the scarp. You must have military permission to visit Ain Della.

The main road continues through the White Desert toward Baharia. As you climb out of the Farafra depression stop to look back on the spectacular plane below. It will take you about a minute to reach the top of the escarpment. Before the paved road, in 1978, it took a four-wheel drive and winch truck a whole day. Camel caravans took four days between the two oases. You travel 50km along the top of this escarpment before you descend into the Baharia depression.

Baharia Oasis (183km from Farafra, no petrol en route.) The first village one encounters in this oasis is **Hayz**, and a fair distance later **Bawiti**, the capital, then **Kasr** and **Mandisha**. All are worth visiting. There are many antiquities throughout the oasis. Accommodations are scanty but there is a campsite, similar to the one at Farafra, at **Bir Etnein** (Well Two) near the airstrip outside of Bawiti. It is not easily accessible via regular vehicle. Contact: Hagg Salah in Bawiti. The gas station is in the center of town. This oasis has golden sand with hills topped by black volcanic rock, a true contrast to the white of Farafra and the pastel of Dakhla. At the outskirts of the oasis is the iron mine linked to the Nile valley by a railway that goes directly to Helwan. The return journey to Cairo from Baharia is 386km. There is a half-way resthouse with a petrol station. You will connect with the Fayoum road outside of Cairo and join the Alexandria road at the old Holiday Inn, near the Pyramids.

Siwa (300km from Marsa Matruh; no petrol en route.) You will need at least six days to visit Siwa Oasis. At least two of these days will be spent getting there. Because it is near the Libyan border,

Siwa is sometimes closed to visitors, and anyone wishing to travel to Siwa must have permission. This permission must be obtained in Marsa Matruh. To get it, once in Matruh drive directly through the town on the main road to the governorate building which is located at the seashore. Turn left and left again. The Tourist Information Office is in the building on the left. You will need a valid passport and visa, three photocopies of each (best to get them in Cairo to save time) and a friendly smile. After completing the formalities at the Tourist Information Office you will have two more stops: the Intelligence Office, where you will be asked a few questions, and the military police, where the final permit will be issued. These steps will take at least half a day. The offices are open morning and evening, but are **closed on Friday**.

Siwa is a straight 300km south-west of Matruh on a well-paved road. Upon arrival at Siwa you must register with the military authorities. They will ask where you want to go and tell you the restrictions. They will also direct you to the hotel. A soldier from the Border Patrol will accompany you to visit certain sites. This is mandatory, so make the best of it. Things to see: the old city of **Siwa, Aghurmi, Temple of Amun, Cleopatra's Baths** and the **gardens**. There is a petrol station near the main square. There are few restaurants so bring your own food and water. You may camp, but there are no facilities.

Recommended reading: Ahmed Fakhry, **The Oases of Egypt**. Vol I, II. The American University in Cairo Press.

To Ras Mohammed, Sinai

Ras Mohammed is a peninsula located at the southern tip of Sinai. It was designated a nature reserve in 1983, and is a true wilderness refuge for a large variety of wildlife. You may visit Ras Mohammed for the day without any restrictions, but to camp you must obtain a permit in Sharm al Sheikh. You will need a valid passport. Permission to stay is granted for as long as you want. Hunting and fishing are forbidden at Ras Mohammed. If you see a violation occuring, the Egyptian Wildlife Service requests you report it to the nearest police station.

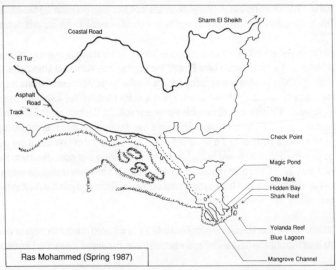

Ras Mohammed (Spring 1987)

شـركة بشـارة لصـناعة المنسـوجات والملابـس ـ العاشـر من رمضـان
Bishara Textile & Garments Manufacturing — 10th of Ramadan City

' Heliopolis office: 7, Ahram St.,

Tel: Cairo 2574120 - 2571350

Tel: 10th of Ramadan 015 / 360450 - 361635

Tlx: 20114 UN — P.O.Box: 47

الادارة التجارية : ٧ شارع الأهرام مصر الجديدة

ت : القاهرة ٢٥٧٤١٢٠ ـ ٢٥٧١٣٥٠

ت : ١٠ رمضان ٣٦٠٤٥٠ ـ ٣٦١٦٣٥ / ٠١٥

تلكس : ٢٠١١٤ UN ـ ص.ب : ٤٧

Ras Mohammed is 50km south-west of Sharm al Sheikh by road, and is accessible by private vehicle or by boat. By car, look for a small sign marking the turn then follow the dirt track. There are several good campsites. The **Shark Observatory**, where there is excellent snorkeling and scuba diving, offers a very good view of the reefs and the sea. The **Mangrove Lagoon** has sandy beach bottoms for children and excellent birdwatching among the mangroves. Throughout the area there is good snorkeling and scuba diving with spectacular coral reefs, colorful fish, sea mammals and turtles. There are no facilities at Ras Mohammed, no fresh water, no food, no shade and no petrol. All are available at Sharm al Sheikh.

For those without transport the following agencies either provide full tours to remote areas or rent vehicles to do it yourself. **Acacia Adventure Travel** 27 Libnan MO 347-4713 345-1022, offers unique safaris with 4-wheel drives to Sinai, Wadi Rayan, the Oases and Siwa, and will arrange additional travel on request; **Max Rent-a-Car** 27 Libnan MO 347-4712/13, rents 4-wheel drives; **Sea and Caravan Tours** 55 Abdel Monim Hafez HE 660978, camper rental; **Sinai Safari** by jeep, American Express 750444 and Isis Travel 847060; **South Sinai Travel** 79 Merghani, 11th floor, HE, arranges camel trips out of Nuweiba; **Starco** 1 Midan Talaat Harb, 4th floor, 392-1205, caravan rental.

TRAVEL IN THE MIDDLE EAST, AFRICA AND ASIA FROM EGYPT

US Embassy travel advisory for the Middle East (The following is an abridgement of a document issued by the Department of State in September 1987)

The policies of the countries in the Middle East vary greatly. To avoid difficulties and serious problems, exercise caution and become familiar with travel requirements and restrictions. Be aware of traditions and respect their limitations. Travel advisories concerning serious health or security conditions are available at US Embassies and consulates abroad and from the Citizens Emergency Center Room 48LL Department of State Washington DC 20520 202-647-5225.

Most Arab countries, except Morocco, Egypt, Qatar and Tunisia will deny entry to any traveler with evidence of travel to Israel in his/her passport. You can request Israeli immigration officials to note your entry into Israel on a separate sheet instead of on your passport. This may not be sufficient if you enter Israel overland. Certain Arab countries do not honor passports with an exit stamp from a place that only leads into Israel. Contact the nearest US Passport Agency for guidance. Some Arab countries refuse to admit persons with passports indicating travel to South Africa.

Kuwait, Oman, Qatar and Saudi Arabia do not permit tourism. All business visitors must be sponsored by a company. Private visitors must be sponsored by a relative or friend native to the country. Entry is by visa or non-objective certificate system (NOC), obtained by a visitor's sponsor and filed with the appropriate foreign government authority.

Some Arab countries require visitors to obtain exit permits from their sponsors in order to leave the country. Do not accept sponsorship to visit a country unless you are sure you will also be able to obtain an exit permit.

US citizens married to foreign nationals should be aware that a woman needs the permission of her husband, and children need the permission of their father, to leave some Arab countries. Do not visit a country unless you are completely confident you will be able to leave. Once overseas you are subject to the laws of the country where you are.

Some countries in the Middle East do not recognize acquisition of US citizenship. If such a person returns to their original country they might be denied the right to communicate with the US Embassy. Dual nationals should also be aware that they may be required to use a passport of the country of their original nationality in order to enter or leave that country. The US government does not object to the use of a foreign passport by a dual national, but regulations require US citizens to use a US passport to depart from and enter the US. Consult the Office of Citizens Consular Services, Room 48L7 Department of State, Washington DC 20520 202-647-6680.

Countries requiring visitors to be certified free from the AIDS virus may require that testing be done in that country.

Tickets Air and sea tickets purchased in Egypt cannot be refunded abroad, and, even though the tickets have been paid in hard currency, refunds are given only in Egyptian pounds. Foreigners buying tickets in Egypt must pay by credit card or in Egyptian pounds with a bank exchange receipt, unless they have a 5-yr residence stamp, in which case the bank receipt is not needed.

Entry information for nearby countries
This information is primarily for US citizens. It may apply to other nationalities as well, but to be sure consult your embassy.

Bahrain Tourist visas are not issued. Transit visas for up to 12 hours and extendable for one week are issued. Return-onward ticket required. Business, work and residence visas are valid for 3 months and require a letter from your company or non-objective certificate from the Immigration Department in Bahrain. Business visas are issued only at your embassy. American Embassy 973-714151.

Cyprus No visa required.

Ethiopia Tourist visa required for stay up to 30 days. You will need one passport photo.

Greece Visa not required for stay of up to 3 months.

India Visa, valid for up to 3 months stay, is required. No visas are issued at ports of entry. Onward-return ticket required, as is a financial guarantee. You will need one photo and $15 or equivalent.

Iran Americans are not permitted to travel to Iran at present.

Iraq No tourists visas are issued. All visitors must be sponsored by their host company. Registration with officials mandatory if staying longer than 15 days. AIDS test within five days of arrival mandatory (performed in Iraq) if staying more than 14 days. American Embassy 964-1-719-6138.

Israel Passport must be valid 9 months beyond arrival. Visa not required for tourists staying up to 3 months. Officials determine eligibility for entry at port by searches and interrogation: extensive security searches are possible. Leave cameras empty for inspection. Passports may be confiscated as a guarantee of departure. Posting of a departure bond may be required. There is an exit fee of $15 or equivalent to leave Israel and LE2.50 for baggage check if returning to Egypt. (Fees subject to change.) If passport is seized ask to see a consular officer or report the seizure to your embassy. **Entry via Rafah** no visa required, only valid passport and LE10. **Entry via Taba** no visa required. For more information refer to the **Travelers' Advisory for Americans**, your embassy, or Department of State U.S(202) 617 5225. Americans are advised to register at their embassy in Tel Aviv 282322. American Embassy 972-3-654338.

Kenya A visa, valid for 6 months, is required.

Jordan A visa, valid up to 4 months, is required. Passports containing an Israeli stamp are rejected. To cross the **King Hussein Bridge** from Jordan to Israel one must submit passport and one photo in person to Jordanian Ministry of Interior in Amman 3 days before crossing. The bridge is open 8-1:30 S-Th and 8-10:30am on Friday. It is closed Saturday and many Israeli holidays. Travelers should arrive at the bridge at least one hour before closing time. **To Jordan via the Red Sea** There are two ferries daily from Nuweiba, one at 8am and another at 11am with a return trip from Jordan at 4pm. Price LE32 one way or LE64 return. Bus service for Nuweiba from Cairo leaves at midnight and arrives at the port at 7am.

If you do not have a 5-year residence stamp it would save a lot of trouble if you exchange money in Cairo and carry the receipt and three photocopies of your passport, visa and 5-year residence with you to Nuweiba. There is a bank at the port, but it is not always open. The procedure is: go to the bank and exchange money, purchase your ticket, walk across the compound and go through customs, and walk or ride by motorized cart to the ship with all your luggage. When you board the ship Egyptian and Jordanian authorities will request your passport for processing. It will be returned to you before you leave the ship. Upon leaving Jordan allow yourself plenty of time. There is a departure tax in Jordan which is strictly observed. On your return journey your passport will again be requested for the same procedure. On arrival in Egypt the authorities may ask you to wait aboard ship. Comply. They are arranging transportation and a quick customs inspection. Those who choose to strike out on their own may find themselves in the midst of returning workers, and customs will take hours. American Embassy 962-6-644371.

Kuwait No tourist visas are issued. Passport must be valid for 6 months beyond arrival. Visas must be obtained before arrival. A transit visa valid for 72 hours is mandatory. Both entry visa and transit visa are obtained at any Kuwaiti embassy. Transit visas are only issued with proof of onward-return ticket. You will need 2 photos. There is no charge. Registration with American Embassy is urged if staying longer than a few days. American Embassy 242-4151.

Lebanon Effective January 1, 1987 US passports are not valid for travel in, through or to Lebanon without express authorization of the Department of State. American Embassy 417774 or 415802/3.

Libya Effective December 10, 1981 US passports are not valid for travel in, through, or to Libya without express authorization from the Department of State.

Morocco Visa not required for stay of up to 3 months. Individual visas must be obtained to enter the cities of Casablanca, Tangiers and Agadir. American Embassy 212-7-622-65.

Oman Tourist visas are not issued. Business visitors require either a business visa (2 photos, 1 entry, valid for 3 months) or a non-objective certificate plus a letter from the individual's company and letter of invitation from a sponsor in Oman. Sponsor should begin application procedures several weeks ahead of travel. Exit permit not required. American Embassy 738-231/738-006.

Pakistan Visa is required and must be obtained before arrival.

Qatar Visa is required. No tourist visas are issued. Passengers may transit Qatar without a visa if they continue their journey within 24 hours. American Embassy 974-864701/2/3.

Saudi Arabia No tourist visas are issued. Visas only issued for short business visits and visits of relatives. Travelers transiting must have a valid visa. Long term employment requires certification to be free of the AIDS virus. Travel to Mecca and Medina is forbidden to non-Muslims. Photographing of mosques, people at prayer and military or government installations is forbidden. American Embassy 966-1-488-3800.

Sudan Passport must be valid 6 months beyond date of entry. Transit visa required for stay from 1-7 days valid for 3 months. Valid visa required for next destination. Single entry tourist or business visa required for stays from 8-90 days. **Overland from Egypt** There are two agencies that offer train and boat services to the Sudan. The **Nile Maritime Agency**, formerly the Sudanese Maritime Agency, 8 Kasr al Nil (in the passageway near the Automobile Club) 740883. This is a private company that has one boat, Zamzam, that leaves from the High Dam at Aswan Tuesdays at 2pm and returns from Wadi Halfa on Fridays at 5-6pm.

Fares	Adults	Children 6-11
First class	64.65	39.70
Second class	45.55	28.70
Third class	26.00	16.60

The **Nile Navigation Company** Ramses Station 753555 has boats leaving from the High Dam on Mondays and Thursdays at 8am. The **Sinai** takes 16hrs for the journey, the **Sixth October** takes 2 days. The **Sak al Naam** will soon be in operation. Tickets may be purchased at Ramsis Station in Cairo or at 13 al Souq al Siahi, next to Misr Travel in Aswan.

Fares	Adults	Children 5-10	Children 1-5
First class	70.00	35.00	free
Second class	38.60	19.30	free

Syria A valid visa must be obtained before arrival. A transit visa is required for a stay of up to 3 days. Visitors must enter and leave via Damascus International Airport. Registration at US Embassy upon arrival is recommended. American Embassy 963-11-333052.

Tunisia No visa is required for a stay of up to 3 months.

Turkey No visa is required for a stay of up to 3 months.

United Arab Emirates Tourist and business visas required, valid for 2 months. Multiple entry visas are issued only to business travelers. American Embassy 971-2-336691.

Yemen Arab Republic Tourist visa or business visa valid for 30 days required. Register with immigration department within 3 days. All persons visiting Yemen must cash $150, or equivalent, at the airport before going through passport control. Travelers must register and receive permission to travel in the country from General Tourism Corporation in Tahrir Square in Sanaa, open only in the morning. You may also arrange for a car and driver at the same time. Rates approximately $80 a day and well worth it. American Embassy 967-2-271950.

COMMUNICATIONS

POSTAL SERVICE

The **Central Post Office** at Midan al Ataba 912356 is open 24 hours a day except Friday and occasional holidays. Most other offices are open from 8:30-3 daily, except Fridays. Mailboxes are located on the streets and in front of post offices; the red ones are for regular Egyptian mail, blue for overseas airmail letters, and green for Cairo and express mail within Cairo. Zip/postal codes were begun in Egypt in 1983; you can purchase a directory at most post offices. Post office boxes can be rented at any post office.

Letters
Local mail letters are 5p regular delivery and 10p for express mail. It costs 15p to airmail (bariid gawwi) a letter of 1-10g to Arab countries, and 30p to any other destination outside Egypt. Delivery of air mail letters and postcards between Egypt and the United States usually takes about two weeks, while letters to and from Europe take about a week. In general, air mail service to and from Egypt is 85% effective; that is, roughly 15% of one's correspondence never arrives. Any letter that has enclosures, such as photographs or clippings, is more likely not to be delivered. Aerograms are available from the main post office. Bring a large quantity of foreign postage stamps to use on letters and postcards sent with travelers to mail abroad. **Surface mail** travels via sea post. An ocean-going freighter takes about six weeks to reach Egypt from its last American port of call. The average delivery time of a sea post letter is about three months. **Bulk Mail** Monthly reduced rates for bulk mail are available at the following rates: International mail, 50 items at 10% discount and 100 items at 15%. Internal mail, 100 items at 10% and 200 at 15%. Inquire at any post office. **Registered Mail** There are two ways to send registered mail: registered, which will cost about 15p above normal charges depending on the destination; and registered with acknowledgment of receipt, which will cost 20-30p above. Registered letters can be sent from any post office. Addresses must be written in blue ink and sticky tape must not be used.

Packages
Receiving: Most people agree that there is no dependable way to mail packages to Egypt. Packages sent by either air or surface mail come through irregularly and are often held up for long periods in customs. Customs duties are high, and the recipient may have to spend a long time at the post office to claim a package. To claim a package, you need the claim notice given to you by the postman, identification, and money to pay the customs and handling charges. Books and records tend to have small assessments, while clothing has a heavier duty. Small gifts or household items usually run from LE1.50-4.00.

Sending: The package rate for overseas is LE3 per kilo. The package must not exceed 20 kilos (44 lbs.) or 1.5 meters total dimensions. Packages weighing more than 2 kilos must be mailed from either the Ataba or the Ramsis post office. There is a customs clearance office at the Ataba post office. All other packages may be mailed from any post office and/or Cairo International Airport. You will need an export license for items which are worth more than LE100 (see Travel section on export licenses). Packages can be sent by **registered** mail only from the Ataba post office. Printed matter like books and magazines can be difficult to register, as it requires a special license.

Special services

Express Mail Service (EMS) is available to 53 countries from the Central Post Office from 8:30-7 daily and at the post offices listed below to 3pm. Postal pickup, for a fee of LE5, is available at your place of business until 3pm. Delivery time within Egypt is approximately 1 day, to Europe 2 days, and to the U.S. 3 days. All items are subject to customs. A customs clearance exists at the Central Post Office at Ataba. For packages weighing less than 100 grams, EMS to Arab countries is LE10; to Europe and North America LE 20; and to other countries LE15. For packages weighing more than 100 grams, the cost is LE15 for the first half kilogram and LE5 for each half kilogram thereafter to Arab countries; LE21 and LE6 to Europe and Africa; LE22 and LE7 to the USA, East Asia, and Canada; and LE23 and LE8 to South America and Australia. Reduced charges for bulk mailings are available.

Participating EMS post offices are: **Abbassia** 127 Midan Abdu Pasha 820469; **Al Azhar** 21E Midan al Azhar; **Bab al Luq** Mohamed Mahmoud 354-6035/8762; **Dokki** Ministry of Land Reclamation Building 702792; **Faggala** 2 Serag al Din 905336; **Giza** 10 Murad 724040.

Heliopolis 3 Bosta 666980; **Hurria** Midan al Tayaran 867332; **Maadi** Road 9 350-2185; **Mohamed Farid** Mohamed Farid 393-2067; **Zamalek** Hasan Sabri 340-1933;

Commercial express mail agencies: Aramex International Courier 85 al Hussein 349-7119; **DHL** 20 Gamal al Din Abul Mahasen GC 355-7301/7118, 34 Abdel Khalek Sarwat 392-9198 393-8988, 35 Ismail Ramzi HE 246-3571/0324; **Federal Express** 1079 Corniche al Nil GC 355-0427; 24 Syria MO 349-0986; 31 Golf MA 350-7172; **IML Air Couriers** 2 Mustafa Kamel MA 350-1160/1240; **Middle East Courier Service** 1 Mahmoud Hafez HE 245-9281; **SOS Sky International** 45 Shehab MO 346-0028/2503; **TNT Skypac International Express** 33 Dokki 348-8204/7228; **World Courier Egypt** 17 Kasr al Nil 777678/741313.

Telefax (also **Facsimile** or **FAX** or **Bureaufax**), photocopying via telephone, is handled at some post offices and local telephone exchanges, daily until 2pm. Both text and graphics can be sent. Fax can be sent to 25 participating countries in North and South America, Europe, Asia and the Middle East. Copies must be clean. The page must not be larger than 250x325cm, and cannot have any glue or metal on it. Costs to UK and Middle East LE10 plus LE5 per additional page; USA, Europe LE12, LE6 per additional page; Canada LE13, plus LE6.50; Asia LE18, plus LE9. To get a subscription to Telefax, go to a participating post office, fill out an application, and pay a deposit of LE200. Any company can acquire a subscription by an official written request to the director of electronic mail. This establishes credit, so that documents can be sent throughout the month and be charged later. If you need to send a telefax after 2pm, businesses and hotels also provide this service. Their rates vary.

Participating Telefax post offices: Ataba 912356; Zamalek 340-1933; Heliopolis 666980; Maglis al Shaab 354-7875; Maadi 350-2185.

TELEPHONE, TELEGRAPH, TELEX

The **Central Telephone and Telegraph Offices** (8 Adli; Midan Tahrir; 26 Ramsis; Alfi) are open 24 hours a day, as are many branch exchanges. Others are open from 7am to 10pm daily. They are equipped to handle all telecommunications needs.

Telephone service Applications for any telephone service are available from the Chairman of the Board of the Telecommunications Organization, 26 Ramsis 354-6035 or the telephone center in your area. Priority installation of a phone, either business or residential, costs LE 1800 for an Egyptian and LE3000 for a foreigner. Service should begin in a few months. Non-priority/ regular installation costs about LE300 for a residence and LE400 for a business; the waiting period is 1-10 years. In case of **breakdown**, call 770055/188/16, or the exchange in your area.

Telephone bills are paid every 6 or 12 months. The payment period is established when the telephone is installed. There are reminders in the newspapers, but at the beginning of January and/or the beginning of July, if you do not receive a bill, you should go to the telephone exchange nearest you.

Telephone exchanges:
Central Cairo 13 Adli 909172 904471; Alfi 934209; Mohammed Mahmoud, Bab al Louk 354-4003; **Heliopolis** al Sawra at Almaza 675522 291-0457; Gisr al Suweis 245-3514/4263; Osiris, Kurba 291-0997/ 0994; **Giza** Midan Giza 720649; **Maadi** 5 Road 9 350-1122/2138.

Types of telephone service
Regular home service enables you to make calls in the Greater Cairo area. It carries a subscription of LE30 for 1500 **periods** a year. Office/commercial service is LE70 for 300 periods. A period is 3 minutes. Additional periods beyond the subscription are about 5p each.

Trunk service adds the facility of making operator-assisted long distance calls inside and outside Egypt (dial 120). It can be arranged at the nearest telephone exchange or at the Telecommunications Organization at 26 Ramsis and requires a LE150 deposit to ensure payment for calls. The balance, if any, will be charged quarterly, but billed with your regular billing. When arranging for this service, you will need 2 copies of either your phone contract or your most recent telephone bill. If the service is for a business, an official letter from your embassy is required.

A **direct international line** permits direct dialing throughout the world. Application is made to the Telecommunications Organization at 26 Ramsis and must be accompanied by 2 copies of either the phone contract or the most recent phone bill, four 35p stamps, LE650 for insurance fees, and, for businesses, an official letter from your embassy. Foreign companies pay LE4,000 for priority installation; private Egyptian companies, LE2,000. Payment is via monthly billing.

Making calls
Local telephone calls can be made to all areas of Greater Cairo, including Helwan, Heliopolis and Kaliubia Governorate. Just pick up the phone and dial the number. Although the system has been greatly improved in recent years, it is still overburdened and exchanges sometimes function slowly during peak hours. Busy signals may indicate that trunk lines into the area are all busy. The **information** number is 768000/141 or 767000/140, but the operators only speak Arabic.

Pay telephones Coin-operated telephones, while fairly scarce, are found outside the telephone exchanges, in front of some public buildings, and in some hotel lobbies. These machines operate with either a 10p coin or a token. Token machines are usually installed in hotels where the coins can be purchased from the registration desk. Another way to make a pay call is to go to a kiosk or coffeeshop. If they have a phone, they will charge you 25p to make your call. You can also make local calls at the exchange.

Long distance and overseas calls. Unless you have trunk service or a direct international line, you must go to an exchange or a hotel to place a long distance or overseas call. At the exchange, the call is usually prepaid, for a fixed duration; if not completed, the money is returned upon presentation of the receipt. The minimum charge is for three minutes. Calls in excess of six minutes during peak hours (8am-8pm) are charged triple the normal amount. One may also **reserve** a call for a specific time to ring at home; this necessitates prepayment. To check on overseas calls be sure to get the code number of the call and the number of the exchange. You may also dial the Overseas Operator, 777120. **Collect (reverse charge)** calls cannot be made. **Person-to-person** calls can be made, but cost more. Most major hotels offer instant telephone service overseas, but you should expect to pay 15-20% more for this service.

Current telephone rates, for the first 3 minutes

Destination	Daytime Rates 0800 to 2000	Nighttime Rates 2000 to 0800	Destination	Daytime Rates 0800 to 2000	Nighttime Rates 2000 to 0800
Africa LE	13-24	10-18	Israel	18	13.50
Arab countries	8-11	6-8	North, East Europe	18	13.50
Asia	24-27	18-20	South America	27	20
Australia	24	18	USA	16.50	12.75
Central America	24	18	USSR	16.50	13
Greece, Turkey	12	9	West Europe	15	12

Long distance telephone codes in Egypt

Abu Qir	055	Fayoum	084	Qaha	013
Akhmim	088	Hurghada	062	Qena	096
Alexandria	03	Ismailia	064	Ras al Barr	057
Ameria	03	Kafr al Dawar	03	Rashid	040
al Arish	068	Kafr al Sheikh	047	Sadat City	049
Ashmun	048	Kafr al Zayat	040	al Saff	018
Assiut	088	Kharga	088	Salhia	016
Aswan	097	Luxor	095	Shebin al Kom	048
Belbeis	055	Mahalla	043	Sohag	093
Benha	013	Mansura	050	Suez	062
Beni Suef	083	Marsa Matruh	03	Tanta	040
Cairo	02	Minia	086	Tell al Kebir	064
Damanhur	045	Mit Abul Kom	048	al Tor	062
Damietta	057	Naga Hamadi	096	Zagazig	055
Desuq	047	Port Fuad	066	6th October	011
Fayed	064	Port Said	066	10th Ramadan	015

The **Cairo Telephone List**, issued in December of each year by the Maadi Women's Guild, provides the English-speaking community with address and telephone listings of individuals, organizations and services. To be included in the List, submit your name (last name first), address, organization or firm, and telephone number to: The Maadi Women's Guild, PO Box 218, Maadi, before 30 September. The Cairo Telephone List may be purchased each December at the Maadi Women's Guild Annual Bazaar at Cairo American College, and as of January from Guild meetings, Community Services Association, American Chamber of Commerce, Maadi Community Church, and Women's Association.

Other services

Telegrams in both Arabic and foreign languages can be sent from all major telephone and telegraph offices (see above). Telegrams must be written in block letters. The rates are 2p per word for a local telegram, 66p to Europe, 55-60p to America and Canada, and 99p to Japan. You will need your passport to send a telegram. Home subscriptions for telephone telegrams are available upon writing to the Telecommunications Organization at 26 Ramsis.

Telefax, or photocopying via telephone, is available at the telephone exchange as well as the post office. See under Postal Services.

Telex In addition to the telephone exchanges listed above, telex services exist at the Cairo International Airport, most first class hotels and various business offices. The charge at the exchange is LE5 per minute to Europe and North America; LE6.50 to South America, Asia, Australia, and Africa; and LE2.50-LE5 to Arab countries. Applications for telex service should be recommended by the Ministry of Economic Affairs or the General Agency for Foreign Investment. In case of breakdown call 938786 919120 930709.

MEDIA

Radio

Local All radio and TV broadcasting in Egypt is from the Radio and Television Building, Corniche al Nil, Maspero, 747120. The channels for **European Radio Cairo** are 557AM and 95FM, operating from 0700-2400. It is a general Western music station playing European classical, pop and jazz music. **News in English** at 0730, 1430, and 2000. **News in French** at 0800, 1400 and 2100. **News in Greek** 1500; **News in Armenian** at 1600; **News in German** at 1800. Ethnic programs follow each news broadcast.

Arabic-language radio stations (medium wave)

al Quran al Karim	864 AM 0425-2400	Quran & religious programs
Program Two	224 AM 0845-2325	popular music
Middle East Program	774 AM 0600-0115	news, ads, music
Arab Voice	621 AM 0500-0200	music, Quran, news at 0530
General Program	819 AM 0600-0550	music, Quran, news on the hour
Music Program	537.6AM 0700-2400	Western classical and pop music
	89.5 FM	

The **Radio Cairo Overseas** station has short wave broadcasts on the 31 meter band, 9475 and 9675 kHz every night from 0200 to 0330 Greenwich Mean Time (GMT), but cannot be received in Cairo. P.O. Box 566, Corniche al Nil, Maspero, 747120.

BBC* World Service broadcasts on short wave throughout the world. Middle East broadcasting is on 639KHz from 0645-1015, 1300-1400, 1500-2100; and 1325KHz from 1700-0115. News is on the hour. **London Calling** is the program journal of the BBC World Service; for subscription information, write to London Calling, P.O. Box 76, Bush House, Strand, London, England, WC2B 4PH. The Cairo address is 19 Al Gabalaya, #41, ZA 341-8546.

BBC regular features

Newsdesk	daily 0400;0600;1800	World News & dispatches
		from overseas & UK correspondents
Radio Newsreel	daily 0015;1200(xS)	news of events as they happen & dispatches from
	1500	correspondents worldwide
News about Britain	daily 0009;0309;1109	British news
Twenty-Four Hours	daily 0509;0709;1309	analysis of main news of the day
	2009	
British Press Review	M-F 0909	a survey of editorial opinion
The World Today	M-F 1645;2209	a thorough examination of
	T-Sa 0315;0545;0915	one topical aspect of the international scene
Financial News	M-F 2230	commodity prices & significant moves in
	r.T-Sa 0450	currency & stock markets
	r.M-Sa 0930	
Financial Review	S 0450 (r.2230)	a look back at the financial week
Letter from America	Sa 1015	by Alistair Cooke
	r.S 0545;1645;2315	

VOA* Voice of America

News is every hour on the hour. For a complete list of programs write or call Voice of America, P.O. Box 122, Dokki, 704986.

Time	Stations**
0300-0330	1260, 7200
0330-0500	7200
0500-0600	7200, 9670, 11925, 15205
0600-0700	1260, 5965, 6095, 7325, 9670, 11925, 15195
1500-1630	1260, 9700, 15205

1630-1700	9700, 15205
1700-1830	9700
1830-2100	9700, 9760
2100-2200	1260, 7205, 9700, 9760

** Stations between 621 and 1580 are found on AM or medium wave; stations above 3980 kHz are short wave stations.

Selected VOA programs

American Viewpoints	Sa 1910	Discussion of provocative magazine or newspaper articles
Concert Hall	S 2010	Performances and interviews with classical musicians
Magazine Show	M-Fr 1730	Reports on science, culture, sports, medicine, & the arts in America
Now Music USA	T-Th 1530;1930	Rock & soul hits
Music USA-Jazz	M-Sa 2010	Willis Conover presents jazz
News in Special English	daily 1630;1830	A slower version of VOA news
Newsline	M-Fr 0310;0410 0510;0610 1510;1710 1910	Correspondents' reports,background on the news, interviews
Press Conference USA	Sa 1530;1930	Interviews with newsmakers
World Report	M-Fr 2110	Review of the day's events

*All times Greenwich Mean Time.

Television
Egypt has three television channels. Channel 1, on the air from 1530 to 2400 (local time), and found on 1 and 5 (or 6) on the dial, broadcasts a full program mainly in Arabic including educational, sports, and religious programs. English language programs include top western musical hits, serials, and a CineClub movie on Saturday nights at 2230. Channel 2, broadcasting from 1500 to midnight daily, and also from 1000-1200 on Fridays and Sundays, has many foreign programs. A movie or serial, either in Arabic or English, is broadcast daily at 1500. Western movies are presented Thursday at 2200, Friday at 1000 (often a classic like Shakespeare) and 2200. Ballet is on Friday evenings at 2100. News in French is at 1900 and News in English at 2000. Channel 3 is a Cairo-only station broadcasting, in Arabic, from 1700-2100. See the Egyptian Gazette for daily television schedules; on Mondays they list all the movies for the week. The Magazine of Radio and TV (in Arabic) also has weekly program schedules. Schedules vary during Ramadan and in the summer.

Newspapers
Arabic language newspapers can be purchased at newsstands and hotels throughout the city. English-language newspapers are usually found at newstands near foreign institutions and at hotels. Both can be delivered to your home. Egypt is the largest publishing center in the Middle East, with four large publishing houses producing all of the large-circulation dailies, weeklies, and periodicals. These houses are regulated by the Higher Press Council and are under the supervision of the Shura Council. They include Dar al Ahram (al Galaa 758333), Dar al Hilal (16 Mohammed Ezz al Arab), Dar Akhbar al Yom (6 al Sahafa 748888), and Dar al Gumhuria (24 Zakaria Ahmed).

Daily newspapers
Arabic

Al Ahram	Al Galaa	758333	oldest; estab. 1875; international
		745666	edition published in U.K.
		755500	
Al Akhbar	6 Sahafa	748469	estab. 1952; Sat. issue =
		766865	Akhbar al Yom
Al Gumhuria	24 Zakaria Ahmed	754133	estab. 1953
Al Mesa'	24 Zakaria Ahmed	754133	evening paper; estab. 1956

Foreign-language

Egyptian Gazette	24 Zakaria Ahmed	741611 751511	English	estab. 1880; Sat. issue=E Mail
Le Progres Egyptien	24 Zakaria Ahmed	741611 751511	French	estab. 1893
Le Journal d'Egypte	1 Borsa Gedida	393-4561 393-1833	French	estab. 1936
Phos	14 Zakaria Ahmed	741611 751511	Greek	estab.1896
Arev	3 Suliman al Halabi		Armenian	estab.1915

Major imported English-language newspapers
Many major international papers from Europe and Arab countries are available; among these are the **International Herald Tribune**, the **Guardian**, the **Wall Street Journal**, **USA Today**, the **London Times**, the weekly **Middle East Times** (39 Hegaz MO 346-5953), and the weekly **Middle East Observer** (8 Shawarbi).

Local community newspapers
British Community Association News (1st floor, 2 Abdel Rahman al Rafai DO 349-8870) monthly.
Helioscope (Heliopolis Community Activities Association, PO Box 2534, HE) monthly; free; has info about events in HE.
Maadi Messenger (Maadi Community Church, Road 17 & Port Said, MA 351-2755) bimonthly; free; found at businesses in Maadi.
Papyrus (1 Digla, MO 349-8036)   German-language monthly; German Community Association publication with cultural, historical, touristic information.

Magazines
Like newspapers, Arabic-language magazines are available at newstands throughout the city. English-language magazines are usually found in foreign neighborhoods and hotels. Subscriptions to foreign magazines mailed from abroad are not reliable.

Arabic magazines

October Magazine	1119 Corniche al Nil	746834	weekly; political, social, cultural, & news, 1st pub. Oct. 1976
Akher Saa	Al Sahafa	748888 758888	weekly
al Musawar	16 Mohammed Ezz al Arab	362-5450	weekly popular
Sabah il Kheir	18 Mohammed Said Pasha		weekly
Rose al Youssef	89A Qasr al Aini		satirical political weekly; f. 1925; monthly English section

al Izaa wat	13 Mohammed Ezz al Arab	weekly; radio & TV programs
Television	1117 Corniche al Nil	
	756928 747190	
al Doctor	8 Huda Shaarawi	monthly
Hawa	16 Mohammed Ezz al Arab	weekly women's magazine
	362-5450	
al Kawakeb	16 Mohammed Ezz al Arab	weekly film & cinema
	362-5450	
Daawa	1 al Tawfikia 743296	
La Femme Nouvelle	French & Arabic women's literary magazine	
al Hilal	16 Mohammed Ezz al Arab	literary monthly
al Azhar	Sharia al Azhar religious magazine pub. by Egyptian	
	Council for Islamic Research of al Azhar, founded in 1931	

Arabic-language children's magazines include **Samir** and **Mickey** (published by Dar al Helal), **Megalla, Maged,** and **al Mezwar** (published by Al-Ahram, al Galaa St.).

English-language magazines

Arab Press Review	24 Digla MO	708556	biweekly compilation of political news.
Business Monthly	American Chamber of Commerce, Suite 1541		
	Marriott Hotel, ZA	340-8888 x1541	Business news.
Cairoscope	34 Gamal Salem DO	348-2503	monthly; current events in Cairo.
Cairo Today	24 Syria MO	355-0427	monthly; tourism,
		355-1063	business, history.
Computer Review	24A Abul Mahasin	344-8169	monthly.
	al Shazli, Suite 1002 MO		
Computer User	23 Shehab,	344-8668	every other month
	Suite 402, MO		
Prism	44 Mesaha GI	348-5842	quarterly; arts

Imported magazines include Time, Newsweek, Architectual Digest, Burda, Economist, International Business Week, US News and World Report, Vogue, National Geographic, and hundreds more.

HEALTH AND MEDICAL SERVICES

One can live comfortably in Cairo, but the stress of adjustment, the change of diet, and the presence of health hazards common to most developing countries require precautions. One Cairo physician recommends that persons with the following conditions should not consider assignment in Egypt: kidney failure requiring regular use of an artificial kidney machine, heavy diabetes requiring hospitalization, uncontrolled epilepsy, severe allergic conditions which might be aggravated by a hot and dusty climate, active cancer, undiagnosed dizziness or fainting spells, hemophilia, collagen diseases requiring constant attention, severe paralysis, and tendencies toward depression, anxiety, or amnesia.

DISEASES

Bacterial infections
Gastroenteritis, salmonellosis (food poisoning) and **dysentery** are all carried by water, milk, or food and may be transmitted by flies or humans. Fly control and good hygiene are the best precautions. Food stalls on the street should be avoided. If symptoms are severe or persist for 24 hours, call a doctor. Vomiting and diarrhea can lead to dehydration, evidenced by weakness and excessive thirst, which can in itself be fatal. Small children should be watched carefully for these symptoms. Dehydration should be treated with oral rehydration solution, available at most pharmacies. An emergency solution is a mixture of 1 tablespoon salt, 1 tablespoon sugar and 1 cup water, or a cola. **Typhoid fever,** which is similarly transmitted, is endemic in Egypt. The incubation period is five to fourteen days and immunization is recommended. Early symptoms are headache, lassitude, aches, fever, and restlessness, and perhaps loss of appetite, nosebleeds, cough, diarrhea, or constipation. A persistent fever develops and gradually rises to 103 or 104 F (39.4 or 40 C) after 7 to 10 days. **Cholera**, also transmitted by bad hygiene, has a short incubation period of one to five days and an abrupt onset accompanied by acute diarrhea and prostration. It is characterized by massive diarrhea with rapid and severe depletion of body fluids and salts, and later, vomiting and severe muscular cramps. Chief dangers are from shock and dehydration, which can be fatal. The threat of cholera is periodic in Egypt, usually in summer, and is met with strict controls. It is advisable to take precautions with your tap water in the summer. **Tetanus** (lockjaw) is an acute intoxication of the central nervous system due to poisons produced by a bacterium that enters the body through open wounds and thrives in airless conditions. It is characterized by rigidity and spasms of the voluntary muscles. All wounds should be carefully cleaned, and appropriate immunizations obtained.

Parasitic and fungal infections

Amoebic dysentery is caused by a microscopic single-celled animal, an amoeba, and the main symptom is persistent, intermittent bouts of bloody diarrhea. Amoebas sometimes spread from the digestive tract to the liver where they form abscesses. Diagnosis is by stool examination. Treatment involves taking specific anti-amoebic drugs, usually for one to three weeks. If left untreated it will spread and cause permanent damage. The symptoms of **Giardia lamblia**, a common parasitic infection, include signs of nutritional deficiency such as weight loss, light stools and a feeling of congestion not unlike that associated with hepatitis. Diagnosis is by stool examination, and it is possible to recover within five days. **Pinworm** is recognized by itching around the anal area. Treatment includes a medication, boiling underclothes, nightclothes and bedclothes and careful cleansing of hands. **Headlice** may be picked up by children anywhere. Both nits (eggs) and lice must be killed and removed. Clothes should be laundered or dusted with chemicals specified by your doctor; Kwell or Eurax can be used on the scalp. **Tinea**, or skin fungus includes ringworm and athlete's foot. Treatments vary, but all medications are available. **Schistosomiasis (bilharziasis)**, infestation with blood flukes or flat worms hosted during a portion of their cycle by snails, is endemic in the tropics wherever there is still or slowmoving water. People become infected by wading or bathing in water containing cercaria (the free-swimming state of the schistosome). Cases among foreigners are rare, but do occur. Symptoms include inflammation, cough, late-afternoon fever, skin eruption, swelling and tenderness of the liver; blood in stools and urine in the more acute stage. Early diagnosis and persistent treatment usually ensure recovery. The Theodor Bilharz Research Institute, Warraq al Hadr, Imbaba 340-5633/4381 341-7181 is a hospital and research center with an outpatient clinic which specializes in treatment of this disease. **Malaria** still occurs in the Nile Delta and some remote areas of Egypt, but it is not considered to occur in Cairo, and you do not need malaria prophylactic medicine unless you are traveling to the far south or into sub-Saharan Africa.

Viral diseases

Rabies exists throughout Africa and can be contracted not only by a bite but also mere contact with the saliva of a rabid animal. It is fatal if not treated in time. Avoid stray animals, or pets that might have encountered stray animals, and seek medical advice at once if there is the slightest suspicion of contact. The suspected animal must be caught and kept under observation to determine if it is infected. If bitten by a stray animal, flush the wound with soap and running water for twenty minutes and go to the doctor. If you have not been vaccinated against rabies you must undergo a series of shots. This vaccine has improved in recent years and currently requires only 3 to 5 shots. The preventative vaccine, which costs from LE30 to LE50, is available from Drs. Adel Naguib and Wasfi Botros, 7 Zaki, Midan Tawfikia, off Ramsis 745204/315 673585, open 9am to 8pm, closed Friday; Dr. Gamil Osman, Shubra al Khalafawy Company, 1353 Corniche al Nil, behind al Nasr Import-Export Company, 943512 8am to 3pm. Closes at 2pm on Thursday, closed Friday; and the Hospital of the Rabies Institute (Maahad al Kilab), Imbaba 346-2042/3. **Hepatitis** is endemic in Egypt. Infectious hepatitis is a virus transmitted through water, contaminated or improperly cooked food, and by contact with an infected individual. Some protection is given by strict hygiene and by gamma globulin. Serum hepatitis is a viral infection spread through the blood, and is most likely to be transmitted by improperly sterilized needles and syringes. Classic symptoms are yellow skin, mucus membranes and whites of eyes, brownish urine, enlargement of the liver, pain, acute sensitivity to smells, excessive fatigue, acute loss of appetite and projected vomiting. Treatment is bedrest, a diet of no fats, followed by reduction of activity. Medication is for symptom relief only. Alcohol must be avoided. The mortality rate is low. **Yellow Fever** vaccinations are not required in Egypt unless the traveler is coming from or going to a country where yellow fever is prevalent, such as sub-Saharan Africa. **Smallpox** has been eradicated worldwide. However, because the last known cases of the disease occurred in Somalia, not far to the south of Egypt, the Egyptian Government has retained the requirement of having a vaccination. Travelers from the U.S. and Europe are not required to have this vaccination (see Travel and Transportation section for information about immunizations).

AIDS (Acquired Immune Deficiency Syndrome) As of February 1988, Egypt has taken several precautions to prevent the spread of this disease. These include: increased use of disposable syringes, listing of victims by authorities, screening of blood kept for transfusion, the banning of importation of blood unless it has an AIDS-free certificate, and increasing public awareness of how to fight the disease. Be especially careful about obtaining gamma globulin, the injection which increases resistance to hepatitis, because this is a blood product and can carry the virus. AIDS is NOT transmitted through touch, respiration, insects, or swimming pools.

HEALTH PRECAUTIONS

Apart from colds and flu, the most common ailments that foreigners suffer in Egypt are food- and water-borne diseases caused by bacteria, viruses, and parasites.

The **water** in Cairo is treated and safe when it leaves the purification plant, but it is possible that it will become contaminated between the plant and your tap. Do not drink the tap water if it is tainted in color or if the water has recently been off. Many people prefer to boil the water (for 10-20 minutes), use a filter or buy bottled water (see Household section). Purification filters can be bought in supermarkets and appliance stores. Precautions must be taken in out of the way places like the oases. Garden water often comes directly from the Nile and should not be drunk. Especially in hot weather, be sure food is refrigerated.

Overindulgence in unfamiliar foods, or eating food that is not peeled or thoroughly cooked such as salads, rare or raw meat, unpasteurized dairy products, or raw seafood may cause **Pharaoh's Revenge.** The main symptoms are diarrhea and nausea. It strikes many people abroad: one does not have to go to a developing country to get it. Do not eat food sold by sidewalk vendors. Peel fruits and vegetables that are eaten raw, and wash those that cannot be peeled in a detergent or bleach solution (1 cupful Clorox to 1 gallon water). Home remedies for diarrhea include a diet of plain toast, boiled rice, and plain tea. **Lomotil** and **Immodium** are dangerous drugs to take without a doctor's close supervision; safer drugs available in Egyptian pharmacies include **Entocid** (take 2 right away and 1 every 6 to 8 hours thereafter or for the next 48 hours) and **Buscopan**. Aspirin and painkillers aggravate gastrointestinal distress. See a doctor if the diarrhea persists for more than 2 days. The main danger of diarrhea is dehydration;

this is treatable with a product called **Rehydrin**, available in any pharmacy (the package has a picture of a mother and child on the front because it was developed to reduce infant deaths in Egypt from dehydration). Other rehydrating liquids include clear broth, unsweetened apple juice, and herb teas. In the event of severe vomiting that lasts more than 24 hours, diarrhea that persists for more than 48 hours, the appearance of blood in the stool, severe dehydration, or a combination of fever, diarrhea, and vomiting all together, see a doctor at once.

Home emergency treatment for **poison** is to have the patient take 2 slices of burnt toast crushed to powder with 4 tablespoons of milk of magnesia and 4 tablespoons of strong tea. For help call the emergency poison center at the Children's Hospital, Ain Shams University, Midan Abbassia, 823314 834114 821455 828212.

HEALTH CARE

The **red crescent** is the symbol of medical services, equivalent to the red cross seen in many countries. It designates hospitals, ambulances and other medical services.

Physicians
Nearly all Egyptian doctors speak English and many have studied in the United States or England. Lists of doctors can be found in the **Maadi Telephone Book.** Companies keep lists for their employees, hotels have doctors on call, and for further information embassies can be consulted. **Working hours** are usually in the evening, and doctors also make house calls. In Egypt, doctor's offices are called clinics or surgeries. Appointments can be made in advance, but you can also walk in. Patients are seen in order of arrival. The fee is approximately LE20 (students are sometimes charged less) and should be paid to the office clerk upon entering the office. **As Salam International Hospital** on the Corniche to Maadi has an out-patient clinic which opens daily at 10am, emergency number 363-8764; 363-8050/4196/8424. The British Community Association has a clinic at the **Anglo-American Hospital**, Zohoreya ZA, next to the Cairo Tower, 341-8630 340-6162-5 x315, open M-Th 9-12 and F-S 9-11.

Alternative medicine includes herbalists who have been operating in Cairo since medieval times. For specific names and services, see the Shopping section.

Hospitals
Hospital service has greatly improved in Egypt in recent years. Several full-facility, well-equipped hospitals have opened. In Egypt it is unusual for a hospital to accept any type of medical insurance; therefore patients should be prepared to pay cash for treatment. **Patients will not be admitted without a substantial deposit.** To this end many companies have placed deposits at specific hospitals for their employees. The newer hospitals offer 24-hr emergency care and are equipped with modern, first-rate equipment and staff, but some of the older hospitals expect the patient to provide nursing care, food, and sometimes even sheets, drugs and blood.

Some of the more modern hospitals are:
Abdel Kader Fahmi Hospital 23 Hassan Aftahoun HE 663138; **Anglo-American Hospital** Zohoreya, next to the Cairo Tower, ZA 341-8630; **As Salam International Hospital** Corniche al Nil, PO Box 388, MA 363-8050/4196/8424/8764; **Agouza Hospital** 178 Al Nil AG 346-2007; **Arab Contractors Hospital** Autostrade, Nasr City 828907 832534 838642 833501/408; **Cairo Medical Center**, Midan Roxi HE 258-0237/0636; **Coptic Hospital** 175 Ramsis 904972/834/435; **Heliopolis Hospital** 1 Hegaz HE 243-0733/3185 245-0986; **Italian Hospital** Abbassia 821433; **Nile Badrawi Hospital** Corniche al Nil MA 363-8688 363-8167/8; **al Salam Hospital** 3 Syria MO 346-7062/3.

Specialized clinics, institutes, and services
Capritage Helwan 784664 offers sulfur baths, paraffin baths, mud baths, whirlpools, short-wave and ultraviolet treatments. You must arrive early Friday morning to visit the doctor, who will recommend the specific treatment.
ETAMS Tours Egyptian Company for Tourism and Medical Services 99 Ramsis, 4th floor, 754721 752462 offers special tours of Egypt with Dr. Sami Bishara, radiologist and physiotherapist, on special buses and taxis, for the elderly, arthritic, or handicapped.
Children's Hospital Abu Riche Hospital, Ali Ibrahim, Munira, Sayeda Zeinab 849063; 846718; 841201.
Hospital of the Rabies Institute (Maahad al Kilab), Imbaba 346-2042/3. Rabies vaccine.
Research Institute for Tropical Medicine 10-11 Kasr al Aini 842494. While the medical and laboratory research units are temporarily closed for refurbishment, a small public service clinic is still maintained on the premises.
NAMRU (U.S. Naval Medical Research Unit) Midan Abbassia 820727/611 355-7371 x2293.
Nasr Institute 1351 Corniche al Nil, Shubra 685261. 24hr emergency medical care.
Poison Center, Children's Hospital, Ain Shams University, Midan Abbassia 821455 828212 823314.
Serum and Vaccine Production and Research Institute Abbassia 821866 820920. Snake bite antivenom.
Theodor Bilharz Research Institute, Warraq al Hadr, Imbaba, 340-5633/4381 341-7181 A teaching institute in schistosomiasis and endemic parisitological diseases with a fully staffed clinic.

Ambulance service
If the patient can still move himself, it is likely to be faster to take a taxi to the nearest hospital. However, the following ambulance services are efficient: **As Salam International Hospital** 363-8050/4196/8424/8764; **Flying Hospital Ambulance Service** al Shabrawishi Hospital, DO 701465 provides ambulances equipped with life-saving equipment/diagnostic tools, drugs, and physicians; the government-owned **Cairo Ambulance Service** 770227 770123 and **Giza Ambulance Service** 720123, offer free services to the nearest hospital. There is a fee for transport to any other hospital.

If **evacuation** from Egypt becomes necessary, there are at least two companies which offer emergency airlifting of medical patients to Europe. The fee for non-members depends upon the cost of the service, and is usually in the range of $35-40,000. **International SOS Assistance, Incorporated** have an office in Cairo. Their service is designed to provide travelers with medical, legal, financial, and personal assistance in case of a medical emergency. The rates are $15 weekly, $45 monthly, and $195 annually. Non-members pay a fee-for-service. Ms. Nevine Wahab, at Cairoscan, 35 Suliman Abaza MO 717553/563/480, arranges emergency transport. The US address is P.O. Box 11568, Philadelphia, PA 19116, USA. **Swiss Air Rescue**, REGA, 8058 Zurich, Switzerland. Tel: 0041-1-47-47-47.

Medical assistance for travelers
IAMAT International Association for Medical Assistance to Travelers has physicians on call 24hrs a day in 125 countries. Membership, by donation, provides health information and a list of participating doctors. Write to 188 Nicklin Road, Guelph Ontario N1H 7L5 Canada; PO Box 5049 Christchurch 5 New Zealand; Gotthardstrasse 17, CH 6300 Zug, Switzerland or 417 Center Street Lewiston NY 14092 USA. **Worldwide Access** (run by Blue Cross/Blue Shield, USA) specializes in healthcare abroad. For more information about their services, write 923 Investment Building, 1511 K St. NW, Washington DC 20005.

Insurance
If you are not covered by a major hospital plan, the British Community Association has a medical scheme open to all foreign passport holders. It includes such benefits as arranging housecalls, guaranteeing deposit at three good hospitals and free service at the clinic at Anglo-American Hospital. Membership costs from LE60-250, yearly and is available for residents, visitors, and companies. 340-6162-5, x315 or 341-8630.

Pharmacies
Pharmacies are usually staffed by competent professionals who can help you in your health care. Many pharmaceuticals are produced in Egypt by such companies as Squibb, Swiss-Pharma, Hoechst-Orient, ABI, PHIZER, EPPICO, CIB, and KAHTRA. Both locally made and imported medication is subsidized by the government and is inexpensive. Some medication requiring prescriptions abroad is sold over the counter in Egypt. Doctors tend to order copious amounts of drugs. Read all labels carefully and be sure you want to take the medication. Antibiotics should be taken carefully.

Medicines available in Cairo known to have dangerous side effects
Enterovioform has been successfully used as a prophylactic for traveler's diarrhea and amoebiasis but has been demonstrated to be potentially carcinogenic and may also cause damage to the retina and eventual blindness. For this reason, it has not been approved by the United States Food and Drug Administration. **Lomotil** and **Immodium**, other drugs used to treat diarrhea, should not be taken without a doctor's supervision. Aminoglycosides, which include **streptomycin, neomycin** (the most dangerous), **kanamycin, amikacin, gentamicin, tobramycin,** and **paramomycin,** can cause kidney damage and permanent deafness, so should be used only in cases of life-threatening infections. **Chloramphenicol** can cause a form of anemia that is sometimes fatal, but it is still one of the drugs of choice for meningitis. **Clindamycin** can cause fatal colitis. **Lincomycin** can cause severe diarrhea. **Corticosteroids,** which include **hydrocortisone, predisolone, prednisone,** etc., can be dangerous, causing mutations at the cellular level. It can stunt the growth of children. Adults should use these drugs only under a competent doctor's supervision, and usage of these drugs should never be stopped abruptly; the dosage should be gradually reduced. **Antibiotics** are useless against colds, viruses or influenza and can cause secondary infections by disrupting the normal bacteria balance of the intestine and other organs. There is also a danger of building up resistance to them, so use them sparingly.

Additional products found in pharmacies are diapers, sanitary napkins, some beauty products, liquid ammonia (nashaadir), baking soda, mothballs (naftaliin), vitamins, and saline solution for contact lenses (contained in IV bottles — make sure seal is good when you open it).

24 hour pharmacies include:
Ataba Ataba Pharmacy 17 Midan Ataba 910831; **Central Cairo** Isaaf Pharmacy 3 26th July, 743369; Seif Pharmacy Kasr Al Aini 354-2678; **Heliopolis** Al Ezabi Pharmacy 1 Ahmed Taysir 663409; Saad Pharmacy 3 Osman Ibn Affan 665854; **Maadi** As Salam International Hospital Maadi Corniche 842188; Esam Pharmacy 101 Road 9 350-4126; Mishriki Pharmacy 81 Road 153 350-3333; **Zamalek:** Zamalek Pharmacy 3 Shagaret al Dorr 340-2406.

Contact lenses & glasses It is probably a good idea to bring an extra pair or two from your home country, but all services and supplies are available in Cairo, including frames, lenses (including plastic and tinted), bifocals, hard and soft contact lenses, solutions and equipment.

WHO Cards see Travel section

Centigrade to Fahrenheit thermometer temperature conversion

C.	35	36	37	38	39	40	41
	Below Normal		Normal		Above Normal		
F.	95	96.8	98.6	100.4	102.2	104	105.8

Veterinary and Pet Care
Pets should be immunized against rabies, and immunization kept up to date; this is especially true for pets acquired locally.

Brooke Hospital 2 Bayram al Tonsi, Sayeda Zeinab 849312.
New Maadi Veterinary Clinic 5 Road 278 New Maadi 352-6693 11-1 and 5-8.
People's Dispensary for Sick Animals (PDSA), al Sikka al Beida (off Salah Salem to Heliopolis) 822294. Outpatient clinic, 83 26th July 772227. Boarders accepted.
Kennels are available at the Brooke Hospital and the PDSA. Any of the above can recommend a veterinarian.

YOUR COMMUNITY

Cairo is an old city in an even older culture. Its people have a long, deep-rooted sense of the past. Traditions and customs, both urban and rural, have been handed down generation after generation. Layer upon layer of foreign influence through centuries of conquest has been absorbed, until what has emerged is a unique, rich array of customs, traditions and cultures in a cosmopolitan and exciting community.

THE PEOPLE

Although the millions of people called Egyptian have a wide variety of lifestyles and backgrounds, three groups of people are unique in Egypt, the **fellahin**, **Bedouin** and **Nubians**. Foreigners, who see within the cities similarities with their own cultures, find the traditional people fascinating because their way of life reflects a different perspective. The **fellahin** are the farmers of Egypt who live in villages along the Nile. They are the backbone of the agricultural economy. Some still live in mud brick homes, farm as they did in the days of the pharaohs, and cling to traditions thousands of years old. The **Bedouin** were originally the nomad wanderers of the desert. They once lived in tents, herded goats and camels and trekked freely over extensive areas of desert and wasteland in search of good grazing for their flocks. This made them excellent trackers and guides. Today there are very few people in the Middle East who still practice this type of lifestyle, but their strong heritage is still evident in desert areas. The **Nubians** have lived in the desert along the Nile spanning northern Sudan and southern Egypt for thousands of years. From 1902, when the first dam was erected at Aswan, the land available has become less and less, and the Nubian culture has been under siege. Today there are more Nubians living outside of Nubia than within the ancestral lands, but the gay and lively tone and atmosphere in Aswan is still dominated by the Nubian culture.

CUSTOMS

The manners and customs of such a diverse culture are abundant and vary from one group of people to another and one part of the country to another. Your Egyptian friends are a good source of information as to how they celebrate special occassions. If you have the opportunity to share such occasions, here are some guidelines.

Birth When a child is born in an Egyptian family it is customary for friends to visit the mother and child. A gift is usually brought for the child. Some families hold a **sabua**, a special celebration held on the seventh day after the child is born.

Death Obituaries are usually printed in the Arabic newspaper Al Ahram. People who cannot offer condolences in person often send a telegram to the family. In both Muslim and Coptic families the men sometimes receive friends for one day in a **chader**, a tent erected especially for the occasion. Copts will also receive condolences in the church. Women do not visit the chader but go to the home where the female members of the family receive visitors. Condolence visits (of both men and women) to the home continue for three days. The 2 major Muslim chaders, often used for funerals of important or famous people, are the one adjacent to the **Omar Makram Mosque** on Midan Tahrir, and **Dar al Munasbat**, beside Merryland in Heliopolis. The funerals of Coptic dignitaries are held in their own parish. A phrase of condolence is **al ba'iyya fi Hayaatak.**

Greetings Egyptians greet each other with a handshake and often a kiss on both cheeks. An especially warm greeting involves several kisses. This is a wonderful custom but there are some social restrictions. Most importantly, it is normally only used by men with men and by women with women. Usually only in cases of close relatives (and even then rarely in public) will a man and woman greet each other in this way. When meeting an Egyptian for the first time, foreigners should not use this greeting. A simple handshake will do.

Meals Lunch is the traditional meal for inviting guests in some families, especially if the invitation is intimate and includes all the family members. It usually begins around 3pm and is the main meal of the day. A dinner invitation is more formal and usually involves a fair number of guests. The meal will be late, often at midnight. The first time one is invited to dinner, a gift, like flowers or candy, is in order. Don't bring anything alcoholic.

Marriage The path to matrimony begins in a Muslim family when the man goes to a male guardian of the woman to ask permission to marry. If they come to an agreement, the man buys the woman a **shabka**, or engagement gift of gold or diamonds and a formal engagement is announced. This is legalized by reading the **Fatha**, the opening chapter of the Koran, which is often followed by an engagement party hosted by the family of the bride. The wedding takes place when the men of the family, in the presence of a religious leader, write a formal contract of marriage. This is called **Katb al Kitab,** the writing of the book. In this contract both parties spell out specifically the arrangements under which they agree to marry. Although couples are officially married at this point, they may choose to live apart until they have completed arrangements for their household. The man's family is usually responsible for providing the living quarters, the woman's the furnishings. Once the contract is signed the marriage is legal. Usually a wedding reception takes place. **Coptic** marriages begin in the same way, with a formal proposal and a shabka. The engagement and the wedding are then held in a church. **Wedding gifts** are part of both Moslem and Coptic traditions. A wedding gift should be something for the house, and should not be given to the couple at the wedding, but on a separate visit. Gifts are rarely opened immediately and in your presence, but will be set aside. Flowers are considered a compliment, not a gift. **Divorce** is governed by religious law in Egypt. The Coptic faith forbids divorce, but under special circumstances divorces are granted. Islam provides for divorce.

CALENDARS AND HOLIDAYS

Calendars

There are three calendars in common use in Egypt. The **western** (Gregorian) calendar (BC/AD) is used for most secular purposes. The **Islamic** calendar (AH), used primarily for religious purposes, is lunar with 12 months of 29 or 30 days. Eleven days shorter than the Gregorian calendar, it moves around the seasons in a 33 year cycle. The **Coptic** calendar (AM) is solar with 12 months of 30 days and 5 extra days each year, with a sixth day being added every 4 years. Used mainly by farmers in managing their crops, it is commonly believed to be the ancient Egyptian calendar. The following lists (which are not a table of correspondence) give the Arabic names of the months in each of the three calendars, starting in each case with the first month of the year:

Gregorian	Islamic	Coptic
yanaayir	muHarram (begins Aug 1, 1989)	tuut (begins Sept 11 or 12)
fibraayir	Safar	baaba
maaris	rabii' il-awwal	hatuur
abriil	rabii' it-taani	kiyaak
maayu	gamaada-l-uula (Jan 89)	Tuuba (mid-Jan)
yunyu	gamaada-l-ukhra	amshiir
yulyu	ragab	baramhat
aghusTus	sha'baan	barmuuda
sibtambar	ramaDaan	bashans
uktuubar	shawwaal	ba'uuna
nufambar	zuu-l-qi'da	abiib
disambar	zuu-l-Higga	misra
		naasi

N.B. The months of the Gregorian calendar are often referred to by their numbers: shahr waahid (January), shahr tamanya (August), etc.

Holidays

There are five secular holidays in the year, when banks, government offices, businesses and schools are closed. They are: **Liberation of Sinai Day,** April 25; **Labor Day,** May 1; **Anniversary of the 1952 Revolution,** July 23; **Armed Forces Day,** October 6; and **Shamm al Nisim,** which is celebrated on the Monday after Coptic Easter. Shamm al Nisim has existed since Pharaonic times and is a spring ritual literally meaning "sniffing the breeze". It is traditional for people to picnic on this day. In Upper Egypt private gardens are opened to the public. It is traditional to eat colored eggs. This is the origin of the western tradition of dyeing eggs.

In addition, the people of Egypt observe special days for various professions. These are not public holidays, and there is business as usual. Some are:

Father's Day February 4   **Mother's Day** March 21
Teachers' Day March 3   **Applied Artists** March 25
Doctors' and Dentists' Day March 18   **Farmers' Day** September 9

For a list of religious observances, including those which constitute public holidays, see under Religion below.

RELIGION

Islam

The official religion of Egypt is **Islam**, revealed to the Prophet Mohammed in Mecca, Saudia Arabia, beginning in 610AD. Islam has five major principles, called pillars. The first is **al Shahaada**, the belief that there is only one God and that the Prophet Mohammed is the messenger of God. The second is prayer, **salaah**. Prayer is performed five times a day and can be conducted in any place as long as it is done facing Mecca. Prayer times when the muezzin will be heard calling people to prayer are at dawn, **al fagr**, noon, **al duhr**, afternoon, **al 'asr**, sunset, **al maghrib** and at evening, **al 'isha**. The main prayer time is Friday at noon, **al gum'a**, when most men congregate at the mosque. The third principal of faith is alms, **zakaah**. By religious law Moslems give a certain amount of their savings to the poor. The fourth pillar is fasting during the holy month of Ramadan (see below). The fifth pillar is pilgrimage, **al higg**, which lasts at least 3 days. All Muslims hope they can make this traditional visit to Mecca at least once in their lifetime. The pilgrimage is performed during the month of Zuul-Higga, seventy days after the end of the Ramadan fast.

There is no priesthood in Islam, but there are religious scholars who can be consulted on religious matters. A **mufti** is a professional jurist who interprets religious law. An **'alim** (plural **'ulema**) is a theological scholar. A **sheikh** is a religious scholar. An **imam** is associated with a particular mosque and leads all prayers there.

Religious observances

(Each entry listed below is followed by the Islamic date and the Gregorian equivalent for 1989. Gregorian dates may differ by a day. For an explanation of the various calenders used in Egypt, see above.)

Islamic New Year, Ras al Sana al Higriya, is a **public holiday** in Egypt. (1 Muharram, August 1, 1989.)

Ashura This is a day of mourning sacred to the Shiite Moslems, the anniversary of Hussein's martyrdom at Kerbala, 10 Muharram, AH 60. However it has become a traditional celebration for all Muslim Egyptians. Some people fast on this day. Traditional foods include **Ashura**, a wheat pudding, and **Bilila**, wheat with milk and sugar. (10 Muharram, August 10, 1989.)

The Prophet's Birthday, Mulid al Nabi, is celebrated with great festivity in Egypt. Traditionally, a procession is held in the al Azhar area of the city, with colorful flags, colored banners and medieval costumes. Special sugar confectioneries are given as presents to children. Tents and stalls specializing in a variety of decorated candy are set up all over the country. A **public holiday**. (12 Rabi al Awal, October 12, 1989.)

Laylat al Esraa wa al Mi'rag This night commemorates the Prophet's miraculous journey. It is believed that during a single night he traveled from Mecca to Jerusalem, ascended to paradise, and returned again to earth. Some people fast. Mosques are decorated with colored lights. Religious festivities are held near al Azhar. (27 Ragab, March 5 1989.)

Ramadan, Islam's holiest month, is a month of fasting. The faithful abstain from food, drink, smoking and sex throughout daylight hours. Children, pregnant women, the sick, and people traveling are among those exempt from the fast. The fast begins just before dawn, at a point called **al imsaak,** when it is light enough to distinguish a white thread from a black one, and ends after sunset with the call to prayer, **al maghrib.** The fast is broken by a meal called **iftar.** If invited to an iftar, punctuality is important, for guests must arrive before the call to prayer. A good gift to bring to the host is **konafa,** a sweet of fine noodles mixed with nuts and raisins and soaked in honey.

During Ramadan the business day begins late and ends early. At dusk the streets are deserted as families gather to break the fast. Evening festivities, which last until dawn, center around al Hussein near the Khan al Khalili, and include musicians, actors, storytellers, acrobats, puppet shows and Koran recitals. Special television programs include the **fawaziir,** a modern-day adaptation of the riddles the medieval storytellers would present in town squares. (Begins April 6, 1989.)

Night of the Worth, Laylat al Qadr, is observed on the 26th night of Ramadan and commemorates the Prophet Mohammed receiving the first **sura,** or chapter, of the **Koran,** the holy book of Islam, from the Archangel Gabriel. It is especially holy and it is believed prayers are answered on this night. (26 Ramadan, May 3, 1989.)

The Feast of Breaking the Fast, Eid al Fitr, also known as the Small Bairam, celebrates the end of Ramadan. Special morning prayers are held in mosques. It is a time of celebration, with family visits, new clothes for children and gifts including **'idiyya,** new money and new coins. Festivities usually last three days and it is a **public holiday.** (1-3 Shawal, May 6-8, 1989.)

The Feast of the Sacrifice, Eid al Adha, also called the Big Bairam, begins approximately 70 days after the end of Ramadan and commemorates Abraham's sacrifice of a sheep in place of his son. The morning starts with the special **Salaat al Eid,** prayer of the feast. Following the prayer, it is traditional to slaughter a lamb and immediately share the meat with the extended family, neighbors, and the poor. Festivities last for four days, and it is a **public holiday.** (10 Zuul-Higga, July 13-6, 1989.)

Coptic Orthodox

The Copts, a minority, are the heirs of the early Christian church in Egypt. The head of the Coptic community is the Patriarch, currently Pope Shenuda III. The hierarchy of the Coptic church is very similar to that of the Roman Catholic church: pope, cardinal, bishop, monsignor, monk, priest, and altar man. Only monks, who are forbidden to marry, are eligible to attain the highest orders in the Coptic faith.

Religious Observances
Coptic New Year, Nayruuz, September 11 (or 12 in leap year). Not a public holiday.

Christmas, Eid al Milad, January 7. The Copts fast for 43 days in preparation for the feast celebrating the birth of Jesus Christ. During the fast the desert monasteries are closed to the public. The fast, which demands abstinence from animal flesh and animal products, is broken on Christmas Eve, following the midnight mass. Some Coptic families exchange Christmas presents and have a Christmas tree.

Epiphany, Eid al Ghutaas, January 19. Epiphany commemorates the baptism of Jesus Christ by John the Baptist and is celebrated by a special evening mass on the eve of Epiphany. All masses between Christmas and Epiphany are full of joyous chanting.

Easter, Eid al Qiyama: **Palm Sunday,** Sha'nin, or Hadd al Za'f, begins **Passion Week,** Esbooa al Alam. Black cloth bands are hung around the church as a symbol of mourning for the death of Christ. All week long there are morning and evening daily prayers, characterized by mournful chanting. On **Holy Thursday**, Khamis al 'Ahad, the priest re-enacts Jesus washing the feet of his disciples at the Last Supper by making the sign of the cross with water on the legs of the men attending the mass. On **Good Friday**, al Gum'a al Hazina, prayers continue from morning to 6pm to commemorate the different events of the crucifixion. On **Holy Saturday,** Sabt al Nur, the reading of the Book of Revelation, which began about 11pm on Friday, is concluded with a sunrise service. Following this mass all the black bands hanging in the church are removed to commemorate the joy of the risen Christ. The Easter service, held Holy Saturday evening, lasts from 8pm till midnight, and is one of celebration. After the service, the fast which began 55 days before is broken.

Pentecost, Huluul al Ruh al Qudus, is 50 days after Easter. These fifty days are considered days of joy, and there is no fasting at all, even on the traditional fasting days of Wednesdays and Fridays. The celebration is concluded with Pentecost, the coming of the Holy Spirit.

Apostles' Feast, Eid al Rusul, July 12. This feast commemorates the martyrdom of the apostles Peter and Paul. Fasting in preparation for this feast begins the day after Pentecost.

Feast of the Virgin Mary, Eid Sayida al Azra, August 22. This feast commemorates the ascension of the Virgin Mary to heaven. Fasting in preparation for this feast runs from August 7 to 21. A church service is held on the morning of the 22nd, after which people break the fast.

Mulids
Mulids are enjoyed by both Copts and Muslims and are celebrations in honor of saints and pious persons. They take place all over Egypt and are usually celebrated on dates related to the lives of the individuals. Festivities include prayer, food stalls and special foods, story-telling, zikrs, dervishes, fire swallowers, tamed animals, parades, games and rides. In visiting a mulid, a foreigner should remember that religious zeal is running high, and conservative clothing, discretion with a camera, and unobtrusive behavior is recommended.

THE FOREIGN COMMUNITY

Adjustment to Egypt may take time and affects different members of the family in different ways. Sociologists have observed that there is an adjustment period of at least six months for

the average newcomer. The period of adjustment includes a phase of alienation, a phase of rejection, a period of wanting to go home, and ultimately, acceptance and enjoyment.

The wage-earner must make adjustments in business practices, routines, and procedures. The homekeeper will find shopping, maintenance, and household duties different. Children must make new friends and adjust to new schools, different types of play areas, and a new set of restrictions. All of these are big adjustments for the family. Support systems to help make this transition exist at schools, churches, and community organizations.

Some Things To Remember

Affection Although one may see an occasional couple holding hands, public displays of affection between men and women are frowned upon in Egypt.

Alcohol is available in Egypt, but excessive indulgence is not acceptable. Islamic law prohibits the use of alcohol by Muslims. Never bring alcohol as a gift to a Muslim family.

Children Egypt is safe for children. They will be helped if lost, guided if confused, and mothered by everyone on the street. Children should be made familiar with traffic patterns and discouraged from playing in garbage dumpsters, which are located on many street corners and can be extremely interesting to children. Stray animals are also an attraction which must be carefully avoided because of the high incidence of rabies. There are few community gathering places or community events for teenagers. Most teenage activities revolve around the school or church.

Crime Cairo is a safe city. Violent crime including rape are extremely rare, but there are pickpockets and purse-snatchers. In recent years, robberies have started to occur in the more affluent neighborhoods. If you are a victim of a crime, report it to the police and your place of business immediately.

Crowds Cairo is a densely populated city of over 14 million people. The downtown streets are extremely congested both day and night. Most people do not seem to need the personal space that most westerners expect; therefore mingling in crowds can be quite uncomfortable for foreigners.

Drug abuse Egyptian law prescribes severe punishments for persons found guilty of using drugs, and even more severe penalties for those selling them. The abuse of canabis and similar drugs such as hashish also carry strict penalties. Smuggling drugs into Egypt can carry the death sentence. For trafficking or dealing in drugs either the death penalty or life imprisonment is mandatory; even being found in possession of drugs is an offence which can result in a long term of imprisonment. A foreigner in Egypt is subject to Egyptian law. Parents should keep in mind that drugs such as barbiturates and amphetamines, requiring prescriptions abroad, are often sold over the counter and easily accessible in Egypt.

Time Egyptians have a relaxed sense of time. If invited to your home, many Egyptians will arrive a discreet half hour to 2 hours late. The abruptness of strangers is often interpreted as rudeness.

An Egyptian never begrudges the time it takes to say hello, nor should you. Even when asking a stranger for directions, it is important to greet him first.

Legal Matters for Foreigners
Birth in Egypt The parents of the new-born child should contact the consular section of their embassy, in order to obtain a birth certificate, and passport for the new citizen. They will need their marriage certificate, the Egyptian birth certificate from the hospital where the child was born, proof of separation if either parent has been previously married, three 2x2 photographs of the baby and a fee of LE80 for Americans and LE100 for British nationals. All documents in Arabic must be translated. For Americans, if only one of the parents is American, that parent must provide proof of having lived in the US for 5 years, 2 of which must have been after the age of 14. The child may receive an individual passport or be added to either parent's passport. The Egyptian government requires all foreigners to register the birth of a child at the Mogamma and apply for the appropriate visa and residence permits.

Death in Egypt A doctor must pronounce the death and issue a death certificate, which must be endorsed by the Public Health Department. The doctor will notify the security police. It is important that the deceased's passport and/or birth certificate be found. The deceased's embassy will help acquire all the necessary documents and help make arrangements for repatriation or burial. It will cost approximately $2,500 to ship an American home, and LE1,000 for a British national. Payment must be assured by the company of the deceased or the next-of-kin. There are several cemeteries in Cairo where foreigners may be buried. Costs will be approximately LE700.

Some Christian Cemeteries in Egypt
Armenian Orthodox Church maintains two cemeteries for persons of Armenian descent. The first, founded in 1950, is located behind Kulliet al Banat in Heliopolis 673407. The second, **Madafen Marmena**, Midan Tibee, next to the Abul Rish Hospital 844580, was founded 300 years ago and is of historical importance because Armenian poets, writers and politicians are buried there. Both cemeteries are maintained by the Armenian Patriarchate 179 Ramsis, next to the Coptic Hospital, 901385 906671.

Coptic Cemeteries There are many Coptic cemeteries in Cairo. Several are located on Sharia Seka al Beida in Abbassia. The area is often referred to as **al Gebel al Asfar**, the Yellow Mountain. Three of these cemeteries are: **Deir al A'bat** 820292, **Deir al Latin** 839180 and **Coptic Catholic** 846263.

Greek Catholic Cemetery 1 Mari Girgis 842293 was established in the 1800s and is maintained by St. George's Church. Maronites and Greek Orthodox may also be buried here. A **Greek Orthodox Cemetery** is located along the same street at 11 Mari Girgis 843683.

Protestant Cemeteries At Sharia Abu Seifein in Old Cairo opposite the Mosque of Amr are two cemeteries. The first is referred to as the **American Cemetery** and contains graves of the early American missionaries to Egypt. The second is primarily a **British Cemetery** at 17 Abu Seifein 841914.

Roman Catholic Cemetery for French and Italians There are two Latin Catholic cemeteries in the north of Cairo. The first, at Sharia Magral Oyun, Fumm al Khalig, 845398 was founded over 200 years ago and is the largest cemetery for Catholics in Egypt. It is maintained by St Joseph's Church, Sharia Emad al Din. The second is in the al Gebel al Asfar area of Abbassia at 51 Seka al Beida 839180. Land is available here on a permanent or temporary lease basis. Contact Louis Gergis 839180. An additional Roman Catholic cemetery is found in Old Cairo across the street from the Mosque of Amr. Often referred to as the **Italian Cemetery,** 845396.

Marriage Two foreigners who wish to marry in Egypt must obtain an affidavit for marriage from their embassy. This affidavit, or letter of no objection, is in two parts, one in English and one in Arabic. The first part must be validated by the embassy. It affirms that both parties are free to marry. If either of the parties has been married before they must provide proof of divorce or death of the previous spouse. For **Americans** this requires an original copy of the divorce papers or death certificate stamped with official stamps and either signed by the Secretary of State of the United States or by the nearest Egyptian consulate abroad. **British nationals** must sign a Statutory Declaration witnessed by the Consul of the British Embassy. Once the affidavit has been notarized by the embassy it must be taken to the Ministry of Foreign Affairs, Sharia Gamat al Dowal al Arabiya MO, where the Arabic part, which is an exact translation, will be notarized. The couple is then free to marry. Although couples may be married in a religious ceremony, the marriage is not legal in Egypt unless it is registered in a civil court. Civil courts exist in all cities, but only two deal regularly with foreigners, one in Cairo at 4 al Mahdi, Ezbekia and another in Alexandria, at Midan Abu Kir. The couple must take the notarized letter of no objection, their passports, and two witnesses to the court. The papers will be ready in two days.

Marriage to an Egyptian The procedures for marriage are the same as those listed above. British women who are marrying a Muslim have the option of registering their marriage in Britain which binds the marriage to British law. This is done by translating the marriage certificate and having the embassy register it at the General Registrar, St. Catherine's House, London.

Money Matters for Foreigners
Personal accounts Foreigners residing in Cairo may open a personal bank account in hard currency at one of the foreign bank branches, such as Citibank, Chase National or Bank of America. Most banks impose a minimum balance of about $2,000 for a personal checking or savings account, and if the balance falls below an average of about $1,000 for any one month, there is a substantial service charge. Also, a check written on an account in an Egyptian bank for payment of a debt in the United States could take months to clear and to be credited to the payee's account. In addition both the Egyptian bank and the payee's bank may deduct a commission from the face value of the check for handling. It is much more practical to maintain a bank account overseas for meeting overseas commitments.

Credit cards VISA, Mastercharge and American Express cards are honored at some banks and businesses in Egypt. You can obtain cash from the Bank of America by presenting your VISA card. They will provide you with up to $150 per day, treated as a loan and billed with interest to your VISA account in the States. With Mastercard you can obtain up to $100 a day in the same fashion. For information about American Express Cards contact American Express, Kasr al Nil 750444 and for Diner's Club cards contact M.E.S.C.O. 48 Bahgat Ali MO 341-6006.

To have money sent from home
International transfer or payment order This way of transferring funds overseas begins with instructions to an overseas bank to order a bank in Cairo to pay the funds to the payee. The payer fills out a form indicating the payee's name, address, the name of the bank in Cairo which is to pay the funds, the name and address of the bank branch to which the payment order is to be sent and the amount of currency to be transferred. The payer should indicate whether payment is to be made in foreign currency. The foreign bank then issues an order by wire, telex, cable or courier service. It is very important that the bank in Cairo be a branch of the same bank overseas. To send an international transfer or payment order to any other bank can cause extended delays. If you have no choice but to deal with a foreign bank that has no branch in Cairo, find out the names of your bank's correspondent banks in Cairo. You do not need to have an account at a Cairo bank in order to receive transfers through that bank. The payer must let you know the money is coming. You will need your passport as identification in order to receive payment.

Bank draft The bank draft is a check written by a foreign bank payable at one of its correspondent banks in Cairo. In this case the payer gives the foreign bank all the same information as is required for a transfer (above); the payer must select a correspondent bank which will do the paying, and the name and address of that bank's branch will be written on the face of the check. The check will be made payable to you. The payer sends the check directly to you and you cash it at the bank and branch written on the check.

International money order This is a service of American Express. To use it, the payer has to go to an American Express office, but does not have to be a cardholder. The face value of the money order can be as much as $200.

Cash transfer via telex can be arranged through travel agents like American Express or Thomas Cook.

Meeting Tax Obligations
US Nationals The **US-Egypt Double Taxation Treaty**, established in 1982 "to conclude a convention for the avoidance of double taxation of income, the prevention of fiscal evasion with respect to taxes on income, and the elimination of obstacles to international trade and investment...", includes regulations governing taxes, business profits, dividends, interest, royalties and relief of double taxation. For a copy of this treaty consult the US Embassy.

US Income Tax Before leaving for Egypt, American citizens should gather as much information as possible about city, state and federal tax obligations at home and about the possible exclusion of income earned overseas. To obtain the latest edition of **Publication 54, Tax Guide for US Citizens and Resident Aliens Abroad** write to Internal Revenue Service or contact the American Services Unit of the American Embassy, which keeps a complete collection of federal (but not state) tax forms available. For more information, there is also the USA Abroad Tax Hotline: 24 hours, 703-276-5550.

Over the past few years, the provisions in the Internal Revenue Code for taxation of income earned overseas by US citizens and resident aliens have been amended several times.

Currently taxpayers may qualify for the foreign earned income exclusion if their **tax home** is in a foreign country and if they meet EITHER the **bona fide residence** test or the **physical presence** test.

Bona Fide Residence Test US citizens qualify for the foreign earned income exclusion if they are a bona fide resident of a foreign country or countries for an uninterrupted period that includes an entire tax year (January 1-December 31). Cases are decided individually, taking into account such factors as the taxpayer's intention and the purpose, nature and length of the stay abroad. Taxpayers may leave the tax home for vacations or business and still be eligible for bona fide residence status.

Physical Presence Test The Physical Presence Test is concerned only with the individual's length of stay in a foreign country or countries. However, intentions with regard to the nature and purpose of the stay abroad are relevant in determining whether the taxpayer meets the tax home test. If, during a period of 12 consecutive months, the taxpayer is physically present in a foreign country or countries 330 full days, he or she meets the Physical Presence Test. The 12 month period may begin on any day. To meet this test, the taxpayer's presence in a foreign country does not have to be only for employment purposes. Some of the qualifying time may consist of vacation time spent in foreign countries.

A taxpayer meeting either of the above tests may exclude up to $95,000 of income earned overseas for services performed during the period of bona fide residence or physical presence. Taxpayers do not automatically qualify for the exclusion merely by having earned income overseas. They must claim exclusion by filing **Form 2555** with Form 1040. The deadline for filing tax returns from abroad is June 15.

To bring either bona fide residence or physical presence into effect the taxpayer may either file his first overseas return as usual, knowing that a refund can be requested after qualification for the exclusion has been determined, or he or she can request an extension of time to file until the qualifications for exclusion can be met.

Tax consultants A representative of the IRS visits the US Consulate in Cairo early each year to advise resident Americans on federal income tax matters. His arrival is advertised in local newspapers and newsletters.

British nationals do not pay taxes on a yearly basis while they are out of Britain. They do not need to file any type of tax return. Upon repatriation they will be responsible for accounting for income earned and paying taxes for all the years they have been living abroad.

Voting
The American Services Unit (open 8-3) of the American Embassy keeps an up-to-date list on US elections, including primaries, and stocks the Post Card Registration and Absentee Ballot Request, Form 76. They also have the **Voting Assistance Guide**. A notary, US Commissioned Officer, Embassy or Consular officer, can notarize your ballots. Your **legal state of residence** for voting purposes is the state where you last resided immediately prior to departing the US.

Any questions which cannot be answered by a voting officer or counselor should be directed to the Director, Federal Voting Assistance Program, Office of the Secretary of Defense, Pentagon, Rm. 1B 457, Washington DC 20301, USA.

British citizens living abroad have the right to vote at parliamentary and European Parliament elections, but not at local government elections. Voting is done by proxy. To be eligible to vote, citizens must complete and register an Overseas Elector's Declaration form and proxy application at the consular section of the embassy each year on or before October 10 for the 12 months beginning the following February 16. Citizens may continue to register for five years. For more information see **Keeping Your Vote When Living Abroad** available from the consular section of the embassy.

Going Home

Returning US citizens As a USA resident, your first $400 worth of merchandise may be brought into the country duty-free provided you have been outside the US for at least 48 hours, you have not already used this exemption within 30 days, your purchases are for personal use or gifts, and you bring your purchases into the US with you. You will need to make a written declaration of items acquired abroad if their total value exceeds $400, otherwise an oral declaration will do. Remember to keep all receipts. The next $1,000 worth of items is dutiable at a flat rate of 10%, while duty rates above $1,400 worth of merchandise vary. US residents who do not meet the 48-hour or the 30-day requirement may bring back up to $25 worth of items duty-free.

US restricted and prohibited articles

Tobacco items are restricted to 100 cigars and 200 cigarettes. **Alcohol** is restricted to 1 liter for persons over 21 years of age. If you exceed these limits you must pay 10% duty, plus a federal and a state tax. **Agricultural** items such as foods, plants, animals and their products are forbidden to enter the US. Contact APHIS Department of Agriculture 6505 Belcrest Road, Federal Building, Room 732 Hyattsville, MD. **Money** in the form of coin, currency, traveler's checks, money orders and negotiable instruments or investment securities may enter, but must be reported to customs if the total amount exceeds $5,000. **Automobiles** purchased abroad must meet US control standards. Contact Environmental Protection Agency, Washington DC 20406. **Research Materials** such as diseased organisms and vectors for research must have an import permit. Contact Foreign Quarantine Program, US Public Health Service, Center for Disease Control, Atlanta, GA 30333. **Cultural Treasures, Art or Artifacts** that have not been approved for export from the country of origin are forbidden. **Endangered Species** including crocodile, lizard, and snake skins; sea turtle products; all birds from Africa, Australia, Brazil, Ecuador, Mexico, Paraguay, Venezuela and Caribbean countries; most wild bird feathers, mounted birds and skins; many parrots; ivory from elephant tusks; furs from spotted cats like jaguar, leopard, snow leopard, tiger, ocelot, margay, and tiger cat; furs from marine mammals like seals and polar bears; coral reef items and plants like cycads, orchids and cacti are all forbidden. Contact US Fish and Wildlife Service, Department of the Interior, Washington DC. **Firearms and ammunition** are subject to restrictions and import permits. Contact Bureau of Alcohol, Tobacco and Firearms, Department of the Treasury, Washington DC 20226. **Medicines containing narcotics** should have a prescription and be in their original containers. **Merchandise** originating in North Korea, Vietman, Kampuchea and Cuba are forbidden.

Status of articles bought in Egypt Certain dutiable items from developing countries may enter duty-free or at a lower rate of duty under the Generalized System of Preferences (GSP). Many items from Egypt fall into this category. For details, see Customs leaflet **GSP and the Traveler**.

Storage Shipments are cleared at the first port of arrival or forwarded in customs custody to another port of entry. You, or someone you designate to act for you, must arrange for customs clearance. You may have a freight forwarder ship your articles and arrange for clearance by a customhouse broker in the US. The fee includes shipment to the first port of arrival. In addition to any customs charges, anticipate charges for inland transportation, broker's fees, and insurance. You may name another person as your unpaid agent to execute the customs declaration and entry by providing that person with a statement addressed to the Officer in Charge of Customs. If shipment is not claimed within 5 days it will be stored at the owner's risk and expense. Items will be sold if not claimed within one year.

Returning UK citizens If you are returning from **outside the EC** you can bring in your belongings free of duty and tax under one of the following conditions: you have lived at least 12 months outside the EC, have possessed and used them for at least six months, can prove that duty and tax have been paid, declare them to Customs, and not sell, lend, hire out or otherwise dispose of them in the UK within 12 months.

You can send belongings to the UK in **advance** of your arrival so long as they arrive no more than six months before you move or return to the UK. You will have to pay a deposit of duty and tax. This will be repaid when you arrive and can prove you qualify for the relief. Your belongings can be imported after your move to the UK so long as they arrive no more than twelve months after the date you move there. For more information call/write to Customs and Excise Dept., Kings Beam House, Mark Lane, London EC3 01-626 1515 Telex: 886231 CEH0LNG.

EDUCATION

Universities and Schools of Higher Learning
The only university in Egypt that offers English language instruction is **The American University in Cairo** 113 Sharia Kasr al Aini 354-2964, and 866 United Nations Plaza, New York, 10017 212-421-6320. Founded in 1919, AUC is the only privately owned university in Egypt. Faculties include Arabic Studies, Economics, Political Science, Mass Communications, English and Comparative Literature, Engineering, Management, Science, Sociology, Anthropology, and Psychology. Centers include the **Abdel Latif Jameel Center for Middle East Management Studies, Arabic Language Unit, Center for Adult and Continuing Education, Center for Arabic Studies Abroad (CASA), Social Research Center, English Language Institute, Desert Development Center, Division of Public Service, Commercial and Industrial Training Center**, and **The American University in Cairo Press**.

Foreigners may apply to all Egyptian Universities. In most instances the language of instruction is Arabic.

Ain Shams University Kasr al Zaafaran, Abbassia, 821455. Founded in 1950, Ain Shams University includes the Faculties of Medicine, Arts, Science, Engineering, Agriculture, Commerce, Law, and Education. Institutes and Centers include **Higher Institute of Nursing, Center for Child Studies, Institute of Environmental Studies and Research, Middle East Research Center, Computer Center, Center of Papyrological Studies and Center for the Development of English Language Teaching.**

Al Azhar University Midan Hussein 904051. Founded in 970 and modernized in 1961, this university is over 1,000 years old. Faculties include Islamic Theology, Jurisprudence and Law, Arabic Studies, Engineering, Medicine, Commerce, Agriculture, and a Women's College with faculties of Arabic and Islamic Studies, Science, and Language and Translation.

Cairo University Orman GI 727343. Founded in 1908, this is the largest university in Egypt, with over 100,000 students, and extensions in rural areas and Sudan. The faculties include Arts, Law, Medicine, Economics and Political Science, Commerce, Engineering, Dentistry, Pharmacology, Agriculture, Science, Veterinary Medicine, Mass Communications and Archaeology. Also **Higher Institute of Nursing, National Institute of Tumours, Institute of Physiotherapy, Higher Institute of Statistical Studies and Research, Higher Institute of African Studies and Research, Institute of Urban Planning.**

Helwan University 7 Mudiriat al Tahrir, Helwan 344-4055. Founded in 1975. Faculties include Engineering, Technology, Commerce and Business Administration, Art Education, Musical Education, Fine Arts, Applied Arts, Social Service, Physical Education, Home Economics, Tourism and Hotel Management, Cotton Sciences, and Science.

Primary and High Schools
The state school system in Egypt is augmented by a large private school system. The language of instruction in these private schools is usually in keeping with the type of curriculum, French, English, German, or Arabic. Some follow the Ministry of Education requirements for education, others follow systems similar to foreign requirements.

Al Alsson School Harraneya GI 539441. Egyptian curriculum K-12.
Al Horreya School 52 Giza DO 348-5857/7894 Egyptian curriculum. K-12.
British International School 5 Michel Lutfallah ZA 341-5959 340-6674. GCE curriculum up to O Levels. British teachers.
Cairo American College 1 Midan Digla, Digla 352-9393 352-9244. American curriculum. K-12. International staff, mainly American.
Centre Culturel Francais, east of Kasr al Aini, Mounira 355-3725. Grades 8-12. French curriculum.
College de la Mere de Dieu 3 Abdel Rahman Fahmi GC 354-8722. Egyptian curriculum. K-12.
College de la Sainte Familie (Jesuit) three locations: Grand College, Sharia Faggala (opposite Ramsis Station) 900411/892; Petit College, Kobeissi Faggala 901583; Petit College, 28 Farid HE 666842. Boys only.

College du Sacre Coeur 5 Beirut HE 258-2232. Girls only. Egyptian curriculum. K-12.

Deutsche Evangelische Oberschule 6 Dokki DO 348-1648/1649/1475. Administered by German Foreign Ministry. German curriculum with some English classes. K-12.

Deutsche Schule Der Borromaerinnen 8 Mohammed Mahmoud, Bab al Louk 354-2226 355-7551. Girls only. K-12. Students are taught English, German, Arabic, and French.

Gezira Language School 12 Abd al Aziz Osman ZA 340-1308. Egyptian curriculum. K-12.

Lycee Francais du Caire 10 Road 12 MA 350-3574. French curriculum. Ages 3-18.

Lycee al Haram Al Shaab GI 850478. Egyptian curriculum. K-12.

Lycee al Horreya Youssef al Guindi, Bab al Louk 354-8080/5236. Egyptian curriculum. K-12.

Maadi British School 26 Hadayek Maadi 350-0329. British primary school with a full primary range of subjects plus French and Arabic. Good sports, creative art facilities. British curriculum and staff. Ages 4-11.

Manor House School Junior School: Lamounba, behind Meridien Hotel off Sharia Oruba HE 668215 256-7110. Senior School: 3 Butrous Ghali, HE 258-1828.

Misr Language School beginning of Pyramids-Fayoum Highway GI 857170. Egyptian curriculum. K-12.

Pakistan International School 13 Abdel Aziz al Dereini, Manial 846889. Foreigners only. Nursery-10. Instruction in English.

Port Said School 7 Mohamed Sakab ZA 340-1506/3435. K-12.

Ramsis College 198 Ramsis 831244 821672. Egyptian curriculum. Girls only. K-I2.

St. Joseph's School 5 Ahmed Sabri ZA 340-1567. English curriculum with Egyptian requirements. Nursery to 6th grade. Girls only to 9th grade.

Victory College Digla 352-8214 352-6191. K-12. English curriculum altered by Egyptian regulations.

Kindergartens, Nurseries and Preschools

Amal Language School Road 105 MA 350-1650. Ages 2 1/2-2. Montessori system. No lunch. October to May.

American Cooky Preschool 6 Road 266 New Maadi 352-0064. English speaking. 7:30-2/4, S-Th. Ages 1-6.

American Montessori School 104 Road 6, Apt 13 MA 351-2860 352-5673, English speaking. 9-12 or 9-1:30 either 4 or 5 days a week. IMI MIA certified. Ages 2 1/2-6.

Barbie Kindergarten 12 Road 107 MA 350-2862. 7:30-4. Ages 4 mo-5 yrs.

British International Playgroup All Saints Cathedral 5 Michel Lutfallah ZA 340-6674 341-5959. Thursday morning playgroup under three years and playgroup for 3-5 yrs.

Cairo International Kindergarten 7 Abd al Monim Sanad, parallel to Ahmed Orabi, MO 347-2858. Ages 2-6. Open 12 months. Language intruction in English.

Cherry Street Nursery School 11 al Negma, off Sheikh Ali Mahmoud HE 245-4240. Ages 2-6. Open 7:30-4, M-F.

Child Home School 112, 119 Tahrir DO 348-6643. Ages 4-6 and 6-12. English language. 8-2 S-Th.

Child World Nursery 70 Abdel Rahman al Rafai MO 348-1396. Ages 1-6. Open all year 8-4 daily, closed F.

Day Care Nursery 40 Baghdad HE 291-9327. 7-3 daily. 1 mo-5yrs.

Der Deutsche Kindergarten, 65 Road 104 MA 351-6102. Playground. Pre school program.

Ages 2 1/2-4. Open 9-1, closed F-S.

Deutsche Oberschule, Mohammed Mahmoud, Bab al Louk 354-2226. 4-year-olds.

Deutsche Evangelische Oberschule 6 Dokki DO 348-1648/9 348-1475. K-12. Egyptians and foreigners.

Disney Baby Home 21 Road 290 MA 352-3156/1878.

Donald Duck Nursery 11 Mussadaq DO. English and Arabic. 2-5yrs. 7:30-3. Closed F.

Ecole des Franciscaines de Marie, 8 Ibn Zanki 340-6539. Pre-school to 7th grade. French curriculum.

German Nursery School Road 12 and 67 MA 350-3174. 3-5 yrs. Enrolment through Deutsche Oberschule, 354-2226.

Happy Baby Nursery 121 Tahrir DO 348-6241. English and French. 40day-5yr. 7_30-4:30. Closed F.

Happy Day Preschool 46 Road 103 MA 350-3662. 2-5 years. 2 classes.

Happy Home 21 Bahgat Ali ZA 340-2550.

International Playgroup 8 Moharram Shawki HE. 8:30-2:30. 4 mo-5 yrs.

Irish Infant Kindergarten 19 Lebanon MO 344-3044.

Jo's Playgroup 55 Misr Helwan Road MA 350-7487. Ages 2 1/2-5.

Al Manar Kindergarten 17 Road 220 Digla, behind Victory College 352-6015. 3mo-5yrs. 8-4. Meals and entertainment.

Mickey Mouse Nursery 5 Ghinea, near Merryland HE 258-0601. 3-4 yrs.

Maadi International Playgroup 75 Road 13 MA 350-0074. 2-4yrs. 5 days/wk, 9-12. Art projects, social skills.

Mere De Dieu 3 Abdel Rahman Fahmi 354-8722. Girls only. K-secondary school.

Nursery School Orabi 58 Road I5 MA 350-3650. 3-5yrs.

Neptune Nursery School 2 Midan al Etahad, corner of Roads 104 and 105, MA 350-5342 1 1/2-6 yrs. Hot meals. 6 days/wk 8-4.

New Maadi Nursery 257 Road 10 MA 352-2134. Hourly day care service.

Pluto Nursery School 3 Midan Hayat al Tadris DO 714206. American curriculum, British and American staff. 8-4 six days /wk. 4 classes. 1-6yrs.

Reiltin Nursery 16 Dessuki AG 347-7152. English speaking. Irish ownership and management. 7:30-4:30 six days/wk. 15mo-6yrs.

Tom and Jerry 11 Dr. Mohammed Goma HE 243-1825. 9-4. Ages 1 1/2-5 yrs.

Tree House Preschool International 27 Road 206 MA 352-0174/3942. British and American systems. 8:30-12 S-Th.

Val's Daycare Center 10 Road 257 New Maadi 352-2134 6mo-5yr. Monthly, daily, hourly. Full English program.

Wee Wisdom American Preschool 5 Road 253 Flat 1 352-7068.

Arabic Language Schools

Ahmed Gamal 24 Road 9 MA 350-0238. Arabic language instructor.

AUC Center for Adult and Continuing Education 28 Falaki Bab al Louk 354-2964; 24 Ibrahim Ramez HE 243-4979; 9 Road 210 MA. **Arabic Language Centre** Mahmoud Azmy, Medinat al Sahafiyin MO 346-3087. Modern, standard and colloquial Arabic.

Community Service Association 4 Road 21 MA 350-5284.

Egyptian Center for Cultural Cooperation 11 Shagaret al Dorr ZA 341-5419.

Gezira Language School 12 Aziz Osman ZA 340-1308/6249.
International Language Institute Mohammed Bayoumi HE 666704.
National Centre for Languages and Translation 33 Road 103 MA 351-4374 350-5174.
Classical and colloquial Arabic. For individuals or groups.

COMMUNITY SERVICE CLUBS AND ORGANIZATIONS

Alcoholics Anonymous Open meetings St Marie de la Paix Church annex Sa 8pm; Holy
Family Catholic Church, 55 Road 15 MA M 8pm. Closed meetings 4 Midan Sheikh Youssef,
Kasr al Aini, behind the US Embassy, T 8pm and Holy Family Church 55 Road 15 MA T 8pm.
Contact US Embassy Health Unit 355-7371 ex2351/2356 or CSA 350-5284.

American Democrats Abroad in Egypt Works to promote awareness of the problems of
overseas Americans, keeps representatives in the US aware of the concerns of overseas
citizens, and facilitates voting in presidential primaries. Contact: John Bentley, Chairman, 353-
1205.

Automobile and Touring Club of Egypt 10 Kasr al Nil 743355. Affiliated to the International
Automobile Association of France and the International Tourist Association of Switzerland.
Established in 1924, the Automobile Club has offices in all ports in Egypt. They issue
international driver's licenses, carnet de passage, etc. Upon request will provide guides of
international driving symbols.

British Community Association 2 Abdel Rahman al Rafai, Flat 2, DO 349-8870. An
independent, non-profit organization established in 1977 to serve the temporary and permanent
British community in Cairo. Annual membership LE10 for individuals, LE15 for a family. Has
a medical scheme at Anglo-American Hospital, open to non-members (see Health section for
more information). Puts out a monthly news magazine. Has a clubhouse for members only at
2 Abdel Rahman al Rifai DO. Membership LE40/60. Monthly coffee mornings in various areas
of Cairo.

Canadian Women's Club Meetings first T monthly October thru May except January, at
embassy residence, 5 Kamel Mohammed ZA. They operate the Nearly New Boutique, a
secondhand clothing store, 22A al Sadd al Aali DO, open 10am-1pm M, T and Th and T 4-7.
Contact: Honey Mansour 704975.

CARE (Cooperative for American Relief Everywhere) International Egypt 18 Huda
Shaarawi Apt 1, PO Box 2019 393-5262 393-2756. CARE began operating in Egypt in 1954
under criteria which address the basic needs of poor people. The aim is to help the poor create
and maintain positive changes in their lives. Projects in Egypt include the North Sinai
Agricultural Development Project, Sinai Social Action Project, South Sinai Fisheries Development Project, High Dam Lake Integrated Basic Services Project and the Village Self Reliance
Program. Accepts donations.

CARITAS Egypt 13 Abdel Hamid Said 751061 762242. Founded in Germany in 1891 and in Egypt in 1967, this organization serves human development for all peoples. It has offices in Alexandria, Bulak, Kafr al Siss, Omrania, Mataria and Haggana. It offers financial, medical and psychological help to refugees, war victims, the homeless and other underprivileged persons. Offers classes in home economics, languages and computers.

Catholic Relief Services 13 Ibrahim Naguib GC 355-8034 354-2404/1360. The official overseas development and emergency relief organization of the American Catholic community, this organization began work in Egypt in 1956. Emphasis is on development and assistance. Programs include agriculture mechanization, food aid to school children, development of fish and duck ponds and development of the silk industry in Egypt. 8-3, closed F,Sa.

Commonwealth War Graves Commission North Africa Area, Nabil al Wakad HE 669351. Established by royal charter in 1917 to maintain and keep records of the graves and cemeteries of the members of the forces of the British Commonwealth who died in the two world wars.

Community Services Association 4 Road 21 MA 350-5284 355-7371 x8232. A non-profit organization founded in 1980 offering services to meet the needs of the English-speaking community in Cairo through education, counseling, social services, recreational programs, newcomers orientations, and entertainment. Contact: Diane Graszik.

Coptic Evangelical Organization for Social Service 4 Midan Halim off Gumhuria 904995 906683. Founded in 1952 CEOSS operates five programs of service in Egypt. The Comprehensive Development Program offers self-reliance through classes, loans and grants. The Resource Service Projects provides training and job opportunities. The publishing houses Dar El Thakafa is one of the largest Christian publishers in the Middle East. The Conference and Study Center provides a forum for discussion and study. Accepts donations.

Egyptian Center for International Cultural Cooperation 11 Shagaret al Dorr ZA 341-5419. Arabic classes, tours to Egyptian monuments, exhibitions, recitals, and cinema. Sa-Th 10-2 and 5-8.

Egyptian Red Crescent Society 29 al Galaa 750558 750397. In existence for over 75 years, this society is a volunteer organization that offers services and supplies to disaster-stricken areas in Africa and Egypt. Partially supported by the Ministry of Social Affairs. Takes volunteers and accepts donations.

Egyptian Society for the Preservation of Nature Established in 1978, the goal of this society is to conserve trees, the environment and the Nile. Special emphasis is to halt the building of high rise buildings in Maadi. Meetings first F of every month at 10am at the Agriculture Syndicate Sharia Galaa, next to the Al Ahram Building. Membership is open to all. Contact: Masooud Shokry 3 Hadika GC, 354-8104.

International Committee of the Red Cross ICRC 20 al Sadd al Aali DO 707587. Open 8-3 S-Th. Founded in 1956, this organization currently disseminates information about the Geneva

Conventions and International Humanitarian Laws via lectures and seminars. Instrumental in finding missing persons throughout the world. No volunteers. Accepts donations.

Maadi Women's Guild A groups of international women affiliated with the Maadi Community Church. Open to any interested woman, meetings are the third T of each month, Sept-May, at 9:30am at the Holy Family Catholic Church 55 Road 15 MA. Year-round **Newcomers' Coffee** on the first T of the month at the home of a member. Organizes the **Moms and Tots Play Group**, Th 10-11:30, 44 Road 15, MA 352-5433. They also host a community **Thanksgiving Dinner** in November at the Maadi House and hold a large **Christmas Charity Bazaar** the first F in December. Publications: **Maadi Telephone Book, Maadi Women's Guild Cookbook** and others 351-2755/2925 352-2040.

Nour wal Amal "Light and Hope" 16 Abu Bakr al Sedik HE 244-1929 243-7772. A non-profit voluntary organization founded in 1954 to help blind girls. Operates a center of rehabilitation which helps educate and train the children. Maintains a braille school, music conservatory, technical and boarding school. Holds a yearly bazaar at the Hilton in mid-November. Membership LE5. Accepts donations and volunteers.

Project Hope 12 Hegaz MO 349-0875 348-0915. An international non-profit organization that offers medical/nursing training in Egypt. Main program is in Assiut, where a Nursing Institute has been established.

Refugee Center of St. Andrews Church 759401. Serves as a last resort for displaced persons. Offers services in education, housing, job placement and permanent homes. Accepts volunteers and donations.

SPARE Society for the Preservation of Architectural Resources of Egypt A non-profit organization staffed by volunteers with a secretariat in Cairo. Its purpose is to serve as a conduit for information related to architectural conservation in Egypt in all its aspects. Occasional newsletter, lectures and historic walks. Open to all. Contact: Elizabeth or John Rodenbeck, 351-8863.

The Tree Lovers Association Founded in 1973, this organization aims to draw attention to the value of trees for a healthy environment and to preserve and propagate them whenever possible. It works through public awareness, preventing abuse, teaching tree protection and taking legal action when necessary. Spring walks in Maadi each year. President and contact: Mohamed Hafez Ali, 36A Road 14 MA 351-1300.

Voluntary Service Overseas 2 Sherif, Flat 90, 8th floor 741590. British-based non-profit organization training locals in language, medical, technical, agricultural skills.

YMCA 72 Gumhuria 917360/877. Founded in 1923 by the International Council of the YMCA, , this organization serves the mind, body and spirit of young people. It serves all religions. Activities include sports, cultural, social, fine arts, camping and handicrafts. It has an outreach program for the underprivileged. Membership is LE50 yearly. Volunteers and donations welcome.

YWCA 11 Emad al Din, 3rd floor 913466 916932. Operates a hostel for university women at 4 Ahmed Shoubri, a special branch in Shoubri offering vocational training and 2 summer camps in Alexandria which provide space for the underprivileged and retarded. Holds an annual charity bazaar which finances most of the yearly activities. Membership is LE5 yearly.   Volunteers and donations welcome.

For a list of social clubs see Leisure section; for business organizations see Business; for scholarly associations see Research.

HOUSEHOLD

LIVING ACCOMMODATIONS

Suburban living is associated with Maadi and Heliopolis. City center radiates from Midan Tahrir. Residential areas with easy access to the city center exist in Mohandiseen, Dokki, Garden City and Zamalek. Lower rent areas that also provide good housing are Agouza, Manial, Abbassia and Madinet Nasr. Living accommodations are predominantly villas or apartments. Most villas are very large, two-storey buildings surrounded by spacious gardens and erected prior to 1954. They exist in all areas of the city, but mainly in Maadi, Heliopolis, Mohandiseen and Zamalek. Some have been renovated for multiple occupancy, but most are single family units. Apartments tend to be spacious with large entry halls, living and dining rooms and often more than one balcony. Kitchens are small by foreign standards. There is often more than one bathroom. Houseboats exist on the Nile at Kit Kat, across from Zamalek near the 15th May bridge.

The cost for renting any type of housing covers a wide range of prices, the most expensive being LE1-2,000 a month for a 2 bedroom apartment to LE3-5000 a month for a villa with a garden. These accommodations would include such features as air conditioning for cooling and heating, modern kitchen, furnishings, telephone (in most instances), and most major appliances. Cheaper, and quite adequate, housing is available from LE200 in most areas of the city. Most housing will come furnished, as Egyptian law allows for higher rents for furnished housing. One may rent on a short-term or long-term basis. **Long term leasing** usually requires an advance payment of from a month's to a year's rent. Although illegal, **key money**, a substantial deposit that is deducted from the rent on a monthly basis, is sometimes required for an unfurnished flat. For foreigners, **buying** property or housing in Egypt is restricted. An Arab foreigner may buy one flat or piece of land under 1,000 square meters. If current legislation is formalized non-Arab foreigners will be able to buy residential property.

Rentals are advertised by word of mouth or in the **Maadi Messenger, British Community News** and occasionally the **Egyptian Gazette.** Ads are also posted on bulletin boards at churches, foreign schools, supermarkets and community centers. Low rent apartments can be found by a **simsar**, a traditional broker. A simsar works informally, and is usually based at a cafe in his area of operations. Ask local residents how to contact one, or just go around cafes in the area of your choice and ask for a simsar (fii simsaar hina?). If the simsar knows of accommodations fitting your requirements he will arrange a viewing and a meeting with the landlord. Some simsars expect a fee for each flat they show you, but the usual arrangement is a fee on signing the contract with the landlord. 10% of the first month's rent is standard. If you rent through a **real estate agent**, payment is usually equal to one month's rent paid by the tenant and again

77

by the landlord. Be sure the agent knows exactly what you are looking for and you know exactly what the agency's terms are.

Some agents include: **American-Swiss-Egyptian Real Estate** 20 Saray al Gezira 9th floor Apt 39, ZA 341-5669; **Arabian American Real Estate Company** 19 Road 151 6th floor MA 351-4571; **Ashraf Agency Real Estate** 2 Road 86 MA 351-6806; **Ammar** 54 King Faisal, Jasmine Tower Apt 2, Pyramids 353-9450; **Bishara Real Estate Agency** 9 Ahmed Wafik HE 258-5022; **Cairo Real Estate** 83 Road 9 MA 350-8939; **Compass Real Estate** 10 Zamzam MO 716083 713976; **al Arroussy** 87 Road 105 MA Gardens 350-3963/6212; **al Sayed Mattar** 83 Road 9 MA 350-3908 351-7068; **Executive Business Services** 7 Lazoghli, Isis Building GC 355-1824; **Handiman Real Estate** 2 Road 23 MA 351-2035 352-8412; **Joe Service** 33 Road 81 MA 350-8538 791422; **Link International** 4 Mazloum 2nd fl. Bab al Louk; **Maadi Real Estate** 85 Road 9 MA 350-4204; **Maadi Real Estate Bureau** 37 al Nada, Golf Area, MA 350-2487; **Seif Nour al Din Real Estate** 4 Midan Mustafa Kamel MA 350-1276; **Smiley Realtors** 19 Road 206 Digla 352-3924.

Things to check include plumbing, water pressure, water shortages and fluctuation, water tanks and pumps, electrical wiring, power cuts, outlets, fuses, telephones, lighting, noise levels at various times of day and night, elevator service, garbage collection, mattresses, comfortable chairs and sofas, condition of furnishings, evidence of pests, balconies and parking. Construction work being done nearby will create high noise levels that may go on 24 hours a day. A nearby mosque may broadcast the call to prayer over a loud speaker five times a day. Nearby schools will mean noisy neighborhoods. Northern exposure allows for cooling breezes. Winter sun is also important.

Before signing the lease repairs should be negotiated. An accurate and exhaustive inventory list should be prepared by the landlord to include the condition of the contents of the flat. It should be checked and signed by both the tenant and the landlord. Keep in mind that a flat without a telephone is probably going to remain without a telephone. Determine whether utilities and services are included in the rent. Make sure they are paid up to the date you move in. Ask to see the receipts, if necessary.

Landlords If the landlord shows you a copy of the lease, takes it away, and later presents you with an "identical" copy to sign, make sure it is indeed an identical copy. Do not sign two different contracts specifying different amounts of rent; the landlord may claim it is necessary for his purposes, but it will ultimately involve you in a lot of unnecessary argument. The landlord is responsible for plumbing, electrical wiring, hot water heater, etc. Insist that the landlord does not keep an extra key to the flat. Obtain and sign a separate list of all the flat's major furnishings and furniture. Agree what is there for your use and find out if the landlord expects to take things out of the flat as he pleases. If the landlord intends to store items in your flat, find out where they will be kept and decide if you want them there. Make sure the landlord does not intend to add other people to your living space (This last item especially applies to students).

It is illegal for unmarried couples to live together in Egypt, especially if an Egyptian is involved. These couples are subject to arrest by the Vice Squad. Single women living alone will find the bowab (janitor) extremely protective, sometimes to the point of interference.

Moving in the city
Moving can be done by hiring workers and a local truck (or donkey cart) and doing it yourself, or hiring a professional moving company. Boxes can be found at local grocers'. You must inform the police of your change of address. If the move involves a change of district, you must inform the police in the district to which you are moving.

Some **moving companies**: (some of these companies will also ship your belongings abroad) **Allied Van Lines** 3 Road 3 Apartment 15 MA 350-1556; **Commercial Services Bureau** 36 Sherif 392-6945; **Expo Services International** 15 Basra MO 349-0065; **Favia International Transport** 18 Adli 758983; **Four Winds International** 11A Corniche al Nil MA 350-1046/0113, American managed, member of IATA; **Freight Systems International** 4 Ali Ibn Abu Talib MO 345-1437 346-9621; **Global International Inc.** 44 Mohammed Mazhar ZA 340-6064 342-0404; **Hansa Transport** 8 Talaat Harb 759918; **International Agency Group** 8 Abdel Rahman Fahmi GC 355-3010; **North American Van Lines** PO Box 366 DO 750404; **Pan World Clearing & Forwarding** 44 Khalifa al Mamun HE 257-6402/4150; **Quick Cargo** 5 Tehran DO 349-2948; **Schenker Liaison Office** 7 Abdel Khalek Sarwat 755642; **Sedra Services** 140 Sudan MO 707179.

HOUSEHOLD MANAGEMENT

Utilities
Minor utility repairs are paid by the tenant, major ones by the landlord. Payment of all utilities is often done by the landlord and included in the price of the rent. If not, payment is usually made to the person who comes to your home to read meters or deliver the bill. If you are not at home, payment must be made at a nearby kiosk or station. These facilities exist in all neighborhoods. Ask a neighbor, your landlord or your bowab to help you.

Electricity
Electrical current is 220 volts alternating at 50 cycles per second. This means most US products, which operate on 110 volts, will require a transformer to work in Egypt, but most British products will not. There are two types of transformers, one for motors and another for heating elements. Transformers come in a variety of sizes, so be sure to check the wattage you will require. They are sold at electrical shops. If you burn out an electrical appliance do not throw it away without checking with a repair shop. Many items can be repaired. Electrical current also fluctuates, so it is advisable to install stabilizers for your more expensive household equipment like refrigerators, televisions, computers and stereos. You may wish to get a stabilizer for the entire apartment. Stabilizers are also sold at electrical shops. **Power cuts** occur infrequently, and major repairs that require power cuts are often announced on television and in the Arabic newspapers. If caught unawares, unplug all major appliances in anticipation of a power surge when the electricity comes back on. Keep candles on hand for power failures. If your building or apartment seems to be the only one without electricity call the electric company. A repairman will be dispatched. If the drought in Africa continues, Egypt will be experiencing electricity shortages by 1989. **Meters** are read monthly. If the reader cannot obtain access to your meter he will leave a small form on which you must record the current reading. It is your responsibility to deliver it to the electricity office. A bill will arrive five to six days later. After waiting five to six days to be sure the slip has been processed, payment is made in cash at your local electricity

kiosk. All kiosks have a lightning bolt on the side. If you cannot find your kiosk, ask your bowab. If the bill is not paid in fifteen days the electricity will be cut. An average monthly electricity bill for a 2 bedroom apartment with air conditioning, a washing machine, dryer and other major electrical appliances is LE50; without major appliances LE20-25.

Sockets and plugs Wall sockets in Egypt are of the round two-pin type. If the plug on your appliance does not fit the socket, plugs can be bought cheaply in any local electrical shop. You may buy a new plug and replace the existing one, or buy a converter or adaptor plug. They will adapt small plugs to larger ones, large plugs to smaller ones and American style flat plugs to round plugs that fit into wall sockets. Do not confuse these with transformers. Converters or adaptors only adjust the plugs, **they do not convert the current.**

Gas
Gas takes two forms, piped and butagaz. **Piped** gas, known as **Petrogas**, will eventually be installed all over Cairo, but currently it exists in Maadi, Heliopolis, central Cairo and Mohandiseen. Petrogas is used for stoves and water heaters; you cannot fuel space heaters with it. The gas meter is read monthly and a bill is delivered to the home. You may pay the bill when it is delivered to your home or at the Petrogas headquarters in your area. **Butagaz** is bottled gas that is delivered to your home on an irregular basis. It is used for stoves, water heaters and space heaters. Cost per tank is LE1.25 delivered and LE.75 if picked up at the station. Butagaz is at a premium in winter and you may have to take your empty tanks to the station yourself. It is a good idea to have an extra tank; however, new tanks are no longer for sale at the Butagaz companies. **Warning: Butagaz is dangerous.** It can leak, explode and kill. All connections must be properly installed. Check for leaks by putting soapy water around all connections. Poor connections will bubble. **Do not check for leaks with a match.** Rubber washers must be replaced regularly. Keep all areas where butagaz is used well ventilated, especially the bathroom. Do not sleep with a butagaz heater on. Never light a water heater while the water is running, it may explode. Butagaz has an odor, learn to notice it. If you can smell it, something is wrong: extinguish all cigarettes, turn off the stove, shut down all tanks, open the windows, don't operate the light switches and contact your local butagaz center. **Kerosene space heaters** are also dangerous. The best advice is not to use them; however, white kerosene or white spirits for heating and primus stoves is available from gas stations.

Butagaz repair
Gas fitters: Abdel Aziz Attiyeh Ali, 6 Osman ibn Affan near Midan Salah al Din HE 675287; **Abou** 3 Brazil ZA 340-8637. **German Service Center** 89 Merghani HE 393-9816.

Telephone
Telephone bills must be paid yearly or at six-monthly intervals. These schedules were arranged when the telephone system was installed. When you receive a bill, payment must be made at the area telecommunication center. You will have a one month leeway. Landlords often include the telephone as part of the rent and therefore they take care of payment. An average yearly bill for regular service is LE30. (For information on telephoning see the Communications section.)

Water

When tap water leaves the filtering plant it is pure and safe; however, there is a possibility of contamination through leaking pipes. Filtering or boiling the water, especially in summer, will ensure its drinking safety. Filters are available in supermarkets. Be sure accessories are available before buying an imported filter. Inexpensive bottled water is available in supermarkets, grocery stores, and kiosks. Bills are delivered to your home every two months. They should be paid at this time, otherwise you must go to the Water Company headquarters in your area.

Services

Garbage is collected at least three times a week and in some areas daily. Usually collection is in the morning, by donkey cart, although a motorized system is under development. Payment is made the first of the month at your door. Average payment is LE2-4 a month.

Laundry is done on a piece by piece basis. You can contract for a **makwagi** to collect and deliver your laundry once a week. Make a list of all items. They will be washed and/or ironed and returned to you in a few days. Laundry services exist all over the city. It is best to get a personal recommendation from a neighbor, friend or your company. Makwagis will also come to the home on a day basis, or your domestic help can do in-house laundry. This can be done in the bathtub if necessary.

Elevators exist in many apartment buildings. Be sure to close all doors when you leave an elevator or it will be inoperable. Do not be frightened if the floor of some elevators, especially in old buildings, sinks slightly when you step onto it, this is simply part of the operating device.

Keeping things cool, or hot Most buildings in Cairo have neither central heating nor air-conditioning. However, thick walls, high ceilings and window shutters provide some relief in the hot summers. Unfortunately these same conditions make the wintertime cold uncomfortable for some. **In summer** shut all windows, drapes and shutters before the heat of the day begins. This will keep the rooms cool and fairly comfortable all day long. Open them again after sunset when the evening breezes begin to blow. This procedure will also help keep out the excessive humidity that has become prevalent in recent years. **In winter** that same humidity turns to dampness. Close doors to all unused rooms to avoid drafts. Dress warmly, in layers, with natural fibers close to the skin. Hang curtains or room dividers in large rooms to cut down unnecessary space to heat. A wide selection of **fans and heaters** can be purchased in any shopping center in the city. **Air conditioners** are available on the market in both domestic and imported brands. Both come with heating and/or cooling units. Filters must be cleaned and changed regularly because of the dust in the air.

Some **air conditioning** retail and repair stores: **AGM Company** 37 Road 7 MA 350-4031; **Airco** York Air Conditioners 3 Ahmed Abdel Aziz MA 350-2448; **Ahramat Engineering and Trading Company** 10 26th July Apt 505 914632; **Arab Traders** 55 Abdel Hakim Hussein, 5th Floor, Flat 10, MO 348-3707 and 3 Fouad al Ahwany ZA 341-6922: contracts for monthly maintenance, plumbing, electricity, air conditioning repairs; **Cairo Cooling Company** 82 Osman Ibn Affan near Midan Triomphe HE, repairs air conditioners and refrigerators; **Carrier Air Conditioning Egypt** 29 Tanta AG 346-2083/1297; **Central Air Conditioning** General Electric 112 al Merghani HE 291-7174; **Climate Cooling Company** 12 Tayaran MN; **Dew Point Company** 7 al Kebly Helwan 781561; **Electro House "Hosni"** 87 Rd 9 (Medical Bldg.) MA 350-3814; **Four C's Air Conditioning** 33 Kasr al Nil 742007; **Miraco** 48 Batal Ahmed Abd al Aziz MO 713730 712503 704272; **Misr Cool** 24 Kamel al Shenawi GC 354-9810; **Samir Bernaba** 10 al Ittihad MA 350-1700.

Household Pests

Be very careful about using sprays and coils to eliminate pests. Sometimes the cure is more harmful than the pest itself. If unsure about a product consult an expert. Do not spray directly on yourself, food, or food-carrying vessels. **Flying Insects:** The mosquito population has diminished recently, but they are still a problem. Although malaria is not endemic in Egypt it is on the increase worldwide with stronger strains for which powerful medicines are necessary. Screen your windows. Sprays, coils and pellets are available from grocers and pharmacies. **Flies** are a big nuisance in the spring and fall. They are aggressive and carry disease. Screen all windows and have fly swatters on hand. **Moths** tend to be abundant in the spring and fall. They are a menace to woolens. They lay eggs that will destroy your fabrics. Be careful of bringing rugs, tapestries and other natural fibers that have been purchased locally into the home. Air, brush and beat them to dislodge eggs. If possible mothproof each item. Mothballs, (naftaliin) are available at pharmacies and supermarkets. All items to be stored should be cleaned first. **Bugs and rodents: Bedbugs** can be brought home from crowded places. To eliminate, put the mattress and all suspected clothing in the sun; wipe wooden slats, supports, bedposts, headboards and footboards with kerosene. Repeat one week later to kill newly hatched bugs. **Ants, roaches** and other household pests can be controlled by an exterminator. It is usual to do this every other year. To avoid having cockroaches or rodents in the house, sweep crumbs and residual food from surfaces and floors regularly. The pests come for the food and may travel through drain pipes and/or toilets. Keep drains tightly covered with tin foil and shut toilet covers at night.

Some **exterminators: Bestox** 16 Huda Shaarawi 243-3156/244-0654; **Drouby** 43 Kasr al Nil 917532; **High Power Pest Control** 76 Teret al Gabal, Hadayek al Kobba 821349 offers one-year guarantee; **Sawco** 48 Kasr al Nil 900267; **Sotaico** 23 Orabi 763748.

Maintenance and Repair

There are excellent repair facilities available for the household if you know how to find them and know the right Arabic words to describe what is wrong.

Appliances Both locally made and imported appliances can be purchased from shops in all areas of the city. Everything from mixers, toasters and irons to stereos and video equipment is available. Most goods are reasonably priced, sometimes below the international market price; however, some are excessively expensive. Check costs before buying. Some of the best prices will be found on Sharia Muski. Some appliances like videos can be rented by the month. All machinery will need oiling more often than in America or Europe, rubber parts will have to be replaced more often. Your neighbors, colleagues or local shopkeepers can advise you of repair shops in your area. See Shopping section.

Some **appliance repair** services: **Admiral Agent** 32 Yehia Ibrahim HE 662850; **AIRCO** 3 Ahmed Abdel Aziz MA 350-2448; **al Araby Company for Trade and Agencies** 3 and 12 Gawhar al Kaed Muski west 908547 924117; **Ayad** 79 Road 9 MA 350-3498; **Bernaba** (washing machine repair) 10 al Ittihad MA 350-1700; **Dawoud Nashed** 4 Brazil ZA 340-9185, repairs electrical appliances, radios, televisions and record players; **Egyptian Automotive and Electrical Company** 15 Giza 728361, appliance servicing; **Electric White Home** 15 Road 153 MA 351-5745; **Electro House Center "Hosni"** 87 Road 9 (Medical Bldg.) MA

350-3814; **FYE** (Installation/Stabilizers/Service-Elec.) 9 Abdel Kawi Ahmed HE 663055; **Fouad Hayek** (sales & repairs) 19 Talaat Harb 741984; **Heliopolis Cooling Company** 10 Osman Ibn Affan, near Midan Salah al Din HE 675353; **Hi-Fi Electronics** end of Palestine Road New Maadi 352-6701, main service center for JVC, National and Mitsubishi, repairs stereos, TVs and videos; **Itacco** 8 Abdel Hamid Lotfy MO 705939. **Kenwood** 15 Mohammed Azmy ZA 341-5635, repairs hi-fi and stereo equipment; **Lahzi Electronic Center** 37 Hasan Hussein ZA 340-0021, repair and maintenance of videos, cameras, TVs, stereos, computers, etc.; **Maadi Electric Center** 72 Road 77 MA 350-7029 351-9950; **Neeasa-Philips** (Philips Brand Appliances) 26 Adli 749245; **Normende** 56B Damascus MO 712125, repairs videos, stereos and TVs; **Raamco Trading Co** 4 Murad al Sherii HE 245-9402; **Radio Masr** 7 Osman Ibn Affan near Midan Salah al Din HE; **Teleshire** 3 Hasan Assem ZA 341-0183 390-5425; **TV Nasr** 4 Granada behind Cairo Medical Center, Roxi, HE 846200 751427; **Yassin Mahmoud al Ashri** 3 Gawhar al Kaed, Muski 904158, imported appliances.

Bicycles in all varieties are available, including second and third hand machines.

Ayad 79 Road 9 MA 350-3498; **Hanafi Mohamed Moussa** 8 Said al Bakri ZA 341-5243; **Ibrahim Khalik** 16 Rushdi.

Carpenters
Aly/Farag 108 Road 9 MA 351-9239; **Dallas Farouk** 38 Road 10 MA 350-4783; **al Shamy** 75 Road 9 MA; **Gallop Furniture & Decoration** 68 Road 104 Maadi Gardens 351-7780; **Garber Mahmoud** 4 Zaki Ali ZA; **Hanafy** 62 Road 9 MA 350-4506; **Ishaak Yousef** 2 Ib al Laq, Roxi HE 258-3512; **Mobica** 20 Harun al Rashid DO 348-8761/8760; **Mohamed al Agami** 21 Bahgat Ali ZA 340-9218; **Rabie Wood Works** 58 Road 104 MA 350-3299; **Sami** Road 9 MA 351-3288; **Shirket al Salam Litigaret al Akhshab** 107 Tahrir DO 716761, also sells wood; **Wood Finisher** 75 Road 9 MA.

Clock and watch repair You can find dozens of clock and watch repair shops in the tiny alleys around Midan al Ataba. They all use the address **19 Midan al Opera, Ataba.** Good buys in second hand watches and spare parts are also found in this area.

Other shops include: **Eterna** 159 26 July ZA and 44 Kasr al Aini 340-7537; **ESTD Co** (Seiko) 55 Nubar, Bab al Louk 354-9285; **Francis Papazian** 3 Midan al Ataba 390-5616; **Hagop Garabedian** 40 Kasr al Nil 392-6067; **Kamil Watch Repair** 38 Magdi HE; **Port Said Watch Repair** 104 Tahrir, Midan Dokki, DO 859355; **Rano** (Rolex agent) 85 Road 9 MA 350-2432; **Swiss** 17 Baghdad HE 291-7809; **Seika** 10 Brazil ZA; **Watch Repair** 95 Road 9 MA; **Watches Magdi** 38 Harun al Rashid HE.

Dry Cleaning: see Rug Repair

Electricians
Ahmed Abdel Hameed, 87 Road 9 MA 350-5426; **Alectronic Osama** 75 Road 9 MA 350-2084; **Aly Abdel Mouhssen** 79 Road 9 MA 350-3485; **Dawoud Nached** 4 Brazil ZA 340-9185; **Electro House Center "Hosni"** 87 Road 9 (Medical Bldg) MA 350-3814; **FYE for Electrical Eng. & Electrical Services** 9 Abdel Kawi Ahmed HE 663055; **El Gihad** 145 Tahrir DO 348-6340; **Saeid Electric** 75 Road 9 MA 350-3614; **Tahan Sami** 5 Ibrahim al Lakkani HE.

Gardening equipment Hand made gardening tools, wooden planters, and other equipment are found on Sharia Ahmed Maher beside Bab Zuwayla in the medieval city. Also **Abu Shady** 58 Gumhuria 917691; see Nurseries below.

House cleaning For carpet and moquette cleaning, furniture and household cleaning and all plumbing and electrical work **Misr Company for Household Services** 38 Ahmed Orabi, Sahafiyin 345-0385. They will also do your food shopping.

Keymakers and locksmiths The cost of duplicating keys varies according to the type of key, but is a matter of piasters. It is usually done on the spot while you wait. For a minimal fee locksmiths will come to the home to open locked doors.

Ahmed 77 Road 9, MA; **Atif Hussein** 79 Road 9 MA 350-5478; **Commercial** 3 Mohammed Adli Khafafi, near Midan Saint Fatima HE; **Hagg Mahmoud Taha** 52 Kasr al Aini GC 345-7593; **Jacques** 18 Ibrahim al Lakkani, in alley next to Amphitrion, HE; **Mahmoud Shaaban Ryad** 58 Mansour, Suk Bab al Louk; **Moftah al Saad** 93 Osman ibn Affan near Midan Triomphe HE; **Mohammad Hassan Makhlouf** 24 Harun al Rashid HE 244-6086; **Sidi** Behlar Building 159, 26th July ZA 340-9142; **Tariq** 20 Ismail Ramzi near Midan al Gama HE.

Painters Imported paint is sporadically available. Local brands can be found around squatter markets, in Bab al Louk market, Ataba market, and in paint shops all over town.

The Egyptian Company for Chemical Trade 19 Abdel Khalek Sarwat, also insecticides, detergents and mothballs; **Engineering Office for Supplies and Contracting** 741786 291-0246; **Far East Company for Irons and Paints** Midan al Bawaki (Ataba); **Fouad** 18 Sadik Mohammed Saad MA 350-4776; **Helmy Mahmoud** 34 Harun al Rashid HE 245-7730; **Hesham al Kawly and Hani Fawzy** 8 Hegazi, Safahiyin 346-3343/7345, also housework; **Mahmoud Abu Gharbia** 136 Tahrir DO 717086, also wallpaper; **Plastic House** 6 Gamat al Dowal al Arabiya MO 347-4067, wallpaper.

Picture framing
Arto 5 Baghdad HE; **Da Vinci** 4 Abd al Hamid Said 755752; **Ibrahim** 8 Ahmed Sabri ZA; **Mohammed Attia** 4 Abdel Hamid al Said, near Cinema Odeon; **Soliman Riyad and Bro.** 14 Harun al Rashid HE 244-5899; **Tewfik Khadr** Kasr al Nil near Lappas.

Plumbers
Abdel Minim Hafez 175 26th July ZA 340-8637; **Bsheer** 76 Road 9 MA; **Ibrahim Mohammad Saleh** 8 Dokki DO 718037; **Magdy** 14 Ahmed Sabri ZA 340-3771; **Mahmoud Bayoumi** 3 Talkha, near Midan Salah al Din HE; **Magdy** Ahmed Sabri ZA 340-3771; **Mohammed al Sayd and Karim Adi** 91 Osman Ibn Affan near Triomphe Square HE; **Plumber,** 21 Damascus HE; **Shahata** 101 Tahrir DO 712003; **Adel Shazlie** 12 Road 106 MA 350-0847.

Rug repair and cleaning Good dry cleaning services exist in most areas of the city and in most major hotels. For expensive kilims and Persian rug repairs and appraisal see **Kazarouni** Carpet Co 14 Sarwat DO 701235.

Assiut 15 Mahmoud Salim AG 349-1191 and 83 al Azhar 903545; **Do It Yourself** 93 Road 9 MA 350-5080; **Ezzat** 75 Road 9 MA 350-2084; **Fouad Gerges** 2 Ali Abd al Aziz MA 350-5469; **Hamam** 56 Kasr al Nil 391-3150; **Ibrahim Mohamed and Sons** 84 Road 9 MA 350-1549; **Klyne** 22 Ahmed Taysir HE; **Massoud Cleaning** 88 Road 9 and 5 Road 154 MA 350-4993; **Meridien Laundry & Dry Cleaning** Meridien Hotel 84-5444; **Victory Laundry** Road 205 Digla 352-9322.

Stoppeurs or invisible menders will re-weave damaged fabrics, including moth holes, cigarette burns and tears.

Galal Brazil, off 26th July, ZA; **Hollywood** 29 Huda Shaarawi opposite Felfela 746180, also a dyer; **Rafa** 36 Baghdad HE; **Raffa al Agati** 10 Harun al Rashid HE 258-2377; **Samir Abdel Aziz Rafa** Ramsis 4

Suliman Gohar DO 717016; **Stoppeur and Teinturerie de Maadi** Road 153 MA. **The Stoppeur** 82 Road 9 MA 350-5421.

Upholsterers
See also Fabric under Shopping.

Afrangi Upholstery 61 Khalifa al Mamun HE; **Hag Othman Abd al Alim** 36 Mosaddaq DO 348-1732; **Hasan Sayed Ahmed** 6 Michel Lutfallah across from the British School, ZA; **Ibrahim Omar** 57 Dokki DO 703688; **Mahmoud Abdel Nabi** 34 Baghdad HE; **Mardini** 34 Kasr al Nil 393-2177; **Moderna** (curtains and upholstery) 23 Talaat Harb 754192; **Ramadan Esmail** Road 9 MA; **Saber al Sayed** 115 Imam Ali HE 678994; **Sayed Amer** 5 Sayyid al Bakri, ZA 340-9673; **Upholstery** 1 Shafiq Ghorbal opposite Heliopolis Sporting Club HE; **M. Younes** 82 Road 9 MA 350-5421. For upholstery fabric **Miss Bohal** 28 Talaat Harb 756315.

Household Help
Because Cairo is very dusty, keeping things clean is more difficult than other places; as a result, basic household tasks are more time-consuming. Recently cleaning companies have come into existence. They can be hired on a day basis to do routine cleaning and/or major jobs like windows and walls. Most people prefer to have domestic help on a regular basis. This would involve hiring an individual for daily full time (6-8 hours a day, except Friday), daily part time (3-4 hours a day, except Friday); twice or three times weekly either full or part time or once a week. Remember, if you choose to have household help on a regular basis, they become a part of the family scene.

Although most domestic help know some English, there will be frustrations because of poor communications. Learning some Arabic will be helpful. Domestic help may be a maid (**shaghghaala**), or houseboy (**shaghghaal**), a cook (**Tabbaakh, Tabbaakha**), a nanny (**daada**), a gardener (**ganayni**), a doorman (**bawwaab**), or a driver (**sawwaa'**). When hiring, ask for a letter of recommendation and a copy of the person's identity papers. These papers provide full name and address which may prove necessary in case of emergency. Hours and work responsibilities should be clearly defined. You should provide tea and sugar during working hours. It is illegal to pay domestic help in foreign currency. Suggested salaries are listed below. **Tipping** is expected on all holidays, including western ones (it should equal a full month's wages spread out over all holidays) and for extra work like staying on duty for parties and dinners. **Firing** No reason is required to fire domestic help, but certain situations require it: when you have lost control or respect; when mental imbalance or unhygienic practices are evident; when things are missing; when food is disappearing in huge quantities; when your instructions are not carried out; when guests have been treated rudely; when tools or appliances have been used without your authority; when strangers have been allowed in the house. **Warning:** Although most domestic help are honest, **most cases of theft in the home can be traced to domestic help.** One must be very careful in accusing domestic help of theft. Be sure the item is not mislaid. If you are sure it has been taken, tell them you are looking for it and hope they can find it by tomorrow. Usually the item is returned the next day. Then fire them. A common practice among dishonest help is for money or other items to be hidden and if you don't miss them, eventually taken. **Things will also be broken.** Leave your good china, glassware and other breakables home, or expect to lose some of them.

Maids and **houseboys** should be expected to do all household chores. Most have their own system. In the beginning working with them to establish routines and expected standards is important. Work should be checked on a regular basis. Monthly salary: LE100-200. **Note that many African, Filipino and Sri Lankan maids are in the country illegally. Employing illegal immigrants is punishable by law.**

Cooks will shop, cook and clean the kitchen. Many have been employed by various nationalities and know how to cook American, French, German and other foods. Teach them your recipes. Keep an account book and have a formal accounting of their expenditures at least once a week. Plan menus with them regularly. These chores are expected of you. Monthly salary LE200.

Nannies You are entrusting the nanny with your children. Be sure they, and all other help, are healthy. You must take the time to instruct them in expected procedures. They should wash, feed, dress and entertain your children. Whether you want them to or not, they will influence the behavior of your children and vice versa. Your attitude toward the nanny will be reflected by your children. LE200-250.

Gardeners are responsible for planting, raking, weeding and watering the gardens. They will expect you to take an interest in their work. You should plan new projects, inspect the garden with them and make an account of the costs. Monthly salary LE100-150. Ask previous tenants or the landlord about the gardener's salary as it varies according to work load.

Doormen clean the stairwells, deal with garbage collectors, wash cars, check on persons entering and leaving the building and run errands. Monthly salary LE10-15 plus LE5 for taking care of your automobile.

Drivers In addition to handling all your driving needs, drivers are also responsible for the maintenance and care of the automobile.

Household Shopping

Things to bring with you This list has diminished over the years and is a matter of personal preference. Most foreigners living in Egypt do very well on the local market. However, there are some things that are not available that you may wish to bring, especially special treats for the family for special occasions. They include: birthday party accessories and presents, foreign postage stamps, non-disposable flashlights, prescription plastic lenses, bathroom scale in pounds, electric blankets, oven and other thermometers in Fahrenheit, kitchen timer, dietetic foods, freeze dried products, cranberry sauce, canned pumpkin, brown sugar, pancake syrup, maple extract, cream of tartar, favorite canned foods, mixes, breakfast cereal, bovril, gravy powder, marmite, salt and sugar substitutes. Note that hard liquor is expensive and scarce in Egypt, so you may want to stock up at duty free on your way in. **Things not to bring** include 110 electrical equipment, and furniture.

Bedspreads
See also Department Stores in Shopping section.

Coucha 21 Kasr al Nil by the Cosmopolitan Hotel 741458; **Decor** 25 Kasr al Nil 392-1459, bedspreads, sheets, curtains, etc.; **M. Younes** 82 Road 9 MA 350-5421, makes American style corded bedspreads, draperies, sheets, upholstery etc; **Ouf** Sharia Tarbiah, al Azhar 905368; **Salon Vert** 28 Kasr al Nil 393-1866/1937, for fabrics, bed linen, tablecloth, mattresses, pillows, blankets, towels, bathrobes, shower curtains etc. Sales twice a year at the end of February and the end of August.

Draperies Drapery rods are found in shops along Sharia Port Said, south of al Azhar. The wire used to hang small curtains tightly across windows is called susta and may be bought by the meter from a hardware store. Drapes are found or will be made at **al Said** 41 Kasr al Nil at Fatarani Carpet Shop 919056. See Department Stores in Shopping section.

Electrical supplies like sockets, plugs, wire, etc., are available in electrical shops throughout the city. Discount center is on Sharia Rowei off Midan Ataba.

Lamps and lampshades
See also Department Stores in Shopping section.

Abd al Kader Hamad 14 Nadi Zamalek Gate DO 344-6258; **Art Corner** 51 Syria MO 346-5625; **Bartoni** 56 Gumhuria; **Basma** 44 Harun al Rashid HE 290-9968; **Design** 3 Shagaret al Dorr ZA 341-0272; **Fathi Mohamed** 26 Adli; **Ghonem** Road 250 MA 351-8324; **Hanfi** 38 Abdel Khalek Sarwat 393-9124; **Kandil** 9 Ib al Laq HE 258-4986; **Khaiifa** 19 Abdel Khalek Sarwat 393-9726, copper lamps; **Rezk** Gamat al Dowal al Arabiya; **S. Barakat** 12 Brazil ZA 340-9651; **Safar Khan** 6 Brazil 340-3314; **Tonico** 38 Sherif, near Adli 976632.

Nurseries for house plants Insecticides and seeds can be found in shops on Ahmed Maher near Bab Zuwayla.

Al Agami 94 Tahrir DO 706649, just before Midan Dokki on the right, several acres of shrubs and potted plants; **Fathi Flowers** corner of al Nada and Road 7 under the overpass MA 350-5026; **Forest Nurseries** 29 Abdel Moneim Riad MO 705453; **Fougere** 24 Omar Ibn al Khatab DO 710493; **Green House Nursery** 15 Batal Ahmed Abdul Aziz DO 475257; **Hadiqat al Zohria** between al Borg Hotel and Cairo Tower, the Ministry of Agriculture's experimental nursery, sells plants and shrubs; **Home Plant Center** 26 Syria MO 349-0661; **Lotus** on the Nile beside the Meridien Hotel; **Merryland Park** Roxi HE, large selection of trees, shrubs, outdoor and indoor plants; **Nile Nurseries** on the Nile behind the Gezira Exhibition Grounds; **Nursery** end of Damascus MO; **Samia Imports** 42 Abdel Halim Hussein MO 706647; **University Bridge Nurseries** at the Giza end of University Bridge, potted plants and flowers.

FOOD AND CLOTHING

Cooking
There is a lot of good cooking to be done in Egypt. As a cosmopolitan city, Cairo offers a wide variety of ethnic foods prepared either in fine restaurants or at home. Most ingredients are available either in grocery stores or speciality shops, or else adequate substitutes are available. As with food preparation in any country, good hygiene and common sense will help avoid difficulties; but you should not feel restricted in your diet. You should however bear in mind that

food here is not fortified with vitamins and minerals and it is important to make more of an effort to eat a balanced diet.

Measures

American measures

3 tsp	=1 tbls	2 cups	=1 pint
4 tbls	=1/4 cup	4 cups	=1 quart
5 1/3 tbls	=1/3 cup	4 quarts	=1 US gallon
8 tbls	=1/2 cup	8 quarts	=1 peck
10 2/3 tbls	=2/3 cup	4 pecks	=1 bushel
12 tbls	=3/4 cup	16 oz	=1 pound
16 tbls	=1 cup	16 oz	=1 pint
1 oz liq	=2 tbls	32 oz	=1 quart
8 oz liq	=1 cup		

British measures

10 fl oz	=1 cup
20 fl oz	=1 pint
2 pints	=1 Imperial quart
4 quarts	=1 Imperial gallon

Conversion from American to British measures

5 US cups	=1 Imperial quart
20 US cups	=1 Imperial gallon
5 US quarts	=1 Imperial gallon

Conversion from American weight to metric weight

1/2 oz	=15 grams	8 1/2 oz	=250 gr
1 oz	=30 gr	1 pound	=455 gr
1 3/4 oz	=50 gr	1 pound 1 1/2 oz	=500 gr
2 1/2 oz	=75 gr	2 pound 3 oz	=1000 gr (1 kg)
3 1/2 oz	=100 gr		

Oven temperatures

	electric	gas	centigrade
cool oven	225 to 250	0 to 1/2	107 to 121
very slow oven	250 to 275	1/2 to 1	121 to 135
slow oven	275 to 300	1 to 2	135 to 149
very moderate oven	300 to 350	2 to 3	149 to 177
moderate oven	375	4	190
moderately hot oven	400	5	204
hot oven	425 to 450	6 to 7	218 to 233
very hot oven	475 to 500	8 to 9	246 to 260

Cooking Substitutes

Baking powder (beeking bawdar) is found in pharmacies and supermarkets. It is single acting; therefore, recipes need slightly more than called for. Add it as the last ingredient to your batter. **Baking soda** (bikarbunaat) and **Borax** are also found in pharmacies.

Brown sugar can only be purchased seasonally from sugar cane factories. For a substitute try 3/4c white sugar and 1/2c molasses ('asal iswid).

Buttermilk is not available on the market. To convert regular milk to buttermilk combine 1 cup milk with 1T white vinegar or lemon juice and let it stand for 10 minutes.

Confectioner's sugar (castor sugar) is not always available. Ask for sukkar budra. To substitute, blend regular sugar to a powder.

Corn meal (oatmeal) is only available in the countryside. Your domestic help may be able to get it for you. Be sure to sift it carefully for impurities. A substitute is semolina, available at grocery stores.

Cornstarch (cornflour) is available in grocery stores. Ask for nisha.

Corn syrup is not available. A good substitute is honey, which is available at supermarkets, groceries or unpackaged from the countryside.

Garlic salt Crush a clove of garlic in 1 teaspoon of salt.

Graham cracker crumbs Use any plain cookies/biscuits like Marie, Lulu or the sweet Tac.

Herbs Use twice the amount of fresh herbs in recipes.

Local Foods

Amareldin Sheets of pressed apricot can be found in grocery stores mainly during the month of Ramadan. These can be used for puddings or to make juice. The sheets are dissolved by covering them with a little boiling water. To dilute for juice blend in a blender with water.

Bread There are excellent traditional local breads on the market. **Aish Baladi**, a brown flat-circular loaf and **Aish Shami,** a white flat-circular loaf are both found in special bakeries throughout the city. Reportedly the best shami in Cairo is at the 16th century bakery of **Suyufiyya**, next to the tomb of Hasan Sadaqa and the Madrasa of Sunqur Sadi on Sharia Suyufia, the continuation of the Qasaba behind Sultan Hasan Mosque. **Aish Shamsi**, bread of the sun, is found only in the Luxor area. It is made in the pharaonic way by setting the dough in the sun to rise. It tastes a bit like sour dough bread. **Aish Battaw**, from the countryside, is wafer-thin and tastes of molasses and the open fire. **Aish Bayti** is a delicious, almost leavened, large, round bread usually made in the home. You may ask your domestic help.

Bastirma is Egypt's answer to pastrami. However, it is loaded with fenugreek and if you don't like that flavoring, forget it. You can buy bastirma in some supermarkets. You usually find it hanging from hooks and covered with a thick outer rind.

Burghul is crushed wheat, used to make Middle Eastern dishes like koubeba, a deep fried meatball with a filling of nuts, raisins and onions, coated with an outer layer of burghul; and Tabbula, a finely chopped green salad of parsley, tomatoes, mint, green onions, lemon juice and burghul. It can be found in supermarkets.

Irfa A cinnamon tea served hot and believed to be good for colds. Ask for it in coffeeshops.

Ersoos Licorice juice made from licorice powder (found in spice shops). You may find it in some juice shops, but it is traditionally sold by a colorful vendor in traditional dress carrying a large glass jar filled with the drink.

Fatta is a special dish prepared with layers of bread, rice, meat, yoghurt, raisins and nuts and drenched in broth, vinegar and garlic. Try it at **Felfela** 15 Huda Shaarawi 742751.

Fitir There are two kinds of fitir, from the countryside and from the city. Countryside fitir is thick layers of thin philo soaked in ghee. It has no filling and is eaten with honey, cream or molasses. It can be found at some bakeries in Cairo. Fitir from the city is sold in fatatri shops. It is thin, made of dough, made to order, and comes with fillings of jam, raisins, coconut, cream, honey, eggs, cheese, or meat. Try **Egyptian Pancakes** 7 Khan al Khalili just off Muski in the Midan; Sharia Tahrir, Bab al Louk.

Fuul The fava bean is the staple of the Egyptian diet. Fuul vendors are on the streets each morning selling beans from pots which have been simmering on a fire all night. Fuul can be prepared a variety of ways, including sandwiches. Try **Felfela** (15 Huda Shaarawi 742751). To buy, be sure you find a clean vendor. Ask your domestic help to bring you some.

Some of the better fuul shops are **Nemah** on the Corniche near the Agouza Hospital; **Nagef** on Sharia Ramsis; **al Gut** in Bab al Louk; **al Tabeii** Orabi, off Sharia Ramsis; **Restaurant al Zamalek** 26th July, 2nd floor, near Shady Bookshop; **al Gahsh (The Mule)** Midan Sayeda Zeinab; and, of course, **Felfela.**

Halaawa A Middle Eastern sweet made of tehina, sugar and nuts, served as a spread or cut into pieces. Most popular brand name is **Rashidi.**

Juices Freshly squeezed juices in season can be found at juice stands throughout the city. They include: orange, grapefruit, banana, carrot, pomegranate, strawberry, guava, mango, tomato, sugar cane, and apricot.

Karkadee A drink, served hot or cold, brewed from the dried petals of the hibiscus flower. The petals are sold in spice stores, a powdered form is found in some supermarkets as are the newly available infusion bags.

Kebab and kufta Kebab, grilled lamb seasoned and marinated in spices, is a speciality of the Middle East. When ground or minced it is called kufta. To try either, grilled over an open fire, go to **Abu Shakra** on Kasr al Aini, in New Maadi next to Cinema Fontana or behind the Sayed Darwish Concert Hall in Giza; or **al Dahan** in Khan al Khalili. To prepare it yourself ask the butcher for kebab meat. For kufta only try **Rakeeb** in Midan Sayeda Zeinab or **Bayn al Asrayn** in front of Show In in Madinet Nasr.

Kushari One of the national dishes of Egypt, kushari is macaroni, rice and brown lentils covered with fried onions and a spicy tomato sauce. Try it at **Goha** on Sharia Emad al Din.

Mahshi Another of the national dishes of Egypt, mahshi is stuffed eggplant (aubergine), tomatoes, grape leaves, zucchini (courgettes) or green peppers filled with rice and/or meat. It is often served as a mezza or as a vegetable with a main course. Try **Ariston** in the alley off Sharia Talaat Harb next to Cinema Miami.

Mefata'a Made of molasses, butter, fenugreek, nuts, and sesame seeds, mefata'a is a traditional jam of the countryside. It is new on the supermarket shelf under the name of **Honey Jam**.

Mezzas Served at the beginning of a meal, mezzas are a variety of wonderful salads like tehina, torshi, kobeiba, olives, cheeses, etc. Try them at **Paprika** on the Corniche near the Radio and TV building or **Amphitrion** Sharia Ahram HE.

Moghat A hot drink of the Delta and northern coast, moghat is a mixture of spices blended with sesame seeds and cooked in butter, then mixed with water and sugar and topped with nuts. Served after a baby is born and considered rich nourishment for nursing mothers, it is also offered to guests who come to congratulate the new mother. It is only found in homes.

Molokhiyya A national dish, the consistency of a thick soup, made from a leafy green vegetable of the same name cooked with garlic. It is often served with rice.

Red carrots Found in November and December and sold only by pushcart vendors, these carrots are eaten raw or made into a cinnamon flavored jam.

Rose water Sold in perfume shops in the Khan al Khalili and in a few supermarkets, rose water is often an ingredient in Middle Eastern recipes. Try adding a drop to fresh orange juice or drinking water.

Sahlab A warm drink made with powdered arrowroot mixed in milk and garnished with coconut and chopped nuts. When available, it can be found in coffee houses like al Fishawi in Khan al Khalili. A powdered form is available from spice shops. If it isn't expensive it has been diluted.

Tehina A dip made from sesame seeds used in cooking and as an appetizer with cut fresh vegetables. Available in supermarkets and grocery shops, it can be blended with garlic, yoghurt and lemon juice. When it is blended with grilled puree of eggplant (aubergine) it is called babaghanoug.

Tamr hindi Served hot or cold, tamr hindi is a drink made from the tamarind fruit, available in spice stores.

Taamiyya or **Falafel** Sold mostly in the morning along with fuul, this is a mixture of ground ful beans, coriander, garlic and other spices, which have been blended and deep fried.

Zaatar A mixed Lebanese/Syrian herb used to garnish yogurt, salad, and pizzas. Herbs include sesame seeds and thyme.

Food Shopping

Alcoholic drinks The only beer available in Egypt is the locally made **Stella** and **Stella Export**. In the spring the company produces **Marzen**, a light ale, and during the winter **Aswan Stout**, a dark bock beer. Stella is available from some grocery stores, but export can only be found in restaurants. There is one winery in Egypt owned by the Egyptian Vineyard Company. **Wines**

include **Gianaclis Village,** white and dry; **Ptolemees,** white and sweet; **Nefertiti,** white and sweet; **Reine Cleopatra,** white and sweet; **Muscat d'Egypte,** white and very sweet; **Castel Nestor,** white and delicately sweet; **Rubis d'Egypte,** a rose; **Chateau Gianaclis,** a red table wine; **Omar Khayyam,** a red table wine; **Ptolemee,** a red dry wine; **Pharaoh's,** a red dry wine; **Vin de Messe,** a sherry and **Cordon d'Or,** a champagne, only available in fall and winter. Wines are available from some grocery stores. Locally made **spirits** include **Gin: Golden Bell, Big Ben** and **Ginner; Vodka: New Star, Abora Green, Cherry** and **Opora; Brandy:** Zottos, **Bolanchi, Vieilli Recolte, Louise** and **Imperatore.** There is also **Zibiib,** Egypt's answer to Ouzo. Imported hard liquor can be bought from **Restaurant Kafeteria,** on the south side of the street which runs beside 15th May Bridge, AG.

Bakeries There are four types of bakery in Cairo.

European bakeries offer everything from rich, exotic pastries to breads in all varieties, dietetic foods, and speciality items like gingerbread houses at Christmas. These bakeries exist in all areas of the city and are often connected to large hotels. This selected list offers some bakeries with unique speciality items.

Baron Hotel between Sharia Merghani and Oruba HE 668701 668289, try the mille feuille; **Chantilly** 11 Sharia Baghdad HE 669026 291-5757, excellent french and onion bread and rolls; **Five Stars** 5 Khalifa al Mamoun Manshiet al Bakri HE 257-7563. includes a restaurant and take away; **Groppi** Midan Talaat Harb 743244 and 46 Abdel Khalek Sarwat 391-1871/2. Groppi's is a landmark in Cairo. It offers a wide selection of goods including syrups, cheeses, smoked meats, fresh cream, eastern sweets, candies, chocolates, glaze, pastas, etc. Will cater; **La Patisserie** Ramses Hilton Hotel 744400 758000; **La Poire** 1 Latin America GC 340-1509 355-1509, exquisite cakes and Um Ali made to order, salty savories, and kobeiba; **Manderine Pastry Shop** 5 Baghdad HE 291-6575; **Marriott Bakery** Marriott Hotel ZA 340-8888, American fruit pies, excellent French bread and a delicatessen; **Meringo Bakery** 100 Corniche al Nil MA 350-4337, 6 Salah al Din ZA 341-2687, also chocolate candy and a coffeeshop; **Miracle** 150 Nile AG 712645, try the cheese filled pastries; **Napoli** 15 Abu Simbel HE 245-4931; **Nile Hilton Hotel** Midan Tahrir 750666 740777, wonderful large loafs of brown bread; **Patisserie Canary** 118 Mohi al Din Abu al Ezz DO 770250, chocolates and wedding pastries; **Saint Moritz** 35 Geziret al Arab MO 345-7572 and 5 Taha Hussein ZA 340-6367, a wide variety of chocolate candy and chocolate croissants; **Saint Germain** 59 al Zahraa MO 717867 711858 and 41 Babel MO 704519; **Simonds** 98 Nile DO 711738/773, 112 26th July ZA 340-9436 and 29 Sherif 393-8519, petit pain, Louis XV sandwiches and pineapple cake to order; **Sweet House** (next to Pearl Hotel) Rd 6 and 82 MA 351-8304 351-7946 and 102B Merghani HE 670105 and 103 al Iraq MO 482422; **Al Tashrifa** 164 26th July, Midan Sphinx DO 344-4996.

Oriental bakeries specialize in the very sweet Middle Eastern pastries. Although they exist in all areas of the city a number of oriental bakeries can be found on or near Talaat Harb between Midan Talaat Harb and Sharia Sherif. Pastries include **Aish Saraia,** (bread of the palace), orange colored finely grained bread soaked in syrup; **Atayef,** nut or cheese stuffed pancakes fried in deep oil; **Baklawa,** philo dough layered with nuts, custard or cottage cheese and soaked in syrup; **Balah al Sham,** a sausage shaped doughnut, dripping in syrup; **Basbousa,** a semolina cake dripping in syrup, and sometimes filled with cream and garnished with almonds; **Bassima,** coconut squares; **Ghoreyeba,** a shortbread cookie similar to Kahk; **Kahk,** a shortbread cookie stuffed with dates, turkish delight or honey and coated with powdered sugar; **Konafa,** cooked shredded batter mixed with butter and stuffed with nuts, cream or cheese, prepared in a variety of shapes; **Lukmet al Adi** fritter-like round doughnuts, fried and then soaked in syrup; **Rawani,** a coconut sponge cake dripping with syrup and

garnished with coconut; **Um Ali,** a rich pudding of bread, nuts, coconut and milk.
Abu Hadi Bab al Louk specialized in aish saraia; **Abd Patisserie** 25 Talaat Harb 392-4407, will deliver large orders; **Alcazar** 4 26th July 391-6853, catering available; **Halawani Abu al Shamia** 50 Continental Passage, Adli 391-8980/3513, has seven branches throughout the city; **Harun al Rashid** 23 Talaat Harb 391-3179 and 56 Midan Opera 391-1673; **Koueidar** 3 Adli 391-0710, 42 Talaat Harb 755189, 19 Ibrahim al Lakkani HE 258-4886 and 17 Lubnan MO 344-5583; **Manisha** 40 Abd al Muneim Riad MO 712109 704243; **Muluki** 46 Syria MO 349-3558; **al Samadi** 47 Batal Ahmed Abdel Aziz MO 344-8671, excellent aish saraia with nuts and cream.

Ifrangi bakeries are European style bakeries that have adapted recipes to Egyptian tastes. They sell local style french bread (fiinu), finger/sandwich bread, croissants, wheat crackers, biscuits, bread sticks, and sometimes fitir. Most do not have names, just addresses. **Abd al Moneim Atteya** 106 26th July and 37 Hassan Assem ZA 340-5462; **Cristal** 5 Talaat Harb 393-0005; 64 Kasr al Aini 355-4332; **El Gihad** 32 Dokki DO 348-3227; **Sameramis** 72 Kasr al Aini 354-4586.

Baladi bakeries make the flat unleavened wheat or white flour breads (see Bread under Local Foods above).

Candied fruit (fawaakih misakkara) Good for fruit cakes or eaten as it is, candied fruit comes nicely packaged. In addition to pears, apples, quince, dates, and chestnuts (now hard to find), there is also orange peel, bitter orange peel, celery, figs, apricots, prunes and sweet potato. The latter is used as a substitute for chestnuts.

In season from **Dar al Barabrah** Sakkara Rd 852289; **Groppi** Midan Talaat Harb 743244; 46 Abd al Khalek Sarwat 391-1874/727; **Koueidar** 3 Sharia Adli, commercial passage 391-4710; **Salem Ahmed Salem** Midan Sayedna al Hussein 910844.

Candy Many familiar brand name candies are now made in Egypt and are available at kiosks and grocery stores. Brand name equivalents (locally available brand in bold type): **Bounty:** Almond Joy (US); **Fruit Tella:** Starbursts (US); **Gersy:** Almond Joy (US), Bounty (UK); **Icat:** KitKat (US, UK); **KatCorona:** KitKat (US, UK); **Mars:** Milky Way (US); **Maxy:** 3 Musketeers (US), Mars (UK); **Rocket:** Brown Cow (US) or Sugar Daddy (US). Candy, when imported, is usually from Europe. **Corona and ICA** are Egyptian brand names. Both make a variety of plain chocolate bars with nut, fruit and nut and other combinations. Other local specialities: **Assaleya** tastes like Bit o Honey, comes in six inch sticks made of molasses with nut centers, found at kiosks; **Bassima,** a coconut candy; **Bonboni,** a hard candy in a variety of flavors; **Fawakeh,** imitation marzipan for decoration; **Fouliya,** peanuts held together in a square bar by a taffy-like sweet. This candy is also made of sesame **simsemeya,** chickpeas **hommoseya,** hazelnuts **bondoeya,** pistachio **fustoeya,** coconut **gouzeya** and almonds **lozeya**; **Halawa,** a candy made of tehina either soft to spread on bread, or hard, to eat with the fingers; **Ladida,** roasted coconut flakes; **Malban,** turkish delight; **Melabbes,** sugar-coated almonds and peanuts.

Candy stores (see also Bakeries above): **Harun al Rashid** 23 Sharia Talaat Harb 751790; **Salem Ahmed Salem** at Midan al Husein 910844.

Catering and supplies Many restaurants or speciality shops will cater upon request. Often these services are not advertised, but passed around by word of mouth. Ask a neighbor, or telephone your favorite restaurant and ask. Many women make speciality items at home for colection. These range from pastries, wedding cakes, and savories to full course meals in a variety of ethnic foods. Look for advertisements in the **Maadi Messenger**, but many of these services are also word of mouth only. Ask around.

Amin 76 Rd 9 MA 350-2857, party equipment; **Ayad** 79 Rd 9 MA 350-3498, party equipment; **Le Chantilly** 11 Sharia Baghdad HE 669026; **Charinos** 87 Osman Ibn Affan, corner of Abdel Wahab al Naggar between Midan Triomphe and Midan Safir HE; **Executive Catering** 10A Rd 275 New Maadi 352-5667; **Gayed/Aida Fahim** 1 Haleem (behind Tawfikia School) Shubra 657983; **Groppi** 46 Abdel Khalek Sarwat 391-1874/727 and Midan Talaat Harb 743244; **al Kammar** 7 al Gawhar al Kaed, al Muski 908-426, party decorations; **La Terrine** 105 Higaz, near Heliopolis Hospital HE 257-8634; **Mina Supplies** 18B 26th July 759526 759348; **Petit Swiss Chalet** 9 Rd 151 MA 351-8328; **Saint Germain** 59 al Zahraa MO 717867; **Sweet Temptations** 6 Rd 278 New Maadi 352-0333, children's entertainment.

Caviar Egyptian style caviar (BaTaarikh) is orange in color and comes pressed into small rectangular bars wrapped in cellophane. It is available at delicatessen departments of supermarkets and at **Shaheen Shop** Strand Building, 183 Nubar Bab al Louk 354-9139.

Cheese Local cheeses tend to be salty, but good. **Dimex** is a Coptic fasting cheese made from non-milk products. **Gibna adima** is aged, strong smelling white cheese. The older it is, the darker it becomes until it is beige in color. The good quality is aged at least a year. **Gibna beida** is a white cheese similar to the Greek fetta cheese. It comes in a variety of forms, both hard and soft, either heavily salted with green peppercorns or medium salted, which most foreigners prefer. **Gibna rumi** is the local equivalent of Parmesan. When fresh it can be sliced for sandwiches, and when hard grated for garnishment. **Arish** is a white cheese made in villages from skimmed milk. It is occassionally available in grocery stores, but more readily found in suks. **Mish** is a cheese made in the countryside and found, upon occassion, in milk stores. It is made from a mixture of cheeses all aged together in the juices of gibna adima. **Nesto** is a processed cheese which can be used for chili con questo. Local **ricotta** is of a wetter consistency than ricotta found in the west.

Coffee Instant Nescafe and the new Misr instant are found in most grocery stores. **Turkish Coffee** comes in the following blends: **maHruu'** very dark, almost burned coffee; **ghaami'** dark blended coffee; and **faatiH**, light, slightly red, blended coffee. To keep it fresh order small quantities. You may also ask for cardamom, mastika and nutmeg to blend with your coffee. The shopkeeper will give you the required amount. These shops will also grind French style coffee or sell you the seeds (khishin) to grind yourself. Coffeegrinders are found in appliance stores or from **Fahmi Ahmed Abu al Adab** 69 Ahmed Maher 923935, the first locally made coffeegrinders in Egypt. When ordering Turkish coffee in a restaurant or cafe you ask for **saada,** no sugar; **'ar-riiHa** 1/2t sugar; **mazbuut,** 1t sugar; and **ziyaada,** 1 1/2t sugar.

Some stores selling coffee beans and ground coffee: **Akbar Matahen Bun Fil Shark** 11 al Kahakeen, al Ghuria and 14 al Ghoulam, al Hussein 908489; **al Arouba** Sharia Tahrir DO; **Coffeehouse** 10 Harun al Rashid HE 259-1154; **La Rose de Moka** 180 Sharia Tahrir, Midan Falaki 354-4083; **Makhazen Bun al Oruba** 103 Tahrir DO 714280; **Shubette** 116 Tahrir DO 709064 and 8 Ahram HE; **Theonis Freres** 53 Midan al Falaki, Bab al Louk 354-2543; **Yemeni** Midan Bab al Louk.

Cooking chocolate Both chocolate bars and cocoa are available for cooking. Make sure to specify which kind you are buying. **Bensdorp Cocoa**, in blue and red boxes, is an excellent brand made in Egypt and sold in supermarkets. The label is in English. Large bars of chocolate used in cooking are also available in grocery stores. They are in plain white wrappers. **Chocolate chips** are not available in Egypt. Substitute chocolate bars. Home made chocolate chip cookies can be purchased by home order, advertised in community fliers like the Maadi Messenger and The Niler.

Cream Sour cream, whole milk and half-cream milk are all available in supermarkets. Local creams are available at milk shops (labbaan), which sell milk, yogurt, cream, honey, rice pudding and pudding. Local cream is **ishta** when it is skimmed from the top of the milk after boiling and **creama** when it is skimmed without boiling. The latter is potentially harmful. Ishta is so thick you spread it with a knife. You can have cream and honey sandwiches at some milk shops.

Alban il Manra 21 Dimishk MO; **Alban Zaher** Harun al Rashid HE; **Au Petit Suisse** 4 Midan Orabi 747511; **Khalifa** Road 15 (next to the fire house) MA; 2 Baghdad HE; **Haj Hussein and Haj Salah** Bab al Louk Market.

Distilled water Used for car batteries, steam irons, cooking and for some types of contact lens solutions. Also called battery water, it can be found in pharmacies and gas stations.

Fish (samak) With seas to the north and south and located on a river, Cairo has an abundance of fresh fish to choose from. Fresh fish markets exist in all areas of the city. Two large ones with a large variety are the Suk Bab al Louk and the Suk Ataba. To buy fish be sure the gills are red and firm and the eyes are bright. Local fish include: **catfish** 'armuuT; **crab** kaburya; **eel** ti'baan; **grey mullet** buuri; **herring** ringa; **John Dory** Huut siidi slimaan; **lobster** istakooza; **Nile perch** bulTi; **oyster, sea dates, mussels, etc.** gandufli; **porgy** shabaar; **prawns** gambari; **red mullet** murgaan; **salmon** salamun; **sardine** sardiin; **sole** samak muusa; **shrimps** gambari; **tuna** tuuna; and **turbot** muusa.

Fruit Fresh fruit in season is one of the best buys in Egypt. For Arabic names of fruits, see Vocabulary.

Gelatin Flavored gelatin or jelly is available in the supermarket. Unflavored gelatin comes in sheets. One tablespoon thickens 2 cups of liquid.

Herbs and spices For a complete list of herbs and spices, see the Vocabulary section.

Markets Every district of the city has a main shopping street where supermarkets, grocery stores, greengrocers, etc. can be found; and a traditional suk where prices are cheaper, produce is fresher, but items are sold unwrapped, unwashed, and in the case of poultry, live. In addition, throughout the city there are large, covered markets which offer excellent produce, fresh fish, meats and other products, also at cheaper prices than local shopping districts. They are: **Suk al Ataba** next to Midan Ataba off Sharia al Azhar going toward Khan al Khalili; **Suk Bab al Louk**

near Midan Falaki behind AUC Greek Campus; **Suk Dokki** in Giza stretching from Sharia Tahrir to Midan Suleiman Gohar; **Suk Al Nasria** in Abdin; **Suk Sohag** at the top of Harun al Rashid just off Abu Bakr al Siddik in Heliopolis; and **Suk Tawfikia** by Midan Orabi in Central Cairo.

Meat and poultry All varieties of meat exist including lamb 'uuzi, veal bitillo, beef kanduuz, and pork. Meat is sold Thursday through Saturday year round except during Ramadan and on religious holidays when it is available daily. All varieties of poultry including chicken firaakh, duck baTT, goose wizz, turkey diik ruumi, pigeons Hamaam, quail simmaan, etc., can be purchased fresh or frozen. Meat may spread bacterial and parasitic diseases, and should be served well done. To kill all potential bacteria or parasites, freeze red meat for two weeks.

Butchers specialize in cuts related to the trade in their neighborhood. In Maadi you can find **T-Bone** steaks and American cuts; in Zamalek, English cuts; in all areas French cuts. **Organs** like heart 'alb, liver kibda, kidney kalaawi, tongue lisaan, tripe kirsha and brain mukh, are also available at the slaughterhouse at Sayida Zeinab and in Bab al Louk Market.

Pork All cuts of pork and pork products are available on the market including smoked bacon, ham and fresh sausage; however, pork is not available in most meat markets. There are a variety of shops at Suk Bab al Louk. Other pork shops include: **Morcos** Ataba 390-5477, Midan al Gama HE 677438, 11 Suk Tawfikia 745070, 55 Sharia Shubra 761521; **Miro Protein Market** 84 Road 9 MA 350-0444; **Viennoise** 3 Mohamed Sabri Abu Alam 756294.

Cold cuts A wide variety of cold cuts are available made from poultry, beef and pork. They include bastirma, a pastrami; luncheon, a type of baloney with a strong garlic flavor; and turkey and chicken loafs. Pork cold cuts include smoked ham, pate, mortadella and salami. Whole pieces of all types of luncheon meats and canned goods are available at wholesale prices in large quantities at Ben Sorain Sharia Muski. **Sausage** (sugu') Excellent highly seasoned sausage made from either beef or pork is available. Try **Kased Harim** 84 Marghani HE 670693 for good beef sausage.

Molasses is usually sold in the spring by itinerant vendors, from pushcarts on the street or in markets like Bab al Louk. It is possible, but difficult, to obtain molasses from sugar cane factories. If bought unsealed it must be boiled three times to purify it.

Nuts and seeds Usually fresh nuts are readily available, but currently hazelnuts bundu' walnuts 'ayn gamal and almonds looz are not being imported and are hard to find. A good substitute in cooking is whole wheat or lentils. Pecans can be found in January. Almonds from al Arish in winter. **Peanuts**, fuul sudaani, are available in a variety of forms, salted and vacuum packed, sand roasted from Aswan, locally roasted, shelled or unshelled. Speciality shops called ma'la exist on all busy streets. They sell lib abiad salted or unsalted pumpkin seeds; lib asmar smaller, darker, pumpkin seeds from the Sudan; lib suri shelled sunflower seeds; lib battikh watermelon seeds; ful sudani shelled, unshelled, plain or heavily salted peanuts; hummus chickpeas, large, roasted and sugar-coated, or small, dried, unroasted; kharrub carob; and fishar, popcorn. Some shops: **Tasalina** 68 Kasr al Aini 355-1135; **Ma'alet** 11 Tahrir DO 702538.

Olives Both green and black olives are available in Egypt. The best ones come from Siwa Oasis. Green olives are found whole; seeded; seeded and stuffed with celery and carrots; and halved, mixed with garlic and spices. Black olives come in two varieties, slim and fat. They are sold plain, in oil, halfed or pureed. Both can be found in grocery stores.

Pasta
Il Capo 22 Taha Hussein in the President Hotel ZA 341-3195/6751; **Drugstore** Ahmed Urabi, Sahafiyin MO; **Groppi** 46 Abdel Khalek Sarwat 391-1871/2; **Lola's** 15 Road 9b 351-5465; **Pates Fraiches aux Oeufs** off Talaat Harb at alley beyond Fu Ching. Fresh egg noodles, ravioli, cannelloni and lasagna.

Philo dough (puff pastry) is found in special local bakeries and some supermarket freezers, and is called gullaash.

Pickles Called **torshi,** pickles include cucumbers, carrots, olives, onions, lemons, and turnips. They are available unpackaged at grocery shops or sporadically in jars in supermarkets. Special pickle shops are found along Sharia al Azhar. Here customers may ask for special blends, spiced to taste.

Pumpkin Available in the fall from most greengrocers, fresh pumpkin can be prepared for pumpkin pie by cutting it in half, cleaning out the inside, baking it in the oven until tender, and then passing it through a sieve. Egyptians prepare cooked pumpkin with sugar, butter, nuts and bechamel.

Salt There are two types of salt available in Egypt, coarse sea salt used for cooking, and fine table salt. The latter requires double the normal quantity. Low sodium salt is just beginning to appear on the supermarket shelf.

Sweets see Candy

Vegetables Brought in daily from the countryside and fresh in season, vegetables can be purchased from greengrocers or supermarkets throughout the city. For Arabic names of vegetables, see Vocabulary.

Yeast is purchased from bakeries or ordered in grocery stores.

Yogurt is purchased in grocery stores and milk shops, either plain or with fruit. The plain can be used in soups, sauces and dips. The best yogurt is found in unglazed ceramic crocks in milk shops.

Clothing
You are in an Islamic country and should dress accordingly. This means no shorts (including men), respectable dress length, and covering the upper arms. The only exceptions to this rule are on the sports field, at beach resorts, hotels, in the swimming pool and in tourist areas. Walking the streets, including Maadi, requires some common sense and respect for your host country.

Synthetics are not a good fabric for Egypt. They are hot in summer and cold in winter. Natural fibers are better. But be careful of moths. It is best to dress in layers, especially in the desert where winter mornings are cold while afternoons are hot.

Shopping for clothing for the family can be frustrating if you don't know where to go. There are many fashionable shops in the major shopping centers in all districts of the city that offer good natural fiber items. At the present time the government has stopped the importation of ready made garments. In February and March of each year the big sales are held in all clothing stores throughout the city. For further details, see the Shopping section.

Clothing Sizes

Men's Suits and Overcoats

British/USA	36	38	40	42	44	46
Continental	46	48	50	52	54	56

Women's Suits and Dresses

British	10	12	14	16	18	20
American	8	10	12	14	16	18
Continental	36	38	40	42	44	46

Men's Shoes

British	7	8	9	10	11
American	8	9	10	11	12
Continental	40	42	44	46	48

Women's Shoes

British	4.5	5	5.5	6	6.5	7
American	6	6.5	7	7.5	8	8.5
Continental	38	38	39	39	40	41

Clothing services

Dressmakers and tailors usually do not require a pattern to duplicate or create a fashion. A photo, drawing, or garment to be copied is enough. Usually good service is passed on by word of mouth. Ask around. For more information on sewing needs see Shopping section.

Abdel Fattah Hegazi 95 Osman ibn Affan near Midan Triomphe HE 672413; **Badawi** Damascus, opposite Epicerie des Familles, HE; **Fifi Tailor** Road 153, across from Benzion, MA; **Fouad Saleh** men's tailor, 4 Abd al Aziz, Abdin 935-632; **Garbouchian** 36 Abdel Khalek Sarwat; **Madam Fatma** 35 Rd 21 Apartment 7 MA 350-5362; **Nassib** 13 Baghdad HE; **Step Down Store** 2 Road 153 MA; **Tazbaz Freres** 27 Talaat Harb 392-9920, makes pleats for shirts, also buttons, lace, and yarn; **Ticketry Tailor** 75 Road 9 MA 350-5125.

Embroidery and beadwork

Alexandria Embroidery 2 Abd al Rahim Sabri DO 707688; **Columbine** 11 Brazil ZA 340-3420;. **The Haberdashery Shop** Sharia Muski between Gold and Midan Hussein southside of street, handbeaded scarves, vests and dresses, will do beadwork to order; **Petit Point** Kasr al Nil beside American Express, duplicates old European and Middle Eastern designs on lamp shades, wall hangings, doilies, etc.

Hand-made shoes

Abd al Fatah Ahmed Sayed Ahmed 14 Abd al Aziz Gawish, Abdin 355-2027; **Farid and Moukhtar** 8 Mostafa Abu Heil 393-0421.

OWNING A CAR IN EGYPT

Owning a car in Egypt may alleviate many commuting problems and it certainly opens all areas of the country to exploration. Cars should be selected not only for comfort, but for reliability and availability of parts. Among the cars recommended are Fiats, Volkswagens, Mazdas, Datsuns, Renaults, Mercedes and Peugeots. The average yearly cost of owning a car, excluding daily needs and repairs is about LE3-500.

Triptyque or carnet de passage en douane Automobiles entering Egypt with a foreigner or an Egyptian who has residence abroad are permitted to enter through any customs port on condition that the owner has an international triptyque issued by an automobile club in the country where the car is registered. The car is permitted to remain in Egypt for three months for the purpose of tourism. An extension for an additional three months can be arranged by the Automobile and Touring Club of Egypt. The owner of the vehicle must have a passport in which the visa has been renewed for the period of time in question. The cost for an extension is LE32. Vehicles entering Egypt without a triptyque from abroad can obtain one from the Automobile Club of Egypt at the port of entry for a fee of LE100, plus insurance equivalent to the value of the customs duties in Egypt. This fee will be refunded when the car leaves the country, or, in cases where the car remains in Egypt, upon payment of the customs duties. The Automobile Club of Egypt has permanent representatives at the harbors of Suez, Alexandria, Nuweiba and Port Said.

International driver's license All Egyptians and foreign residents in Egypt may obtain an international driver's license to be used outside of Egypt by making application to the Automobile and Touring Club of Egypt 10 Kasr al Nil 743355. They are open daily from 9-1, closed Friday. This licence is not valid in Egypt. You will need your Egyptian driver's license and two photocopies, your passport and a fee of LE15. Your Egyptian license must be at least one month old and/or three months away from expiration. To obtain an international driver's license in your country of origin to be used abroad, including Egypt, application must be made to an automobile club.

Egyptian driver's license International driver's licenses may be used in Egypt for only one month. To apply for an Egyptian driver's license the applicant must take a passport, two photocopies each of the identity page, date of issue page and all current visa pages, a stamped certificate from an opthalmologist (he/she will need an additional two photos and your passport), and a certificate from a physician (both letters in Arabic) plus LE30-5. Foreigners must take all the documents to the Egyptian traffic office in Gezira, in front of the Gezira Club, under the October Bridge. Each applicant is given a road test and an oral examination in Arabic or English. The license is valid as long as the person's work permit and passport are valid (usually one year). To renew a driver's license, take a passport, photocopies of the documents listed above, former license, and four photos to the place you obtained your original license.

Importing a car into Egypt It is expensive and complicated to import a car into Egypt. A person wishing to import a car must be resident in Egypt for a minimum of three months. Customs duties are high (up to 250%), based on the number of cylinders, age, and value of the car. For example a Peugeot of 5 cylinders is taxed at 160% of its value. Accessories such as air conditioning, radio, sunroof, etc. receive an additional tax at a rate of 85-165%. Vehicles older than 2 years may not be imported. Tourists or individuals who are temporarily in Egypt may obtain a temporary importation license from their local automobile club. (See above) For more information, consult the Egyptian Automobile Club, Kasr al Nil, or the paperback (in Arabic) Car duties 1987-88 by Taha M. Kosba, available in Arabic bookstores, approximately cost LE5.

In order to import a car on **temporary admission** (duty unpaid) one must make arrangements for **a letter of guarantee** from the owner's place of employment. This letter facilitates acquisition of a **temporary admission certificate** valid for one year. This certificate is issued under the following conditions: the vehicle is for personal use of the owner and his or her immediate family; the owner will not sell or otherwise dispose of the car; the car must be exported upon termination of employment in Egypt. The yearly customs fee for cars imported on temporary admission is LE40, payable when the license is renewed. Failure to renew the license carries a fine of 10% of the value of the car. In case of theft, the owner must pay a customs duty of 150% of the value of the car. Insurance companies assess the car at this value.

Under certain conditions cars with temporary admission certificates may be sold to another person with the same customs privileges. Proof of sale will be required. To complete the transfer of property to the new owner, the car has to be shipped outside the country and brought back in under the new name.

Importing a car from the free zone markets A great variety of foreign cars, payable in dollars, are available for immediate delivery from one of the free zone markets in Egypt. Once the vehicle is purchased, it is regarded as imported and is subject to customs duty under the conditions listed above.

International Trading Company of Duty Free Cars 99 Sudan MO 349-9556/9519.

Buying and selling a car in Egypt. The **civil registration office** (shahr il 'iqaari) where the car was originally registered will register the buying and selling of an automobile. The buyer pays a percentage of the car's price as a registration fee. This fee is usually between LE100-150. If the car is sold for more than LE2,000, the seller has to deposit the amount received for the car into a national bank. If the money deposited is in dollars then it must remain in the bank for two years. If the money deposited is in Egyptian pounds, it must remain in the bank for a minimum of thirty days, after which it can be withdrawn. If you are selling a duty free car, its value must be assessed by the Nasr Car Company on Sharia Alfi. This assessment is not related to the selling price, but will be the amount of money that must be deposited in the bank.

Yearly registration
The owner of a vehicle with a private license plate must go to the Cairo Traffic Department with his car and a valid driver's license to renew his registration. Failure to renew the license within one month of expiration date incurs a fine of 1/3 of the regular yearly fees. The procedure for yearly registration takes about an hour or two.

Cairo traffic departments and registration offices
Abbassia Midan Abbassia, in front of the Misr Travel building; **Agouza** Sharia Masr Sudan near the bus station; **Central Cairo** Midan Ataba next to Ezbekia gardens; **Darrasa** Salah Salem, about 100 meters after Sharia al Azhar meets Salah Salem; **Gezira** opposite the Gezira Sporting Club under the October Bridge; **Giza** Ben al Sarayat near the Coca Cola factory; **Heliopolis** Midan al Gama; **Madinet Nasr** Raba al Adawaya, on the expressway the second street after the Sadat Memorial; **New Maadi** Road 77, behind Golf shopping area; **Old Cairo** Sharia Ain al Sira, off the Corniche near the Nilometer.

Imported cars with duty unpaid must register at the Central Office, Customs Traffic Office on Sharia Ramsis in Madinet Nasr, next to NAMRU. Prior to registration all traffic fines must be paid at the traffic office in Midan Ataba. The receipt must accompany all other documents.

Types of license plates Private license plates for Cairo and all points south are black with white lettering; for Alexandria and all points south up to, but not including, Cairo, white with black lettering. Green plates are for diplomatic vehicles, orange for taxis, red for trucks, and khaki for military vehicles. Imported cars in the country on a duty-free status carry the following plates: white with blue from Alexandria; green with white for Suez; dark blue with white from Port Said; and yellow with black or yellow with red from Nuweiba.

Insurance varies according to engine size, horsepower and value of the vehicle to be insured. **Liability Insurance,** third party, is obligatory and is charged to you at the time of yearly license renewal. **All Risks Insurance,** theft, accident, etc. and **Total Loss** are voluntary. All insurance costs are at fixed rates with discounts for non-claim. These discounts begin at 15% for the first year of non-claim, rising at a rate of 5% per year to 45% after six consecutive years of non-claim. Be prepared to have dents inflicted by hit and run drivers. Sometimes fender benders are settled on the spot by agreeing to a fee. Repairs are increasing in price, but are still relatively inexpensive.

Insurance companies There are two types of insurance company in Egypt, government and private sector. Both offer the same services.
Government: **al Shark Insurance Company** 15 Kasr al Nil 740994; **Misr Insurance Company** 7 Talaat Harb 740130; **National Insurance Company** 41 Kasr al Nil 391-8751 390-0192.
Private Sector: al Mohandis 36 Batal Ahmed Abdel Aziz MO 701074; **Delta Insurance Company** 26 Batal Ahmed Abdel Aziz MO 714263; **Suez Canal Insurance Company** 7 Nabil al Wakkad DO 711048.

Car Maintenance
The type of car repair you receive depends on the type of dealer you patronize. Authorized car dealers and modern garages will repair your car with imported or factory made parts. Some car repair shops will use hand made parts. The latter method is often inexpensive and involves ingenious ways of replacing and repairing. The former way is more expensive, often because of imported parts, but leaves the car in its factory condition. Authorized dealers offer the best and most reliable service, but if they say something cannot be fixed, you may find a baladi dealer who can solve your problem.

Car dealers: **Audi and Volkswagen** Egyptian Automative and Electric Company, Sharia Mourad in front of the zoo, 751964; **BMW** Abou Futouh, Gamat al Dowal al Arabiya MO; **Buick and General Motors** Magar 19 Talaat Harb, 744063 744162; **Chrysler** Anglo-Egyptian Motor Co 27 Adli 745032 745103 745411; **Chrysler, Cummins, Case, International Harvester** Elektessadia 2 Mohammed Farid Wagdi, Manial 842215, service 352-0707, trucks 126 Bassatin near New Maadi, cars 847B Sharia Port Said, Ghamra; **Fiat Representaive Office** 1097 Corniche al Nil 5th fl, GC 354-9660 355-7596 354-2562; **Ford and Citroen** Anglo-Egyptian Motors company, 27 Adly 745411, Auto Car Service, 84 Rd 9, MA 350-5946, Coop Gas Station, Maadi Corniche entrance 350-2696; **International Trading Company** duty-free cars 99 Sudan MO 349-9556 349-9519 349-0275; **Mansour Chevrolet** Gamat al Dowal al Arabiya, MO 460087; **Mercedes** Mercedes Agency Ramses near the Maaref area, **Mercedes Benz** Engineering Car Co. 14 Rd 9 MA 351-3128 350-0931; **Nissan** Albha Trade Center 2 al Zafran, behind Giza gov't, GI 861988 851946; **Orfanelli and Mansour,** 9 Falaki Bab al Louk, 547782; **Mitsubishi and American Chrysler** Electessadia, 2 Mohamed Farid Wagdi, Manial, 842215; **Peugeot** 4 Wadi al Nil MO 463069 650394; **Peugeot** Abaza 20 Sharia Adli 756553; **Renault** Renault agency, 37 Lutfi Hassouna, DO; **Suzuki and Datsun** Saudi, Midan Missaha DO; **Toyota Egypt SAE** P.O. Box 154 346-5560 346-5562, **Toyota** Alpha Trade Center 2 Zaafaran GI 851946; **Volvo** Volvo Agency 26th July, opposite Cinema Rivoli.

Additional car repairs: **Abbasy Spare Parts & Car Repairs** New Maadi, in front of al Nasr 351-3593 350-0238; **Amer, Tewfik** (Car repair & Mechanic) Rd 9 (behind bakery & Imam's) MA 350-3725; **Auto Car Services** (Parts & Repair) 84 Rd 9 MA 350-5946; **Egypt Diesel** (Diesel Service) 36 Iran DO 348-3005 / 9339; **FADYCO** Spare Parts & Repair 6 Serag al Din, Faggalah near Midan Ramses 901620; **Misr Fiat** (Fiat Nasco Service) Madinet Nasr after Sadat Monument 608745/9154/3290; **Sahara Automobile Service Club** 14 Teeba, MO 491472, 480399; also 10 Rd 4, MA 350-5388; **Shorty's Car Repair,** Rd 9, next to Gomaa, MA 350-5916; **VW Repair Service** 108 Rd 9, MA; **Zamalek Auto Service** 32 Hasan Asim ZA; **Zamalek Car** 15 Brazil ZA 419530.

Gasoline, called benzene, is sold by the liter in two grades **super** (81 octane) at 30p per liter and **regular** at 25p. Prices are controlled by the government. **Oil** is sold by the liter. Most gas stations do oil changes and small maintenance. Attendents expect to be tipped. Gas stations exist in all areas.

Tires Tires are repaired and purchased at special shops usually found near gas stations or along main thoroughfares. They usually have large piles of tires in front of the shop. Again, attendents expect to be tipped.

Rules of the Road
Because of the lack of visible controls and the special satus they believe they enjoy, many foreigners drive carelessly, discourteously and recklessly in Egypt. **You are also governed by the rules of the road.** Traffic tends to jam because most drivers are trying to jockey for a better position instead of remaining in lanes and being patient.

Mile-kilometer conversion tables
Distance 1 mile=1.6 km; 5 miles = 8 km.
Speed 30mph=48 km/h; 40=64; 50=80; 60=95; 70=112.
Road signs are similar to European symbols.

Accidents Minor accidents in which no one is injured occur often. If your car is inoperable, call the police, get the license plate number and driver's license number of the other driver and call a tow company and your insurance company. If you are involved in a serious accident where a person or domestic animal has been injured or killed, do not stop. **Although Egyptian law requires all persons to stop at the scene of a crime, foreigners are advised, for security reasons, to drive directly to their embassy, place of business or the nearest police station and report the accident.** Tow company: Tamco 844529.

Checkpoints Barricades exist on most secondary roads in the countryside. If the way is not completely blocked a vehicle should slow down and unless waved to the side by the police officer, should pass on through. All vehicles must stop at blocked barricades. Depending on their location, these barricades are manned by the border patrol, local police or military police. Be prepared to give the officers your car papers and the passports of all occupants of the vehicle. Usually the officer will check the papers and pass you through. If any of the papers are not in order you will be detained, and in some instances your car will be impounded until the papers are updated. Unless there has been some trouble in the area, it is rare that the vehicle will be inspected.

Desert travel Do not venture on long desert journeys with a car that is in poor condition. Be sure you have a good spare tire and proper jack. Equip you car with spare parts like fan belts. Do not leave the main road unless you are traveling in tandem with another vehicle and have a good sense of direction. If your vehicle becomes disabled, stay with it. Do not attempt to walk in the hot sun. Unless you are on a track, another vehicle will soon pass and help you. For two ways of finding true north, see the Restricted and Difficult Travel section of the Travel and Transportation chapter.

Losing your license If a policeman takes your license because of a traffic violation, he will issue you a receipt. You may claim your license the same day at the traffic office in the district in which the offense occurred. Upon presentation of the receipt and payment of the fine you will receive your license. If you wait until the next day you must collect your license and pay a larger fine at the traffic office in which your car is registered.

Night driving is very dangerous, especially on the roads to Upper Egypt and Hurghada. Most headlights seem to be pointed straight ahead instead of down on the road, blinding the oncoming driver. To compound the problem drivers insist on blinking their lights as they approach, further blinding anyone headed in their direction. There seems to be no cure for this phenomenon except to stay off the road at night. If you find yourself traveling at night, a good tip is to travel in tandem with another vehicle. If you stay behind it, the vehicle cuts the glare of oncoming lights while its tail lights give you a good focus on the road ahead. Needless to say you should stay a safe distance behind to avoid an accident.

Parking Parking space is at a premium in Cairo. Street parking is often bumper to bumper. The cars are watched over by an attendant called a **menadi**. You must tip him for his service, usually 25p a day. Traffic police will issue a ticket for illegal parking. If the car is obstructing traffic it may be towed away. If your car is towed away you must collect it and pay a fine at the traffic office in the area in which the car was parked. You can ask the traffic officer where he took the car. The fine will be from LE10-50. Multi-storey **car parks** exist in Midan Ataba; Midan Opera; off Sharia Gumhuria near Alfi; and behind the Ramsis Hilton.

Radar The traffic police use radar on major highways in the country. If you are clocked going over the speed limit you will be issued a ticket.

Speed limits Highway speed limits for private vehicles, often enforced by radar, are 90km on all roads except the Cairo-Alexandria highway where the limit is 100km.

Traffic tickets Traffic tickets are issued for most traffic violations. In most instances a driver is not stopped, but the ticket is written and submitted to the traffic office. Illegal parking tickets carrying large fines are pasted on a window of the automobile. Except for those tickets posted on vehicles, a driver has no access to his fines until it is time to pay the traffic violations at the time of registration renewal or selling the car.

SHOPPING

If you look long enough there isn't anything you can't find in Cairo; it's just a matter of knowing how and where. From shawls from Kashmir and the Maghreb, animal skins and elephant tusks from Africa, and silver and gold jewelry of distinctive Middle Eastern designs, to European designer fashions, perfumes and high tech equipment—if it is fashionable, exotic, unique, or only an idea in your head, you can find it, or have it realized, in the shops and workshops of the city.

TYPES OF OUTLETS

Besides ordinary shops, supermarkets and a few shopping malls, there are a number of other types of outlet. **Kiosks** are located in all areas and at almost every street corner in the city. They usually sell cigarettes, candy, ice cream and cold drinks, but they also sell speciality items related to the area in which they are located. If near government buildings, kiosks will have stamps; by a school, stationery; near a hospital, gift items, tissues and some medicines. **Vendors** exist all over the city. Some set up permanent locations and can be found at particular times of the day, like the fuul man in the morning; others are mobile and move from district to district with their carts. These vendors sell molasses and fruits in season, bamboo flutes, garland flowers, plasticware, baskets and other portable products. **Suks** Nearly every district of the city has a traditional suk where everything from vegetables to charcoal is sold. Items are usually cheaper, fresher and in more variety, but are not as hygienically packaged as in modern shopping areas. Be prepared to pick your poultry live. **Flea markets** are found everywhere in the city. Some are open one day a week, others on a continuous basis. They sell everything from old bottles to spare parts for Russian made products. **Government Stores** There are two types of government stores, one for foodstuffs and a second for household goods. The food shops are used primarily by people eligible for government welfare services; however, non-Egyptians can shop there. They often have imported cheese and canned goods. The older shops are painted blue, the newer are orange and white pre-fab buildings. The household goods are usually all natural fiber blankets, bedspreads, towels and rugs; kitchen items like dishes and pots and pans; and some clothing. Prices are fixed and cheaper than in other stores. **Co-operatives** are similar to government stores, except they are joint efforts on the part of farmers and retailers. They offer fresh produce at cheaper prices than in the suks. Anyone can buy from the cooperatives. **The National Food Security Company** is such a cooperative. It is usually an open wooden building painted red and white and located near the government stores.

SHOPPING DISTRICTS

Most Middle Eastern shopping is in the medieval city, but there are shops specializing in oriental products in almost every district of Cairo. In most of these shops, buying is leisurely and you can expect to be invited to a refreshment, either Turkish coffee, mint tea or a cold drink. Where once bargaining was a way of life, today more and more shops operate on fixed prices. If bargaining is in order, it is traditional to make your first offer less than one half the asking price and slowly move up while the shopkeeper moves down. You should meet at around half the original asking price.

Khan al Khalili
The Khan al Khalili is one of the greatest Middle Eastern suks in the world. Although the area we know today is a far cry from the intriguing and mysterious arena it once was, it is still a cornucopia of exotic items. Originally referring to a warehouse built in 1382 by Amir Karkas al Khalili, Sultan Barquq's Master of the Horse, the name has now come to represent a series of small streets and alleys bordered by the Mosque of al Hussein on the east, Gold Street on the west and Sharia Muski on the South. The Khan, as it is called by locals, houses shop after shop catering to the taste of both tourist and collector. It is a place that draws the shopper back time and time again.

The Gamalia
The Gamalia, or camel market, is the northeastern area of the medieval city beginning at Bab al Nasr and ending at the Mosque of Hussein. Not to be confused with the modern-day camel market at Imbaba, the street runs parallel to the Qasaba (see below). Although mostly filled with shops catering to inhabitants of the area (groceries, poultry stores and the like), the street contains many Islamic buildings and some interesting shops.

The Qasaba
The Qasaba is the main street of the medieval city, bisecting it north to south from Bab al Futuh to Bab Zuwayla. It is one of the busiest thoroughfares in Cairo, passing through dozens of suks and changing its name almost as many times. Starting in the north the first shopping area of interest straddles both sides of the street in front of the Mosque of Barquq. These shops sell all items used in the coffeeshops of Cairo: water pipes in brass, copper or glass, coffee urns, small cooking fireplaces, and kanakas for making Turkish coffee. They even have coffeehouse furniture like brass topped wrought iron tables and games such as backgammon, chess and dice.

The next shopping area along the Qasaba is just south of the Mosque of Qalaun, where the street is sometimes called Suk al Nahaseen, the Street of the Coppersmiths. Here, where the Fatimid palace kitchens once stood, copper and brass shops have existed for over 1,000 years.

Beyond the Suk al Nahaseen is the Suk al Sagha, Bazaar of the Goldsmiths. The Qasaba, now called Gold Street, forms the western border of the Khan al Khalili. There are dozens and dozens of gold shops, silver shops, workshops and jewelry equipment shops, not only along the street, but in the haras (alleyways) leading off to the west. This is the suk. It is here that the rare and unusual pieces of antique gold can be found. The villagers, who use gold as an investment, bring to the merchants necklaces, earrings and bracelets of traditional design to change for hard cash. Most of the items sold in this suk are 21k gold.

At the edge of Suk al Sagha, Sharia Muski cuts its way through the Qasaba. This is the Times Square or Picadilly Circus of the medieval city, for it is the busiest intersection. Everything from the itinerant coin collector to the pushcart vendor selling luffas can be seen here. After the Qasaba crosses Muski, perfume, bridal, notions (Brit: haberdashery) and herb shops abound. Just off the Qasaba, between Muski and Sharia al Azhar is **Ouf,** a large department store filled with natural fiber products. It is one of the true finds of the medieval city.

From Bab al Futuh to Sharia al Azhar, the Qasaba bears yet another name. It is often called Muizz li Din Allah, after one of the early Fatimid rulers of the city.

Beyond Sharia al Azhar the Qasaba enters what was once the **Silk Mercer's Bazaar.** Today, unfortunately, the cloth shops, which once offered silks from China, are gone and the only items remaining from that era are two **tarboush shops;** but running parallel to the Qasaba is the spice market, also called the **Sudanese Suk.** Here in the tiny passageway can be found the largest collection of herbalists in the medieval city. They vie for space with rug and blanket merchants.

Back on the Qasaba, now called **Sukkaria,** the sugar bowl, because of the many pastry shops once found in this area, we continue until we approach the Bab Zuwayla. Inside the gate are candle makers, while outside is the only covered suk remaining in Cairo, **Suk al Khayamia,** the Bazaar of the Tentmakers. Here, in small cupboard-like shops, men sit and patiently sew the colorful appliqued tenting used on ceremonial occasions. This is probably the only truly Egyptian art form among the Islamic crafts. From the Suk al Khayamia, the Qasaba continues literally to the Red Sea for after it works its way through the city, it becomes part of the old trade route to the east. But for our shopping trip the street is no longer of interest.

Muski
Contrary to what most people believe, the Muski and the Khan are two different places. Once Salah al Din ibn Ayyoub decided to allow foreign merchants to open shops in Cairo, he designated a new street, Sharia Muski as the only place where these shops could be located. Sharia Muski begins at Midan Hussein in the east and runs along the southern edge of the Khan al Khalili in a straight line past the southern edge of Suk al Sagha to Midan Ataba, over a kilometer away. It reached its heyday during the British occupation when it housed fashionable hotels and emporiums. Today, the street hosts many of the wholesalers of the city with shops selling beads, sequins, notions, embroidery threads and yarns, slowly yielding to party decorations, paper and art supplies, and ultimately to imported electronic equipment like stereos, radios and televisions. Like the Qasaba, the street bears many names, but all of it is the Muski.

Beside Bab Zuwayla
During the Mulid al Nabi (Prophet's Birthday) celebrations, one of the oldest candy stands in Cairo sets up shop just outside the Zuwayla gate. From Sharia Port Said to Bab Zuwayla along

Sharia Ahmed Maher are shops for wood, tin, marble, bird cages, tools, canvas chairs, beach umbrellas and other items. Once the street reaches the Qasaba the tone changes and so does the name. It is now **Darb al Ahmar**, the Red Alley. Darb al Ahmar continues east with gold shops, rag rug weavers, bakeries and fuul stands vying for space among medieval mosques, apartment houses, palaces and schools. Along its way to the Citadel it becomes **Bab al Wazir**.

Ezbekia

Moving west from the medieval city we come to **Ezbekia**, first developed as a suburb by the Amir Azbak in the fifteenth century. In the nineteenth century, Ismail Pasha renovated the area as part of his plan for Europeanizing Cairo, destroying the old palaces around Ezbekia and much of historical Cairo in the process. After the transformation, Ezbekia was one of the most fashionable squares in the world. Today the gardens have little of their former glory left. The streets around the gardens contain a number of outdoor stalls selling religious items, second-hand books and magazines. The major streets flowing into this area include **Gumhuria**, running east/west; **Alfi; 26th July**, formerly Sharia Fouad, with cafes, shopping and cinemas; and **Abdel Khalek Sarwat**, filled with bookshops, jewelers, and hosting Groppi's Garden.

City Center

Since the 1952 Revolution **Midan Tahrir**, formerly Midan Ismail, has been the center of the city. The square is a hub of travel agents, airline offices, transportation depots and government agencies. **Kasr al Aini** which runs south out of Tahrir houses many banks and government offices. The streets which run north between Tahrir and Ezbekia are the busiest, liveliest parts of downtown. **Talaat Harb**, formerly Suliman Pasha, and **Kasr al Nil** host many of the city's older well-known cafes and cinemas, as well as travel agencies, book stores, department stores, doctors' offices and business offices. This was the main shopping center of Cairo from the turn of the century to recent years and many of the old, established, distinguished shops remain.

Zamalek

Zamalek began as a horticultural station where exotic trees and plants from all over the world were transported to Egypt. After the erection of the Gezira Palace (Marriott Hotel), the ambience of a quiet residential area of stately villas and old world charm developed. The villas which remain have largely been leased to embassies for use as official residences, or to businesses for office space. The rest were razed to make room for the high rises which crowd the island. Most shops and services are concentrated on several main streets and the alleys which lead from them. The principal street which traverses the island from southeast to northwest is **26th July**. Its two primary intersections are **Sharia Brazil**, which south of 26th July is called **Hasan Sabri**, and **Shagaret al Dorr**. This area is teeming with boutiques, restaurants, shoe stores and bookshops.

Giza

Giza is another governorate and another city, but it blends into Cairo until it is hard to tell one from the other. Once considered a healthful place to convalesce, the **Dokki** area alone contains seven hospitals. The trend from garden and villa to high-rise began in the 50s. The main commercial streets are **Tahrir**, which is a hodge-podge of government offices, businesses and shops; a street called **Dokki**, to the north of Tahrir; and **Wizaret al Ziraa** to the south. This street has some excellent restaurants and a lot of service-oriented businesses, including auto repair. **Mohandiseen** is the largest and fastest-growing area of Giza. There are several excellent shopping areas. **Gamat al Dowal al Arabiya,** often referred to as The Mall, features a large variety of shops including car sales, kitchen equipment, furniture and clothing stores. **Batal Ahmed Abdel Aziz** is the continuation of Wizaret al Ziraa. **Syria** and **Damascus** have very good restaurants.

Maadi
South of the city is Maadi, a pleasant suburb with building restrictions which once limited buildings to only three stories and shops only to Road 9. Both these restrictions have been ignored in recent years, and Maadi's character is changing. Road 9 is still the largest shopping area, with many new shops and restaurants including outlets from the Khan al Khalili. The Golf area offers grocery, pharmacy and boutique shopping. Digla remains the least developed for shoppers, while **New Maadi** is growing with restaurants and retail stores.

Heliopolis
North of the city is Heliopolis, also called Misr al Gedida (New Cairo). Planned as a garden city by the Belgian businessman Baron Empain, it featured wide, straight, tree-lined streets. Today it is the largest of Cairo's twelve districts, and much of it is quite congested. Among the numerous shopping areas are **Sharia Baghdad, Midan Roxi,** and **Midan al Gama.**

SHOPPING

Most shops in Cairo are open 9-1 and 5-8 in summer, and 10-6 in winter. Pharmacies and food stores generally stay open until 10pm. Shopping hours during the month of Ramadan vary widely: some shops close all day and open at night, others follow more regular times, but open later and close earlier. Most shops close on Sunday, with a few choosing to close on Friday.

Retail shops in Cairo are opening at such a rapid pace it is difficult to keep up with all of them. It is also impossible to list all the shops and services in a city as large as Cairo; therefore our shopping list is selective. We have tried to present you with the best, the unusual, the hard-to-find or unique items. A trip in any main shopping area will help you find clothing, florists, grocery stores, stationery shops, appliances and such, and word of mouth will tell you of newly opened shops and services. Services, like repairs and household services, have been listed in the chapters to which they relate. So have specialized items. However, every service and shopping item that appears in this book is listed below and cross-referenced to the appropriate chapter. Although we recognize that there are more areas to the medieval city than the Khan al Khalili, where the medieval city is listed as a separate unit within an entry, it is listed under the name Khan al Khalili.

It should be noted that one street address often covers all the shops and businesses in the same building, and that building numbers do not necessarily run in ascending or descending order.

Air conditioning see Household
Alcohol see Household

Amber

Amber is a translucent or opaque resin from a prehistoric species of pine tree that is now extinct. There are many varieties of amber, including pale yellow, honey, brown, red, white (called bone amber), and almost black. Pressed amber is a cheaper variety, where bits are pressed together. Transparent amber is very highly sought after, especially if it is fossilized. Note that opaque amber stays opaque, it does not become transparent with age. True amber will float when put in saltwater, and when heated has a distinctive smell. In days gone by, amber was considered a part of a fellahin or Bedouin woman's wedding gifts and was worn by people all across North Africa. Today many women bring the amber to the shops listed below to trade for money and other items. The shopkeepers in turn fashion the amber into necklaces and prayer beads which they sell to customers.

Mohamed R. El Kady Khan al Khalili (opposite Atlas) 906886, dealer in wholesale and retail amber, black coral and other specialities including individual beads, prayer beads, necklaces, pipe parts, etc.; **Shaban el Khrat and his sons** 10 Shewikar Building, Khan al Khalili 903369, amber, ivory and black coral worry beads.

Antiques

Note that the line between antique and secondhand can be thin. Genuine antiquities dealers must be licensed by the government's Department of Antiquities. Best buys are European items. Genuine pharaonic items are carefully monitored and cannot be taken out of the country without approval of the Department of Antiquities. This is also true of Islamic items that can be proved to be from the Islamic era. Islamic antiques are overpriced in Egypt, and are cheaper in Europe and the USA. However, if you like it, bargain and buy it, for you may never find it again. US customs allows antiques into the country duty-free. In central Cairo there are many little antique shops in the Bank Misr area off Kasr al Nil and Sherif. A few more are to be found on Kasr al Nil beyond Midan Mustafa Kamel, as well as in Khan al Khalili.

Khan al Khalili
Ahmad al Da'a and Son 907823; **Fathi Mohamed Mahmoud Tantawi and Company** 8 Wekalet al Makwa, Khan al Khalili 914667, old tables, chairs, marble, scarabs, antique pharaonic reproductions, beads, coins, inlay; **Khan Khalili Bazaar** 12 Sharia Khan al Khalili 903366, antique brass beds, mashrabia chairs, sofas and mirrors, inlay chairs, new mashrabia on order, gold, silver jewelry, stones, leather, used musical instruments, will ship, AX, VISA; **Lotus Palace** 7 Khan al Khalili 907400 905835 901190, the owner maintains four shops in the Khan, items include French, German and King Farouk antiques, jewelry of all kinds, no shipping, accepts AX, VISA, MC and Eurocard; **Oriental Gifts** 4 Sekket al Badestan, Khan al Khalili, Chinese and Japanese porcelain; **Oriental Souvenirs** 5 Sekket al Badestan, Khan al Khalili 902142, established for over 100 years and selling Chinese porcelain, Jordanian and Turkish antiques; **Ahmed Dabha and Hamdi** 5 Sekket al Badestan, Khan al Khalili 907823, antiques of all kinds including carpets and Chinese porcelain.

Other
Ali Ahmed Ibrahim 16 Huda Shaarawi 392-0259, French, Italian, Persian, Turkish tables, chairs, gramophones etc. gathered from mansions in Cairo; **Au Temps Jadis** Mohammed Marashli at Mohammed Mazhar, ZA; **Gallerie Classique** 32 Bahgat Ali ZA 341-1719; **Gallerie Gaby** corner of 26th

July and Mohammed Azmi ZA; **Hamada** 44 Kasr al Nil 756053, objets d'art; **Hussein Ahmed** 16 Huda Shaarawi 392-0259, specializes in Persian and Turkish carpets, but has large selection of furniture; **Lola** 19 Yehia Ibrahim ZA 341-7933, Persian carpets, furniture; **Mashroos Mohamed Al Assal** 21 Huda Shaarawi 393-8852, French, English, Italian, Japanese, Arabian sofas, chairs, vases, chandeliers, mirrors and statues; **Mohamed Mahmoud Ahmed** 1 Ibrahim al Laqqani HE; **Mounir** 83 Road 9 MA 350-5176; **Renoir** 17 Sherif 759760, mostly French clocks, tables, cabinets, trays, vases and plates; **Restoration and Conservation** 1 Mamaar Behlar (off Kasr al Nil) Apt 5, 7th floor 770299; **S. Barakat** 12 Brazil ZA 340-9651; **Sami Abdel Hamid Shehata** 5 Huda Shaarawi 393-3047, Turkish, French Syrian vases, chandeliers, mirrors, tables, furniture, clocks and silver; **Sanabel Gallery** 4 Road 216 Digla 352-4978, European antiques; **Senouhi** 54 Abdel Khalek Sarwat, fifth floor 910955; **Shahrazad** 30 Sherif 393-5764, Islamic mirrors, tables, chairs and coins; **20 Mansur Mohammed** at that address ZA; **Zamalek Antique Dealer** 106 26th July ZA 340-1385.

Appliances

Every street in every shopping center has an abundance of shops selling appliances. Probably the best prices in the city are found on Sharia Muski near Midan Ataba. For a list of repair services see Household chapter. For a list of secondhand items see Flea Markets.

Arabi Company for Trade and Agencies 12 Gawhar al Kaed (Sharia Muski) 908544 924117, televisions, antennas, tape recorders, Toshiba; **Arab Company** 3 Gawhar al Kaed 904158, all imported appliances available in Cairo from small kitchen appliances, clocks, fans, to video games, cassettes and tapes.

Some Agents
Akai and Pioneer Sherket Awlad al Moulrad al Togaria, 1 Talaat Harb 392-7360 and 162 26th July AG 347-1193; **BASF** 11 Abul Feda ZA 699184; **Braun** Maarad Garden City, 2 Gamal al Din Ibrahim Mahasin GC 354-5513; **Kenwood** Egyptian Maintenance and Supply, 15 Dr. Mahmoud Azim ZA 341-5635; **Minolta** Khalex, 7 Issa Shaheen; **National** Yacoub and Ibrahim Nassif, 22 Kasr al Nil 392-5979; **Philips** 10 Abdel Rahman Rafei MO 349-0922; **Singer Sewing Machines** 8 Talaat Harb 759911; **Sony** 2 Suliman Halabi 754771 752411.

Aqua gear see Leisure
Art galleries see Leisure

Art Supplies

Many shops with artists' supplies are found on Sharia Sherif between Kasr al Nil and 26th July. Supplies can also be found at art schools.

Ahmed Abdel Kerim 17 Mohammed Mahmoud; **Al Arabi** 60 Kasr el Aini, agent for letraset; **Art Corporation** 21 Sherif 393-8722, oils, acrylics, calligraphy, stained glass colors; **Book Center** 8 Ibrahim al Lakkani, HE; **Bucellati** Midan Mustafa Kamel; **Dar Saad** 23 Sherif; **El Noor Stationery** 8 Ahram (Selehdar Corner) 358-4563; **Khodeir** 3 Shawarbi, high quality stationery and office equipment; **Salama** Papeterie des Beaux Arts et de l'Architecture, 44 Sherif; **Standard Stationery** 30 Abdel Khalek Sarwat, on the corner of Sherif, periodic bargains on imported supplies from China; **Rafaat Hassan Shehata** 30 Sherif 392-5821 393-9618, art and office supplies; **Talens**, near Wimpy MO, paints, acrylics, etc.

Auction Houses

Auctions take place regularly. Special sales are often announced in the Egyptian Gazette.

Catsaros 22 Gawad Hosni 746123; **Al Masri Auction Hall** 9 Beirut HE 258-8915/6031; **International**

Auction Hall 4 Midan Mustafa Kamel 758478;   **Osiris Auction Hall** 17 Sherif (facing National Bank) 746609.

Automobile dealers, repairs, spare parts see Household
Bakeries see Household

Baskets

Many baskets are sold at the curbside or by vendors. They include work from Cairo, Fayoum, Luxor, and Aswan.

Al Sadd al Aali Midan Finney DO;   **Latin America** across from US Embassy GC;   **Greek Store** Road 9 MA.

Bathrooms see Furniture below

Beads and Precious Stones

Most precious stones are imported into Egypt. **Amethyst, aquamarine** and **topaz**, all different colors of the same stone, are imported from Brazil. To test for authenticity place the stone on a white paper in artificial light. Real ones have only two shades within the stone. Most **Emeralds** in Egypt are not of good quality. Good emeralds are a clear, dark green. **Rubies** are imported from India and Burma. If they are transparent or very large they are fake. **Sapphires** must be dark and opaque. **Tourmaline** comes from Burma and Bangkok. **Garnets** from Britain. **Pearls** are from Bahrain, the Emirates and Japan. To authenticate, tap the pearl on your teeth. If it feels like glass it is real. **Onyx**, imported from Germany, is authentic if it makes a sharp sound when dropped onto glass. Onyx should be opaque. **Lapis Lazuli** comes from Egypt, Afghanistan, Chile and Russia; **malachite** from South Africa; **white coral** from the Red Sea; and **red coral** from Tunisia. **Turquoise** is from the United States, Iran and Sinai. Real turquoise has different shades, streaks and impurities to the stone.

Khan al Khalili
Agit Bazaar 6 Saromatia 902077, beads and ivory; **Ahmed Zaki** 15 Shewikar Building Passage, Khan al Khalili 923665, works with all stones including scarabs and turquoise, will make to order, will string, no settings, workshop on premises, AX;   **Ali Ahmad al Kolaly** 5 Khan al Khalili 931458, fixes and repairs all precious stones and mountings, especially pearls;   **Ali Koborrassany** 12 Khan al Khalili 902496 906732, open for sixty years, sells diamonds, pearls, gem stones and all kinds of beads;   **Farouk Abd al Khalek** 6 Khan al Khalili 931452, black agate inlayed with silver and other natural stones; **Farouz** Saromatia, Khan al Khalili 924782 964786, Jade, diamonds and turquoise; **Gurguis Azer** al Makassiss, Suk al Sagha 920518, repairs precious stones; **Hagop Hagopian** 6 Saromatia 914916, makes diamond jewelry to order, workshop on premises, also other precious stones; **Hag Kadri Abu Al Abeed** 32 al Mashhad al Hussein, Gamalia, 926713, antique beads including sandalwood, ivory canes, cocktail picks, brass, some incense; **Hassib** 6 Saromatia, Khan al Khalili 929867 928298, all types of stones and beads malachite, lapis, coral; **Ibrahim Abdel Afifi's Baghdad Store** 8 Khan al Khalili 937647, Necklaces and prayer beads; **Emeil Sif Falamon** Khan al Khalili 906168, precious stones of all kinds, ask to see old silver and Bedouin jewelry; **Sadek Mohammad al Mansoury** Sekket al Badestan, Khan al Khalili, open only from 10-1, sells beads and pharaonic items, will ship, AX, MC, VISA; **Mohamed Al Yousf** 25 Sharia Muski (west of Gold St.), glass beads by the ounce; **Zomorod** 6 Khan al Khalili 931458, precious stones including emeralds, aquamarine and lapis.

Bedspreads see Household

Belly Dancing Costumes
Haberdashery Shop 73 Gawhar al Kaed (Sharia Muski) 927452. Exquisitely worked bellydancing costumes, shawls, ballet shoes, beaded scarves, and bellydancing supplies. Excellent craftsmanship. Made to order. Sells to bellydancers all over the world. Will ship.

Bicycles see Household
Books, Bookbinders, Bookstores see Research

Brass and Copper
Specialities of the medieval city, brass and copper have been consumer items in Egypt for over 1,000 years. Almost anything can be found or duplicated in the workshops of the city.

Khan al Khalili
Abd Al Fattah Badr and Fils Mohamed 19 Muizz li Din, Qasaba, established for 150 years, makes fuul bean pots for use in the local industry; **Ahmed Gomaa Hassan** 5 Khan al Khalili 915806, in existence for over 100 years, sells brass, copper and Muski glass, will copy old styles; **Ahmy Mohsin** 5 Rabeh al Selehdar, Khan al Khalili 922639, items made to order including Christmas ornaments, candle holders, sayings, mugs, nameplates and mirrors; **Aly Abd Al Aziz Al Khawanky** 13 Khan Abu Takle, Gamalia 934070, brass pots and trays; **Also Bazaar** 12 Khan Gaffai, Khan al Khalili 904958, old copper plates, trays, urns, vases and shishas; **Bazar Kallown** 99 Suk al Nahhaseen, Qasaba 906026, old brass work; **Hassan Mohamed Said** 99 Suk al Nahhaseen, Qasaba 930284, engravers, brass, silver and copper; **Ibrahim Al Askary** 106 Suk al Nahhaseen, Qasaba 904042, in addition to selling brass items this craftsman works on restoration of domes and minarets; **Kin Saleh Baxar** 80 Suk al Nahhaseen, Qasaba 930511; **Mohamed Al Gamil and Son Galal** Sekket al Kabwa 900734, 200 year-old shop specializing in old and new copper and brass items including frames, will copy old brass, will ship, AX; **Mohamed Mousa** 99 Suk al Nahhaseen, Qasaba 903021, old and new brass and copper including coffeegrinders, kohl pots (mak-hala), and coffee pots; **Sayed Fahmi and Co.** Suk al Nahhaseen, Qasaba, minaret tops in brass and copper.

Bridal Items
Bride Gallery 26th July, south side of Zamalek Bridge, MO; **La Poupee** 21 Kasr al Nil 393-3734, in existence for 75 years, all bridal wear and wedding accessories; **Um Gaber** Darb al Barabra, made to order, bridal crowns, also ornamental flowers for dresses.

Butchers see Household
Cameras see Photography below

Canvas
The main area of the city for buying all types of canvas is Sharia Ahmed Maher by Bab Zuwayla. There are dozens of shops in this area.

Other
Hussein Mohamed 347 Ramsis 820968. Camp chairs, beach umbrellas, etc.

Carpenters see Household

Carpets
Egypt has a big carpet industry, manufacturing a wide variety of carpets and rugs. They include Helwan and Assiut Kilims, tapestries used as wall hangings, rag rugs, Bedouin rugs, oriental

rugs, and others. Weaving villages include Kerdassa, Harrania, Desia in the Fayoum, Mahalla, Kafr al Sheikh, Akhmim near Sohag, and the oldest in Egypt, Nakada in Qena. Types of carpets include kilims which are wool on wool; **Adi**, which are usually geometric designs; **Oda**, which usually have a religious inscription; **Asais**, which are hand woven without a loom from left-over material; and **Molawen**, which have Arabic geometric designs. See **Egyptian Carpets**, an AUC Press publication. For repairs see Household.

Khan al Khalili
Abdel Azim al Hosari 14 Hosari al Tarbeyya, blankets, rugs, wool; **Ahmed al Agouz** 12 al Mashhad al Husseini 909046, handmade wool carpets, saddle bags and silk carpets all with Islamic patterns and bright colors, will ship; **Ahmed H Al Rashedy** 11 al Fahameen, al Azhar 909533 904329, hand and machine made geometric design rugs, imitations of Tunisian, Bedouin and Alexandrian kilims, Sudanese shawls; **Ayman Farag Awad** 11 al Fahameen, al Azhar 922201, geometric and pictorial handmade rugs in plastic, silk, or wool, prayer rugs, kilims, made to order: needs your image and takes six months, cost LE1,500 per square meter; **Carpet Technical Company** 5 Khan al Khalili 909343 919146, Chinese, Egyptian, Bedouin carpets and tapestries, will ship, AX, VISA; **Egyptian Exhibition for Carpets and Furniture** 2 Khayamia 923429, wool and cotton rugs and straw mats for mosques; **Al Kahhal** Khan al Khalili 909128/173 and Nile Hilton 779045 ex1626, Oriental, Persian, Turkish Carpets, all made in Egypt with New Zealand wool, German and Swiss dyes and silk from Japan, all sizes, will ship retail or wholesale, all credit cards; **Hamid Ibrahim Abdel Aal** 5 Fahameen, al Azhar 934162, five generations of the same family have worked in this shop making and selling rugs, patterns include Menufia, camel wool, wool cotton patterns and some Sinai and Bedouin rugs, will ship; **Mahmoud Zakareyyiah Mohammad** 1 Khayamia 938152, wool carpets, prayer rugs, sandals, chair cushions, couch cushions, foam; **Marc Antoine Fouad Hajj** 5 Sekket al Badestan, Khan al Khalili, rugs made by families in Fayoum and Assiut, geometric designs, village scenes; **Mahmoud Benis** Fahameen, al Azhar 927125, blankets, rugs and carpets in acrylic, wool from Kafr al Sheikh; **Rashidi** 11 Fahameen, al Azhar 904940, Inexpensive rugs; **Shahatta Talba Manna** 11 Fahameen, al Azhar 929211, all types of rugs, synthetic and wool, factory and hand made, blankets, all can be made to order, speciality carpets.

Other
Abdou Moustafa 21 Sherif, hand-knotted carpets 756092; **Al Assiouti Seggad** 7 Batal Ahmed Abdel Aziz MO 345-1499, kilims, Chinese silks; **Ashraf Exhibition** 17 Sherif 743408; **Fatarani** Kasr al Nil, east of Midan Mustafa Kamel 919056; **Ismail Ali** Midan Opera, hand-knotted carpets; **Kazarouni** 22 Kasr al Nil 754119; **Kilim** 3 Dr. Fouad al Ahawani ZA, large variety of rugs; **Wahdan Export Office** 13 Sabri Abu Alam.

Kerdassa The shop keepers say the village gets its name from its vocation, **kana wa dasa** meaning "leg of the loom and preparation of the yarn." Regardless, Kerdassa has been a weaving center for many years. It served all the weaving needs of the people of the Oases. Today many of the shops have been usurped by other types of oriental gift items, but weavers still work in some of the traditional shops. The dyes are synthetic. Weavers advise cleaning by brushing only. If you hold a kilim up to the sun and see holes, it is not woven well.

Mohamed el Fooly Sharia Kerdassa, carpets, tapestries; **Mohamed and Ahmed Eisa** 29 Sharia Kerdassa, carpets, woven curtains in cotton and silk, bedcovers, sheets, shawls; **Mina Bazaar** 20 Sharia Kerdassa; **Nasr Nour Salem** 24 Sharia Kerdassa and 42 Midan Opera 391-3373.

Wissa Wassef Harrania School Harrania. Owned by the Wissa Wassef family, this school has received international attention, not only for its fine weaving, but for the exceptional manner in which the weavers are trained. There is an exhibition hall. Natural vegetable dyes are used. Also has batik and pottery.

Other types of carpets and rugs
Al Amal Carpet Company 19 26th July MO 347-8529; Carpet City 19 Road 151 MA 351-4625 22 Kasr al Nil 754119, 33 26th July; Khalek Bank Misr 748966, sells carpets by the square meter; Wall to Wall Carpets 39 Sherif 392-9441 393-3052; Zamalek Carpet 14 Gamat al Dowal al Arabiya MO 341-7803.

Cartographers and Maps
Maps of Egypt are sold in most bookstores. Recently, excellent maps of the city have come on the market, including individual district maps by Naguib Amin, and the Cairo A-Z. You can purchase older maps, including copies of the maps drawn by the Napoleon expedition from the Egyptian Survey Authority Sharia Giza, south of Orman Gardens, 348-8003. To purchase you must have a letter of intent and be prepared to wait a week or so for authorization.

Georgette and Samir Shaker Saba PO Box 247 MA 350-3525. Naguib Amin 2 Maarouf 746724; Remote Sensing Center 101 Kasr al Aini 355-7110, satellite maps; Trapetco Data Services 24 Kamel al Shennawi GC 355-0318, mainly survey maps.

Catering see Household

Cigarettes
Cigarettes are purchased at Kiosks. International brands include Rothman, Marlboro, Marlboro Lights, Camel, Kent, du Murier, and Kool. Local brands include Belmont, Port Said (a menthol), Cleopatra luxe, 100's, lights, and silkcuts. See Household.

Clearing agents see Travel and Transportation
Clock and watch repair see Household

Coffeeshop Supplies
These speciality shops have all the items used in traditional coffeeshops including coffeemakers, shishas (waterpipes) in brass, copper or glass, brass-top tables, dominoes, dice, backgammon, etc. Retail and wholesale items.

Mohammad Hassan 143 Muizz li Din, Qasaba; Mahmoud Eid 143 Muizz li Din, Qasaba.

Clothing
One of the fastest-growing retail trades, clothing shops cater to all tastes and offer some of the best buys in Egypt. Natural fiber products, many featuring excellent quality Egyptian cotton, are used to create fashionable designs at very reasonable prices. For ethnic clothes see Crafts below.

Unisex
Balloons 75 Road 9 MA 350-6916, excellent jeans, shirts and casual wear; Banana Wear 68 Gamat al Dowal al Arabiya MO 348-8907/718832, casual Benetton 114 Mohammed Farid, 23 Shehab MO and Road 9 MA 392-8473; Boutique First 38 Batal Abdel Aziz MO 712270; Comanch 25 Dr. Michel Bakhoum

DO 715578, jeans of all types; **Flash** 23-4 Gamat al Dowal al Arabiya MO 345-1717 346-0593, clothing and shoes for men and women; **Kamar el Zaman** 5 Baghdad 691381; **Magasins Cladakis** 39 Sherif 393-9383, hats, shirts; **Maison Unisex** 15 Abdel Khalek Sarwat 744491; **Mobaco Sportswear** 19 Talaat Harb 393-4603 and 242 Sudan GI 346-1368, men's and women's casual wear, own designs; **MAM** 64 Shehab MO 347-1368, casual and sportswear; **S.A.Y.** 39 Abdel al Magnum Riad MO 348-3373, two boutiques side by side, one for women and one for men; **Stop n Shop** 1 Malek al Afdal ZA, excellent men's work and casual shirts, pants and women's casual and beach wear; **Swista Co.** 2 Abdel Hamid Lotfi MO 714115; **Tahan** 24 Talaat Harb, in the Cinema Radio passage, 748903, casual wear and jumpsuits.

Children's
Arafa and Dajani 24 Kasr al Nil 393-1505, children's and teen-age clothes; **Baby Land** 55 Midan Roxi HE 258-4949 and 55 Abbas al Akkad MN 617919; **Baby Mode** 64 Shehab MO 345-0459; **Baby World** Road 151 MA and Shagaret al Dorr ZA; **Baraka** 35 Abdel Meneim Riad MO 717937; **Le Berceau** 16 Abdel Khalek Sarwat 393-7530, infants to 9 yrs; **Capri** 2 Damascus, Roxi HE 258-0517; **El Gallion** 37 Kasr al Nil 392-2655, infants to 6 yrs, library for children with TV and videos; **Raymond's** 7 Brazil ZA 804013 806043, Midan Salah al Din HE 69377 and 9 Ahmed Sabri ZA 808347; **Silvia** 17 Kasr al Nil 392-0264, infants to 14 yrs.

Men's
Biba Casual Wear 31 Geziret al Arab MO 346-6721, casual wear and Arena bathing suits; **Cecile** 1 Batal Abdel Aziz MO 347-3495; **Draperie Maurice Hanna** 43 Sherif 393-6922, vestiaco, local; **Eid Stores** 35 Talaat Harb 392-5264, specialized in wool bathrobes and scarves, VISA, AX; **HERA** 27 Damascus MO 347-6871, evening and formal wear; **High Fashion Home for Gentleman** 3 Monshaat al Kataba, Shawarbi 393-9209 393-8356; **King George's House** 19 Talaat Harb 392-5777, wool bathrobes, safari suits, alterations; **Mix and Match** 23 Baghdad HE, casual wear; **Mr. Love** 64 Shehab 352-9156, casual and underwear; **New London House** 41 Kasr al Nil 391-3500/5437, complete line of men's wear; **Playboy** 26 Sherif 392-5595/0764, casual, own designs; **Rouby** 34 Kasr al Nil 392-2039, undergarments, bathrobes, ties, shirts; **Salome** 19 Baghdad HE; **Selverge** 40 Mosadek DO 702014, casual and formal wear.

Women's
Aime Louis 6 Shawarbi 393-4598, dresses and bags; **Boutique Fatima** 157 26th July ZA 341-9951, Islamic style hats, veils and dresses; **Boutique Five** 106 26th July ZA 340-0896 and 6 al Selouli DO 349-2347, casual clothes; **Boutique Swiss** RA 6 Shawarbi 393-4326; **Boutique Valentina** 58B Damascus MO 349-0221; **Chez Renee** 26 Kasr al Nil 392-4276; **Class** 56 Shehab MO 347-6657, Evening and casual wear; **Fantastic** 5 Brazil ZA, 35 Hassan Assem ZA and 28 Osman Ibn Affan HE 340-0151, evening wear and Islamic veils, hats and dresses; **For You** 19 Mansur Mohammed ZA 340-5717; **Jungle Wear** 69 Shehab MO; **Lingerie Mouve** 11 Shawarbi 392-8621; **Lingerie** 162 26th July AG 346-1573; **Maison Francaise** Kasr al Nil 392-8310, specialize in handmade blouses and wool yarns; **Margaret's** 159 Behlar Mansions off 26th July ZA, casual wear in natural fibers, own designs; **Mervat Shenouda Boutique Finesse** 6 Brazil ZA 341-5691; **Mix and Match** 21 Midan Mazhar ZA 340-9602, European imports; **Nelly** 32 Shagaret al Dorr ZA 340-4955, evening dresses; **Om Habiba** 2 Behlar Passage off Kasr al Nil 392-21671, exclusive women's clothing; **Al Ridaa** 10 Midan Ibn al Walid DO 348-0148, Islamic veils, hats, dresses and evening wear; **Right Stuff** 8 Gamat al Dowal al Arabiya 344-6699, chic, casual and sportswear; **Samia Import** 42 Abdel Halim Hussein MO 786647 American fashions, swim wear, leotards and tights; **Set al Hosn** 9 Baghdad HE, evening and afternoon wear; **Stefenel** 157 26th July ZA 341-1115, casual and evening wear, own designs; **Trendy** 1 Sayed al Bakri ZA 342-0358 and 60 Hussein MO; **Timanad** corner of Hassan Sabri and 26th July ZA 340-0893, casual wear; **Up 16** 114 26th July ZA 341-8459, own designs; **Veronique** 114 Mohammed Farid and 161 26th July ZA 341-0403, imported French clothes; **Virginia** Gamat al Dowal al Arabiya MO 479875, teens' and young adults' jazzy casual clothes; **Zan's** 20 Ismail Mohammed ZA 340-0169, casual wear.

Special
Medical Clothes 4 Baghdad HE 660779.

Coins see Silver below and Leisure
Computers see Business

Crafts

Al Patio 6 Road 77c, Golf Area, MA, excellent and unusual pottery, rugs, dresses; **Assila Gallery and Applied Arts** 98 Mohi al Din Abu al Ezz DO 709719; **Baracat** 12 Brazil ZA 340-9651, jewelry, pottery brass and copper; **Choice** Corner of Abdel Hamid Lotfi and al Anaab MO; **Desert Exhibition** 8 Road 203 Digla 353-1491, palm tree furniture, pottery, bed covers and original fashions; **Emeraude** 54 Abu Bakr al Siddik HE 243-1524; **Gallery Diar Alhana** 9 Road 100 MA, rag rugs, jewelry, gift items; **Haddouta Gallery** Sharia Amira, New Maadi 352-4352 pottery, photography, furniture; **Khan Karoun** 150 Corniche AG 462928, some old pieces, pictures, ceramics; **Mit Rihan** 13 Maraashli ZA 340-4073; **Morgana** Road 9 MA, Oases dresses, native crafts; **Nomad** Shopping Galleria, Cairo Marriott ZA 341-2132, crafts, traditional clothing, jewelry, basketware, pottery and fabrics; **Om el Khair** 107 Misr Helwan Road 351-4463, excellent selection ceramics, woodwork jewelry, pottery; **Om el Saad** 58 Mosaddaq DO 349-8685; **Safar Khan** 6 Brazil ZA 340-3314, textiles, tapestries, pottery; **Sornaga** Labanas, off Kasr al Nil, just north of Lappas, government pottery shop with intricately painted vases using arabesque and pharaonic designs; **Senouhi** 54 Abdel Khalek Sarwat, 5th floor, 910955, Wissa Wassef rugs and batiks, jewelry, old etchings, drawings and water colors; **Shahira Mehrez** 12 Abi Emama DO 348-7814 dresses and fashions from traditional designs.

Department Stores

Department stores exist in all areas of the city, and many of the downtown stores have suburban branches. **Omar Effendi** is Egypt's answer to Woolworth. Sales are twice a year in February and August.

Benzione 39 Kasr al Nil 707605, Road 153 MA; **Gentillesse** 16 Ibrahim al Lakkani HE 258-1938; **Happy Home** Marwa, behind Cairo Medical Center, HE 258-3563; **Hazeen Stores** 21 Madina al Munawara DO 348-2856; **El Naghi** 44 Kasr al Nil 758673, primarily shoes and clothing for men and women; **Nostoire** Ibrahim al Lakkani HE 258-5098; **Omar Effendi** 2 Talaat Harb 759848, Roxi HE 258-5883, Maadi 351-4155, and Adli, Abdel Aziz, Ibrahim al Lakkani HE, Tahrir DO, features wonderful, inexpensive fabrics, especially for upholstery; **Salon Vert** 30 Kasr al Nil 393-1866/1937, three major stores all in the same area featuring linens, fabrics, houseware, clothing; **El Shabouri** 36 Sherif 393-9854; **Shalon** Kasr al Nil 393-1026, pharaonic bedspreads, towels and tablecloths; **Sidnawi** Kasr al Nil 393-7990, household items, fabric; **6M** 38 Gamat al Dowal al Arabiya MO 346-9017, large store featuring mainly men's and women's clothes; **Tredco al Sayad** 46 Sherif 392-7684/7533, knitting machines,safes, telephones, exercycles; **Trois-S** 33 Mohammed Mazhar ZA; **Versaille** 47 Gamat al Dowal al Arabiya MO 349-5206, formal wear, wedding clothes, etc.; **Yahya Houry** Midan Mustafa Kamel 391-1958.

Distilled water; Draperies; Dressmakers and tailors; Electricians; and Embroidery: see Household

Emporiums

There are many shops in the medieval city that hold a variety of items usually of interest to tourists.

Berti Said 5 Sekket Khan al Khalili 919314, primarily ivory and mother of pearl, but also inlay, brass, copper, camel bone products, will ship, accepts credit cards; **Al Mosslem Market** 95 Suk al Sagha

932176, manufacturer of oriental souvenirs, jewelry, silk brocades, Assiut shawls, tapestries, tentwork, inlay, ivory, mother of pearl, leather work, camel saddles, gold, silver and brass; **Al Sayadh Store** 8 al Adawi at Midan Hussein—the owner had a Woolworth's shop in Port Said which was lost during the war, speaks excellent English, French, Italian, German and Arabic—oriental goods, ashtrays, scarabs, plates, lamps, candleholders, poufs, handbags, inlaid boxes, amber necklaces, keychains; **E. Hatoun and Sons** 7 al Sabaa Kaat al Baharia (off 29 Muski) 905605, a unique shop established in 1878 hidden away through passages, but known to all on Muski, just ask—rugs, silks, arms, brass, fixed price; **Hosny M Hassan** 5 Khan al Khalili 918316, leather, trays, dolls, sandals, boxes, alabaster, etc., will ship, accepts credit cards; **Khan il Khalili Bazaar** 12 Khan al Khalili 905366, mixed assortment of leather, ivory, gold, silver, old stones, galabias, etc.; **Mohamed Al Gamil and Son Galal** Khan al Khalili 900734, brass planters, mashrabia, wall hangings; **Mohamed Ibriham Ouf and Company "Ouf"** Sharia Tarbiah, al Azhar (off Gold Street to the right after it crosses Muski) 905368, first floor: Cashmere shawls from India in muted colors with embroidered designs, cotton, silk, camel hair, wool materials by the meter, 2nd floor: wool scarfs (kufiyya) worn by men in traditional dress in a variety of muted colors and in six sizes, silk shawls for women in traditional black and a variety of colors, velvet shawls in fluffy cotton in bright colors, and wonderful woollen off-white large shawls useful for bedspreads or dresses; **Said Mohamed Mansy** 8 Ganabikia 903443, pharaonic and Islamic wall hangings, leather handbags, poufs, inlaid boxes, etc.; **Sopha** Um al Gholam al Gedid, scarves and shawls in wool and nylon, fur and leather caps, heavy gloves, long johns, embroidered shawls from India.

Exterminators see Household.

Fabric

There are more fabric shops than clothing outlets in the city. They offer a wide variety of imported and local fabrics with selections that rival any place in the world. Fortunately, most are located in one central area along Kasr al Nil, and the side streets around it, Midan Mustafa Kamel, Gumhuria and Talaat Harb. In addition, every section of the city has fabric shops. Some of these shops cater exclusively to Egyptian made fabrics, others to imported fabrics. Egyptian fabrics include cottons, wools, linens, and chiffons. Many department stores have excellent fabric departments. Hand-loomed fabrics from Akhmim, Garagos and Kerdassa are sold in boutiques and speciality shops. Factory outlets exist in the cities in the Delta where many of the local fabrics are made. In selecting fabrics pay careful attention to flaws and dye quality. Notions (haberdashery) are not sold in fabric shops. See Notions below.

Bandong Company Harun al Rashid HE 245-9210; **Belle Dame** 21 Kasr al Nil 392-1458, both local and imported fabrics wedding dress material; **Bohal** 34 Adli, men's fabrics; **Champs Elysee** 32 Kasr al Nil 392-4686/4530, Egyptian silk, cotton, wool, linen, gabardine and synthetics; **Madame** 29 Kasr al Nil 392-0981, all imported fabrics, evening wear, Italian cotton, African designs, Italian silk, designer fabrics; **Moderna** 23 Talaat Harb 754192, mostly imported fabrics; **Mohamed Nour Salem** 42 Midan Opera 391-3373, men's fabrics, cotton, wool, linen, gabardine; **Salon Vert** Kasr al Nil, three department stores devoted almost exclusively to fabrics, first store: houseware, bedding, etc, second: dress fabrics, upholstery, and patterns like Butterick and Vogue, third: men's fabrics; **Wooltex** 21 Talaat Harb 392-1703, all wool materials and yarns for clothes and blankets.

Firearms see Sports
Firewood see Household

Flea Markets

For anyone who enjoys wandering around flea markets looking for bargains, Cairo is a paradise. The variety is endless and the good finds are still there.

Army Surplus Suk Askari, Midan Ahmed Hilmi. Daily. All army supplies including clothes, insignias, tents and equipment. This market is somewhat difficult to find. When facing the Ramsis railroad station, walk left around the side and over the bridge. A flight of steps leads down into the suk behind the station. The items sold here are official military issue. Many have been traded in by ex-soldiers. Be sure to wash all items carefully before using.

Bird Market Suk al Asafeer. There are several bird markets in the city. Most of the suks are open-air and sell and trade birds, dogs and fish. They are open from around 10-2:30. The coffeeshops in the area are a good place to meet bird lovers. **Suk al Gom'a** Friday market: at the southern end of Midan Salah al Din on the side street south of the Salah Salem overpass. This road leads to Basateen and New Maadi. **Suk al Hadd** Sunday market: at the Giza railroad station. As you face the station go to the right side. **Suk Itneen wi Khamis** Monday and Thursday market: located in the Abu Rish area of Sayeda Zeinab. Turn east on Kasr al Aini at the intersection south of Kasr al Aini Hospital. Go one block, passed the Children's Hospital and over the overpass. The market is on the far side, under the overpass.

Car Swap Midan al Ittihad at Road 105 MA. Every Friday from 10-3. Car broker available for a commission. Sell or buy.

Imam al Shafie Market in Basateen along the street leading to the Mosque of Imam al Shafie. This market, selling mostly secondhand goods, has been functioning every Friday for several centuries. It includes a **scrap** market where everything from old bottles, bolts, and nails to occasional antique finds can be bought; the **canto** market for old clothes and material; a **grain** market, a **poultry** market; and a **sheep and cattle** market.

Paper Market Midan Ataba at the beginning of Sharia al Geish. All types of paper supplies, art supplies and dyed leather hides. Daily.

Suk Lazoghli At Midan Lazoghli near Ministry of Internal Affairs, Sayeda Zeinab. Car repair and spare parts. Open daily.

Suk Talaat Sharia Ashria near Um al Masriyeen Hospital GI. Tuesdays only. Medical tools and supplies, food, furniture, etc.

Wekalet al Balah Abul Ela, Bulaq. Everything from cars, spare parts, Russian-made spare parts, hardware, tools, clothes, etc. Probably the largest selection of fabrics in the city offering everything from the finest silks to remnants. Open every day.

Furniture
Every section of the city has fine furniture shops featuring a wide variety of products at reasonable prices.

Bamboo The major shopping areas for bamboo furniture are on Sharia Ramsis just north of Midan Ramsis and on Sharia Baghdad HE near the Greek Orthodox Church.

Bamboo Aton 195 Ramsis, rattan and bamboo furniture and baskets; **Bamboo Barbary** 153 Ramsis

907335; **Bamboo Decor al Assiuti** 153 Ramsis 902465; **Bamboo al Wishi** 21 Ramsis 939800 924633; **Bamboo Kong** 149 Ramsis 904565; **Bamboo al Shark** 157 Ramsis 904664; **Hammad Freres** 176 al Tahrir, Bab al Louk 742621; **Hassan Ali Hammad** 199 al Tahrir, Abdin.

Islamic A very special shop which is preserving all the medieval arts of furniture and decoration is **Nadim** National Art Development Institute of Mashrabia 47 Suliman Gohar, south of the Coca Cola Bottling Company, DO 715927 714219. Islamic furniture can also be found in antique shops and craft shops (see above). Local carpenter shops will make to order. See also Mashrabia and Inlay Wood below.

Modern
At Home 26 July at Brazil ZA; **Ceramica** 38 Batal Ahmed Abdel Aziz MO 716121, bathrooms; **Contistahl** Gamat al Dowal al Arabiya DO 347-9031, kitchens; **Decor Center** 27 Baghdad HE 664037; **Design Center Cairo** 7 Baghdad HE 669752; **El Diwan Gallery** 27 Abd el Meneim Riad MO 706062, excellent quality modern furniture; **Happy Home** Marwa, behind Cairo Medical Center, HE 258-3503; **Ideal** 8 26th July at Adli, metal furniture; **Integrated Interiors** 10 Geziret al Arab MO 348-0479; **Mansoura Furniture Company** 17 Gamat al Dowal al Arabiya MO 344-6919; **Mamelouk** 4 Hassan Assem ZA 340-2437; **El Marwa** Harun al Rashid HE 245-6051, metal curtains; **Mobica** 8 Ahmed Sabri ZA 341-0117 and 2 Harun DO 348-6726; **Queen** Abd al Meneim Riad MO and Basateen 352-0466; **Rich Gallery** 59 Mohi al Din Abu al Ezz DO 349-1785 and 96 Mosadek DO 705098; **Rustico** 91 Merghani HE Spanish-style furniture; **El Salam** 44 Harun al Rashid HE 243-8596; **Saraii Center** 20 Tahrir DO 248-8651; **Selection** 35 Mohi al Din Abu al Ezz DO 349-7779; **Verosol** 139 Tahrir DO 348-2266, Venetian blinds and window shades.

Galabias
These comfortable long robes are the traditional clothing of the countryside. They have been adapted for lounge wear, sleepwear and exotic evening wear for women. They come in a variety of traditional styles and patterns. Available almost anywhere from Kerdassa to posh boutiques and in any fabric from cotton to hand-loomed silk, they are a real buy in Egypt.

Khan al Khalili
Abbas Higazi Khan al Khalili 924730, made-to-order with some ready-made available in a variety of styles and sizes, primarily galabias, abayyas, kaftans, will ship, accepts credit cards; **Atlas** Khan al Khalili 906139, galabias, dresses, robes, tablecloths, towels, hand-loomed Akhmim cotton, Egyptian silk by the meter or made to order, fashionable designs, ask for catalog of fabrics and designs, extensive waiting period, be sure to fix the price when ordering and keep all receipts; **Hassan al Derei** Khan al Khalili; **Modes Crocodil** 2 Sekket Khan al Khalili 936054, traditional galabias, specializing in abayyas and hand-decorated Lybian jackets; **Wahba Fashions** 19 Hotel al Hussein Passage 934286, traditional galabias for all ages including toddlers, specializes in velvet Moroccan vests trimmed in gold or silver.

Other
Ammar 26 Kasr al Nil; **Galabela Center** 40 Kasr al Nil and 20 Shehab MO 348-8513; **Garbis** 8 Brazil ZA; **H. H. Shops** 2 Kasr al Doubari GC 354-7366, handpainted silks; **Ibis** 24 Khalifa al Mamoun HE 245-8180, pharaonic designs; **Touch Wood** 20 Mansour Mohammed ZA 340-3095.

Garden tools see Household

Glasses and Eye Needs
See Health for more information.

126 SHOPPING

Baraka Optical Company 10 Baghdad HE 678165 and 159 26th July 342-0343; Ibrahim abd al Hamid 5 Sherif 392-0058, Leonard, Porsche, Pole-optik; Maadi Optician 118 Road 9 MA 350-7079, Bausch and Lomb, plastic lenses; Mounir Nassif 30 Talaat Harb 745505/6, Bausch and Lomb contact supplies and glasses of all varieties; Sphinx Opticals 160 26th July.

Gold see Jewelry below
Groceries see Household
Haberdashery see Notions below
Handicrafts see Crafts above

Herbalists and Spice Shops

Some spice shop owners are herbalists practicing traditional medicine with cures for everything from minor indigestion, worms, bloatedness, constipation, nervousness, diarrhea, to allergies, diabetes, weight control, eczema, burns and ulcers. Others are experts in the growing and harvesting of herbs and spices, and still others sell spices merely for use in cooking. Spices available in Egypt include anis, bayleaf, cardamom seeds and powder, cinnamon sticks and powder, cloves, curry, ginger roots and powder, saffron, white and black pepper in corns or powder, vanilla sticks or powder. You can see spices being roasted and prepared off Sharia Muski near the Mosque of Barsbay. The main street for spice shops is Fahameen, running parallel to the Qasaba beginning at the Ghuri monuments. Most of the shops were established over 200 years ago and are owned by members of the same family. They carry everything you could possible want in the way of spices, herbs, dried flowers, henna, etc. Some specialities are a special diet recipe of 20 herbs; mefatta'a, a jam of molasses and herbs for energy; potions to prevent hair loss, kidney failure, diabetes; and an incense to protect against harm. This area is also called Suk Sudan.

Abdul Latif Mahmoud Harraz 39 Ahmed Maher 923754, founded in 1885, has its own farm, area of specialization is seeds: poppy, rare white mustard seeds, tree seeds, flower seeds and plant seeds, including ballout, a seed for bad breath originally from Lebanon, but grown on the shop's farm; Ahmed Abdel Halim 14 Fahameen 904329, in addition to the regular spices offers hair oils to reduce baldness; Ahmed Sadek Zalat 10 Sheikh Mohammed Abdu, al Azhar 903773, in addition to traditional spices and herbs, including incense, specializes in herbalism and spiritual healing, products are available for rheumatism, kidney problems, skin diseases and weight control; Donia al Henaur Qasaba, in front of Ashraf Mosque 912722, a 200 year-old establishment selling spices, perfumes, candles, incense and like products; Etaret al Ghouria on the street of the same name 930249, in addition to spices has medicinal herbs, especially for losing weight; Hosri Abd Al Haleem, Fahameen 904639; Khedr al Attar Muizz li Din, in front of Ashraf Mosque, 900865, the proprietor is a herbalist who offers traditional cures for body ailments, among the cures are leeba murra for diabetes, balah kabl for blood pressure, boiled ginger and cinnamon for colds; Magdi Abu Afia Ghuria, in addition to selling herbs and spices this shop is the candle distributor for Cairo; Tarek Mohamed Safwat Ghuria 904805, the speciality here is pinecones and hedgehogs used to cure fever for children; Wekalet Abu Zeid al Hamzawi al Saghir, over 23 shops throughout the city, established for 200 years, have 4,000 types of potions for cures including remedies for coughs, constipation, fertility, and rheumatism.

Houseware see Household
Insurance see Owning a Car under Household

Ivory

Ivory is one of the endangered species products that are forbidden to enter the US, Britain,

Australia, Germany and other participating countries. Egypt has stopped legally importing ivory, which was formerly imported from French Africa and Ghana. True ivory has grain lines running through it; bone, which is often used as a substitute, does not. To test, hold a hair against the object and then try to set the hair afire. If it burns, the object was not ivory. Tusks and unworked ivory are sold by the weight. A tusk is sold for LE500 a kilo. Ivory is delicate. It should never be washed, and turns yellow from perfume. Most of the shops that sell ivory are slowly turning to other products, but it is still available on the market.

Happy Palace 12 Khan al Khalili 914417, ivory, rhino horn, camel bone and stones; **Faberka** 12 Darb al Attar, behind al Azhar mosque, 925373, ivory from the Sudan and Africa carved into pharaonic statues, animals and jewelry made to order or ready made, you can even buy tusks—prices are lower here, as this shop is a distributor for the Khan merchants; **Ishak Ibrahim al Assiuti and Brothers** Khan al Khalili 910589/944767, ivory, wood, buffalo horn and camel bone made into detailed small animals, excellent craftsmanship; **Lamai Abdel Malek** Khan al Khalili 906168, ivory pendants, earrings, letter openers, bracelets and animals; **Saad** 9 Wekalet al Makwa, Khan al Khalili 917466, ivory and ebony animals, beads, will make to order.

Jewelry
Jewelry is one of the best buys in Cairo. The variety of styles, both modern and antique, is overwhelming: pharaonic jewelry both in authentic reproductions and modern adaptations; Islamic jewelry in exquisite calligraphy, Koranic pendants and folkloric reproductions; Middle Eastern jewelry from the suks of Yemen, Jordan, Syria and Saudi Arabia; Bedouin jewelry with distinctive heavy silver and base metal materials and unique designs; fellahin jewelry including Coptic crosses; Turkish, Art Deco, Art Nouveau, modern gallery work, the list goes on and on. You can even design your own and have it produced in the workshops. There are thousands of jewelry shops in Cairo. Almost all offer an extensive variety of chains, charms, Koranic inscriptions and cartouches. Listed below are shops that offer unique services.

Gold
Gold jewelry includes 21 karat for traditional fellahin, Nubian and Bedouin gold, and 18k for Middle Eastern and European chains and charms, and gold-plate. Gold is sold by weight with a percentage added on for workmanship. Prices are listed daily in the Egyptian Gazette. Note that there are about 28 grams to the ounce. All gold is stamped with a small mark indicating the percentage of precious metal in the item. Antique or older village and tinker work is often not stamped. A gold camel in the window of a gold shop indicates the items are gold-plated brass.

Khan al Khalili (only) Listed here are a few well known shops in the Khan al Khalili that offer a wide variety of gold objects. Your choice should be by price and workmanship.
Gouzlan 6 Sekket al Badestan, Khan al Khalili 904721 and 88 Road 9 Maadi; **Hareem** 6 Seramatia, Khan al Khalili 929491, also stones; **Milhran and Garbis Yazejian** Khan al Khalili 912321, in addition to standard cartouches, chains and pendants offers Russian wedding rings; **Sirgany Jewelers** corner of Gold and Muski 901255 901670 914903, and Abdel Khalek Sarwat, Central Cairo 913044 917780, and Sonesta Hotel HE 609444 609262. Founded in 1776 this is one of the oldest gold shops in the city. All types of services are available: gold, diamonds, platinum, precious stones, rare coins, pharaonic, Bedouin, fellahin, Nubian jewelry, antique pieces. Anything made to order. No shipping. VISA AMEX.

Suk al Sagha This is the gold market of Cairo. The actual suk runs from Sharia Muski in the south to just short of the Mosque of Qalaun, along the Qasaba. At this point the street is called Gold Street. The small alleyways on the west side of the street are filled with gold shops. Many of the shops do not open until 12 noon. There are a few other traditional gold shops located out of the suk itself. They have been included in this list. Many of these jewelers do not speak English. All of them offer unique, unusual, sometimes one-of-a-kind items. Some have antique items or will produce antique items on order. Craftsmanship can be a problem.

Adly Fam 72 Gawhar al Kaed (Sharia Muski between Midan Hussein and Gold Street) 921500, specializing in 21 carat fellahin jewelry: crescent-shaped gold earrings called **makhrata** (vegetable chopper), some done with a single wire; oblong diamond shaped necklaces called **Hab il Zeitoun** (olive seeds); and lace-like multi-strand necklace with tiny discs with picture of Cleopatra called **kerdan**—very good workmanship, small selection; **Adel Rizk** Bab al Awal, Suk al Sagha, first shop on right off Gold Street, one of two jewelers remaining who specialize in gold jewelry for people from the Oases—includes Baharia earrings called **al Sakia** (the waterwheel); also some fellahin jewelry like **faroni** a necklace with a pharaonic motif as the centerpiece, be careful of workmanship; **Al Gamal Jewelry** Gold Street, specialized in gold-plated brass traditional jewelry, wide variety of necklaces, earrings, and bracelets all of Bedouin, fellahin, Nubian designs, reasonable prices—the shop is one of several with a large gold camel in the window; **Gundi Shenouda** Bab al Talet, Suk al Sagha 904370, established for 65 years, one of two remaining shops that specialize in 21 carat gold work for people from the Oases, some original pieces available for copying, bracelets, necklaces, earrings, selection limited, made-to-order—earrings from Dakhla Oasis called **al Hanani**, earrings from Baharia called **al Sakia**, original **faroni** necklace worn by fellahin from Upper Egypt; **Sabri Fayek** Bab al Talet, Suk al Sagha, traditional 21k gold fellahin earrings and necklaces, styles vary and include faroni, kerdan, etc.; **Sigal** Gold Street 907750, tons and tons of gold-plated fellahin jewelry, excellent quality and designs, very reasonable prices; **Youssef Moustapha Sudani** 16 Sharia al Makassis, Suk al Sagha 915852, Nubian traditional jewelry goldsmith, work is handtooled and by stamp, all 21 carat—some pieces: **fadawi**, typical circular Nubian earring, **zumam**, circular earring with flat 1/4 inch insert through ear, **akish**, circular wide-bottomed earring with tree designs, **dougaha**, choker necklace.

Other Gold shops can be found on every major shopping street. In central Cairo look in the shops near Groppi Garden on Abdel Khalek Sarwat and in the small street Sekket al Manakh, leading off it on the west.

Silver
Silver has been the traditional metal of jewelry in the Middle East. Usually in large designs, antique pieces are still available in the suks around the Khan al Khalili. Modern silversmiths tend to adapt traditional motifs into modern designs. In most jewelry shops one will find an abundance of earrings, bracelets and necklaces to suit all tastes.

Khan al Khalili
Amir Agha Jeweler Khan al Khalili, south of Atlas, specialized in handmade necklaces, earrings and bracelets with traditional motifs. Will make to order from your design. Also sells clasps, balls, stones and other parts for jewelry, excellent English, excellent workmanship; **Azmy** Gad Wekalet al Gawahergia, Suk al Sagha 900452, interesting silver items, electric lamps, candlesticks, church censors, crosses, etc.; **Fils Mahmoud al Manakhli** 99 Gold Street, 905848, 902571, in addition to regular silver items has old Bedouin bracelets, necklaces and rings; **Mohamed Amin** 70 Gold Street 921214, Bedouin bracelets, necklaces and old gold and silver coins; **Moustafa Mobarz** 2 Wekalet al Gawahergia and Gold Street, excellent collection of old Bedouin silver, bracelets from all over the country; **Saad of Egypt** Khan al Khalili 921401 909370, and Ramsis Hilton 777444 758000 ex3109, only jeweler in the Khan to copy from the famous European houses like Cartier, plus excellent craftsmanship on calligraphy, plates, platters, urns, picture

frames, etc, some jewelry; **Samir's Silver** 95 Gold Street, silver bracelets, necklaces and old coins; **Silver Shop** 10 al Makassis, Suk al Sagha 936519, tucked into a small courtyard deep in the Suk al Sagha, in operation for over 100 years, specializes in silverplate—houseware, candlesticks, book covers, picture frames and omom, a vessel used to sprinkle perfume in the home—will repair as well, prices reasonable, good workmanship; **Wassef Silverware Company** Wekalet al Gawahergia, Suk al Sagha 932460, silver household items including trays, candlesticks, etc, also bags and bags of Bedouin silver, necklaces, bracelets, old coins, Coptic and Ethiopian crosses, also Nubian gold items, prices are excessive— bargain.

Keymakers and locksmiths see Household

Knitting
Abdel Hadi 7 26th July; **La Donna** Abdel Khalek Sarwat and Mohammed Farid; **Maison Francaise** Kasr al Nil.

Lamps and lampshades see Household

Leather
Cairo has a very active leather industry and ready-to-wear leather products are exported to the European market. Leather shops can be found all over the city.

Khan al Khalili
Bazaar Mahmoud Khalili 5 Rabeh al Selihdar 921644, jackets, handbags, skirts, wallets and pants all made from cow leather, will make to order; **Ibrahim** 5 Khan al Khalili; **Kasr Khan al Khalili**, Jackets, handbags, skirts, trousers and wallets in cow leather; **Hussein Abdel Fattah** 8 Sekket Khan al Khalili 928121, gazelle, lamb, crocodile, serpent, lizard bags, belts, wallets; **Loulout Khan Khalili** 8 Wekalet al Makwa 917517, jackets of buffalo leather; **Sayed Abbas Said** 2,5 Sekket Khan al Khalili 906718, Gucci-like brief cases, bags, wallets and belts made of cow, moose, goat, sheep and snakeskin; **Rasha Bazaar** 2 Haret al Wekala, Khan al Khalili 910783; **Al Sayed Gasfar Moharram and Company** 1 Haret Dar al Touffah, off Ahmed Maher beside Bab Zuwayla 362-5424, raw leather sold by the foot; **Tiger Bazaar Company** 5 Khan al Khalili Bazaar 900887, moose, gazelle and cow leather sandals and camel saddles.

Other
Bellina Talaat Harb, leather purses; **La Boutique** 36 Kasr al Nil 393-5543, design their own leather bags, purses and belts; **Dabbour** Shawarbi 393-4453, bags, shoes and belts; **Leather Home** 106 26th July ZA 340-5715, 3 Ishak Yaqoub ZA 340-8267, 34 Yehya Ibrahim ZA 340-7072 and 107 Road 9 MA, leather clothing; **Santus** 9 Lebanon MO 344-0310, jackets, skirts, pants; **Shalan Leather Works** 12 Kasr al Nil 764637, coats, jackets, dresses, skirts; **Vero Chic** 19 Talaat Harb 393-1895, jackets, skirts, bags, rabbit fur jackets, make to order.

Lumber see Wood below
Magazines see Communications

Marble
Abbas Khalil Attiya Ali 12 Ahmed Maher, beside Bab Zuwayla, 938654, marble to order with English, Arabic or French engraving, plaques, tombstones, nameplates, etc, both imported and Egyptian marble from Aswan and Assiut; **Hagg Hassan Abu Hameda** 69 Ahmed Maher 919738, alabaster figurines, statues, castles, coffee tables and fountains; **Hanafi Ahmed Youssef** 27 Sami al Baroudi, Bab al Khalk; **Ibrahim Khalil Ibrahim** 15 Darb al Khoshira, beside Bab Zuwayla 922385, wholesale floor tiles, polished

Islamic design stone and marble, both imported from Italy and Belgium, and alabaster from Beni Suef, can cut to size; **Michailides** 26 Ahmed Maher; **Said Ahmed Othman** 3 Ahmed Maher 924432, marble from Aswan and Upper Egypt, fountains, tables, surfaces, all colors and qualities, engraving.

Mashrabia and Inlay Wood

These two crafts are traditional to the Middle East, and a piece or two is usually included on everyone's shopping list. Mashrabia is usually made from red birch or oak, neither indigenous to Egypt. For additional shops see Furniture above.

Mashrabeya Factory 5 Rabeh al Selihdar, mirrors, frames, plates, wall hangings, chess tables, backgammon tables, will make to order; **Arabesque Ali Hamama** 5 Wekalet al Kotn, Khan al Khalili 907244, mashrabia and wood products retail or made to order, credit cards, will ship; **Hassan and Ali Abdel Aal** Khan al Khalili 903361, inlay work of all kinds using ivory, mother of pearl, various woods, etc, will make to order; **Ibrihim Zayed** Chevikan Building, Khan al Khalili, manufactures own backgammon, wooden plates, tables; **Mother of Pearl Products** 6 Khan al Khalili 932985, inlay wood, mother of pearl, camel bone, jewelry boxes, Koran stands, chest sets; **Saleh Badr Ali Sherif** 5 Rabeh al Selihdar 919219, inlay boxes from mahogany, sandalwood, ebony, camel bone and mother of pearl.

Meat see Household

Medical Supplies

Circle Trading Company 347 Sharia Sudan, Sahafiyeen 347-1155, sports, medical and scientific equipment; **Medical Equipments** 30 Sherif 393-0871; **SSC Medical** 40 Geziret al Arab MO 346-3844/5998.

Milk, Moving companies see Household

Musical Instruments

The best shopping area for musical instruments, both for purchase and rental, is Sharia Mohammed Ali. In addition to selling imported western musical instruments, these shops specialize in oriental ones including **Duf**, a Sufi drum; **Kanoon**, like a zither, **Muzmar**, a wedding horn; **Nay**, a flute; **Oud**, lute; **Rababa**, a Bedouin violin; **Ri**, a tambourine; **Simsimia**, a sailor's guitar, **Tabla**, a drum.

Eastern Music Exhibition 154 Mohammed Ali, oriental instruments and imported Spanish, Yamaha, German and Chinese guitars, Chinese and Egyptian violins and bongos; **Elegant Exhibition for Musical Instruments** 154 Mohammed Ali 391-0892, ouds made by well-known craftsman Samir Amin, other instruments also available; **Egyptian Music Exhibition** 160 Mohammed Ali 391-0465, ouds, nay, muzmar, kanoon, drums, ri, bongos and flutes; **Gamil Georges** 170 Mohammed Ali, ouds made by owner, a well-known craftsman, also hand-made imported old violins and old Italian mandolins; **Hankash and Sons** 23 Mohammed Ali 390-1036, ouds, bongos, nay, ri and others; **The Jewel of Music** 2 Atef Ouf off Mohammed Ali, sells and exports ouds, guitars made in China, drums, bongos, ri, muzmar, and Italian violins; **Maged Al Rushdi** 54 Mohammed Ali 391-5243, all oriental musical instruments, spare parts; **Marco's Musical Instruments** 160 Mohammed Ali 391-7935, antique Italian, German and French violins, cellos, old and new ouds, clarinets, oboes, old and new kanoon, synthesized guitars, amplifiers, trombones, saxophones and guitars; **The Modern Oud Exhibition** 164 Mohammed Ali 390-1016, ouds, dufs and muzmars; **The New Music Corner** 170 Mohammed Ali 931236, oriental instruments and drums, recorders and flutes; **Oud House** 164 Mohammed Ali 390-1970, sells and repairs oriental instruments; **Piano Marzouk** 34 Abdel Khalek Sarwat 758944, large supply and variety of guitars, pianos, organs,

drums; **Rashad Al Agel Difts** 39 Sherif 745947, sells electronic musical instruments and Yamaha key-board synthesizers; **The Sound of Music** 168 Mohammed Ali 390-0974, oriental musical instruments; **Star** 40 Sherif 747723, specializes in electronics, large variety of Casiotone keyboards and synthesizers; **The World of Music** 6 Mumtaz off Mohammed Ali 909488, specialized in selling, repairing and making ouds.

Muski Glass

Muski glass is an inferior glass made of recycled bottles in traditional factories in the Gamalia section of the medieval city. It comes in five main colors: Navy blue made from cobalt oxide; brown make from Stella beer bottles; turquoise blue made from pounded brass; green made from 7-up and Stella beer bottles; aqua from coke bottles; and purple made from Old Spice bottles. The factories are primitive, and can be visited.

Al Daour Glass Factory al Beerkedar, Gamalia, candle holders, tumblers, vases, pitchers, plates, lamp-shades, lanterns, creamers and small rings; **Hassanein Ismail al Tahan** 61 Haret al Beerkedar, Gamalia 936869; **Sayed Abd al Raouf** 8 Khan al Khalili 91466, sells only.

Newspapers see Communications

Notions

The wholesalers to the entire city in the area of notions, threads, yarns, buttons, appliques, trimmings, sequins and beads are mainly located on or around Sharia Muski.

Madinet Al Akada 75 Gawhar al Kaed, Muski between Midan Hussein and Gold, deals in all Egyptian-made products including cotton thread for crocheting, wool yarn by the kilo, applique, buttons, trimming, sequins, belts and trimmings; **Suez Company** 72 Gawhar al Kaed, beads and spangles in all colors and sizes from Italy, Germany and Taiwan sold by the kilo and in large quantities only (at least 5 kilos), strings of sequins, ropes of artificial pearls.

Other
Adel and Mamdouh Bros. Company 4 Harun al Rashid HE 256-0315, tricot yarn; **Abdel Hady** 7 26th July 915056, variety of yarns, embroidery equipment, crochet and knitting needles, cotton, silk, wool threads, wool yarns; **Au Petit Point** 15 Kasr al Nil, needlepoint supplies including imported threads, canvas, rare kilim designs and Islamic motifs on canvas; **Boubajian** 33 Kasr al Nil 776993, sewing notions, zippers, buttons, Dritz scissors; **FAF Company for Yarn** 7 Harun al Rashid HE 674303; **Garbis** 8 Brazil ZA; **La Poupee** Kasr al Nil, buttons and other supplies; **Maison Garbis** 8 Brazil ZA 340-7644; **Mercerie** 5 Brazil ZA; **Pfaff Sewing Machine** 20 Iraq MO 349-0173 348-4092, sales and repair.

Nurseries see Household
Office equipment see Business
Painters, Pasta see Household

Perfume

Essence, as the shopkeepers prefer to call it, is one of the bargains of Egypt. Most essences like jasmine, geranium, roses, violets, camomile and orange blossom are grown and processed in Egypt. Musk is imported from India, sandalwood from Hawaii. All of these essences are exported to France to be used by the famous French perfumeries. Essence, which will maintain its natural aroma indefinitely, is sold by the ounce and can be used as is to scent closets, in ashtrays to cut smoke and freshen rooms and, dissolved in alcohol, to wear. Dissolve one part essence to 9 parts alcohol for perfume; 1-20 for eau de toilette; 1-30 for eau de cologne. One ounce of essence costs from LE6-15. The shops duplicate all the famous perfumes from famous houses like Chanel, Yves St. Laurent, Christian Dior, etc. These shops also sell amber paste, considered by some as an aphrodisiac and often drunk in coffee or tea. To one cup of liquid add the equivalent of the head of a match; and kohl, the original eye make-up of ancient Egypt. Kohl comes in all colors and is sold in little vials.

Khan al Khalili

Amber Perfumes 34 Tarbiah (near Ouf) and 73 Gawhar al Kaed (Muski) 905075; Ali Mahmoud Habib 16 Midan al Hussein 935721, combines a perfume shop and bead shop, beads include amber and black coral, perfumes include jasmine, rose, gardenia, musk, violet, sandalwood, all credit cards; Doaa Perfumes 9 Sekket al Badistan, Khan al Khalili 926196, all credit cards, will ship; Kattab 83 Gawhar al Kaed 902721, a 200 year-old establishment on the left-hand side as Sharia Muski meets Midan Hussein, claims to be the first perfume firm in the east, interesting decor of mastabas, old crystal bottles (some for sale) and very oriental atmosphere; Mohamed Abd Al Hodar Al Hennan Ghuria, in addition to regular perfume stocks has green perfume and concentrated Amazon oil for falling hair; Mostafa al Hennaoui Muizz li Din 911488.

Other

Imported perfumes are not expensive in Egypt. They can be found in most shopping districts in cosmetic shops and some boutiques. Beach 8 Brazil ZA; Boutique al Nil 3 Talaat Harb 393-2774, Aqua Velva, Old Spice, Yardley, Nivea, Faberge, Panache etc; Burda Road 9 MA, passage beside Isis Butcher; Elle 28 Mohammed Mazhar ZA; Fidji 11 Shawarbi 757455, most famous brands; Je Reviens 5 Shawarbi 744435, most famous brands; Shalimar 59 Khalifa al Mamun, Midan Roxi, HE 258-4343, most famous brands including Georgio.

Pharmacies see Health

Photography Equipment

There are many photo stores in Cairo, most offering good service. Film brands available include Ilford, Tudor, Kodak, Agfa and Fuji. Film can be purchased from stationery stores, hotel shops, bookstores, kiosks in tourist areas and many other locations. Photo finishing is available in all shopping areas. Consult Travel and Transportation for passport photo facilities. Most major brand cameras are available on the market. Darkroom equipment and materials are harder to come by, but can be found.

Actina 4 Talaat Harb 767236, Agfa and Kodak film and lab materials; BKY 68 Road 9 MA, photo finishing, portraiture, passport photos; Cairo Photo Store 36 Sherif 392-7216, AV products, screens, slide projectors, overhead projectors; Egypt 2000 6 Alfi and 11 Sherif 743914/3975, photo finishing; Kodak Egypt 20 Adli 749037/9399, 3 Harun al Rashid HE 290-8265, and Road 9 MA, photo finishing, darkroom chemicals and paper at the Adli address; Minolta Agent Khalex 7 Issa Shaheen; Nikon Agent Ali Naggi 915463; Nile Hilton Camera Shop Nile Hilton, filters, cameras, film, equipment; Philippe Color Lab 88 Abdel Salam Arref GI 348-5181, professional color work, workshop with studio lighting, Ilford enlargers, camera equipment including Hasselblad; Ramsis Lab Sharia Ramsis 833507, professional finishing; Tudor Egypt 44 Zamalek Club Shopping Center 346-2330, 57 Road 9 MA, photo finishing.

Plumbing see Household

Pottery and Porcelain

Traditional pottery is usually sold on street corners. Some places to find it: along Sharia al Ahram GI; near the Mosque of Amr in Old Cairo; along the Corniche from Maadi to Cairo. Modern pottery is often sold at exhibitions, see Leisure; or in craft shops, see Crafts above. If you want to do your own, pottery clay is available from the street vendors. See Crafts for retail outlets of individual artists, and Leisure for galleries.

Rosenthal Glass and Porcelain 17 Mohammed Mazhar ZA.

Printers, Publishers see Research
Real estate see Household
Rugs see Carpets above

Safes

Amanco Misr Travel Tower, 14th Floor, Midan Abbassia 282-2372. Distributor for Chubb Safe Equipment Company. Burglar-resistant, fireproof safes, data and paper protection cabinets, high security locks.

Secondhand Shops

Canadian Women's Club secondhand boutique 28 Gezira ZA; **Ezbekia Gardens** near Midan Opera, secondhand books; See Flea Markets above.

Sewing see Notions above

Shoes

There are probably more shoe stores in Cairo than any other kind of shop. They are found in all shopping areas, but are especially prevalent on Kasr al Nil and 26th July where it meets Midan Opera. The list below offers the most popular or speciality shops featuring unique or handmade items.

Abd al Meneim abu Zeid 8 Brazil ZA 341-8623, shoes made to order; **Bedros** 20 Talaat Harb 759109, good selection of men's shoes; **Bellina** 20 Talaat Harb, shoes and handbags for women; **Boutique Nabila** 15 Taha Hussein ZA 340-3227/3063, exclusive designs; **Gadalla** Kasr al Nil 392-1539; **Jasy** 107 Road 9 MA; **Lotfi** Midan Talaat Harb, funky canvas shoes and boots, bright colors for young people; **Lux Shoemaker** 75 Road 9 MA, makes riding boots; **Red Shoe** 11 Shawarbi, women's shoes and boots made to order.

Signmakers

Ali Taha and Sons 30 Baghdad HE 291-0666; **Moftah** 119 Ramsis 741521, hand-painted signs in English and Arabic on cloth, wood and other surfaces.

Silver see Jewelry above
Spices see Herbs above
Sports equipment see Sports under Leisure
Stamps see Leisure

Stationery

See Art Supplies above; see Research

Dar Saad Stationery 12 Sherif 391-1057 392-5966, also drafting supplies; **Mattar Stationery** 17 Sherif 393-9028, cross pens; **Samir and Ali Stationery** 27 Abbassia, 21 Sherif, 25 Sherif, 7 Zaker Hussein HE, also engineering, architectural and drafting equipment.

Supermarkets, Stoppeurs see Household.

Tarboush

The tarboush (fez) is now found only in two shops, both on the Qasaba in Ghuria. There are two types of tarboush, the Effendi, once worn by all government employees and gentlemen in Egypt, and the Umma, for religious personages.

Mostafa Hassan 36 Ghuria 901003; **Ahmed Mohammedy Ahmed** 908331.

Taxidermists

Contact the Cairo Zoo.

Tentmakers (al Khayamia)

Farahat Sarudi Sou'di Darwish Khayamia 920951, pharaonic and Islamic wall hangings, cushion covers; **Hanafi Mohamed Ibrahim** 18 Khayamia 939831, tenting for rent for funerals, weddings and parties, makes large tents for local and foreign clients, also pharaonic and Islamic wall hangings, pillows, etc.; **Mahmoud Zaki Abdel Atif** 18 Khayamia 939146; **E. Mokhtar Hamed** 24 Khayamia 902623, mostly canvas; **Mahmoud Farag** 19 Khayamia, pharaonic and Islamic tents, cushions, hangings; **Mohamad H. Abas Mohamad** 29 Khayamia 936158; **Sayed Sayed T and Sons** 18 Khayamia 922387; **Yosry M H Ouf** Khayamia 939327.

Toys

Toys can be found in many bookshops, supermarkets and stationers.

Atfal Toys 23 Road 151 MA; **Bazaar al Zamalek** 10 Brazil ZA 341-0591; **Carnival Zamalek** 5 Brazil ZA; **Elibbary** 19 Shagaret al Dorr ZA; **Al Shark** 5 Brazil ZA; **Hobby Center** Malek al Afdal ZA; **House Care** 13 Baghdad HE 670899; **Le Galion** Kasr al Nil; **Le Petit Coin** 7 Brazil ZA; **M and A Kardour** 28 Hasan Asem ZA, art supplies, Texas Instruments and Casio; **Papillon** Mahmoud Bassiouni; **Pussycat** 9 Shawarbi; **Star** 7 Brazil ZA Fisher-Price, Barbie.

Upholstery see Household
Veterinarians see Health
Video clubs see Leisure

Walking Sticks

Ahmed Hassan Orabi 5 Sekket al Badestan, Khan al Khalili 917409, also blue ceramic objects and some beads.

Windsurfing equipment see Sports

Wood Products

Attiya Suliman Abd Al A'l and Company 93 Ahmed Maher 921186, mostly tools, whips, canes, shovels, rakes, mallets, will make items to order; **Gomaa Ali and Sons, Company** 1 Mamaar Geara (Ahmed Maher) 935689, this 100 year-old shop makes barrels of all sizes including planters, garden chairs with canvas seats, tables, etc; **Mohammed Mohammed Hendi** 15 Ahmed Maher 920026, this family was originally in the tentmaking business, but now make beach items exclusively—umbrellas, chairs, stools, tables, tents all ready-made or made to order; **Mustafa Fathi Abd Al Gawad** 5 Ahmed Maher 930159, ladders, rolling pins and wood cut to order; **Said Abd Al Halim Nafei** Ahmed Maher 937888, bird and animal cages, houses, feather fans for fires, birdseed; **Shirket al Salam Litigaret al Akhshab** 107 Tahrir DO 716761, wood by the plank.

LEISURE

Cairo has always had more than its share of exciting things to do and see, but in recent years there has been a bonanza of new activities. Venues are improving and increasing. Museums are being restored and improved. Monuments have undergone amazing face-lifts, while the areas around them have been spruced up. With the creation of the new opera house, the performing arts are on the verge of a new renaissance. Sport has always been a high priority activity for residents, and with the development of the Egyptian and Red Sea coasts, snorkeling, scuba diving, windsurfing and a host of water activities have also developed. Whatever your leisure time interests you will find something to do in and around Cairo.

CINEMA HOUSES AND VIDEO CLUBS

Egypt was one of the first countries in the world to be photographed for the film industry. As far back as 1896 short documentary films featuring the beaches of Alexandria and the arrival in Egypt of important dignitaries were being shown in private salons. The legitimate Egyptian Film Industry was founded in 1927 in the era of silent films. Sound came to Egypt in 1930, just a few years after its invention. Since then Cairo has become one of the major film centers of the world. Currently 60-80 films a year are produced, with distribution mainly in the Arab world, but also in Europe, and North and South America. Films are shot on location, mainly in Cairo, and premieres, with major Egyptian stars, are a regular feature of the nighttime downtown scene. Some major Egyptian film stars are Ahmed Zaki, Adel Imam, Soad Hosny, and Faten Hamama, once married to the most famous Egyptian film star of all, Omar Sherif. Among the most prominent directors are Youssef Shahin, known internationally for **The Land** and **Adieu Bonaparte**, and Salah Abou Seif who won first prize at the Comedy Film Festival in Switzerland for his film **The Beginning.** The most famous internationally acclaimed Egyptian film is **The Night Of Counting the Years** (The Mummy) about tomb robbers in the Valley of the Kings, directed by Shadi Abdel Salaam.

International films with Egyptian themes are plentiful. Among the best known are **The Ten Commandments, Cleopatra, Land of the Pharaohs, The Egyptian, Sphinx, The Awakening, Live and Let Die** (James Bond) and **Death on the Nile.**

Cinema Houses
Most cinema houses in Cairo are large, elaborate theatres built in the first half of this century when film was in its heyday. They are worth visiting for the faded elegance of a time gone by. Unfortunately, most are in bad condition with poor sound and projection systems; however, there are several new theatres which are up to international standards. Smoking is permitted

in most theatres; the audience, primarily male, is sometimes more audible than the soundtrack; and vendors move up and down the aisles during the show selling soft drinks and confections. In addition to the houses listed below, most sporting clubs have outdoor cinemas and there are neighborhood theatres in most areas of the city. Films are shown at around 10am and 3, 6 and 9pm. Some theatres have five showings daily during Ramadan. Tickets are about LE1. Usually a newsreel, coming events, a cartoon and advertisements precede the feature. Occasionally a documentary will also be shown. There is rarely a double feature.

Cairo Palace Saray al Ezbekia 745350, mostly Arabic films; **Diana Palace** 17 Alfi 924727, Arabic films only; **Faten Hamama** 1 Roda, Roda Island 849767, films run one week only; **Hyatt Al Salam Hotel** Abdel Hamid Badawi HE 245-5155, foreign films at 6 and 9pm Th-S, Ramadan at 9 and midnight; **al Hamra** Midan Roxi 258-2866, open air; **Kahira** 7 Emad al Din, currently under repair; **Karim I, Karim II** Emad al Din 924830, two new theatres offering current international films of high caliber; **Kasr al Nil** 6 Kasr al Nil 750761 753715, once the venue of Om Kalthum concerts, it features mostly foreign films; **Metro** 35 Talaat Harb 757566, owned by Metro Goldwyn Mayer, showing mostly foreign films, during Ramadan offers a different foreign film each evening at midnight; **Miami** 38 Talaat Harb 745656, only Egyptian films; **Normandy** 31 Ahram HE 258-0254, two theatres, one open air; **Odeon** 4 Abdel Hamid Said 758797, until recently showed only Russian films, now basically martial arts films; **Opera** Midan Opera 915543, one of best equipped theatres in Cairo, mainly Arabic films; **Palace** Sharia al Ahram HE, two cinemas, one open air; **Pigalle** 23 Emad al Din 938594, mostly Arabic films; **Radio** 24 Talaat Harb 756562, once leased by Warner Brothers, second biggest cinema in Egypt, mainly foreign films; **Ramses Hilton** summer poolside cinema 758000; **Rivoli** 23 26th July 743249, largest cinema in Egypt showing mostly Arabic films; **Roxi** Midan Roxi HE 258-0344, mostly Arabic films; **Sphinx** Midan Sphinx MO 346-4017, open air, double feature.

Video clubs
There are hundreds of video clubs in Cairo and one is sure to exist in your neighborhood. Most have a yearly fee for membership and a charge per film rented. Almost all are PAL/SECAM with either VHS or Beta. One video club that offers NTSC is the **American Community Center Video**, behind Gupco in New Maadi, 352-0289.

COFFEEHOUSES

The coffeehouse was introduced to Egypt with the arrival of coffee from the Yemen in the Middle Ages. First introduced by the religious community, the coffeehouse has had a colorful and interesting history. Through the centuries coffeehouses, mainly patronized by men, were often banned because coffee was believed to be narcotic. It was in the coffeehouses of Cairo that storytellers would weave the famous epic tales of **Abu Zeid, Kalilah and Dimnah** and tales from the **1001 Nights**. Today coffeehouses are still a place where men gather. Different coffeehouses have become famous because of their clientele, others for their good beverages or the caliber and type of tobacco in the shishas, either **ma'asil** or **tombac**. Tradesmen often congregate at a particular coffeehouse, while small businessmen will use the coffeehouse as their office. Truck and bus drivers tend to congregate at cafes near Midan Ahmed Helmi, Midan Giza and al Kulali; film extras off Emad al Din; Nubians in Abdin; a pre-Revolution atmosphere can be found near Cinema Diana; backgammon players gather at the **Phoenix** on Emad al Din and in the cafes along 26th of July. There is even a coffeehouse where the deaf and dumb congregate, and another for people who are cult followers of Om Kalthum. The following coffeehouses are places both men and women can visit.

Atelier 2 Karim al Daoula, off Mahmoud Bassiouni near Midan Talaat Harb, 746730, a small coffeeshop with garden and art gallery usually patronized by literary personalities; **Cafe Riche** Talaat Harb, just west of the Midan, features an outdoor cafe for light drinks, for years listed in guide books as frequented by literary personalities and the site where the Free Officers planned the revolution—today there are more people looking for personalities than personalities, but the gracious service and pleasant atmosphere makes a visit worthwhile; **Fishawi's**—tucked into a small corner of the Khan al Khalili, Fishawi's is more of an alleyway than a coffeehouse, a mishmash of old mastabas and gilded baroque mirrors. More traffic flows through the cafe in an hour than on some streets of the city. Vendors sell everything from lottery tickets to shoeshines. The oldest coffeehouse in the city, it is the place where the rich met and mingled late into the night during King Farouk's day. Everyone should visit Fishawi's at least once. Open 24hrs; **Groppi's** There are three Groppi's in Cairo, one in Heliopolis, another on Midan Talaat Harb and a third, the well-known one, on Abdel Khalek Sarwat. This Groppi's offers a garden and was made famous by British soldiers during the war. Here, some long-standing literary personalities, who work in the Al Ahram building nearby, breakfast in the early morning hours; **Sukaria Cafe** near Khan al Khalili. This is one of the coffehouses famous for their clientele. Often frequented by fortune-tellers and magicians, it can offer pleasant entertainment.

FAMILY FUN FOR CHILDREN

Cairo offers ample opportunity for the family to get together for fun. Some outings like going to a bookstore, felucca rides on the Nile, camel or horseback riding at the Pyramids, picnics and camping in the desert, swimming at local hotels and clubs, and snorkeling and scuba diving at the Red Sea can be enjoyed at any time. There is also an endless list of sightseeing available in the city to suit everyone's taste. Here are some things just for the kids. Be sure to scout out toilet facilities before you go.

Amusement Parks
Cooky Park Sharia Eryani behind the Jolie Ville Hotel near the Pyramids 857446, offers pony rides, a ghost train, a room of mirrors, rides, a shooting gallery and magicians, a restaurant, 12-10 daily, later on Thursday evenings, admission 50p; **Merryland Park** Roxi HE 244-8090, opened in 1964, offers swings, a mini zoo, a lake with tropical fish and boat rides, a playground, a restaurant, picnic tables, a nightclub and even a hall for weddings, 9am-2am in winter and 9am-3am in summer, admission 50p; **Sindbad Amusement Park** on the Ismailia Road near the Cairo International Airport 291-3351, entertainment includes 15 different rides including bumper cars, a mini roller coaster and lots of rides for small children. There is a cafeteria. 12noon-10pm in winter, 5pm-2am in summer, 7pm-2am during Ramadan.

Aquarium Sharia Wadi al Gezira ZA 340-1606. Fish and other marine life exhibited in a pleasant garden grotto constructed during the reign of the Khedive Ismail. There are 32 aquariums with 192 kinds of fish of which 70 are found in Egypt. Map of grounds is available at the door. Picnics possible. 8:30-4 daily.

Cairo Puppet Theatre Ezbekia Gardens 910954. Although in Arabic, the story line is easy to follow. Puppet characters include Sindbad the Sailor, Ali Baba, and Red Riding Hood. Both resident and visiting puppeteers perform Thursday through Saturday at 6:30 and Friday and Sunday at 11am in the theatre on the fringe of Ezbekia gardens. Admission LE1-2.

Cairo Zoo Sharia Giza GI 726314/233. Established in 1890, the Cairo Zoo is one of the oldest in the world with a most comprehensive animal collection. In addition to the fun of watching the animals, children may join the **Friends of the Animals Club** which meets every Friday at 1:30 at the club building in the zoo. Children are introduced to the behavior, care and personalities of zoo animals. Entrance to the Zoo is 20p.

Egyptian National Circus Sharia Nil, south of the Balloon theatre, AG 346-4870. Winner of the Gold Medal of the 1983 Monte Carlo Festival, the circus is a good 2 1/2 hour one-ring extravaganza performing nightly in Cairo with two traveling troupes. The circus, complete with acrobats, clowns, animals, lion tamer, pantomime, tumble and trapeze artists and musicians, was founded in 1966 and trained by Soviet experts. Nightly at 9:30pm. Entrance LE5, 3, or 2.

Fattouta An Egyptian clownish figure developed by Samir Ghanem, an Egyptian film star, who performs at special programs often held in hotels, especially on holidays. Usually advertised in the newspapers. Although the language is Arabic, the storylines are simple and can be enjoyed by all.

Felfela Village along the Mariutia Canal GI. Friday and Saturday afternoon horse shows, folk dancing and good food. No reservations accepted and very popular.

Gezira Planetarium Gezira Exhibition Grounds 812453. Nightly star shows in Arabic. Special English-language children's shows can be arranged by appointment. Contact Dr. M. Ahmed Soliman 341-2453. Hours 7pm daily except Friday. Ramadan hours 8pm. Admission Foreigners LE1, Egyptians 50p.

Heliopolis Kids Club Meets the second Friday of each month at the Baron Hotel in Heliopolis from 12-3. For information call 291-5757.

International Dolphin Show Meridien Hotel, Corniche al Nil 845444. Three shows at 11, 1 and 3 on Friday, Saturday and Sunday. Tuesday and Wednesday for reserved groups only. Thursday for schools.

Al Salam Friday Kid's Movies 245-6111. Special children's movies, primarily in English are held Friday at 11am at the Hyatt Al Salam Hotel. Schedules are available by phone. Admission LE2.50.

FINE AND APPLIED ARTS

Cairo's lively art scene is stimulated by many organizations including the Council of Arts of the Ministry of Culture, which sponsors galleries and arranges twice-yearly exhibitions; the

HILTON INTERNATIONAL EGYPT

WE OFFER YOU EGYPT A LA CARTE

Whether your friends and business associates from overseas are coming to Egypt on business or on holidays , Hilton International has something exciting waiting for them . In Cairo the **Nile Hilton** and **Ramses Hilton** offer delux accomodations, fine dining, first class entertainment and up to date business services. On the Nile, the **M.S. Isis / M.S. Osiris** takes them on a fascinating cruise among the treasures of ancient Egypt. At the **Fayrouz Village Sharm El-Sheikh**, they will enjoy sea, sun and sand in an area known to be one of the best diving places on earth. In Luxor, **Hilton International Luxor** is the perfect resort hotel from where they can explore the greatest of Upper Egypt monuments and - at the same time - enjoy a carefree holiday.

University of Helwan Faculty of Fine Arts; the Syndicate of Artists; and private schools, galleries and cooperatives.

The season for exhibitions, at which art works are usually offered for sale, runs from late September through May. Most galleries have openings on Thursday evenings, with shows lasting about two weeks. Usual hours are 10-1 and 5-7. Summer hours are later. Many galleries are closed on Fridays.

Information about shows may be found in the **What's On** column of the Egyptian Gazette and in the monthly magazines **Cairoscope** and **Cairo Today.** Major shows include the **Biennale d'Alexandrie** with exhibitions of plastic arts, photography, sculpture, drawing and engraving and the **Biennale du Caire** sponsored by the National Centre of Plastic Arts.

Galleries and Workshops
Aida Gallery Sakkara Road, 6 kilometers after El Dar Restaurant 538141. Exhibitions by famous Egyptian artists in all media. Also caters lunches and dinners for small groups. 10-2 and 5-8. Closed F.

Al Ain 73 al Hussein MO 349-3940. Handcrafted jewelry by Azza Fahmy, fanous lamps handcrafted by Randa Fahmy, and Islamic furniture handcrafted by Nabil Ghali. Excellent craftsmanship. Periodic exhibitions. Winter 10-1 and 4-7. Summer 10-2 and 4-8 and 9 on M,Th.

Al Salam Gallery 1 Sheikh al Marsafi ZA 341-8672. Basement of Mohammed Mahmoud Khalil Museum (behind the Marriott Hotel). Contemporary gallery with entrance to the right side of the museum. Often shows pottery, sculpture and jewelry, as well as fine art. 10-1 and 5-8 daily. During Ramadan, 11-2 and 8:30-11:30.

Arabesque 6 Kasr al Nil 759896. Lobby of the Arabesque restaurant, next to Kasr al Nil Cinema, in central Cairo. Contemporary art. Some well-known names. 12:30-3 and 7-11:30.

Atelier du Caire 2 Karim al Daoula 746730. Artists' cooperative with two galleries. Avant-garde work and exhibitions of lesser-known artists. Also coffeehouse where literary personalities gather. 11-2 and 8-12.

Baraka 2 Sharia Dr. Mahrouki off Ahmed Abdel Aziz MO 347-9390. Mashrabia furniture and fine art, mainly lithographs. Occasionally some international artists. 8:30-3 and 5-8:30. During Ramadan, 10-2 and 8:30-11. Closed S.

Mashrabia 8 Champollion, near Thomas Cook 778623. Group and individual shows of well-known artists. 11-2 and 5:30-8.

El Patio 6 Road 77c behind the Government building in the Golf area of Maadi 351-6654. Occasional exhibits in the upstairs gallery. 10-6. Closed S.

Government Galleries
Center of Arts (Mogamaa al Fenoun) also called the **Akhnaton Gallery** 26th July at Abul Ela Bridge, across from the Marriott Hotel, ZA 340-8211. Three galleries, a fine arts library and a small cinema hall are housed in an old mansion. The galleries are Akhnaton I, II, III. I, on the ground floor, is the premier gallery of Egypt featuring new works of contemporary artists, usually

leaning to the abstract and avant-garde. II, entered from the front stairs, features representational works, large retrospective exhibitions, and some visiting shows. III, on the second floor exhibits smaller shows. Hours 10-1 and 5-8 daily except F. During Ramadan 11-2 and 8-10.

Egyptian Center for International Cultural Cooperation 11 Shagaret al Dorr off 26th July, ZA 341-5419. Mixed media, crafts, fine art. 9:30-5 daily except F.

El Nil Exhibition Hall Gezira Exhibition Grounds at Tahrir Bridge (Kasr al Nil) on Gezira Island 341-8796. New government-sponsored gallery in a well-lighted modern building. Large shows including Cairo Biennale and the Salon du Caire in which most of Egypt's leading artists participate. 10-1:30 and 5-8 daily. During Ramadan, 11-2 and 8-10. Free. Closed F.

Faculty of Fine Arts Helwan University 4 Mohammed Thaqeb ZA. 10-1:30 and 4-6. Exhibits of students and faculty members.

Historic houses where artists work
Beit Sennari, 17 Haret Monge, south of Saneyya Girls School at Midan Sayeda Zaynab, 932543. The hara is named after a savant of the French Expedition to Egypt in 1798. The building, used as a headquarters by the French, is an Islamic home in an excellent state of repair. The current occupant is the **Institute of Applied Arts** which provides working space for fifteen artists.

Manisterli Palace 2 Malek al Salah, on the tip of Roda Island next to the Nilometer, 986931. Built in 1851, the palace is now the **Center for Art and Life**, a cultural institute investigating the arts of the Egyptians. Calligraphic work and some students' work is for sale. 9-3 daily, closed F. Admission 25p.

Musafirkhana Palace Darb al Tablawi, north of al Hussein Mosque in the Gamalaya, 920472. This 18th century Islamic-style house was used by the khedival family and is the birthplace of the Khedive Ismail. Restored by the Ministry of Culture, it is used by several artists in various disciplines. A tour of the building is a must. 9-4.

Wekalet al Ghuri two blocks west of al Azhar Mosque before the Qasaba crosses Sharia Al Azhar, 909146 920472. The building is one of the few Islamic caravanserais remaining in Cairo. Recently restored, it is now the home of about thirty artists. Work includes batik, stained glass, inlaid wood, oil paintings, glass and pottery. Items made to order. Two yearly exhibitions Nov 1 and March 21. Hours 10-2 S-Th. Entrance fee LE1.

HOBBIES

Birdwatching
If you've never birdwatched before, Egypt is a wonderful place to begin. With a variety of habitats, and located on the main migratory pathway between Europe and Africa, Egypt hosts

a bird population which is among the most diverse in the world. March-May and September-November are the best seasons to see birds in Egypt. Migrations occur in the fall and spring. There are two basic types of migrations. The **broad front migration** is usually when small birds like **warblers, thrushes, shrikes, wheatears, plovers, quails, rails** and **terns** cross the Mediterranean, hitting the entire Egyptian coast as they pass on their way to their winter homes. The **narrow front migration** is when birds are forced to follow set routes. This migratory path is usually followed by large birds, which cannot take advantage of wind drafts and must follow land masses. One such route is the **Suez Flyway.** In the Suez Flyway the migrating birds fly along the coast of Israel, down the coast of Suez and along the Red Sea turning inland at Qena and turning south at Aswan.

Although heavily populated, Cairo is still a good place for birdwatching. At the **Giza Zoo,** in addition to the birds that live at the zoo, a number of birds like the **Nile Valley Sunbird** and the **Greenfinch** winter there. The **Giza** and **Sakkara** plateaus host a good variety of desert species all year long. Other good areas to watch birds in the greater Cairo area include the **Barrage** and **Abu Rawash,** beyond Kerdassa.

The **Northern Coast** of Egypt has excellent winter habitats for birds, especially around the lakes of Manzala, Burullus (needs military permission), Bardawil (needs police permission from al Arish), Mariut and Idku. **Wadi Natrun,** on the Alexandria-Cairo desert road has winter, migrating and resident birds. The long ribbon of the **Nile Valley** serves as a wonderful habitat for resident as well as migratory birds.

In the **Fayoum** and the **Oases** of the Western Desert one finds a large variety of birds in the winter including **ducks, gulls, herons, grebes, coots, harriers and waders.** Probably the best spot in the Fayoum area is **Wadi Rayan** (needs a guide), because of its isolation, but excellent facilities also exist at **Lake Qarun.**

Although the **Red Sea Coast** and **Eastern Desert** are good places to see birds all year round, they are especially good in spring and autumn when the birds are in migration. **Hurghada** and the surrounding islands have typical Red Sea birds while the remote area of **Gebel Elba** (needs a guide and military permission) hosts a variety of rare tropical birds and an occasional Ostrich.

In Sinai, from the **Wadi al Arish** to Rafah along the northern coast, one can find local birds, winter birds and birds in migration. **Feran Oasis** and the **St Catherine's** area host typical Sinai birds like the **Egyptian Vulture** and **Verreaux's Eagle,** while the Sinai coast is good for sea birds, and Ras Mohammed for migrating birds.

For further reading see **Common Birds of Egypt** and **The Birds of Ancient Egypt,** both AUC Press publications.

For further information contact **Ahmed Riad** 2 Granada, Roxi HE 258-1082 or **The Egyptian Wildlife Service** at the Cairo Zoo 726314. For international information contact **International Council for Bird Preservation** 219c Huntingdon Road, Cambridge CE3 ODL England; **International Waterfowl Research Bureau** Slimbridge, Glos. GL2 7BX England; **World Wildlife Fund** Avenue du Mont Blanc CH-1196 Gland, Switzerland; **International Union for Conservation of Nature and Natural Resources** Avenue du Mont Blanc CH-1196 Gland, Switzerland; **United Nations Environment Programme** UNEP/CMS Secretariat, Wissenschaftszentrum, Ahrstrasse 45, D-5300 Bonn 2, FR Germany; **US Fish and Wildlife Service** Department of Internal Affairs, US Department of the Interior, Washington, DC 20240.

Bridge

Bridge in Egypt is supervised by the **Egyptian Bridge Federation,** a member of the International Bridge Federation and affiliated to the Higher Council for Youth and Sports. The Egyptian federation participates in international and Olympic tournaments. The bridge season starts around mid-October. There are ten official tournaments including open double, mixed double, four member team tournament and a marathon. An international tournament, organized during the first two weeks of each February at the Ramses Hilton, is attended by players from all over the world. The different sporting clubs promote the game via tournaments and bridge lessons. Tournaments start at six in the evening and any amateur player is encouraged to participate. Foreigners are welcome. You need not belong to the club to play. Fee is approximately LE4 per person. For further information contact Wahid Garana 746441 or Hany Garana 758950. The **Bridge Club of Heliopolis** meets every Monday at 9am at the Baron Hotel Heliopolis. Contact 290-8119. The **Maadi Duplicate Bridge Club** meets every Tuesday at the home of one of the members.

Chess

There are 21 chess clubs which are organized by the Chess Federation located at the Gezira Sporting Club 340-6000. Membership is LE20 yearly. Egyptian clubs participate in several major international competitions yearly: African Competition, Middle Eastern Competition, Arab World Competition and World Champion Competition. Local competitions are divided into two divisions and are held in summer in Alexandria and in winter in Cairo. They follow the Swiss tournament rules. The federation provides the individual clubs with umpires and schedules and organizes tournaments. Brochures and details are available, in Arabic, at participating sporting clubs including Maadi, Gezira, Heliopolis and Heliolido. Individual clubs also have their own tournaments. The Maadi Club has four: open club tournament; second class tournament; lady's chess tournament; and 17 and under tournament. All take place in the summer. There is also a Ramadan Tournament.

Coin collecting

Many of the silver and gold shops on or around Gold Street in the Khan al Khalili area of the city have old coins and paper money for sale. Street dealers can also be found in the Khan, just ask around. Organized meetings no longer exist. For a list of silver shops offering coins see Silver in the Shopping section.

Pigeon racing

There are 10-15 clubs devoted to pigeon racing in Egypt. The **Cairo Pigeon Club**, founded in 1939, is located on Sharia Toushomar, behind the Tahrir (formerly Mohammed Ali) Club and in a straight line in front of the Lufthansa offices. Meetings are held every Thursday evening 6 or 7pm, depending on the season. There are two main racing seasons for pigeons. From mid-January to the end of March races are held for year-old and over pigeons and from June to July for yearlings. The races are governed by the Ministry of Youth and Sports. A series of races beginning with short distances, like Minya to Cairo, and ending with long distances, from Aswan to Cairo, make up the season. Most pigeons for these races are of European stock.

Stamp collecting

The first stamp was issued in Egypt in January 1866. The most famous stamp is an issue of 1869 featuring the Sphinx and the Pyramids. It was used for 50 years and was the first stamp in the world featuring a building. Rare Egyptian stamps include the Suez Canal Company stamps. Buyers should exercise caution when buying stamps as there are plenty of forgeries of Egyptian classics and of the many Egyptian and Sudanese overprints on the local market. Stamp dealers congregate nearly every day at the Cafe Mukhtallat 14 Ataba Khadra, 50 yards from the Egyptian Postal Museum. The Philatelic Society of Egypt 16 Abdel Khalek Sarwat 3rd floor meets on Saturday evenings. Publication: Zehery Catalogs and the Journal L'Orient Philatelique. The Egyptian Postal Museum, with a magnificent collection and display of stamps and postal artifacts, is at the main post office at Midan Ataba. Open mornings only. Stamp series are available from any Post Office.

Alfi Zaklama 4 Emad al Din, second floor 355-0042, medium-sized stock with some specialists' material, very genial service; F. Cifariello and Company 31 Sherif 748761; Mrs Arthur Michel 16 Abdel Khalek Sarwat, second floor, small stock, some specialists' material and some European stamps; Oriental Philatelic House 79 Continental Arcade, Midan Opera, 939984, large stock with lots of specialists' and foreign material.

MUSEUMS

Agricultural Museum Mathaf al Zira'a, next to the Ministry of Agriculture, off Sixth of October Bridge, DO 700063 702879 702933. Founded in 1938, the museum is the oldest existing agricultural museum in the world. The grounds cover 42 feddans on a site formerly belonging to Fatma Ismail, the daughter of Khedive Ismail, and include an excellent variety of trees, picnic facilities, parks and large exhibition halls with permanent displays. The first building is the Museum of Ancient Egyptian Agriculture with 15 halls featuring agricultural implements, products and agricultural methods used in pharaonic Egypt. The second building houses the Natural History Museum with 30 halls devoted to reptiles, mammals, birds, fish and insects, portrayed in their natural environment. The Botany Collection is housed in the third building. The fourth building is the Social Life of Arab Nations with wonderful displays of arts and crafts, jewelry, costumes, musical instruments and life size scenes of craftsmen at work. The final building is the Cotton Museum which outlines the history of cotton from its introduction to Egypt during the reign of Mohammed Ali. It is currently under renovation. There is also a cinema and conference hall available for rental via the Director of the Museum. 9-2 daily except M. Entrance 10p.

Ahmed Shawki Museum 6 Ahmed Shawki off Murad GI 729479. The home of the eminent poet has been renovated to house his memorabilia. Ahmed Shawki not only composed poems but wrote ballads which were sung by such famous Egyptian singers as Abdel Wahab and Om Kalthum. Hours 9-3. E 50p, F LE1.

Beit al Siheimi Darb al Asfour in the Fatimid city off the Qasaba near Qalaun Mosque. This museum features an excellent perspective on living accommodations in Ottoman times. Features include decorative details, high-carved window seats, Damascus tiles, domed bath, painted cupboards, marble facings and mashrabia casements all showcased in a cool courtyard, and public and private rooms in an Islamic home. Hours 9-4, closed Friday during 12-1. LE1, students 50p.

Center for Art and Life in the Salamlek of the Manasterli Palace, 2 Malek al Saleh, Roda Island 986931. This palace, build in 1851, contains a cultural center with artisans working in textiles, pottery, and glass from all periods of Egyptian history. 9-3, S-Th. 25p.

Center for Reviving Ancient Egyptian Art 3 Adel Abu Bakr ZA 340-7045. This center, which is involved in the restoration of ancient artifacts, houses an exhibition hall of pharaonic, Coptic and Islamic artifacts. It also has a library and bookstore. 9-2. closed F. Admission free.

The Coptic Museum Mari Girgis metro stop in Old Cairo 841766. This museum, set in a pleasant garden in the Fortress of Babylon, was founded in 1910 and offers the most extensive collection of Coptic artifacts in the world. Completely renovated in 1983-4, the museum features objects and architectural pieces, both religious and secular, of Coptic art, a uniquely Egyptian art form which evolved during Egypt's Christian era. Displays include embroidery, textiles, manuscripts, icons, ivory work, metalwork, woodwork, pottery and glass. Hours 9-4 daily, F 9-11 and 1-3. During Ramadan 9-3, F 9-11 and 1-3. LE2.

The Cotton Museum see the Agricultural Museum above.

The Egyptian Antiquities Museum Sharia Mariette Pasha 754319. Founded in 1857 by the famous Egyptologist Auguste Mariette, the Egyptian Antiquities Museum is one of the great museums of the world. Located at Midan Tahrir, next to the Nile Hilton, the museum and its grounds contain the most exhaustive collection of ancient Egyptian artifacts to be found. Exhibits cover all eras of the ancient Egyptian civilization, with much of the second floor devoted to the famed Tutankhamun collection. It is from this museum that the great touring exhibitions of Tutankhamun and Ramses II were mounted. Hours 9-4 daily, F 11:30-1:30. LE3.

Entomological Society Museum 14 Ramsis, near the train station. This small museum maintained by the society features displays of birds, resident and migrant in Egypt, as well as an outstanding insect collection. There is an on site laboratory for insect identification. 9-1 daily except S, and 6-9 Sa, M and W.

The Ethnological Museum 109 Kasr al Aini in the Geographic Society building, ground floor, 354-5350/5450. This small jewel of a museum features displays depicting the ethnographic heritage of Egypt. Items include jewelry, furnishings, crafts and costumes. Currently under renovation and closed to the public.

The Folklore Center 18 Bursa al Adima, Tawfikia, fourth floor, 752460. The center, located off Sharia Ramsis near Gumhuria newspaper, has a one-room exhibition of dresses from the

Oases and Nile valley and some jewelry, basketry and implements. 10-1. Closed F. Free.

Gayer-Anderson Museum (or Beit al Kritlia, House of the Cretan), 4 Midan Ahmed Ibn Tulun 847822. Located between the two outer walls of the mosque of Ibn Tulun, this museum is two houses of the sixteenth and seventeenth centuries reflecting the early Ottoman styles of architecture. Restored and refurnished by Gayer-Anderson, a British army officer who made his home in Egypt, the museum includes his mementos. 8-4 daily; closed Fridays during 11-1. E 10p, F LE1. Photograph permissions E LE1, F LE5.

The Geological Museum at the beginning of the Corniche going toward Maadi with entrance on Atar al Nabi, Misr al Adima (old Cairo), 982608/2580. Recently moved from its home on Sharia Sheikh Rihan to this temporary location, the museum is part of the Geological Survey of Egypt. Specimens on display include vertebrates, like the Fayoum Animal from the Eocene Period; invertebrates; rocks and minerals, including moon rocks, meteorites and gemstones; fossil skeletons, building stones and old Stone Age implements. 9-2, closed F. Entrance free.

Gezira Museum Agricultural Society pavilion in Gezira Exhibition Grounds, entrance on Sharia Tahrir at the Galaa Bridge, 806982. The museum houses a collection of rare paintings, sculptures and art objects including Islamic antiquities and Coptic tapestries that once belonged to the ex-royal family. The collection includes rare Bohemian crystal glassware and ancient glass; metalwork from the Islamic period; pottery from Persia, Greece, Egypt and Asia Minor; Persian carpets; and paintings and sculpture from the French, English, Italian and Flemish schools of art. The collection includes works by Rubens, Renoir, Rodin and others. Unfortunately up to now only 10% of the vast collection has been on display; however, the museum was closed in the spring of 1988 to undergo an extensive renovation. Plans are to expand the space to include the entire building, restore the collection, and reopen within a year with enough space to display most of the pieces.

The Islamic Museum (Museum of Islamic Art) Sharia Port Said at Midan Ahmed Maher 903930. This museum, founded in 1880 to save masterworks from local buildings, contains the greatest collection of Islamic art in the world. There are over 78,000 items covering all periods of Islamic art, including the Ommayad, Abbassid, Tulunid, Ayyubid, Fatimid, Mameluke and Turkish eras. The collection covers carpets, tapestries, metalwork, woodwork, pottery, glass, tilework, lustre, doors, minbars, windows, fountains, illuminated Korans and calligraphy. 9-4, F 9-11. E 10p F LE2.

Jewel Museum in the Jewel Palace (Qasr el Gawhara) at the Citadel 926187. Built by Mohammed Ali in 1814 for his harem and the scene of the execution of the Mamelukes, this palace houses Oriental and French furniture, a gilded throne, Turkish paintings, clocks, glass, and 19th century costumes. Special features include King Farouk's wedding throne, moved here from the Abdin Palace, and Khedive Ismail's bedroom furniture. Hours 9-5. E 25p, F LE2 (included as part of Citadel visit).

Mahmoud Khalil Museum 1 Sheikh Marsafi, opposite exit gate of Gezira Sporting Club, ZA 341-8672. Donated to the state by the political leader and his wife and housed in an exquisite

Islamic building once belonging to Amr Pasha, a member of the ex-royal family, this is an excellent collection of impressionist paintings and sculptures including works by Van Gogh, Renoir, Degas, Manet, Monet, Gauguin, Toulouse-Lautrec, Rousseau, Delacroix, Rubens, Pissarro and Rodin. Guidebook. 10-1 and 5-8. E 50p, F LE1, students free.

The Manial Palace Museum 1 Saray Manial, on Roda Island and adjacent to the Club Med, 987495. The palace was built in 1901 for Mohammed Ali, the youngest son of Khedive Tewfik and the uncle of King Farouk. On the right is the salamlek, a reception building with a series of large lavish rooms. In the garden is the hunting museum. A mixture of Turkish and European styles in architecture and furnishings, the collection includes illuminated manuscripts, embroideries, ceramics, rugs and paintings. 9-4. E 25p, F LE1, students 50p. Photography permission LE1, video permission LE25.

Military Museum at the Citadel 936124. Begun in 1937 and moved to the Citadel in 1947, the Military Museum, recently restored, is located in three palaces built by Mohammed Ali as his official residence. The museum exhibits include military equipment, clothing and items from pharaonic, Islamic and Modern Egypt including some Napoleonic items. Included are 220 oil paintings of military battles, historical events and political personalities; 750 antique weapons, including historic and modern artillery; 145 uniforms; 250 statues; orders and decorations; dioramas, including scenes of the inauguration of the Suez Canal; and maps. Two of the most outstanding items are the military chariot of Tutankhamun and a carriage of the Khedive Ismail. 9-5. E 25p, F LE2 (in addition to Citadel admission).

Modern Art Museum Formerly located in Dokki, this museum has been incorporated into the Cairo Opera House complex. The collection consists of 13,000 modern art pieces, primarily paintings, sculptures and graphics done by Egyptian artists since 1908.

Mukhtar Museum, Sharia Tahrir, Tahrir Gardens, across from Gezira Exhibition Grounds, entrance before the Galaa Bridge, 340-2519. The works of Mahmoud Mukhtar, the famous 20th century Egyptian sculptor, considered the founder of the Egyptian modern art movement, are on display in this museum erected especially to house the collection. There are over 100 statues in bronze, marble and stone as well as memorabilia connected with the artist's life. Additionally his work includes the statue of Saad Zaghloul in the square of that name at the Gezira end of the Kasr al Nil Bridge, and the famous statue **Renaissance of Egypt** on Sharia Giza at the end of University Bridge. 9-1:30 T-S.

Museum of Hygiene and Medicine Sharia Sakakini. Originally established in 1927 by King Fuad under the guidance of the Dresden Museum of Hygiene, this museum contains displays of human anatomy, physiology and pathology. Today it is housed in the elaborate rococo Sakakini Palace built in 1898 and once belonging to Henri Sakakini. The building alone is worth a visit. 9-2 daily. Closed F.

The Mustafa Kamil Tomb and Museum below the Citadel, Midan Salah al Din 919943. The tomb, in highly polished marble, is just inside the entrance. The additional rooms contain the great nationalist's correspondence, photographs, clothing and library. Also buried here are

Mohammed Farid and Abdel Rahman al Rafi. 9-3. Ramadan 10-3. 50p. Groups 25p each, students 5p.

Nagi Museum Chateau Pyramids. Works and memorabilia of Mohammed Nagi, a painter and leader of the modern art movement in Egypt. Closed F.

National Museum for Civilization (Museum of Egyptian Civilization) Gezira, entrance to the old Exhibitions Grounds by Galaa Bridge, 340-5198. This small museum contains paintings and models depicting the history of Egypt from prehistory to the present period. 9-3 daily, closed Friday. E 50p, F LE1.

Natural History Museum Giza Zoo Sharia Giza GI 726314/233. This small museum contains an excellent display of birds, reptiles and mammals from all over the world. Fee 20p.

Police Museum at the Citadel 927094. Recently restored, this museum covers a large portion of the Citadel grounds and includes a prison, with towers, dungeons and mannequins of the Islamic era; a hall of historic fire engines, featuring a fire engine from 1776 and another from 1885; a garden museum, with cannons, one of which is fired each sunset during Ramadan to announce iftar; and the main museum. The main museum displays police equipment from the pharaonic era to the present including manuscripts and illustrations of political assassinations and famous crimes; a collection of counterfeit coins; police weapons including rare swords, daggers, pistols, axes, and equipment for punishment; uniforms, mainly from the Islamic era; and vehicles. There is a guide book in English and Arabic with a history of police and prisons in Egypt. 9-5. E 25p, F LE2.

The Post Office Museum Midan Ataba 390-9686. Located on the second floor of the main post office this museum contains exhibits depicting the Egyptian postal service through the ages, including memorial stamps. 8-1:30, closed F. 10p.

The Railway Museum east end of the main station at Midan Ramsis 763793. Established in 1933, this museum contains early steam engines, railway coaches, the Khedive Ismail's private train, and models of trains and stations throughout Egypt. 9-2, 9-11 on F, closed M and holidays. E 50p, F LE1.

The Royal Carriage Museum 82 26th July, Bulak 774437. With all the renovations that have occurred recently connected with the museums of Egypt, it is hoped that this exceptional museum is high on the list of priorities for consideration. Housed in the original building used by the Khedives as the Royal Stables and Carriage House, the museum now shares its space with a factory and a car park. The visitor must pass through these areas to get to the museum, which is well worth the effort. There are two floors, the first devoted to the carriages, the second to costumes and trappings. There are 78 royal carriages representing 22 different types of vehicles. Most were presented to the rulers of Egypt as gifts. One of the most impressive is a berlin given to the Khedive Ismail by Napoleon III and the Empress Eugenie in celebration of the opening of the Suez Canal. There are 7 displays and 20 cupboards on the second floor containing metals, saddles, uniforms, livery, trappings and oil paintings. There is also a rare

collection of engineering drawings illustrating the construction of the carriages. Excellent catalog in Arabic with details on types and uses of carriages, descriptions of livery and trappings. 9-3:30 daily. E 10p, F 25p. A second Carriage Museum with carriages borrowed from this collection exists at the Citadel.

The Saad Zaghloul Museum (or Beit al Umma, House of the Nation), 2 Saad Zaghloul, at the metro stop of the same name, 354-5399. This, the former residence of the Egyptian statesman, contains memorabilia of the influential politician who was prime minister of Egypt in 1924. It is directly across the street from his tomb, which is built in pharaonic style. 9-3, closed F. E 50p, F LE1.

The Solar Boat Museum on the southern side of Khufu's Pyramid 857928. This museum houses the oldest known boat in the world (4,500 years old). Discovered in 1,200 pieces in a pit now under the museum, the 43m boat has been restored and maintained in controlled temperature and humidity conditions. 9-2:30 LE6.

The Wax Museum Ain Helwan Station, Helwan. This museum is very small and in a shabby condition with inferior wax models depicting events in Egyptian history. 9-5, closed F. E 25p, F LE1.

Additional museums include: **Airport Museum** Cairo International Airport 291-4277, open 24 hours; **Helwan Palace Museum** 340-5198, currently closed to the public; **Mohammed Ali Palace and Museum** Corniche al Nil Shubra, currently closed to the public.

NIGHTLIFE AND DISCOS

Gambling Casinos Although gambling is not a big feature of nighttime Cairo, a few casinos, exclusively for foreigners, exist in some of the five star hotels. The casinos offer blackjack, roulette, craps, baccarat and slot machines. Play is in foreign currency and passport identification is necessary.

Nightlife Almost every hotel has a **nightclub** which features both western and oriental style entertainment. Oriental Nightclubs exist throughout the city, but mainly on Pyramid Road. **Discos** also exist independently and at hotels. For a list of current nightlife entertainment consult **Cairo Today** and **Cairoscope**.

PERFORMING ARTS

Egypt's rich heritage in performing arts began as far back as ancient Egypt when dances, music, and theatrical performances were held in praise of the Gods. A second and greater influence has been the Islamic heritage of the country. Islamic music, dancing and storytelling have all left a base upon which many of the modern performing arts are built. Finally, there has also a been a strong foreign influence on performing arts. This influence, primarily French, blended with the rich heritage from the past to create an interesting, unique and rewarding atmosphere. With the opening of the Cairo Opera House, the city is on the verge of an exciting performing arts explosion.

Performance venues for the performing arts will change with the opening of the Cairo Opera House. Consult **Cairoscope, Cairo Today** and the **Egyptian Gazette** for time and place. Month-long festivals are held each year in October, July and during Ramadan featuring dance troupes, drama, bands and orchestras performing at the Floating Theatre, Balloon Theatre, Al Samer Theatre and Children's Theatre. Entrance is free. The schedule for these events is announced each summer.

Dance

Cairo Ballet Located on Pyramids Road in the City of Art, the Cairo Ballet was founded in 1966 and originally trained by Soviet experts. The ballet school has a special section for 9-11yr olds. Among the repertory are **Shopaniana, Giselle, Don Quixote, Carmena Borana,** and **Carmen**. The venue for the Ballet is the new Opera House (see Venues under Theatre below), where the season will be the month of January.

Folk Dance Troupes There are over 150 folklore dance troupes in Egypt. They perform a variety of programs keeping alive ethnic traditions from all over the country. In Cairo they include the **National Troupe** and **Reda Troupe** both supported by the Egyptian Authority for Dance and Music, with offices at 27 Abdel Khalek Sarwat and the Balloon Theatre (6-10pm) 347-7457/ 1718. Performances are held regularly at the Balloon Theatre in Cairo and the Mohammed Abdel Wahab Theatre in Alexandria. The National Troupe has been in existence since 1960. It founded the folkdancing school in 1967. The Reda Troupe was founded in 1959. Among the dances performed by these groups are **The Bread Baking Dance, New Nubia, The Horse, The Gypsy Dance, The Mameluke, The Handkerchief,** and **The Peasant Wedding.**

Free Spirit Dance Ensemble Creative Dance Studio 44 Road 82 MA 350-5523. This is a newly formed small dance company of seven performers featuring modern and classical dance. They will offer four presentations yearly.

Music

Arabic Music Troupe (Shirket al Musiqa al Arabia) al Galaa Building, Sharia Galaa 742864. Organized in the 1960s and also called the Classical Orchestra and Choir of Arabic Music, this group is under the auspices of the Cairo Symphony Orchestra. Orchestral pieces represent the samaei type of Arabic music. The all male choir performs songs for mixed voices, solo and group, and classical pieces. Performances are on alternate Thursdays at Gumhuria Theatre.

Cairo Conservatoire City of Art, along Pyramids Road 851475/561 850727/291. Founded in 1959 as a school of music, the conservatoire offers instruction in piano, string, wind, percussion, composition, singing and musicology. It is staffed by instructors from Germany, England, America and Egypt. Matriculation is by audition. Performances include solo, group, and the

Cairo Conservatoire Orchestra. Performances are generally held at the Sayed Darwish Concert Hall (see Venues under Theatre below).

Cairo Opera Company Founded in 1869, the Cairo Opera Company was displaced by a devastating fire at the old Opera House in 1971 that destroyed not only a variety of sets, instruments, scores and costumes, but also the priceless original sets and costumes of **Aida**. The company moved to Gumhuria Theatre, where the season commences each March and has 12 performances. The 1989 season is scheduled to take place at the new Opera House and will feature **Aida, Cosi Fan Tutti** (in Arabic), **Don Pasquali** and **Madam Butterfly**.

Cairo Opera Choir Performs with the Opera Company and occasionally with the Cairo Symphony Orchestra.

Cairo Symphony Orchestra The forerunner of this orchestra was the Haifa Symphony Orchestra that featured Egyptian and Palestinian musicians as well as prominent musicians from Europe. On many occasions it was conducted by Arturo Toscanini, and performed in Cairo in Ewart Hall at The American University in Cairo. The current orchestra is under the auspices of the Egyptian Authority for Theatre and Music. The current maestro is Yousef el-Sisi. The orchestra performs mainly at the Gumhuria Theatre 12 Gumhuria 391-9956 390-6606 every Friday at 8:30 from September to mid-June and is scheduled to perform in the Cairo Opera House during the 1988-89 season.

Folkloric Orchestra of Egypt (Ferqet al Alat al Shaabia al Mousiqia) Internationally acclaimed orchestra under the auspices of the Egyptian Authority of Mass Culture 735153 728004. This famous orchestra, also known as the Nile Music Orchestra, performs with ancient Egyptian instruments.

The Om Kalthum Classical Arabic Music Troupe An exceptionally fine orchestra of the Higher Institute of Music, which performs Sept-May, Th 8:30 at the Sayed Darwish Concert Hall.

Theatre
The legitimate theatre season in Cairo runs from September to May with many groups moving to Alexandria in the summer; however, there is a summer season running July and August. Theatre performances are advertised in the local daily newspapers. Shows usually start at 9:30pm, 10:30 during Ramadan. Most theatres are dark on Tuesdays or Wednesdays; however, all times are subject to change without notice. Comedy in Egypt tends to be farce, with a great deal of puns and ad libs. Drama tends to be allegorical. There is censorship. The following is a selective list of theatre companies and venues.

Government troupes
These troupes are sponsored by the Egyptian Authority of Theatre and Music EATM, 27 Abdel Khalek Sarwat or the Egyptian Authority of Mass Culture EAMC Bahr al Azam GI 725153. The season is planned in advance with shows usually running 4-6 weeks in each of the venues.

Avante Garde Theatre Venue is the Talia (meaning Avante Garde) Theatre, Midan Ataba

937948 763466. The theatre has two halls, the Zaki Tolaimat and the Salah Abdel Sabour. The latter is also known as the Pocket Theatre. The company consists of about 15 directors and 150 actors presenting modern plays in Arabic, including translations of western writers. Showcase for new actors. EATM.

Children's Theatre Metropole Theatre, Sharia Alfi 933334. Founded in the 1980s. EAMC.

Comedy Theatre Various venues, including the Mohammed Farid Theatre Sharia Mohammed Farid 770603, and the Floating Theatre, next to University Bridge, Manial 849516. The Comedy Theatre presents star-studded productions. Lots of ad lib and lots of fun. EATM

Modern Theatre Al Salam Theatre 101 Kasr al Aini 355-2484 354-3016. This theatre group offers three shows nightly beginning at 5:30. Performs mainly contemporary plays, but will begin offering children's plays in 1989. Closed T, W. LE2-10. EATM.

Manf Behind the Balloon Theatre AG. A fringe group semi-attached to EAMC, this group offers exploratory theatre with new forms and formats. Announcements by word of mouth.

National Theatre (Qawmi) Midan Ataba 917783/911267. Founded in the 1930s this is the oldest extant theatre group in Cairo. The troupe is composed of established actors and directors. Performances are usually Arabic plays, and foreign plays translated into Arabic. Performs regularly at the George Abiad Theatre (named after an Egyptian tragedian), more often called the Ezbekia Theatre or the National Theatre, the best equipped theatre in the city (after the new Opera house, of course). EATM.

El Samer Troupe El Samer Theatre Sharia al Nil AG. Down the street from the Balloon Theatre. Performs the works of contemporary Egyptian playwrights and traditional folkloric drama. Admission often free. The El Samer Theatre is due to be renovated as one of the newly created Palaces of Culture. EAMC.

Youth Theatre Abdel Wahab Theatre, Ramsis 763466. Founded in the 1980s, this theatre group is designed for young actors, actresses, and playwrights to gain theatrical experience. 8:30 or 9:30. Closed T,W. LE2-10. EATM.

Private theatre companies
The private theatre companies tend to have different performance schedules from the government-operated companies. They offer more variety and feature individual performers.

The American University in Cairo Theatre Company 354-2964. Performs in Wallace Theatre and Howard Theatre. Plays are in English, French or Arabic. Performances are advertised in local papers. The season, running from October to May, usually offers two major English language plays and a French and an Arabic play. Runs tend to be short.

Fayez Halawa Troupe performs primarily political allegorical comedies at the Miami Theatre Talaat Harb 748102. Closed Monday.

Galal Sharkawi performing political satire in Arabic at the Farid al Atrash Theatre, Galaa 750689.

Samir Ghanem Troupe A comedy troupe usually performing Arabic- language comedies at the Bab al Louk Theatre Midan Falaki 355-3195.

United Artists Theatre (Motahedeen Theatre) consists of two companies. The first, performing at the Hurria Theatre, Sheikh Rihan 355-0702, features the most famous and extraordinary comedian in Egypt, Adel Imam. This is Egyptian comedy at its best. The second company now features Fuad al Mohandis, performing at the United Artists Theatre 30 Ramsis 775393.

Al Warsha (The Workshop) 10A Abdel Hamid Sayed 779261. An exploratory theatre troupe of theatre and film professionals performing translated and new Egyptian plays.

Amateur theatre groups
There are three English language amateur theatre groups in Cairo open to anyone interested in any aspect of theatre. They usually perform 3-4 plays yearly.

Cairo Players A predominantly British theatre group performing 3-4 short-run English plays a year, mainly in Zamalek and central Cairo. Open auditions. Contact: 712862.

Heliopolis Players Sponsored by the Heliopolis Community Association, this group performs an annual Christmas pantomime and 2 or 3 other English-language plays yearly. Open auditions. Contact: Jacqui Ringenoldus 291-7892.

Maadi Players Well-established, mainly American, theatre group performing 3-4 English-language plays yearly, often offering top quality performances. Venues include Holy Family Catholic Church 55 Road 15 MA and Cairo American College Theatre MA. Open auditions. Contact Krish Sorenson, 350-3193.

Venues
Balloon Theatre (Om Kalthum Theatre) 26th July and Sharia Nil AG 347-1718. From October to May nightly plays, music, or folkloric dance companies perform here. Mostly in Arabic with an occasional visiting troupe. Seating for thousands. Can be rented.

Cairo Opera House (The Egyptian Education and Culture Centre) This long awaited complex is enjoying its first season in 1988-9. Built with the cooperation of the Japanese in the Gezira Exhibition Grounds on Gezira Island to replace the original house which burned down in 1971, the new facility will include three theatres (the largest containing about 1,000 seats), an art gallery, conference rooms and a library. There will be 10 entrances and a car park for over 2,500 cars. The premier season will include, in addition to local performing arts, Japanese Kabuki, the London Festival Ballet, the Paris Opera, the Vienna Radio Symphony Orchestra, and other internationally acclaimed groups.

Gumhuria Theatre 12 Gumhuria 852137 919956. Once a movie theatre, this site was refurbished on an interim basis to replace the original opera house. It will continue to serve as a venue for the performing arts.

Sayed Darwish Concert Hall Gamal al Din al Afghani GI 852473. Located behind the City of Art off Pyramid Road, this theatre is primarily used by the classical Arabic orchestras, Arabic-language drama and student performers of the conservatory and Academy of Arts.

Sphinx Theatre, at the foot of the Sphinx, GI 856006. Sometimes plays, ballets and musical concerts are performed during summer in this open air theatre. Also nightly Sound and Light shows. Rental available.

Additional venues include **Floating Theatre** Bahr al Azam GI; **Misr Theatre** Mohammed Farid 771863, comedy and satire; **Mohammed Abdel Wahab Theatre** Sharia Ramsis; **Negm Theatre** off Sharia Dokki DO 705892, comedy and satire; **Rihani Theatre** Mohammed Farid 913697, named after Naguib al Rihani, the Charlie Chaplin of Egypt; **Zamalek Theatre** 13 Shagaret al Dorr 341-0660.

SIGHTSEEING

There is so much to see in the greater Cairo area and so many excellent guide books to help understand pharaonic, Coptic and Islamic history and monuments that the list below, although inclusive, serves only as a checklist of important popular sites. Modern Cairo, which is often presented in a superficial manner, has been given expanded coverage.

Pharaonic
Most of the pharaonic monuments near Cairo are in the desert, on or near the vast pharaonic necropolis on the west bank of the Nile. This necropolis runs from Giza to Maydum.

Giza Plateau. 4th dynasty.
　　Pyramid of Khufu, one of 7 wonders of ancient world
　　Pyramid of Khafre
　　Pyramid of Menkaure
　　Sphinx
　　Solar Boat
Memphis, the ancient capital of the Old Kingdom
Obelisk of Senusert I at Mataria
Pyramids of Dahshur, including the Bent Pyramid
Pyramid of Maydum, the first true pyramid of Egypt
Sakkara funerary complex of Zoser, 3rd dynasty, including:

Step Pyramid, the first monument ever constructed of stone
Pyramid of Unas containing earliest pyramid texts
Tombs of Ptah-Hotep, Ti and Mareruka with the finest tomb reliefs of the Old Kingdom
Serapeum, burial gallery of the sacred Apis Bulls

For further reading: **The Ancient Egyptians, The Birds of Ancient Egypt, The Egypt Story, Gods and Myths of Ancient Egypt, In the Shadow of the Pyramids, The Obelisks of Egypt**, all AUC Press publications.

Coptic
Located south of the city center near the Mari Girgis Metro stop, what we call Coptic, or Old Cairo, is in fact the earliest known settlement within the city and contains Coptic, Jewish and Islamic monuments. When visiting Coptic churches one should dress modestly, and women should wear a headscarf.

Coptic Cairo
Fortress of Babylon, 1st century Roman fortress
Convent of Saint George, with outstanding reception hall
Church of al Muallaqa, the Hanging Church, built over the gates of the Fortress
Church of Abu Serga, with the cave of the Holy Family
Church of Sitt Barbara, with exceptional woodwork
Coptic Museum, best collection of Coptic art in the world
Ben Ezra Synagogue, oldest in Cairo
Virgin's Tree in Mataria

For further reading: **Coptic Egypt, The Holy Family in Egypt, The Copts in Egyptian Politics 1918-1952**, all AUC Press publications.

Islamic
Cairo is the richest city in the world in Islamic monuments. There are 622 listed in the Index to Islamic Monuments. Visitors should wear modest clothes when visiting these sites. When entering a mosque shoes must either be removed or encased in slippers provided at the door. Shoulders should be covered. Do not enter a mosque while prayer is in progress. Prayer takes about ten minutes, except for the major prayer around noon on Fridays, which lasts about an hour.

Old Cairo
Fustat, ruins of Islamic city founded by the invading Arabs
Mosque of Amr ibn al-As, the first mosque erected in Egypt
Mosque of Ibn Tulun, the oldest complete mosque in Cairo
Beit Kritlia, two Ottoman homes
Citadel Area
Citadel, the fortress city erected by Salah al Din
Midan Salah al Din
Mausoleum of Sultan Hasan one of the most impressive monuments in Egypt

Rifaʻi Mosque, contains the tombs of rulers of modern Egypt
Fatimid City
Bab al Nasr, Bab al Futuh, Bab Zuwayla, gates of Cairo
Qasaba, the main street of medieval Cairo
Mosque of al-Hakim
Musafirkhana Palace, home of a rich family of the 15th century
Mosque of al-Aqmar
Mausoleum of Barquq
Mausoleum of al-Nasir Mohammed
Mausoleum, Muristan and Madrasa of Qalaun
Mosque of Saleh Talai, only extant Fatimid mosque built outside the city walls
Azhar area
Mosque of al-Azhar, oldest university in the world
Wekalet al Ghuri, a commercial hotel of the medieval period
Ghuria
Fakahani Mosque, built during the Ottoman era
Mosque of Muayyad, with twin minarets atop Bab Zuwayla
Street of the Tentmakers
Darb al Ahmar
Mosque of Qajmas al-Ishaqi
Mosque of Aslam al-Silahdar
Sabil-Kuttab of Mohammed Katkhuda Mustahfizan,
Mosque of Ahmed al-Mihmandar,
Maridani Mosque, with an exceptionally fine mashrabia screen
Beit al-Razzaz, a palace originally built by Qaytbay
Mosque of Aqsunqur, also called the blue mosque
The Northern Cemetery, inaccurately called Tombs of the Caliphs
Sultan Inal
Amir Qurqumas
Complex of Barquq
Tomb of Sultan Barsbay
Complex of Sultan Qaytbay, considered the crowning achievement of Mameluke
architecture
The Southern Cemetery
Tombs of Sayeda Atika, Mohammed al-Gaʻfari and Sayeda Ruqayya, all members of
the Prophet Mohammed's family
Tomb of Sayeda Nafisa
Tombs of the Abbassid Caliphs
Khanqah and Tomb of Shahin al-Khalawati, on the Mokattam Hills
Mosque of al-Guyushi, with the oldest minaret in the city
Mausoleum of Imam al-Shafʻi
Hosh al-Basha, tomb of the family of Mohammed Ali
Aqueduct, over 3km long, linking the Nile to the Citadel
For further reading: **Islamic Monuments in Cairo, The Minarets of Cairo,** AUC Press publications.

Modern Cairo

Ain al Sira The only sulfur baths located within the city are found between Fustat and the Southern Cemetery. These are the most western of a series that begins in Sinai at Hammam Faroun, appear again across the Gulf of Suez at Ain Sukhna, and, in almost a straight line, reappear in Helwan and Ain al Sira. The mud from Ain al Sira is used at the Capritage in Helwan for medicinal mud baths. In addition to swimming in the sulfur water, there is a picnic area, a restaurant and other facilities. There are other sulfur springs in the western desert.

Baron's Palace Located on Sharia Oruba HE, on the right just after the Merghani underpass, this architectural extravaganza, built at the turn of the century by Baron Edouard Empain, the developer of Heliopolis, is patterned after a Hindu temple and is covered and surrounded with Hindu reliefs and statues. It is said the structure is built on a railway turntable which once rotated to face the sun. The palace has been abandoned for many years, and it is dangerous to enter the building. No admission.

Barrages At Qanater, 20 miles north of Cairo, where the Nile divides into the Rashid and Damietta branches, stand the two dams begun during the reign of Mohammed Ali. The Damietta Dam is the larger with 71 sluices, while the Rashid Dam, separated from the former by a kilometer, has only 61 sluices. You may drive over the dams. Park facilities offer bicycling, boat rental, carriage rides and picnic areas. Can be reached by car, along the Corniche, or river bus (Friday and Sunday mornings only) from Maspero Station across from the Radio and TV building. Journey time is 2 hours. The last bus from Maspero is at 5pm. Very popular crowded spot.

Cairo Tower Gezira, near the Gezira Exhibition Grounds, 341-0884. This lotus-shaped tower, built during the Nasser Era, is 187 meters or 68 stories high and offers a panoramic view of the city including the barrage to the north and the Giza, Sakkara and Dahshur plateaus to the west. There is a restaurant on the 14th floor, cafeteria on the 15th and an open air view on the 16th. 9am-12pm daily. E LE2, F LE3.

Cairo International Fair Grounds Sikka al Beida, Medinat Nasr. The largest exhibition ground in Egypt, the fair ground houses a number of pavilions used for exhibitions including the Cairo International Book Fair.

Cairo Zoo Sharia Giza GI 726314/233. Founded in 1891 and one of seven zoos in Egypt (Alexandria, Mansura, al Arish, Fayoum, Sohag and Tanta), the Cairo Zoo never closes. In addition to visiting the 400 varieties of animals, there are pony rides, a Natural History Museum, grottos, picnic facilities and 3 restaurants. The zoo is spread over 52 acres which once belonged to the Orman Gardens designed by Barrillet-Deschamps of France for the Khedive Ismail. The mosaic pavement of the pathways is original. Daily from 9-5, extremely crowded on Fridays and official holidays. English language map available. 10p, special exhibits, 20p.

Camel Market Located just beyond Imbaba near the Imbaba Airport, the market begins at dawn on Friday and Sunday. Camel herders from the Sudan and farmers with goats, horses, donkeys and other livestock bargain. Tack is also available.

Often a short hop to Switzerland gives you a pleasant head start.

With all the advantages Swissair has to offer, flying worldwide via centrally-located Switzerland will seem like a hop, skip and a jump. A short stopover at the ideal Zurich or Geneva airports, and you're off to the destination of your choice in Europe, Asia, Africa, or the Americas. Pampered and served by our much praised cabin crew, you travel a lot more pleasantly than if you had skipped the hop via Switzerland and the amenities of a Swissair flight.

swissair

For information and reservation please contact Swissair: Reservations, Tel. 392 1522, Ticket Offices: 22 Kasr El Nil Street, Tel. 393 7955, Heliopolis, Tel. 664 760, c/o Bon Voyage, Maadi, Tel. 350 1240, Alexandria, Tel. 482 4834.

Cemeteries In addition to the pharaonic, Islamic and Coptic necropolises, there are many foreign cemeteries in Cairo. Several are located side by side across the street from the Mosque of Amr in Old Cairo. The **Italian Cemetery** (Catholic Cemetery) contains many graves of early foreign residents in Egypt, including Theodor Bilharz. The **British Cemetery** 17 Sharia Abu Siffeen 841914. The entrance is along the metro tracks one block west of the Mosque of Amr. This is a very spacious cemetery maintained by the British government, which contains among others the graves of British soldiers from World Wars I and II. The **American Cemetery** is a small cemetery located just before the British cemetery along the same street. This 50-100 meter plot was acquired by special petition to Khedive Ismail in 1875 by Andrew Watson, head of the American Mission in Egypt and father of Charles Watson, the first president of The American University in Cairo. Although burial still takes place, most of the graves are of the early American missionaries to Egypt including Andrew Watson and his wife. The cemetery is enclosed by a high wall and has many trees which offer a cooling shade even in summer. The epitaphs written on the tombstones often give vivid details of the lives of the people buried here. A fourth cemetery worth visiting is the **Heliopolis War Cemetery** Nabil al Wakkad at the junction with Shaheed Ahmed Tayseer HE, which commemorates the dead of two World Wars.

Dahab Island located south of Roda Island with a dock along the Corniche 986156. Three feddans of parks, a restaurant, a children's playground with pedalos, and a conference hall are located on this island. Access is via a felucca which departs every 10 minutes from the dock. 9am-11pm, S9am-1am. LE10.

Gamal Abdel Nasser Mosque and Tomb 26th July, Abbassia. Built after the death of Nasser in 1970, the tomb is located behind the mosque.

Garden City For Art Deco and Art Nouveau lovers, a walk through Garden City will provide plenty of examples of both art forms. Originally the site of a refuse dump for the city, Garden City was chosen by Ibrahim Pasha as the site for his palace amid a forest of new trees in 1835. When the British set up their official residence in the area in 1906, the palace was demolished and foreigners began to develop the area. By 1920 buildings were going up at an unprecedented rate. Many of them still stand. It is these buildings, standing on the serpentine streets, that are the most interesting. Many facades, doorways and entrance halls, all accessible to the curious, are in their original form.

Gardens (public)

Andalus Garden, along the Nile in front of El Borg Hotel, ZA. A small but pleasant garden with a promenade along the river.

Ezbekia Gardens off Midan Opera. Once one of the most fashionable gardens in the world, Ezbekia was laid out along French lines during the great rebuilding of Cairo in the 1860s. Today, bisected by 26th July, little of its grandeur remains, and it has diminished in size. Bookstalls line the sidewalks outside the gardens, puppet shows are held regularly in the Puppet theatre here.

Orman Botanical Gardens next to the zoo in Giza 728272. Designed by the French landscape artist Barillet-Deschamps, who died before his work here was completed, the gardens originally were 5 1/2 miles long and 3 miles wide. In 1891 the northern portion of the gardens were used to create the Cairo Zoo. Today the grounds cover 29 feddans in the heart of Giza. Many trees, shrubs and plants are labeled. Students from Cairo University often frequent the garden. Cafeteria. Picnic facilities. Annual spring flower show, usually in March. Map of grounds available. Hours 8-5 in summer and 8-4 in winter. Entrance 10p. Cameras 50p, video LE10.

River Garden along the Nile, north of Andalus Garden, continues the quite peaceful atmosphere beside the river.

Tahrir Garden Sharia Tahrir, opposite the Gezira Exhibition Grounds at the southern tip of Gezira Island. In addition to pleasant walkways shaded by trees and free-standing sculptures which grace the area, these gardens contain the Mahmoud Mukhtar Museum, the Cairo Sporting Club and at the tip of the island, the Gezira Sheraton.

Gezira Exhibition Grounds Sharia Tahrir, Gezira. Contain a number of exceptionally fine museums including the Museum of Egyptian Civilization, Gezira Museum, the Planetarium and the newly constructed Cairo Opera House.

Harrania Village 2 miles off Pyramids Road on the Sakkara Road 850403. This village, built in traditional style, hosts the world famous Ramses Wissa Wassef School for coarse weave tapestries. The school complex has won an Aga Khan award for its distinguished architecture. Some items on display are for sale, but can also be bought from Senouhi 54 Abdel Khalek Sarwat, 5th floor, 391-0955. Harrania exhibit hall open from 9-5, weavers at work 9-12 and 1:30-4:30.

Midans of the city

Midan Abdin, officially called Midan al Gumhuria, this area was originally the site of the palace of Abdel Rahman Katkhuda, which was demolished in 1874 by the Khedive Ismail to make way for his European-style Abdin Palace. It was in this midan that Ahmad Orabi, in the 1880s, presented his petition for Egypt for the Egyptians, and where, after the revolution of 1952, Gamal Abdel Nasser gave his official speeches to the people of Egypt.

Midan Mustafa Kamil, named after the nationalist who fought for Egyptian independence at the turn of the century, and **Midan Talaat Harb**, named after the industrialist who founded Bank Misr, are linked by Sharia Talaat Harb. The latter was once called Soliman Pasha, after a French officer who was commissioned by Mohammed Ali to reorganize the Egyptian army. Between and beyond to Midan Opera is a section of Cairo reminiscent of Paris and sometimes referred to as the Gold Coast.

Midan Opera was named after the famous Opera House that was erected here in 1869 (burned October 1971), and was once the most fashionable area of Cairo. It has recently undergone restoration and is a pleasant place to visit. Although many of the hotels in the area are not as elegant as they once were, they still retain an aura of the past, especially the Continental Hotel on the square and the Victoria Hotel on Sharia Gumhuria. The statue in the square, created by Charles Cordier in 1872, is of Ibrahim Pasha, who ruled Egypt after Mohammed Ali. Ezbekia Gardens are nearby.

Midan Qasr al Dubara was once the site of Ibrahim Pasha's palace. The palace was demolished in 1906. Today the square is very small and in its center is a statue of Simon Bolivar donated to Egypt by Venezuela.

Midan Ramsis is located in what was once the Islamic port of al-Maks, the customs point. Access was via the Bab al Hadid, Gate of Iron. The area was demolished by Mohammed Ali to build the railroad station which was completed in 1851. Today it is one of the busiest squares in the city with not only the rail station but several bus stations. A statue of Ramses II, discovered at Memphis in 1880, dominates the square. It is worth a visit, especially the railway station and its museum.

Midan Saad Zaghloul is located at the Gezira end of Kasr al Nil Bridge just in front of the Gezira Exhibition Grounds. The statue of Saad Zaghloul, nationalist leader and Prime Minister of Egypt in 1924, located in the center of the square, was created by Egypt's foremost modern sculptor Mahmoud Mukhtar, whose museum is just down the street.

Midan Sadat is the largest and busiest square in Cairo. Formerly called Midan Khedive Ismail, whose statue once stood atop the fountain in the center of the square, then Midan Tahrir after the Revolution, the area is currently undergoing a facelift. The area has a heavy concentration of airline offices, bus terminals and government buildings.

Mokattam Hills For an excellent panorama of the city and, on a clear day, a view of the pyramids from Giza to Dahshur, one must visit the Mokattam Hills. The hills stand 700 feet above sea level and are part of an extensive range that stretches from North Africa to China. Created of limestone during the Eocene period, the Mokattam is riddled with caves and fossilized stones. Some of the area is restricted, but the remainder is an interesting place to explore. The plateau contains houses, restaurants and tree lined streets. It is a favorite place in the summer when the cooling breezes offer a respite to the heat on the plain below.

Palaces of the city
Abdin Palace Erected by the Khedive Ismail in 1874 as his official residence, this is the most magnificent European-style palace in Egypt. Its grounds cover 24 feddans of grottos, parks, and kiosks located in gardens landscaped along European lines. Site of Ismail's dismissal as Khedive, Farouk's capitulation to the British and other events that led to the downfall of the ruling family, the palace is considered unlucky by some, fulfilling the prophecy of Mohammed Ali, who reputedly stated that "as long as my descendants occupy the Citadel their rule will be supreme". Among its many distinguishing features are a crystal banister, an alabaster staircase, a Byzantine Room, a Suez Canal Room, a library of rare books and personal memorabilia of the ex-royal family, and many antique furnishings. Recently restored, the palace will soon be open to visitors.

Al Gawhara Palace Located at the Citadel, this palace was one of two constructed by Mohammed Ali as his royal residences. It was here in 1811 that Mohammed Ali hosted the infamous banquet after which he slaughtered all the Mamelukes in order to rid himself of their interference and power. The rooms, patterned after French influence, are highly decorated. Partially burned in 1972 during an attempt to steal the Khedival jewelry that was housed inside, the palace is now open to the public.

Gezira Palace ZA 340-8888. A former palace of the Khedive Ismail, this is currently the centerpiece of the Marriott Hotel. Erected in 1869 just in time to accommodate the royal guests attending the opening of the Suez Canal, the palace was called the Palais des Fetes, and royal parties were held here regularly. Confiscated to pay Ismail's debts, the palace was turned into a hotel and later sold to a private family. Its varied animal collection was sent to Giza to found the Cairo Zoo. Among its distinguishing features are several onyx fireplaces, a marble grand staircase, a wood-paneled billiard room, excellently crafted grill work from foundries in Germany, and hundreds of antique chairs, mirrors, and furnishings in Islamic and European designs. Restored in the 1970s, many of the public rooms contain original furnishings. 24hr access.

Kubba Palace Kubri al Kubba HE 243-1915. Containing 400 rooms, this palace was erected in 1863 and became the residence of the Khedive Tewfik. Among its treasures were the collections of matchbox covers, rare coins and stamps that King Farouk was fond of collecting, a diamond and gold coffee set given to Ismail by the Empress Eugenie of France, and a Faberge thermometer. The library of this palace was housed in 27 rooms and contained rare and important manuscripts and Korans. Much of its contents were sold at public auction in February of 1954. Public access is limited.

Shubra Palace Erected in 1808 by Mohammed Ali, the Shubra Palace was the summer retreat of the court throughout the Khedival era. Its gardens were among the finest in Cairo, filled with rare trees, grottos and pavilions.

Papyrus Institute (Dr. Ragab's), 3 al Nil GI 348-8676/9035. Located on a houseboat between the Giza Sheraton and the University Bridge, the Institute contains an exhibition of copies of famous papyri; some are for sale. Papyrus plants grow in the garden and a demonstration of how papyrus is made can be seen. Hours 9-7 daily.

Pharaonic Village (Dr. Ragab's) on Jacob Island, Sakiet Miky, GI 729186 729053. A boat to visit the island leaves every half hour from Sharia al Nil at Bahr al Aazam, 2 kilometers after Casino de Pigeons. The visit takes 1 1/2hrs. You visit the island by boat and see over 300 people, some dressed in ancient Egyptian costume, practicing agriculture and handicrafts for the benefit of visitors. Features include a wealthy man's house and a peasant's house. 9-4 daily. Ramadan 9-2:30. E LE5 F LE30.

Planetarium Gezira Exhibition Grounds 341-2453. Features evening skyshows in Arabic nightly except Fridays at 7pm. English-language shows are available by appointment. Entrance 25p.

Victory Memorial Sharia al Nasr Parade Ground, MN. The victory memorial in the shape of a pyramid was erected to commemorate the victories of the Egyptian army in the October War of 1973. It was here that Anwar al Sadat was assassinated during a military parade on October 6, 1981. He is buried beneath the memorial. Free admission.

Day Trips from Cairo

Ain Sukhna is a picnic spot on the Red Sea a few hours drive from Cairo. It can be reached by either the Suez Road or the Digla-Ain Sukhna Desert Road (the first 40km of this road are not in good condition). This is a good spot for picnics, swimming, snorkeling, limited scuba diving, and wind surfing. Some of the beaches near Ain Sukhna are enclosed with barbed wire. **Under no conditions should one venture onto these beaches. They were mined during the recent conflicts in the area and some mines still remain.**

Digla Desert A good day's outing is to explore the area east of Digla off the Digla-Ain Sukhna desert road. There are hundreds of tracks leading off into the desert. It is best to go with more than one car, but if you get lost, just head north and you will find the main road once again. If by accident you head south you will eventually come to the Wadi Hof-Helwan Road. There are many wadis and butts to explore. Be sure to bring water. Flies are a problem in the spring and fall.

Helwan, south of Cairo along the Corniche, was once the garden spot of Cairo, and the Khedive Tewfik would move his entire court to the city for a month each year while he underwent a cure in the sulfur springs. Today, with the industrialization of the area, the city's gardens are suffering toxic poisoning and Helwan is not as it used to be. However, sites to see are the **Japanese Gardens** with pagodas, buddahs and, on Fridays, traveling musicians, fortune tellers and entertainers; the **Helwan Hot Springs**, where one can bathe and take the cures; the **Capritage**, a health spa; the **Wax Museum**, depicting scenes from the history of Egypt; and **King Farouk's Resthouse**, on the Corniche, with a museum and a restaurant. There are also access roads leading into the desert behind Helwan for people who like to explore. The desert behind Digla and Helwan is exceptionally beautiful once one gets off the main road and beyond the industrial areas.

Lake Manzala Located east of Port Said along the northern coast, and averaging a depth of only one meter, this lake, the largest in the Delta, is a protected area for wildlife. This is a full day's outing, so start early and bring a lunch.

Petrified Forest Located in an area called Gebel al Khashab and covering a 25 square kilometer area, the petrified forest is east of Digla on the Digla-Ain Sukhna desert road. One joins the road from the new expressway by turning east at the Zabbalin village. Twenty-five kilometers later the entire area on the left-hand side contains the petrified forest. Look for tracks going off to the left, any one of which will take you into the forest. Do not expect standing trees. This area is covered with fragments, and sometimes entire logs that have become petrified. A good place for a picnic. No shade. Legislation to create a protected area is pending.

Suez Canal Completed in 1869, the Suez Canal is one of the most important canals in the world.

Linking the Mediterranean to the Red Sea, it is a vital waterway for shippers. The easiest way to visit the canal is to visit one of the three canal cities. **Port Said,** along with its sister city **Port Fouad,** stands at the northern entrance to the canal. There are many seaside restaurants, some on the top floors of buildings, that offer a good view of the harbor and the entrance to the canal. There's also good shopping in Port Said. **Ismailia** stands at the midway point of the canal. It is where the Suez Canal Authority is located and, in addition to superb views of the canal, one can swim and watch the ships go by in the Lakes. There is also the **De Lesseps Museum,** with mementos of the builder of the canal. **Suez** is at the southern entrance to the canal. Here one can walk along the promenade at the entrance to the canal and watch the ships as they enter.

Wadi Digla is a very miniature Grand Canyon. It is a beautiful spot for a picnic, rock collecting, walking, climbing or just sitting and enjoying. Reached from the Digla-Ain Sukhna desert road about 30km from the new expressway. As you reach the top of the hill after the petrified forest and begin the descent on the other side look for a dirt track on your right. There are several, each will lead you to the main track. The best one runs parallel to the main road for about half a kilometer before it turns into the desert. This is the beginning of the main track. All the tracks hook up with this track as it heads east-west. Follow it west, back toward Digla. You will meander through small wadis until the way is blocked by the Wadi Digla. It is best to go with more than one car and have someone with you who has a sense of direction. Bring water, food and shade.

Wadi Hof lies between Digla and Helwan off the expressway. There is no access via the expressway, and you have to go to Helwan to enter. The road from Wadi Hof runs to the Red Sea across the Eastern Desert. There are many side tracks for exploring the area.

Wadi Rayan Found in a depression west of the Fayoum, the Wadi Rayan is a natural environment for birds and mammals including rare falcons, the fennec fox and gazelles. This is a long trip and portions of it need a four wheel drive.

SPORTS

It is impossible to list all the sports facilities and activities available in Cairo. Most organized sports are under the auspices of the official federations and/or the sporting clubs. The sporting clubs are listed below, the federations in the Directory at the end of the book.

Participating Sports
Baseball
The **Maadi Baseball Association** and the **Cairo American Softball League** offer a variety of ball activities for all age groups. The **Men's Softball League** plays two seasons, September to December and February to May. There are 17 teams that play, beginning each Friday at 9am and weekday evenings at 6pm. Each season ends in play-offs. The **Women's Softball League** has 6 teams. The schedule runs in tandem with the men's. Both leagues play at the

Victory College, Digla. Anyone can play. The **Maadi Little League** is for both boys and girls ages 5-15. The divisions include **T-Ball Division I** for 5-7 year olds; **T-Ball Division II** for 7-8 year olds; **Little League Division I** for 9-10 year olds; **Little League Division II** for 11-12 year olds; and the **Senior League** for 13-15 year olds. Organized play begins each year in February and runs through April. There are play-offs in April and May. Games take place at Cairo American College each Saturday beginning at 9am.

Gliding

Gliding takes place each weekend at Imbaba Airfield. Lessons are available from The Egyptian Gliding Institute and The Egyptian Aviation Society. Both can be contacted via the airfield. For those interested in sightseeing only, hour-long trips can be arranged over the Pyramids and portions of Cairo. Long-distance trips require special permits. Arrangements can be made via the Institute or the Society. Approximate fee for one hour, LE30.

Golf

Nine-hole golf courses exist at the Gezira Club in Zamalek and the Mena House Oberoi at the Pyramids. Equipment available. Tournaments are organized through the sporting clubs. See Yearly Events.

Horseback and camel riding

Short rides, mainly for tourists, are available at the Pyramids. For more serious riders the stables located along the desert south of the Pyramids are a must. Horses may be rented by the hour or purchased and stabled. Lessons are available. Some features include desert rides to Abu Sir and Sakkara; sunrise, sunset or moonlight riding; and desert picnics complete with roasted lamb, musicians and dancing horses. All for a fee. There are also accommodations at sporting clubs and hotels.

MG Sphinx Mohamed Ghoneim, owner, Pyramids 853832 851241; **AA** Abdel Aziz, owner, Sharia Abul al Hol, Pyramids 850531, specialized in large groups and parties arrangements featuring dancing horses and BBQ, also offers excellent lessons for adults and children with emphasis on safety; **Eurostables** Pyramids 855849; **Ferrosea Riding Club,** south edge of Gezira Club, 800692 ZA; **Gezira Sporting Club** 340-6000; **Hyatt Al Salam Hotel** 61 Abdel Hamid Badawi HE 245-5155; **KM, SA,** and **FF,** all in the Pyramids area. For horse racing and Arabian horse farms see below.

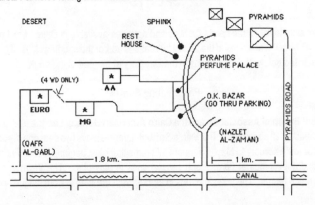

Hunting

Hunting is an organized sport in Egypt. Protected species include **falcons, eagles, osprey, bustards, crocodile, monitor lizard, Nubian ibex, Doreas gazelle, Barbary sheep** and **ostrich.** Restricted areas include the area from Saint Catherine's Monastery to Ras Mohammed in Sinai, where such animals as gazelles, hyena, fox, hyrax, ibex, wolf and Sinai leopard make their home; and Gulf of Aqaba, Zaranik, Lake Bardawil, al Tina, and Tiran, where major bird habitats are found. You must be 21 to own a gun in Egypt. In order to hunt you will needs a gun license and a hunting permit. Tourists can get license and permit at the airport. All foreigners may get licenses and permits at Room 12 in the Mogamaa, Midan Tahrir. In order to buy a gun you must have a letter from your embassy and approval from your local police station. The Shooting Club, see below, provides services for hunting for members, including ammunition at discount prices. They own four estates for hunting. Blinds are allotted at the beginning of the season on three lakes. Hunting usually takes place on Fridays. Automatic membership to Port Said Sporting Club. Duck season begins first Friday in December and ends the last Friday in March, **dove** from April to May, **snipe** from November to December, and **pigeon** all year round.

To buy firearms: **Ahmed Mandi** 50 Gumhuria, Tawil Building 910940, hunting rifles and ammunition; **Al Seglaby** 1 Adli, 917401 and 10 Midan Opera, Continental Hotel Building; **Belgian Agency for Firearms and Sports Equipment** 9 Road 261 MA 352-1957; **Islaha al Islamia** 24 Sabri Abu Alam 745918; **Safari** 24 Digla at Shehab MO 348-9469.

Pharaoh's Rally

The Pharaoh's Rally is a spectacular 12 day 4,000km race first held in 1981, for three categories: cars, motorcycles and trucks. Beginning and ending at the Pyramids, the course takes in the Western Desert from Siwa to Abu Simbel, and the Eastern Desert. Entries for participants are accepted until the end of July, with racing in October. Local contact: Rami Siag 285-6022. International contact: Fenouil SA des Pharaons, 47 Rue Emile, Roux 94120, Fontenay-Dous-Bois, France.

Tennis

Tennis facilities exist at most clubs and hotels. For tournament information see Yearly Events.

Spectator Sports

Horses

Horse racing is available every Saturday and Sunday on alternating weekends at the Heliopolis Hippodrome Course and the Gezira Racetrack from mid-October through mid-May. Post time is 1:30. Race card appears in the Saturday Egyptian Mail. Pari-mutuel betting for win, place, twin tote, double. Race horses are exclusively Arabian, with beautiful conformation and gait. The horse racing journal **L'Echo Sportif**, in Arabic, is sold at most newsstands. **Heliopolis Racing Club** 245-4090 offers riding lessons.

Arabian horse farms: **Egyptian Agricultural Organization,** EAO El Zahraa Station, Sharia Ahmed Esmat off Gisr al Suwais 243-1733. This is the famous government-owned Arabian horse farm with pure bred blood lines. Home of famous Arabian Al Zahraa. Visitors are welcome. 8-1 daily.

To buy:
Al Badeia 340-0166 535297 owned by Nasr and Hassan Marei is the largest and oldest privately owned

farm with 95 horses; **Hamdan** owned by Ahmed Hamza with 25 horses; **Shams al Asil** owned by Wegdan Barbary with 25 horses. Horse shows take place on a periodic basis and are advertised in the newspaper.

Hockey
The hockey season runs from September to March. Ten teams participate in two divisions with playoffs for the National Cup held each spring.

Soccer
The national pastime of Egypt. Any place there is an open piece of land one will find boys playing soccer. Professional soccer is played from September to May with League Championships and Cup Tournaments concluding the season. There are three leagues in Egypt with twelve teams to the league, each having its own field where games are played. Because of the popularity of Ahly and Zamalek, these two teams play at Cairo Stadium in Heliopolis. During the season each team plays 22 times. For each game a system of points has been established to ascertain the league winner. At the end of the season the two lowest-standing teams drop to the league below, while the two highest-standing teams of the second league rise to the first. Games are played on Friday and Sunday afternoons beginning at 3pm. Admission is from 50p-LE10 depending on seating. Tournaments include the **Egypt Cup, Africa Cup**, and **World Cup**. These competitions take place in the spring and early summer. **Soccer Teams** in the first league include **Ahly, Zamalek, Mahalla, Itihad al Sakandary, Olimbi, al Marikh, Tarsana, al Masri, Ismaili, Domiat, Arab Contractors, Naseig Helwan.**

Water Sports
Boating
A wide variety of boating activities may be enjoyed in Cairo. **Feluccas** can be rented by the hour for picnics and joy rides. Although they can be rented almost anyplace along the Nile, the most popular spots are in Maadi and downtown. In Maadi docking is on the Corniche north of the Good Shot restaurant. The trip goes south to Helwan and north to As Salam Hospital. Downtown, for cityscape sailing, docking is north of the Meridien Hotel, across from the Hilton Hotel, and in front of the Cairo Tower. Privately owned **sail boats** can be docked at the Cairo and Maadi Yacht Clubs, see below. **Sailing competitions** sponsored by the Cairo and Maadi Yacht Clubs are from September through June. Races are scheduled, primarily between April and October, for the Nile class, a five meter dinghy, and the International Finn class. Membership in the two yacht clubs is reciprocal.

Corals
The coral reefs along the shores of the Gulf of Suez and Gulf of Aqaba in the Red Sea are considered among the best in the world. Corals are living organisms which are protected by law in Egypt. It is forbidden to take them from the sea. Many reefs are close enough to the shore that even the novice swimmer can enjoy the beauty of the corals.

Fishing
The fisherman can find Egypt a true adventure. Sport fishing is available along the Nile, on the Red Sea, and on the Mediterranean. There are also the lakes along the northern coast, in the Fayoum and at Aswan. Protected areas where it is forbidden to fish with either nets or explosives

include the Gulf of Aqaba from Taba to Ras Møhammed. The Egyptian Wildlife Association urges persons seeing violations to report them to the nearest police station. The non-competitive fisherman can make arrangements year-round to fish at Hurghada and Marsa Allam on the Red Sea. For the competitor, the Egyptian Game Fishing Federation sponsors four tournaments a year. In February and July international tournaments are held at Hurghada. In April and November tournaments are held at Sharm al Sheikh. **The Shooting Club**, see below, has premises at Marsa Allam on the Red Sea for fishing and can arrange all details for fishing expeditions for members. Equipment available from **Mohammed Amin** 2 Sabri Abu Alam 762007.

Rowing

Ten rowing clubs exist on the Nile from Giza to Imbaba along the eastern shore. Competitions usually run from November through April every Friday. See Rowing Clubs below for more information.

Scuba Diving

Egypt is blessed with year-round dive weather, water temperatures of 70-80 degrees, underwater visibility up to 150 feet, and some of the greatest coral reefs in the world. Lessons are available at dive clubs in Cairo (see below) and dive centers on the Red Sea. Trips are organized on a regular basis. Restrictions include spear fishing in protected areas and removal of reef life. Facilities include professional dive centers with American and European equipment including 72 cubic feet steel and 80 and 90 cubic feet aluminum tanks with standard J and K valves, and decompression chambers. **Dive spots** include: **Ain Sukhna** Ridge reefs and sandy beaches, no dive facilities, easy snorkeling; **Hurghada** Abundant sea life, reefs, islands for camping and a diversity of dive shops with full equipment for rental; **Safaga** Rough sea beds, for experienced divers only, abundant sea life including hammerhead sharks, dive shops with full equipment rental; **Sharm al Sheikh** Many diving spots including Ras Umm Sid for dolphins and turtles, The Tower for barracuda, Naama Bay for turtles and the Near, Middle and Far Gardens for sea fauna, three dive shops and boat rentals with full facilities; **Islands of Tiran and Sanafir** Serviced from Sharm, fast currents and dangerous reefs; **Dahab** Features include The Canyon and a blue hole, dive shops with full facilities; **Nuweiba** Easy diving, good for novices, dive shops with full facilities; **Ras Mohammed** Serviced from Sharm, best diving in the Red Sea, several dive areas for variety of terrain: rocky, sandy and reef dives.

Diving Schools: Egyptian School for Scuba Diving 13 Mona DO 348-6698. Diving courses both theoretical and practical for all levels. Registration all year round. Provides all equipment except mask, snorkel and fins. MDEA PDIC.

Aqua Equipment: Adawat al Sayd 2 Sabri Abu Alam 745918, underwater fishing equipment, spear guns, snorkels; **Ahmed Mandi** 1 Adli 917401 and 10 Midan Opera, Continental Hotel; **Kyros Paschalis** Madrasa al Fransiya, Maarouf, underwater gear, spear guns; **Smiley Realtors** 19 Road 206 Digla 352-3824, diving tanks filled.

Sea shells

One of the best beaches in Egypt for collectors is the beach area of Ras Sidr on the Gulf of Suez Sinai coast. Over 100 variety of sea shells wash up on shore and are easily gathered.

Swimming
Sporting club pools are available to members. Hotel pools may be used on a daily basis for a fee which often includes lunch. Some hotels offer yearly memberships for all sporting facilities.

Sporting Clubs and Associations
British Golfing Society Meets regularly the last Saturday of every month at 10am at the Mena House golf course for competitions. Open to British passport holders, not strictly enforced. Newcomers may play as guests. Nominal fee for membership. Contact Andy Matthew, 353-2342 352-0495.

British Sub Aqua Club 31 Lebanon MO 346-1105/09/10/23. Primarily a diving club, this organization also offers monthly meetings every third Monday at 8pm, slide shows, underwater videos, trips, limited equipment for hire. Initial membership £45 with £20 yearly.

The Cairo Diver's Club Meetings every first Monday of month at Intercontinental Hotel 7:30-9:30. Aqua Diving instructions and certificates (PADI). Diving trips. Open to divers and non-divers.

The Cairo Hash House Harriers Weekly Friday afternoon runs at Pyramids, in the desert and other locations followed by picnics and social hours. 712674.

Cairo Rugby Club 2 Road 161 MA. Founded in 1980. Weekly training every Wednesday at 5pm at Victory College, Maadi. Social hours every Wednesday and Friday evening at club house. Facilities include dancing, pool, softball and soccer. Sponsors annual Nile River Raft Race in October. Arranges tours twice yearly to nearby countries. Membership, open to non-players, by approval of committee. $50 yr for players and non-players and $10 yr for students. Contact Dave Jenkins 353-0301, Robert Jones 350-3340 and Andy Heath 346-7962.

Cairo Sporting Club in front of the Galaa Bridge next to the Gezira Sheraton 340-1204. Two swimming pools, squash courts, tennis courts, motorboat rentals.

Cairo Yacht Club Sharia al Nil, beside the Sheraton Hotel, GI 348-9415. Rentals, lessons, moorings, races for sailboats. Membership LE600 with LE28 yearly. Mooring charges LE1 per meter per year.

Gezira Sporting Club, Saray al Gezira ZA 342-0800 340-6000. This 67-acre facility includes 20 tennis courts with professional instruction, a golf course, olympic size swimming pool, smaller heated pool, racetrack, bowling lawn, squash, basketball, volleyball and handball courts, playing fields, children's playground, gymnasium, sauna, riding stables, and more. The office is open from 9-1 daily except Thursday. Supervises many of the local competitions in sports. The winter cricket tournament is played here. Yearly rates for foreigners: married $300, single $270. Diplomatic corps married $290, single $260. Tourist temporary membership one week married $50, single $30; month married $100, single $55.

Health and Fitness Clubs
New Life Health Club and Beauty Center Meridien Hotel 845444 ex575 and 8 Road 101 MA 350-1232,

swimming, squash, health club, game room, acupuncture, jacuzzi, monthly and annual fees 9-9 daily;
Sheri Nile Health Club 3 Essam al Dali GI 349-6225 and Meridien Heliopolis 671411 670190 and Ramses
Hilton 777113, game room, health club, massage, beauty treatments, daily, monthly or annual fee 9-9
daily, accepts credit cards; **Valentine Fitness Centre** 70 Merghani HE 291-4756, health club, massage,
health and beauty treatments, dance, exercise, sauna, weight training, sportswear shop, daily or annual
fees, closed Friday 9-9; **Samia Imports** 42 Abdel Halim Hussein MO 706647.

Heliolido Sporting Club 4 Mahad al Ishteraki, Midan Roxi, HE 258-0070 258-0045. The club
includes tennis courts, swimming pool, squash, volleyball and basketball courts, gymnasium,
dining, etc. Life membership is LE2,000 plus a small annual fee. There are also monthly and
daily rates.

Heliopolis Sporting Club 17 Merghani HE 671414. Pool, squash, tennis, playground, croquet,
billiards, basketball, volleyball and many other facilities. Membership is LE3,000 for the first
year and LE40-60 each additional year. Foreigners may use the facilities in summer only,
LE100 for 3 months, LE3.50 per day.

Maadi Sporting Club 8 Damascus Midan al Maadi MA 350-5693 350-5504. Facilities include
sailing, water-skiing (at Maadi Yacht Club), 12 tennis courts, 6 squash courts, riding and
boarding of horses, swimming pool, croquet, football, basketball, cricket, judo, karate, bridge,
sauna, barber shop, beauty salon, cooperative, dining facilities, open air cinema and a nursery.

Maadi Yacht Club Corniche al Nil, next to the Good Shot, MA. Affiliated with the Maadi Sporting
Club. Lessons by appointment. Races every Friday.

National Sporting Club (Ahly) south of the Gezira Club, ZA 340-2112. The club includes tennis
courts, swimming pool, an active gymnasium program, courts, playing fields, and other sports.

Rowing Clubs There are ten rowing clubs in Cairo including the **Arab Contractors Rowing
Club**, the largest; the **Armed Forces Rowing Club**, the oldest; and **The Egyptian Rowing
Club** (formerly the Royal Rowing Club). Membership is available at The Egyptian Rowing Club
11 Sharia Nil, behind the Giza Sheraton Hotel, GI 348-9639. Rental of boats for members only.
Annual membership, including rowing lessons for Egyptians LE300 and for foreigners six
months for LE500 and one year for LE1,000.

Sakkara Country Club Off Sakkara Road 12km from Pyramid Road 534307. Flood-lit tennis
courts, golf, swimming pool, horseback riding and lessons. Egyptians LE1,500 initial fee and
LE400 yearly. Foreigners $500 per family per year and $400 per single per year.

The Sakkara Palm Club Sakkara Tourist Road 018-200791 or 921031. Swimming pool, 2 clay
tennis courts, 2 squash courts, horses, sauna, playground. 56 bungalows for rental, disco,
BBQ. Membership required.

The Shooting Club Sharia al Seyd DO 704333 704535. Specializes in all kinds of shooting
including trap, skeet, pigeon and rifle range. Also has tennis courts, swimming pool,
playground, etc. The club provides game shooting and has premises on the Red Sea for fishing.

Shooting sessions are held in summer every day except Monday, with evening sessions on Saturday, Tuesday and Thursday. In winter every afternoon except Wednesday and Friday. Bets may be placed. See Hunting above for more information.

Tawfikia Tennis Club Ahmed Orabi, Sahafiyeen 348-1930. Tennis courts, 2 swimming pools, squash courts, basketball, table tennis, children's playground, restaurant and open air cinema. Hosts the Open Tennis Championship of Cairo. Membership LE750 for the first year and LE70 for each additional year. Foreign membership LE1,500 and LE150 yearly.

Tayaran Club 14 Ahmed Fuad HE 243-2265. Swimming, squash, tennis, billiards, basketball and many other facilities. Membership LE1,200 for first year and LE50-60 each additional year. Foreigners by daily ticket only.

Tivoli Heliopolis Tourist Establishment Omar Ibn al Khattab, Midan Almaza HE 290-6496 670743. Swimming pool, playground, night club, restaurant. Membership fee LE380 yearly, LE275 for six months; LE215 for three months, LE150 for two months and LE80 for one month.

Zamalek Sporting Club 26th July, Mit Okba, MO 346-6665. Three swimming pools, squash courts, tennis courts, croquet, jogging, football fields, game rooms, playground. Membership first year LE2,000 and second year LE18 for husband, LE7 for wife, LE7 for children over 16 and LE5 for children under 16. Foreigners pay by daily ticket.

Sports Equipment and Repair

Belgian Agency for Firearms and Sports Equipment 21 Saad Zaghloul, near Kasr al Aini 354-3754; **Clay Sports** 11 Zakaria Ahmed 753643, tennis equipment including Dunlop, Slazenger, Davis, etc; **Hag Mahmoud Ahmed Sarhar Co.** 6 Bab al Akhdar Midan Hussein 925698, guns, fishing gear, snorkeling gear, harpoons, 10-2:30 and 4-7 closed Sundays; **Klonaris Freres** 23 Abdel Khalek Sarwat 747376; **Lebnan Sports House** 14 Saray al Ezbekia 913418, also Arabic scrabble and monopoly; **MCI Egypt** 15A Ibn Radwan al Tahib GI 987441, camping gear, tents; **Modern Sports Center** 34 Hegaz HE 438572; **Mohamed A El Attar** 61 Ahmed Zaki, Ain Shams 779706, 98 Mohammed Farid 347-5899 and 1 Nadi ZA 343-7554, sports equipment including children's bicycles; **Al Nahda al Hadisa** 11 Syria MO; **Olymps** 62 al Nasr New Maadi, sportswear and equipment; **Picnic Sports and Camping Equipment** 20 Nasr New Maadi 352-5679, sports and camping equipment including a wide variety of tents; **Segallaby's** 1 Adli 917491; **Sport House Marzouk** 11 Sherif Pasha 759181; **Sport House Marzouk** 11 Sherif 393-9181, squash rackets, tennis equipment, roller skates, exercycles, ammunition and library; **Sport Palace** 159 26th July ZA 340-7631; **Tamco Supermarket** 58 Misr-Helwan Road MA 350-4134, tennis, soccer, weights, etc.; **Tennis rackets and restringing** at any sporting club.

LEISURE CLUBS AND ORGANIZATIONS

All Nations Women's Group 340-2405/7927/8059. One meeting at a member's home and one outing somewhere in Egypt monthly for a group limited to 40 members, 4 from each country. Membership by inquiry with placement on waiting list and eventual acceptance when space permits. Trips to historic sites and local factories, crafts shops or art galleries. Annual membership LE20.

The Archaeology Club is an outreach program of ARCE, 2 Midan Dubara GC 355-3052. It was organized to increase appreciation of Egypt's past by informing people of the latest archaeological research in Egypt. Monthly lectures and meeting at 24 Syria MO. It offers four yearly field trips to archaeological sites and a six to eight week lecture series. Membership $75 yearly and $125 for families.

British Women's Coffee Mornings Open to British women only. Second and fourth Wednesday monthly. 10:30 St. Michael's Church Hall 8 Seti HE 668476 and first Wednesday of every month 11am at the British Embassy residence.

The Cairo Art Guild c/o Women's Association 3 Salah al Din MO 346-3521 355-7371 x8328. Open to any artist or those interested in the visual arts. Meets second Monday at 7pm at Women's Association Building for lecture or slide demonstration. On fourth Monday group trip to local gallery or artist's studio. Sponsors an annual Arts and Crafts Fair and a Fine Arts Exhibit.

Cairo Drivers An auto club established for persons interested in restoring antique cars. For information contact Mike Nicolas, 354-8211 ex3257 or Mohamed Megahed 354-8211 ex3287.

Cairo Petroleum Wives Open to all members of the community. Lectures, games, car rally, cooking, news, lectures, bridge, tennis, golf and tours. Meetings fourth Monday monthly 9:30. Membership fee LE10 yearly prorated. Contact Mrs. MacDowell 352-4987.

Fine Arts Lovers 3 Ahmed Pasha GC 354-1425. Meetings every Thursday at 6:30. Lectures, exhibitions, competitions by artists, poets and musicians. Open to foreigners. Membership LE10 for the first year, LE5 thereafter.

Heliopolis Community Association Founded in 1983, this non-profit organization provides community activities including tours, drama group, annual pantomime, dinner, theatre, bridge, mah-jong and the like. Monthly meetings fourth Wednesday at the Baron Hotel in HE at 8pm. Monthly newsletter. Newcomers coffee third Wednesday 10am. For more information contact Jacqui Ringenoldus 291-7892.

International Women of Egypt Open to foreign women married to Egyptians. Membership by invitation only and restricted to no more than 3 members from any nation. Meetings at member's home second Thursday of each month. Lectures, games, potluck, outings, some charity work. 340-8059.

Maadi House 21 Road 19 MA 350-2293. Sponsored by US Embassy for US direct-hire ex-pats only. Open to the foreign community for special events and on Tuesdays from 12-2 for a salad bar, Thursdays from 5-8:30 for tavern on the patio and Saturdays 8:30-11:30 for breakfast.

Secretaries' Club of Heliopolis Meetings third Sunday at 7pm at Baron Hotel Heliopolis. Contact: Amani Haggag 291-5757 x2018. Special rates and facilities at Baron Hotel, fashion show, make-up demonstrations, ladies' interests. Social club.

The Spanish Speaking Women's Club Coffee morning first Tuesday at 10:30 at members' homes. Contact Maria Elena Domingo 726330.

Women's Association 3 Salah al Din MO 346-3521. An English speaking women's group meeting the second Wednesday of every month at the Marriott Hotel, Aida Ballroom. Area meetings, monthly, bridge groups, lectures, cultural trips, bazaars.

RESEARCH

Cairo is a fertile field for researchers in a wide variety of disciplines; but unless the researcher is affiliated with a local center that is acquainted with what is available and how things operate in Cairo, the mysteries of language, accessibility, government permissions and laws may be overwhelming. Scholars affiliated with institutions abroad with no base in Cairo, freelancers, and anyone contemplating a project related to Egypt may be frustrated as to how to begin. For all of these, and anyone who has a need to know, the following overview offers some insight into the procedures researchers must follow.

PERMISSIONS

All academic research involving anything other than information in the public domain or the use of public or private libraries requires permission from the government body or agency which supervises and coordinates research in the discipline. For example for archaeological work in the fields of Arabic Studies, Coptic Studies and Egyptology, proposals and appropriate documents must be submitted to the Egyptian Antiquities Organization. In the field of Natural History, the governing agent is the Undersecretary of State for Zoos and Wildlife, and for journalists the Press Center.

Military clearance To enter areas of the country under military control, regardless of the type of research, a security clearance from the military authorities is necessary. Military clearances can take two to three months to come through, and are usually given only to members of recognized institutions. These clearances are arranged only after the research project has been approved by the proper authorities.

Finances All projects must have a budget which will be approved by the same government agency to whom the proposal is submitted. The project must have adequate funds in Egypt to cover all costs. Foreign projects must transfer money to a local bank or institution and obtain a letter of guarantee and, in some instances, bonding.

Importing equipment All materials imported into Egypt for approved projects must be bonded by a local bank and re-exported upon completion of the project.

Examples of Permission Procedures

Although different disciplines are governed by different laws and different government bodies or agencies, many of the steps involved in acquiring the necessary documents are similar. What follows is an overview of the necessary procedures for obtaining permission to do research in two fields: data gathering and documentary filming. These illustrations present a picture of the processes individuals and institutions must follow to abide by the law in Egypt.

Data gathering
Government Agency: **Central Agency for Public Mobilization and Statistics (CAPMAS)**
Sharia al Oruba, MN 601083 601020.

Research studies not involving a field situation, work based on secondary data, analysis of survey data already available, and study of an organization's own operation do not require special permissions in Egypt; however, any area involving a field situation and data collection does.

An individual not affiliated with an institution may encounter great difficulties in obtaining clearance to work in the field. In addition there are restrictions on the involvement of foreigners in field work. In many instances field work must be done by Egyptian staff members. In cases of research undertaken in cooperation with a government agency, the results must be cleared with the agency prior to dissemination.

Further, researchers must abide by the provisions set forth in the following laws: Presidential Decree No. 2915 concerning the establishment of CAPMAS; Decree No. 231 for 1968 issued by the Director of CAPMAS concerning censuses, surveys, opinion polls, etc.; and Decree No. 488 for 1987 issued by the Director of CAPMAS.

Prior to undertaking any field study, a request for a research clearance should be submitted to the Director of CAPMAS by the director of the institute, department or center with which a researcher is affiliated. The following documents should be presented with the request: Three copies of the Research Proposal (the proposal should provide the following information: title of study; name of institute(s) and collaborating agencies (if any) conducting the study; names of researchers to be involved in the study; research problem(s); objectives; study area(s); methodology; population sample and size; and duration of the study with beginning and termination dates); three copies of every instrument and any guide-list of questions to be used for date collection.

Permission will take a minimum of three months.

Film
For foreign companies or individuals to be able to film in Egypt in any media including film, video, and still photography for the production of feature, documentary, commercials, or other films, the following procedures must be followed:

Once a producer has script in hand he must acquire an Egyptian agent who will see the process of permissions through in an orderly and correct manner. The agent should discuss all procedures with the producer. Once all is agreed a contract should be signed.

Censorship The first step is to send three copies of the final script and fees (approximately LE5) to the censor for approval. The cinema censor (Talaat Harb, 3rd floor, next to Cinema Radio, 759100/041) is not a formality. The script will be read for vice, religious prejudice, or anything insulting to Egypt. This process should take about two weeks. If the censor has rejected the entire script or a portion of it, the producer will be informed what is offensive and why it is offensive. He has the right to appeal to a higher council within the censorship. If the censor approves the script it will be returned. Each page will be stamped approved and a censor will be assigned to stay with the film until it is completed. The censor will also inform the General Union for Film Makers (20 Adli, opposite Kodak, 756687), who will claim a fee of LE1,000 for the first two weeks of filming.

Permissions While the script is at the censor's the agent will submit the appropriate applications to the Ministry of Interior. All foreigners working on the film must be given a security clearance. All sites to be used in filming must have clearance. In most instances this is a formality; however, in restricted areas permission must be obtained from additional ministries or agencies. This process will take approximately four weeks.

If sites include antiquities, an additional application must be made to the Egyptian Antiquities Organization 4D Midan Abbassia. If approval is given, fees must be paid for the privilege of filming in these areas. For exterior scenes the fee is LE200 a day; for interior scenes LE200 an hour. This process can be concluded in a matter of days. If sites include privately owned places, negotiations must be with the owners.

All the above permissions must be renewed annually and must be obtained for each production filmed in Egypt.

Finances The finances of the film are also governed by Egyptian law. While the script is at the censor's an Egyptian budget should be prepared with the guidance of the agent. This budget is passed to the Ministry of Culture for approval, then taken to a foreign currency bank where arrangements will be made for the total amount of foreign currency to be transferred to Egypt. Once the money is in Egypt, the bank will issue a certificate to be used for customs and bonding.

Equipment A detailed list of all equipment to be imported, with complete specifications for each piece, must be submitted to the customs authorities. They will assess the percentage of customs duty on the total. This assessment must be presented to the same foreign currency bank for the issuance of a **bank bond** in favor of the customs department. The bond is a guarantee for temporary admission of all items on the customs list and an assurance that all will be exported once the project is finished. Once the filming is completed and all items have been exported the bond is cleared.

Rushes Once filming begins the censor continues to play an important part in the production of the film. With censor-approved script in hand the censor attends all filming sessions. Each can of exposed film must be signed and sealed by the censor. This, together with a letter signed by the censor and the appropriate fees, is sent to the censor department at the close of each day's shooting. The censor approves them and sends them to the Ministry of Culture, which approves them and sends them to the customs. The customs department deducts the number

of meters of film in the can from the raw film imported into the country and issues a certificate. The rushes can now be sent out of the country. This process takes approximately three days.

Technicians Egyptian technicians are required to work on all films shot in Egypt. The union has set a policy of one Egyptian technician for each foreigner, but this policy is currently being reviewed.

Documentary filming shortcut For documentary filming there can be an alternative. If one member of the foreign unit can provide evidence that he/she is affiliated with a legitimate foreign television network, a different and shorter procedure can be followed. Contact is initially made with any Egyptian cultural attache abroad. They will inform the State Information Office who will in turn inform the Press Center Office at the Radio and Television Building. It is advisable that a local agent be mentioned at this time. Next the producer must send a brief 1-2 page synopsis along with all location requests and a list of all foreign crew to the Press Center. In this instance, if filming has been approved via the Ministry of Interior and other organizations listed above, no censorship, bank bond or duty is required. Even rushes go directly to the Press Center for expediting through customs.

Equipment entering Egypt under these arrangements must be accompanied by a crew member who should have four copies of a detailed packing list and a separate list of raw film stock and sound tapes. A Press Office official will meet the crew member at customs and help clear the equipment on a temporary basis. The four copies of each list are verified and stamped. One copy stays at customs, another goes to the producer, a third to the Press Center and the final one is held by the production unit.

Agents:
Kasr al Nil Films for Cinema and TV. Production and Distribution. Agent: Ahmed Sami 37 Ibrahim, Roxi, HE 258-8166. Credits include: The Night of Counting the Years; The Spy Who Loved Me, Death on the Nile, The Awakening, Gallipoli, Sphinx, Love Boat on the Nile, and Sadat's Eternal Egypt. Will also do small budget productions.

Misr International Films 35 Champollion 3rd floor 748033. Agent: Youssef Shaheen. Credits include: King Tut, Fortunes of War, and assistance in some of the major productions listed above. Also does commercials.

DATABASE RESEARCH

Several facilities have been established in Cairo in recent years which open the entire world of scholarly research to the local scholar. Simply stated, On-line Information Systems is a research library; but instead of being limited to a single library or group of libraries it is accessed world-wide and compiles the research for you via databases stored in computer files. All you need to use this service is a need to know. If you are doing research in a particular field and want to find information, go to someone who has subscribed to the service.

Where to find it
The American Cultural Center Library 4 Ahmed Ragheb GC 355-0532. On line to **DIALOG**. Additional services for on-line users include: checking library holdings; checking holdings of additional libraries and information centers in Egypt; requesting assistance from their center in Washington DC; and off-line printing of full texts when available. These services are restricted to five citations at a time.

British Council Library 192 al Nil AG 347-6118. Requests are submitted by pouch to the main office of the British Council in the UK. The search is done via databases in the US, UK and Europe and returned to Egypt via pouch. There is a flat fee for the service, which takes 3-4 weeks to complete.

Cairo American College Midan Digla, Digla MA 352-9393/9244. On line to DIALOG in the US and Telegram Gold in the UK. This service is available to Cairo American College faculty and students only.

ENSTINET Egyptian National Scientific and Technical Information Network, 101 Kasr al Aini 355-7253, is a public information utility sponsored by the Academy of Scientific Research and Technology in co-operation with Georgia Institute of Technology. It acts as a gateway to databases in Europe and the US. ENSTINET is also compiling databases in Egypt including Egyptian Sectorial Bibliographical Database, Union Lists of Foreign Periodicals Database, Egyptian Journal Database, Directory of Current Agricultural Projects, Directory of Agricultural Institutes, and soon to come, Egyptian Banks Database, Egyptian Bibliographic Database in Arabic, Directory for Egyptian Databases. ENSTINET offers a public service called **Instant Computer Line Retrieval,** 101 Kasr Al Aini 355-7253.

How does on-line retrieval work?
You go to the local service and ask to research a subject. A person will work with you to find out exactly what you want to know and help create a series of words to research in the databases. For example, if you only request **EGYPT BETWEEN 1850-1900** you may get the response that there are 30,000 references in the databases you selected. That is a lot of sources to look through. But if you narrow the field to **SUEZ CANAL-OPENING CEREMONIES-NOVEMBER 18, 1869**, the response may be 300 references. Adding an additional word, **EUGENIE** may bring the references down to 20. The information you are looking for is about the Empress Eugenie on November 18, 1869 during the Suez Canal opening. 20 of the 30,000 articles on line deal with, or at least refer to, exactly that subject.

You now have three choices: you may ask for a bibliographic citation, an abstract, or the entire article. Any one of these can be sent to you instantly via the computer or by mail. You may also go to a nearby library with exact references in hand. Your choice may depend on your budget. In reality this service is not expensive when you consider the time-saving aspect, the accuracy and the reward, but on-line questions can add up. The search described above, including abstracts of eight articles, cost $30 plus the fee of the local service.

Can I do this myself?

Yes you can. You will need a good working knowledge of computers, a computer and a modem. The computer must be asychronous, and the modem must be compatible with Bell 103 and/or Bell 212; or CCITT V 22 and/or Bell 212. The modem connects to your telephone which is the life-line to the databases. You should also have a Telecommunication package which will enable you to store the data you receive over the modem in your computer for later use. The first step is to join a gateway (see below). Once you arrange to be on-line, each time you want to use the service you telephone the telecommunications center access numbers, which you will receive at the time of application, and you will then be on-line. Then you must access the database you wish to use.

Gateways

Gateways are companies who have established access to a variety of databases. These systems have made the databases in the United States and England available in Egypt:

Channel Communications. Flat 7 27 Gezira al Wusta ZA 341-3438. Information services currently available TYMNET, TELENET, NILENET. Required hardware: Microcomputer and Modem. Terminals must be asynchronous, operating at 300 or 1200 BPS with 8 bite ASC, 11 characters and no parity, one stop bit. Modems must be compatible with the following: Bell 103 or 212 (300 Baud), CCITT V 22 or Bell 212 (for 1200 Baud). Required software: PC Talk, Perfectlink, X Talk XVI, etc. Hook up time: two weeks. Hook up charge: $150. Ministry Charge: LE500 (deposit) LE 100 (monthly minimum). Access: 740400 or 752344. On line charge: 27 piasters per minute used. 81 piasters per kilocharacter. Function: Access to US stock quotes, credit reports, news, air fare and schedules, interest rates as well as linking with other subscribers' computers.

Telecommunications Authority Data Packet Switched Service ARENTO Sharia Ramsis 777517 775085. They will link you to the international databases. The fee is LE100 per monthly subscription that will not be charged in months you do not use the service and is deducted from your on-line time, a LE500 deposit, and 27 piasters per minute of use and 81 piasters per kilocharacter of information. Charges average about LE2.50 per minute for transmission of data.

For more information: **Compu Serve Information Service** 5000 Arlington Centre Blvd. Colombus, Ohio 43200. (800) 818-8990. **The Source Telecomputing Corporation** 1616 Anderson Road, McLean VA 22102. (783) 734-7500.
Publications: **Directory of On-line Databases** by Ruth N. Cuadra et al, Santa Monica, Cuadra Associates Inc. 1982; **The Information Broker: How to Start amd Operate Your Own Free Based Service** by Kelly Warnker, R.R. Bowker Co. 1981; **Creating an Information Service** by Sylvia P. Webb, an Aslib Book 1985; **On Line Publications,** Pinner Green House, Ash Hill Drive, Pinner, Middlesex HA5 2AE, UK.

RESEARCH FACILITIES IN CAIRO

When going to a research facility to apply for permission you should bring identification in the form of a passport, identity card, CV, and/or letter of introduction from an institution. In some instances these documents may prove unnecessary; but having them handy may save a lot of frustration.

Archaeological Centers

The government agency governing all archaeological research, museums, historical restoration, antiquity sites and excavation in Egypt is the **Egyptian Antiquities Organization**, 4D Fakhry Abd al Nour (opposite the Police Academy) Abbassia 839637. 9-3 daily. Closed F-Sa. Publication: **Annales du Service des Antiquites de l'Egypte.**

Austrian Archaeological Center 6A Ismail Mohamed, Apt 62 ZA 340-6871. Open to recognized scholars only, 8:30 to 2:30 except Sundays. Work in progress includes Vienna-based seasonal excavations at Tell al Dah'a in the eastern Delta.

Canadian Institute 32 Road 103 Maadi 350-7214. Open 9-4 S-Th. Supported by the Society for the Study of Egyptian Antiquities, the University of Toronto, and the Royal Ontario Museum, the Canadian Institute has excavated in East Karnak, Luxor, Dakhla Oasis and Tell al Madkhutah near Ismailia.

Chicago House Sharia al Nil, Luxor 82525. Founded in 1924 by the Oriental Institute of Chicago, Chicago House supports scholars in the pursuit of research pertaining to the ancient monuments in Luxor. Work includes precise facsimile drawings which preserve the decorations on the walls. Library for scholars only. Chicago House sponsors the **Friends of Chicago House**, with members helping to support the facility.

Egypt Exploration Society c/o The British Council, 192 al Nil AG 345-3281/84. Founded c.1882 to aid Egyptology, the Society co-ordinates efforts of British researchers working in Egypt. It is currently supporting projects at Sakkara, Memphis, Tel al Amarna, and Qasr Ibrim in Nubia. Membership is open to anyone who pays annual subscription fee. Apply to the British Council. Lectures and field trips are open to the public. Publishes an annual journal of current research and a newsletter distributed to members. No library.

German Archaeological Institute 22 Gezira al Wusta (entrance on 31 Abd al Feda) ZA 340-1460/2321. A center for research in Egyptian history. Library of 40,000 volumes on Pharaonic and Islamic Egypt is open to scholars with appropriate identification from their supporting institutions. Open M-Th 8-1. Ongoing excavations at Aswan, Luxor, Abydos, Dahshur, Abu Mena and Old Cairo.

Institut Francais d'Archaeologie Orientale 37 Sheikh Ali Youssef, off Kasr al Aini 354-8245. Founded in 1880. Open 9-1 daily except Sa and S. Library of 60,000 volumes on Pharaonic and Islamic Egypt, open M-Th from 2-6. Access available to scholars and students upon approval of director. Ongoing excavations at Oasis of Kharga, Dakhla and other sites. Extensive publications including **Annales Islamologiques**, monographs, and 20 books per year.

Italian Institute of Archaeology 3 Sheikh al Marsafi, upper floor of the Italian Institute, ZA 340-

8791. A small research center primarily for Italian scholars conducting archaeological excavations in Egypt. The small archaeological library is open to responsible researchers with permission of the Italian Cultural Institute. Library hours 10-1:30 daily except Sa and S. Current projects include digs in Upper Egypt and the restoration of an historic theatre in Cairo.

Netherlands Institute of Archaeology and Arabic Studies 1 Dr. Mahmoud Azmi ZA 340-0076. Hours 9-2 M-F. Small reference library of 8,000 volumes in Arabic and western languages on Arab Studies and archaeology. Six newspapers. Student I.D. required. Current excavations include Sakkara and in the Delta.

Polish Center of Mediterranean **Archaeology** 14 Baron Empain HE. Supports Polish archaeologists and researchers working in Egypt. The very small reference library is open to recognized scholars only. House S-Th 9-1. Current projects are in Upper Egypt, Cairo, Sakkara and Alexandria.

Swiss Institute 11-13 Aziz Abaza ZA 340-9359. Exclusively for Swiss archaeologists. No access. No requests.

Libraries and Cultural Centers
Academy of the Arabic Language Library 15 Aziz Abaza ZA 340-5026/5931. Founded in 1932 as a general library of 50,000 volumes and periodicals in all languages emphasizing Arabic language and heritage. The library contains rare Arabic books and biographies of members of the Academy. Open to any responsible researcher with a specific study topic. No borrowing. 8:30-1:45 daily, closed F,Sa.

The African Society 5 Ahmed Hishmat (rear) ZA 340-7658 341-9543. Founded in 1972 to promote and encourage research on Africa. Lectures, seminars, conferences, exhibitions on topics of interest or concern to African nations. Library is open to members from 5-7 on Sa and Tu and contains books by African writers, political, economic, and cultural documents, and recent periodicals. Membership available at LE1 to students from African Universities resident in Cairo. Publications: **African Newsletter** published in Arabic, English and French on problems and issues in various scientific and cultural fields.

Ain Shams University Library Khalifa al Mamun, Abbassia 820230 822030. Founded in 1950 as a university library, it now contains 90,000 books in Arabic, English, French and Persian. Special collections include books about Kadria Hussein, daughter of Hussein Pasha, and the books of Dr. Shafik Ghurbal. Access with Ain Shams student ID only. 9-5 daily, closed F.

Al Azhar University Library Darrasa, near main building of University 906154. The general library of the University is the Library of the Faculty of Islamic and Arabic Studies with 80,000 volumes including 20,000 manuscripts and rare books. Each of the 36 faculties has its own library all under the supervision of the General Manager. Identification necessary for access. 8:30-2 daily except Friday.

The American Center 4 Ahmed Ragheb GC 355-0532 (library) 354-9601 (center). Founded in 1974 to present cultural programs and provide information about the United States. Library of over 15,000 volumes and periodicals. On-line database access. Hours 10-4. M,W till 8. Closed F. Center open from 10-8. Services include films, lectures, exhibitions. Membership is open to any resident over 20 years of age and to university students. To apply bring two small photos and identification. Processing will take one week.

All Saints' Cathedral Library Michel Lutfallah ZA 341-8391. General lending library for general reading. Open every day at discretion of librarian. Call for hours.

American Research Center in Egypt Library, ARCE 2 Kasr al Dubara, GC 355-3052/8239. A reference library for fellows and members. No public access.

The American University in Cairo Library 113 Sharia Kasr al Aini 354-2964 ex6901/5/14. Founded 1919. 210,000 volumes, 1,600 periodicals. English, French, Arabic. Special collections: **Creswell Library** of Islamic Art and Architecture, **Debanne Library, Labib Habachi Library on Egyptology,** and the newly acquired **Saba Library** (not yet available to the public). Open 8-8 except S 10-8, closed F. AUC ID required. Special membership is available at LE15 for one month, LE25 for 3 months, and LE60 for an academic year. Applicants for special membership should have a serious research interest and a letter of introduction from a supporting institution.

Arab League Information Center Library Midan Tahrir 750511 ex270. Founded 1945, this library contains 20,000 volumes in Arabic, English, French and German, and 16 periodicals on history, government and societies of all Arab League countries. Serves as a reference library for the General Secretariat in the same building. Open to serious graduate researchers by application at office on top floor. Hours 9-2, closed F.

Austrian Cultural Center 1103 Corniche al Nil Apt 7 354-7436/4063. Founded in 1958. Small reference library of Austrian and German literature (in German), history and contemporary Austrian life (in English). Hours 9-1 M-F. Open to the general public.

Bibliotheque Francaise French Consulate 5 al Fadl, off Talaat Harb, 774922. Hours M,W 2-4 and T, Th, F 9-2; and 27 Sabri Abu Alam HE. Hours M,T,W,Sa 9-1 and W,Th,Sa 4:30-8. Arabic literature translated into French, and French literature. Open to the public.

The British Council 192 al Nil AG 347-6118 345-3281-4. Teaching center for English language, computer skills, British GCE O Levels. Fees for all classes. Also lectures, plays and exhibits. Open to the public.

The British Council Library 192 Sharia Nil AG. 345-3281-4 ex153. Founded in 1963. 38,892 volumes, 85 periodicals. On-line database services to UK. Hours 9-2 and 3-8 M-Sa. Annual membership LE10. Borrowing for members only. Special 3 week membership LE 1.50.

Cairo American College Library Road 253 Digla 352-9393/5244 ex140. 30,000 books, 160 magazines and 8 newspapers, as well as 8,000 audio-visual items. 7:30-5 daily except W till 4 and F, Sa 10-4. Yearly membership for non-CAC families restricted to adults. Fee: LE100. On-line database service to US and Europe restricted to students and faculty. Special summer membership open to all.

Cairo Demographic Center Library 2 Libnan, opposite Naniwa Restaurant, MO 346-2002. Containing the largest collection of demographic materials in the Middle East, this library has 25,000 books and 110 periodicals in English, Arabic and French on fertility, immigration, population trends and mortality in the Arab countries, Africa and Asia. Open to any responsible researcher. Borrowing privileges for center students only. Publishes all research reports and center studies. 9-5 except F.

Cairo Evangelical Seminary Library 8 Sikka al Beida Abbassia 820574. This library has 25,000 volumes in English, Arabic and German on theology, missions, Judaism and New Testament studies. Primarily for students at the seminary, any interested scholar with appropriate identification may have access. No borrowing privileges. Hours: M-F 8-6; Sat: 8-12.

Cairo University Library Orman GI 727581/8426. Founded 1908. 1,029,900 volumes, 7,043 periodicals on all fields in Arabic and other languages. Cairo University ID required. Winter 9-5; Summer 9-2. Closed F.

Canadian Cultural Section Canadian Embassy, 6 Mohammed Fahmi al Sayed GC 354-3110. Information center about study in Canada. Large documentary film library about Canada in English, French and Arabic available for loan to schools and organizations. Hours M,W,Th 7;30-3.

Catholic Egyptian Office for the Cinema Library 9 Adli Passage, 3rd floor, 911568. Established in 1947, this small Franciscan archive possesses an Arabic-language collection of all Egyptian film reviews from newspapers and magazines since 1927. Small collection of books in Arabic, French and English on cinema and Egyptian film. Open to any interested person. Sponsors an annual film festival to choose the five Egyptian films which most promote universal brotherhood and strengthen the human family. Publishes a bimonthly review of current Egyptian films in Arabic.

Central Library of the Agricultural Research Center University Street, Giza 723000 ex331. Founded 1920. 25,000 volumes. 9-2, closed F,Sa. Limited access.

Chinese Cultural Department 10 Ibn Battuta GI 852261. Small general library in Chinese, Arabic and English of less than 500 books and periodicals on Chinese literature and history. Open to the general public. Publications include **China Builds**, a periodical about Chinese life. 9-1 and 4-6 daily except F.

Creswell Library of Islamic Art and Architecture The American University in Cairo 113 Kasr al Aini. Open only to bona fide students of AUC and recognized scholars with permission from the library director. 8-5 S-Th. 10,000 volumes, many rare editions in the fields of Islamic art and architecture, and history.

Egyptian Library Abdin Palace. Originally the private library of the Mohammed Ali dynasty, this restricted library contains 20,000 volumes, mostly rare and special editions given to the Khedives as gifts. No access at the present time.

Egyptian National Library (Dar al Kutub) Corniche al Nil Bulaq 753254. Founded in 1870, Egyptian equivalent to Library of Congress. Containing 1,500,000 volumes, of which 1/3 are in European languages, the National Library has 11 branches with 250,000 volumes in each plus a special children's library at Roda, 15 al Manial 840312 with books in different languages, and a music library at 5 Champollion 753254. Extraordinary collection of rare manuscripts. Reading rooms open from 9-6 daily except Fridays. No borrowing privileges.

Entomological Society of Egypt Library 14 Ramsis 2nd floor 750979. Founded in 1907. Contains over 31,000 volumes and exchange publications with 300 entomological societies and scientific institutions over the world. 9-3 and 5-8. Closed Th evenings and all day F.

Egyptian Center for Cultural Cooperation 11 Shagaret al Dorr ZA 341-5419. Arabic classes and tours to Egyptian monuments for non-Egyptians. Exhibitions, recitals and cinema. 9-2 S-Th. Exhibitions open to 8pm.

Food and Agricultural Organization Library The General Cooperative Society Building for Agrarian Reform, 7th floor, Sharia Wizaret al Ziraa, next to Agricultural Museum, DO 705029/182 702789. Contains 40,000 books, reports and periodicals in English and Arabic on agriculture and related fields. Primarily a working resource for the FAO staff, this library is open to the public daily from 10-1. Interested researchers register at the desk. No borrowing privileges. Closed F,Sa and July and August.

French Cultural Center 1 Al Huquq al Faransiya, Mounira 355-3725 354-7679, and 27 Sabri Abu Alam HE 663241. Literary lectures every Monday at 6, seminars every Wednesday at 6, French cinema, drama and documentaries on a regular basis, exhibits, elementary to advanced courses in conversational and written French, university placement exams.

Geographic Society of Egypt Library 109 Kasr al Aini GC 354-5450. Founded in 1875 by Khedive Ismail the library has books mainly on Middle Eastern geography as well as manuscripts and maps dating to the 14th century. The Society maintains two libraries, one of 10,000 volumes on all subjects relating to world geography with maps and periodicals, and a second 4,000 volume collection of Dr. Suliman Huzayyia emphasizing geographical subjects. Hours are 9-2 daily; 9-4 M,W and Sa. Closed F. Borrowing privileges restricted to Society members. Information about membership application available at the library. Current research papers are published yearly in the Society's **Bulletin** available in Arabic, French and English editions.

Giza Zoo Libraries Giza Zoo, Sharia Giza GI 726233 ex217. There are two libraries at the Giza Zoo, both open to the public, neither with borrowing privileges. **Egyptian Wildlife Service Library** is a small library for research in ecology, conservation, management and wildlife protection. **Giza Zoo Library** is larger, with books on wildlife, diseases and ecology. Books are mainly English-language. 9-2 daily.

Goethe Institut: Program Department 5 Abd al Salam Aref 759877. Cultural activities, seminars, concerts, lectures, scientific and general library. Monthly brochure can be mailed if requested. 8:30-1:30 except S.
Language Department 6 al Sherifeen 393-1169/1088. German language instruction at all levels. Placement exam necessary when not at beginning level.

Goethe Institut Library 5 Abdel Salam Aref (formerly Bustan) 2nd floor, 759877. A general library of 12,000 volumes on German culture and history with 200 scientific periodicals on applied natural sciences, engineering, veterinary and human medicine. Reading room open to the general public. Borrowing privileges for members. Membership available with ID. Hours M,W,Th 11-7; T,F 9-2.

Indian Library 37 Talaat Harb 745162 745243. A reading room for information on all aspects of Indian life, history and general culture. Free to the public. Hours S to Th 9-2:30; 9- 5:30 on T, Th. Closed F,Sa.

Indonesian Cultural Center 13 Sharia Babel DO 702822 702826. An information center on Indonesian history, culture, religions, tourism, trade and development. Bimonthly bulletin of events and exhibits. The small reading room is open to the public every M and Th 10-12 and 5-7.

Institut Dominican D'Etudes Orientales Library Masnaa al Tarabish, Abbassia 925509. A Priory library of 50,000 volumes on Islamic Philosophy and History of Islamic Science. Publishes **Melange**, a review of research done by Institute scholars every two years. Institute coordinates work of scholars in Cairo. Open to any interested scholar. Hours M-F 10-2 and 4-7.

Institut Francais D'Archaeologie Orientale Library 37 al Sheikh Ali Youssef off Kasr al Aini 354-8245. Houses a library of 60,000 volumes on all aspects of history and archaeology in Egypt. Open to recognized scholars. Hours M-F 9-1 and M-Th also 2-6.

Israeli Academic Center in Cairo 92 al Nil, Apartment 33 DO 349-6232. Reference library of books and periodicals on Israeli life, literature and history written in Arabic, Hebrew and English. S-Th 9-5. Open to the public.

Italian Institute of Archaeology Library 3 Sheikh al Marsafi ZA 340-8791. Housed on the upper floor of the Italian Institute and open to responsible scholars with permission of the director. Hours M-F 10-1:30.

Japanese Cultural Center 106 Kasr al Aini, 3rd floor 355-3964. Reference library of materials on Japan. Also films on W at 6pm. Exhibits. Language courses for Egyptians. Hours S-Th 9-2.

Jesuit Center attached to the College de la Sainte Familie, 1 Bustan al Maksi (across from railroad station off Midan Ramsis). A reading reference center with books on theology and

philosophy in English, Arabic and French. Founded in 1975 and open to any student with university ID. No borrowing privileges. Hours 5-10pm, closed Th.

Library of the Central Bank of Egypt 44 Ramsis, 4th floor, 732360 742287. Founded in 1950 with materials on banking, economics and commerce in Arabic and English. 5,000 volumes in Arabic, 10,000 in English. Also periodicals and journals in English and Arabic. Open to anyone with an ID card, but borrowing restricted to bank employees. Daily 9-2.

Library of the Egyptian Museum 6 Mariette Pasha, Midan Tahrir 772352. An estimated 40,000 volumes on two floors of the Egyptian Museum open to responsible researchers by application at library office on the ground floor of the museum. Materials cover ancient Egyptian art, architecture and history. Hours T-S 10-4, F 9:30-11:15.

Library of the Ministry of Education 16 Ismail Abaza, off Kasr al Aini 354-1449. Founded in 1927, this library contains 65,000 volumes on education in European and Arabic languages. May be used by any interested researcher but non-Egyptians need an ID. Borrowing privileges only for Ministry of Education employees. 8-2:30 daily, closed F,Sa.

Library of the Ministry of Justice Midan Lazoghli 355-1176. Founded 1929. Over 90,000 volumes and periodicals in Arabic, French and English in the fields of law and social science. Restricted to judges and legal authorities. Hours: 9-2:30, closed F,Sa.

Library of the Christian Center for Music Services Middle East Council of Churches, 1127 Corniche al Nil, near TV building Maspero 747063. Begun in 1964, a full service library of materials on church music which is open to the general public. Includes books, records, tapes and sheet music in sacred, classical and popular disciplines. Also a few instruments that can be rented. Hours M-Th 3-7, F 10-1.

National Information and Documentation Center Tahrir DO 701696. Founded in 1955. Operates in all languages and specializes in science and technology. Five departments: Libraries, Scientific and Technological Information, Reprography, Editing and Publishing, Training. Publications **Arab Science Abstracts** and 18 journals. Open to any researcher with permission of the Director. 9-3 closed F,Sa.

Soviet Cultural Center 127 Tahrir GI 731416/355/035/638.

Spanish Cultural Center 20 Adli Passage 756476. A small library of 6,000 volumes in Spanish and Arabic on Spanish culture, history, geography and literature. The center organizes Spanish language classes from October-May with intensive courses during July and August. Fees for all classes. Exhibitions and lectures on various aspects of Spanish life and culture. Open 11-4 M-F.

Society for Coptic Archaeology Library 222 Ramsis, Abbassia 824252. Founded in 1934 to promote Coptic studies, the library contains over 13,000 volumes and 40 periodicals on late antiquity, Coptic language, literature, history, art, archaeology, theology and liturgy. Open to any interested person upon application. Fee: LE4. Members receive annual Bulletin of current research and information. Bulletin available to non-members for LE 12. 3:30-6 MWF.

US Agency for International Development Information Center Cairo Center, 10th floor, Kasr al Aini 354-8211 x3225. Founded in 1978, this information center is primarily a working resource on economic development in Egypt for AID projects, officers, contractors and others interested in the field. It contains 6,000 reports and documents on development in Egypt; 22,000 microfiche on USAID projects elsewhere. No borrowing privileges. ID required. 9-4:30 daily, closed F,Sa.

UNESCO Library 8 Abdel Rahman Fahmi (formerly Salamlek) GC 354-5599/3036. Collection of educational, scientific, general culture, media books on the social sciences, mostly in English and French. Open to public, but no borrowing privileges. Sa-W 9:30-3.

International Organizations with Offices in Cairo
American Mideast Educational and Training Service AMIDEAST 6 Kamel al Shennawi GC 354-1300 355-2946/3710. Founded in 1951 as a private, non-profit voluntary organization to increase international understanding, offices were opened in Cairo in 1956. It provides information on all aspects of American education and training at post-secondary school level. It maintains a comprehensive microfiche catalog of all colleges and universities in the United States with additional reference materials about graduate studies. Serves as local representative for the Educational Testing Service of Princeton NJ and registers candidates for TOEFL and GRE exams. Provides information on FMGEMS and ECFMG exams for medical internships and residences. Open to the general public. Hours: 8:30-3, S-Th.

American Research Center in Egypt (ARCE) 2 Midan Kasr al Dubara GC 355-3052 354-8239, and The Kevorkian Center, New York University, 50 Washington Square South, New York, NY. Established to give American scholars specializing in ancient, medieval and modern Egypt a permanent archaeological and research base in Cairo. Subsidized by private support. Library for members or by permission of director. Sponsors lecture series and The Archaeology Club. Fellows live on houseboat "al Fustat". Supports up to 20 fellows yearly on topics covering humanities, social sciences, art and archaeology. Applications by November each year. Individuals may join ARCE. Membership entitles one to a quarterly newsletter and the yearly **Journal of the American Research Center in Egypt** as well as access to the library.

Ford Foundation 1 Osiris, 7th floor, GC 355-2121 354-4450/9635 and 320 E 43rd Street, New York. A regional office for grant-making in Egypt, Sudan, Jordan, West Bank and Gaza, Lebanon, North Yemen, Syria, and Tunisia. The Foundation is presently interested in projects in agricultural development, human rights, child survival, international relations, income and employment generation, community development and preservation of traditions. It responds to local initiatives from individuals, institutions or governments. The Foundation welcomes ideas for grants in these fields of interest. A report of its work is available upon request. A small reading room with books and periodicals on these topics is open to the public 8-3 daily except F, Sa. No borrowing privileges.

Fulbright Commission 1081 Corniche al Nil 354-4799/8679. The office administers exchange of scholars between Egypt and the US through a variety of programs. The Fulbright Commission serves both the US and Egyptian academic communities with an educational and cultural exchange. The core program oversees an exchange of post-doctoral professors for lectures or research in all fields. The commission administers other educational and cultural exchange programs: The Hubert H. Humphrey North-South Fellowship Program, Eisenhower Fellowships, Fulbright-Hays Foreign Curriculum Consultant Program, Operation Crossroads Africa, Salzburg Seminar, American University Women Fellowships, Edward S. Mason Fellowships, and Rockefeller Foundation Fellowships. Americans must apply through the Council for International Exchange of Scholars, 11 Dupont Circle, NW Washington DC 20036. Egyptians must apply through the Fulbright Commission, address above. Apply to the commission office for more information. 8:30-4, except F,Sa.

International Center for Agricultural Research in the Dry Areas (ICARDA) 15G Radwan Ibn al Tahib, eleventh floor, PO Box 2416 GI 723564 724358 728099. One of 13 international centers funded by a consortium of governments and private American foundations. This office supports applied agricultural research in the Nile valley including Egypt, the Sudan and Ethiopia. Aids Egyptian scientists, and workers plan and execute research in improving the quality and productivity of fava beans. Reports on current research are published in annual bulletin. Open to the public. Hours: 8-3 S-Th.

International Development Research Center, Canada (IDRC) 4 Pakistan GI 738760 735419 738926. A regional office of a Canadian government organization which funds research projects of an applied nature: agriculture, food utilization, forestry science, social science, health science, information science and engineering and earth science. Founded in 1971, the office opened in Cairo in 1977. The Cairo office supervises projects from Pakistan to Morocco. The center accepts proposals from institutions only. Publishes a quarterly newsletter in French and English and an annual journal in Arabic.

Middle East Foundation 4 Road 105 2nd floor MA 350-8604. Founded in 1976, the Cairo office is a branch of a Cyprus-based foundation which publishes general educational materials for young people. Publishes a monthly magazine **Huwa wi Heya** focusing on family or social relations.

Agencies, Institutes and Centers
Academy of the Arabic Language 15 Aziz Abaza ZA 340-5026/5931. Founded in 1932 to incorporate new scientific and technical terms into Arabic, to watch over Arabic linguistic development and to maintain and revive the Arabic heritage in all fields. Composed of 40 members, elected for life for their outstanding professional accomplishments. Specialized committees meet weekly to conduct ongoing research. Annual meeting for presentation and discussion of current materials, which are subsequently published in their **Annual Journal** in Arabic. Library.

Academy of Scientific Research and Technology 101 Kasr al Aini 355-1047. Founded in 1971, this government agency oversees Egypt's science and technology. It initiates and coordinates scientific research aimed at socio-economic development, informs and educates the public about scientific and technological systems and helps develop appropriate management to integrate new research and achievements within the society. It works through several centers: **Central Metallurgical Research and Development Institute; Institute of Astronomy and Geophysics; Institute of Oceanography and Fisheries; National Information and Documentation Center; National Institute for Standards; National Research Center; Petroleum Research Center; Remote Sensing Center;** and the **Theodore Bilharz Research Institute.** Individuals must apply at the various centers for permission to do research. Publication: **Research Reports.** Hours 8-3, closed F-Sa.

Agricultural Research Center Ministry of Agriculture. DO. Affiliated institutions: **Agricultural Economy Research Institute** GI; **Agricultural Guidance Research Institute** Nadi al Seyd DO; **Animal Health Research Institute** Nadi al Seyd DO; **Animal Production Research Institute** Nadi al Seyd DO; **Central Laboratory for Design and Statistical Analysis Research** Cairo University GI; **Cotton Research Institute** Cairo University GI; **Desert Research Institute** Mataria; **Field Crops Research Institute** Cairo University GI; **General Department of Agricultural Research Stations,** Cairo University GI; **Horticultural Research Institute** Cairo University GI. Researchers must apply at the various centers for permission to do research.

Arab Council for Childhood and Development 7 Midan Misaha DO. Founded in 1987 and funded by Arab governments to conduct projects to support development of children in all Arab countries, this group works with educational and vocational training, literacy, and the handicapped.

Cairo Demographic Center 2 Libnan MO 346-2002/6373. An inter-regional center affiliated with Cairo University which trains demographers from Egypt, Africa, Arab countries and Asia through to PhD level to conduct demographic studies in their own nations with local data. Activities conducted in English or Arabic. Publishes an annual Newsletter, monographs, occasional papers, and a working paper series. 9-5 except F.

Center for Restoration and Records of Egypt's Artistic Past 3 Adel Abu Bakr ZA 340-7045. Founded in 1956 this center serves as a reference for artistic information on all ages of Egyptian arts. Has a large collection of books for sale in English and Arabic about museums, centers, artists, etc. 9-2:30. Closed F,Sa.

Central Metallurgical Research and Development Institute al Tabbin Helwan 790775. Founded 1972. Affiliated with the Academy of Scientific Research and Technology. Research in extractive metallurgy, ore beneficiation, technical services, metal forming and working. Publishes research reports. Hours 9-3 except F,Sa.

Desert Development Center The American University in Cairo 113 Kasr al Aini 354-2964 ex5330. Research on economically viable agriculture energy and community development on arid lands. Maintains two sites: Sadat City and South Tahrir. Publishes a newsletter which reports on research. Small library in English and Arabic on desert development topics.

Egyptian Authority of Folkdance and Music 27 Abdel Khalek Sarwat 347-7457. Ministry of Culture organization mandated to supervise the National Folklore Troupe, the Reda Troupe, Youth Music and National Circus.

Egyptian Authority for Mass Culture Bahr al Aazam GI 725153 728004. Mandated to teach Egyptian and Arab culture to the people. Responsible for three orchestras, five chorus and choral groups, and six folkloric troupes. Theatres under its supervision are the Floating Theatre, the Balloon Theatre, Al Samer Theatre and Children's Theatre. Supervises October, July and Ramadan cultural festivals.

Egyptian Authority for Theatre and Music 27 Abdel Khalek Sarwat 393-6091 392-6235. Responsible for eight theatres in Cairo, three in Alexandria, and seven acting groups. Arranges all schedules, performances, budgets and advertising.

Egyptian Geological Survey and Mining Authority 3 Salah Salem, Abbassia 829662. Founded in 1896, this government agency deals with geology and mining in Egypt. It grants mineral exploration and exploitation rights and does surveys and maps on a regional basis. It supervises the Geological Museum. Its **Geological Information Center** contains 30,000 books and materials on geology and mining in Egypt. Open to the public. Publishes research reports in English. Hours 8-3, closed F,Sa.

Egyptian Petroleum Research Institute Medinat Nasr 607433. Founded in 1976. Affiliated with Academy of Scientific Research and Technology. Deals with all aspects of petroleum and renewable energy resources issues. Publishes reports. Hours 8-3, closed F,Sa.

Egyptian Wildlife Service Giza Zoo, Sharia Giza GI 726233. Established by the Ministry of Agriculture under the directorship of the Giza Zoo. This service develops and manages existing protectorates in Omayad, Gebel Elba, St. Catherine's, Lake Bardawil and Ras Mohammed. It drafts proposals for laws of preservation and protection, designs and implements public awareness programs, surveys Egyptian wildlife, both flora and fauna. Rangers recruited from the Veterinary College.

Folklore Center 18 Bursa al Adima, near Midan Tawfikia, 3rd floor, 752460. A government center for all Egyptian folk materials: exhibits of dress, crafts and skills, musical instruments, cosmetics and the environment. Contains a small reference library of folkloric, humanistic books and archives of tapes, films, photographs. An ID and specific study topic necessary for use of reference materials. Publishes **Journal of Folklore.** Hours 10-1. Closed F.

Hydraulics and Sediment Research Institute Delta Barrage. Founded in 1949 for research on current meters, pumping stations, hydraulic structures, hydrographic surveys, water control and management. Publications: **Technical Report.**

Institute of Arab Music 22 Ramsis 743373. Founded in the early 1960s, this government agency is a small information center of tapes, documents and records about music and musicians in the Egyptian National Theatre. Part of the **National Center for Theatre and**

Music, it publishes an occasional newsletter with information about the national theatre and music in Egypt. Materials, mostly in Arabic, available to any serious researcher. 6-9pm daily.

Institute of Astronomy and Geophysics Helwan 782683. Founded in 1903 for research in astronomy, geomagnetic and seismic phenomena, this institute is affiliated with the Academy of Scientific Research and Technology. Includes **Helwan Observatory; Kottamia Observatory; Misallat geomagnetic observatory; Helwan, Aswan, Matruh seismic stations; satellite tracking stations at Helwan and Abu Simbel.** Library of 10,600 volumes. Publication: **Helwan Observatory Bulletin.**

Middle Eastern Regional Radioisotope Center for the Arab Countries Sharia Malaeb al Bamaa DO 700569. Provides training on radioisotopes in medical, agricultural and industrial fields. Conducts research in hydrology, tropical diseases and fertilizers. Publications: **Annual Report, Bulletin.**

National Center for Criminal Social Research Midan Ibn Khaldun, Imbaba 347-3655 346-1440.

National Center for Educational Research, Ministry of Education Building 12 Falaki 355-2357/1945. Co-ordinates educational policy among various institutes both national and international. Conducts educational research throughout Egypt and coordinates educational policy among various national and international institutes. Current projects include compiling national data on curriculum changes in both general and technical education at pre-university levels. Publications: **Contemporary Trends in Education, Educational Information Bulletin,** both in Arabic; and biannual **Report About Education in Egypt** for UNESCO in English and Arabic. 9-2 daily, closed F.

National Institute of Oceanography and Fisheries 101 Kasr Al Aini, 14th floor 355-1381. Founded in 1931 to conduct research on oceanography, the environment and fisheries, the Institute has stations at Alexandria, Hurghada on the Red Sea, and an inland station at the Barrages. Research includes fish culture, fisheries, physical, chemical and biological oceanography. Affiliated with the Academy of Scientific Research and Technology. The Institute of Inland Fish Culture 10 Hasan Sabri ZA 340-1616 at the Aquarium is a branch. 8-3:30 daily, closed F,Sa. The Aquarium is open 8-3 daily. Publication: **Bulletin.**

National Institute for Standards Sharia Tahrir DO 701835. Affiliated with the Academy of Scientific Research and Technology. Researches in meteorology; has custody of and maintains the national standards for physical measurements through its Scientific Instrument Center. This institute designs, develops and manufactures special standards devices requested by research institutions and universities.

National Research Center Sharia Tahrir DO 701010. Founded in 1956, this center does research in pure and applied sciences in agriculture, the environment, engineering, biology, health, energy and natural resources. Publishes a research bulletin four times a year. Hours 9-3, closed F,Sa.

Nutrition Research Institute 16 Kasr al Aini 2nd floor 847476. Founded in 1955, the Institute does academic and applied research on foods and human nutrition in both urban and rural environments. It serves as a consultant to other government institutions and international agencies. Publishes occasional research bulletins. Small library open to any interested researcher. 8-2 except F.

Public Health Laboratories, Ministry of Public Health 19 Sheikh Rihan 355-0096 354-7371/ 7376. Founded in 1885 these labs, under the Ministry of Health, provide services in bacteriology, toxicology and chemistry for the supervision of food control, water, sewage and waste, and epidemiological surveys in Egypt. Hours 8:30-3:30, Th 8:30-1:30, closed F. Publishes a research bulletin. A small library is on the premises for lab personnel only. No public access.

The Press Center Radio and TV Building, Corniche al Nil, Maspero 756884. Coordinates all foreign press personnel in Egypt through three sections, one for permanent correspondents, another for visiting correspondents, and a third for record-keeping. Issues press cards, facilitates access to places and people, arranges press meetings. Maintains 48 Press Information Offices throughout the world. Hours 9am-10pm daily.

Remote Sensing Center 101 Kasr al Aini 355-7110. Founded 1972. Affiliated with Academy of Scientific Research and Technology. Conducts basic research in remote sensing and its applications in all scientific fields for Egypt, various regional governments and private companies. Provides short-term training in remote sensing for specialists in geology, engineering, agriculture, etc. Current projects include industrial pollution, water surfaces, and urban planning. Research reports published in Arabic and English. Hours 9-3.

Research Institute for Tropical Medicine 10 Kasr al Aini 842494. Founded in 1902. Includes clinical parasitology, helminthology, entomology, biochemistry, physiology and pharmacology, radiology, radiotherapy and radioisotopes, bacteriology, pathology, haematology, endoscopy, serology, urology, immunology, malacology, animal house and field research. Library of 4,000 volumes. Temporarily closed for refurbishment.

Social Research Center The American University in Cairo 113 Kasr al Aini 354-2964 ex6940. Established in 1953, this center was the first in Egypt and the Middle East to train and support workers in social science research methods. It conducts broad academic research to create understanding of how changing technologies and socio-economic development affect the individual, the family and the community. The center consults and collaborates with government ministries, non-governmental institutions and other universities to produce and integrate its research into public policy and everyday life in Egypt, the Middle East and Africa.

State Information Service 22 Talaat Harb 974111 756821 756884. The State Information Service is part of the Ministry of Information, and is responsible for informing Egyptians about publications, cinema, and audio-visuals. It prints and translates all political speeches into English, French, Arabic, and German, and issues 2 magazines: **Al Mustaqbal** (The Future) and **Magallit al Gara'ed al Alamiyya** (The Magazine of International Newspapers), which compile translations of Middle Eastern articles from papers worldwide. In addition it receives press attache reports from the world and passes them on to the appropriate government officials. Governs the Press Center and all foreign press representatives in Egypt.

Theodor Bilharz Research Institute Warrak al Hadr, Imbaba 341-7181 340-4381/5633. Founded in 1979 and affiliated with the Academy of Scientific Research and Technology, this regional center trains workers from the Arab world and Africa to do research in schistosomiasis (bilharziasis) and endemic parsitological diseases. It works with field studies in the lab and in clinics. Publishes research reports and the **Journal of Bilharziasis**, in English. Currently expanding a small working library into a large information center which will be open to the public. Hours 8-3, closed F,Sa.

Telecommunications Training and Research Institute Madinet Nasr. 603623 604370 839999. Research into all subjects related to telecommunications.

United States Agencies in Egypt
Library of Congress 20 Gamal al Din Abu al Mahasin GC 354-2167 355-3871. Collects Egyptian publications for the Library of Congress and other research libraries in the US and elsewhere, and procures current materials regardless of language from all Arabic-speaking countries. Publishes a bimonthly accessions list on the Middle East sent to over 700 libraries worldwide.

Naval Medical Research Unit-3 (NAMRU-3) Salah Salem, Abbassia 355-7371 ex229. This US Naval unit is doing research into schistosomaisis and other diseases.

USAID see Business

United Nations Agencies in Egypt
Food and Agricultural Organization of the United Nations The General Cooperative Society Building for Agrarian Reform, Sharia Wizaret al Ziraa, next to Agricultural Museum, DO 702789 705182/029. At Egyptian governmental request the FAO works within the Ministry of Agriculture to find and promote improved methods of agricultural production throughout Egypt. Current projects include work to control brucellosis, develop improved irrigation and sanitation methods, and promote better ways to preserve and conserve foods. Th 8-3, Sa 9-2.

International Civil Aviation Organization 16 Hasan Sabri ZA 340-1463/1532 341-8163. Established as a UN-affiliated regional office in 1950, this organization executes the provisions of the 1944 Chicago convention on International Civil Aviation. It coordinates the implementation of regional air navigation plans, holds meetings to educate and inform on newest procedures on telecommunications, meteorology and air traffic control. Further, it serves as a liaison between civil and military aviation in the Arab countries and monitors their progress in maintaining up-to-date approved aviation procedures. M-F 7:30-2:30.

United Nations Children's Fund (UNICEF) 8 Adnan Omar Sedki DO 701766 710578 700815. The Fund carries out UNICEF's work for children in Egypt in child development, protection and survival, and in women's development through its educational, informational, medical and skills training programs. S-Th, 8-3.

United Nations Development Programme 29 Taha Hussein ZA 341-5577 /2244 340-6476. Governs all UN development programs in Egypt through its Fund for Population activities and World Food Program.

United Nations Education, Science, Culture Organization (UNESCO) 8 Abdel Rahman Fahmi (formerly Salamlek) GC 354-3036/5599. Liaison office for Egypt. Holds seminars and meetings on education, science and culture as they apply to local conditions and needs.

United Nations High Commission for Refugees 8 Dar al Shifa GC 354-0393. Office established in 1954, deals with education and resettlement in a third country of all refugees except Palestinians.

United Nations Information Center 1 Osiris GC 355-0682. Established in 1949 to inform the public of all UN decisions and activities and to report to the UN the official Egyptian government reaction to these decisions and activities.

United Nations International Labor Organization 9 Taha Hussein ZA 340-0123 341-9290/ 9961. A regional office for Egypt and the Sudan, this agency provides technical cooperation for development of human resources in statistics, planning, vocational training and rehabilitation, employment, occupational health and social legislation. Houses a small library of ILO materials with general borrowing privileges by application at the desk.

United Nations Relief and Works Agency for Palestine Refugees (UNRWA) 2 Dar al Shifa GC 354-8502/4. Provides liaison between Palestinian refugees in the East and West Banks, Gaza, Jordan, Lebanon and Syria with UN agencies, the Egyptian government and the embassies of other governments in Cairo.

United Nations Truce Supervision Organization, Observer Group, Egypt 18 al Thawra HE 662456 665310. Maintains a UN observer presence in Egypt with five outposts in Sinai and one in Ismailia. Also acts as a UN liaison between governments. M-F 7-2.

World Health Organization 29 Taha Hussein ZA 341-2156/2244. The Cairo office is a liaison between the WHO regional office in Alexandria (Sharia Sultan Abdel Aziz 483-9240/0090) and government offices and embassies in Cairo. It works through institutions to further educational, informational, medical and preventative programs in fighting disease, with special attention to immunization and AIDS. S-Th 7:30-2:30.

INTERNATIONAL ORGANIZATIONS WITH MIDDLE EAST INTERESTS

Aga Khan Program for Islamic Architecture of Harvard University and the Massachusetts Institute of Technology. Room 10-390, Massachusetts Institute of Technology, 77 Massachusetts Avenue, Cambridge, MA 02139. 617-253-1400. Provides professorships, visiting

appointments, graduate study, financial aid, travel grants, conferences, seminars, publications and awards.

American Arab Anti-Discrimination Committee 1129 20th Street, NW Washington DC 20036. 202-293-5900. Newly established. Plans newsletter, seminars, lectures and a library.

American Council for the Study of Islamic Societies. 138 Tolentine Hall, Villanova University, Villanova, Pennsylvania 19085. 215-645-4738. Annual meeting. Membership: $25.

Center for Christian-Moslem Relations Seloy Oak College, Birmingham, England. Extensive library.

Dumbarton Oaks (Harvard University)—Center for Byzantine Studies 1703 32nd Street, NW Washington DC 20007. 202-342-3240.

Institute of Christian Oriental Research ICOR 620 Michigan Avenue NE Washington DC 20017. 202-635-5088. Finest collection in the United States on Coptic studies. Also material on Arabic, Syriac and Hebrew. Library. Permission necessary in advance.

Institute of Muslim Minority Affairs 46 George Street London WIP 1FJ UK.

Islamic Center Library 2551 Massachusetts Avenue, NW Washington DC 20008. 202-332-3451. Majority of collection in Arabic. 10-4 daily.

Middle East Association 33 Bury Street, St James's, London SW1Y 6AX.

The Middle East Institute 1761 N Street NW Washington, DC 20036. Annual meeting. Publication: **The Middle East Journal.** Membership regular $40, student $30.

Middle East Studies Association MESA Department of Oriental Studies, University of Arizona, Tucson, AZ 85721. 602-621-5850. Founded in 1966 to promote high standards of scholarship and instruction in Middle East Studies, to facilitate communication and foster cooperation. Annual meeting each November in North America. Publications: **International Journal of Middle East Studies** (quarterly); **MESA Bulletin** (semiannual); **MESA Newsletter** (thrice yearly); **Roster of Members** (biannual) and **Directory of Graduate and Undergraduate Programs and Courses in Middle East Studies** (biannual). Membership: full/associate $50; student/retired, $25; joint $60; institutional $500.

National Council on US-Arab Relations 1625 Eye Street NW Suite 904 Washington DC 20006. 202-293-0810. Telex 989927 NCUSAR WASH. Provides speakers, bureau, teacher training workshops, public education grants, and Arab world study tours. Sponsors The Joseph J. Malone Faculty Fellows Program in Arab and Islamic Studies and The Malcolm H. Kerr High School Scholars Program in Arab and Islamic Studies.

Project of Translation from Arabic PROTA 47 Homer Avenue Cambridge MA 02138. 617-876-6877 and 34 Hereford Square London SW7 England (01) 370 3159. A non-profit project dedicated to the dissemination of Arabic culture and literature abroad. Purpose is to make available in English some of the best contributions of the Arab creative talent in the domains of fiction, poetry, drama, folklore, medieval and modern. Catalog available.

LOCAL SCHOLARLY CLUBS AND ORGANIZATIONS

Egyptian Association for Archives, Librarianship and Information Sciences Faculty of Arts, University of Cairo DO. Information available through the Library Science Department of Cairo University 728532/811/623. Founded in 1986, this organization consists of a professional group of librarians. Holds lectures and monthly meetings.

Egyptian Association for Psychological Studies 1 Osiris GC. Associated with the Faculty of Education, Ain Shams University, Abbassia. Founded in 1948. Meetings first Thursday of the month. Publication: **Yearbook of Psychology.**

Egyptian Botanical Society 1 Osiris GC. Organizes conferences, lectures and field trips for collecting, preserving and identifying plants. Publication: **Egyptian Journal of Botany.**

Egyptian Geographical Society 109 Kasr al Aini, at Ministry of Public Works, 354-5450. Founded in 1875, reorganized in 1917. Library with manuscripts and maps dating to the fourteenth century. Membership by formal application to library. Publishes bulletin of current research. 9-2 daily; 9-4 M,W,Sa; closed F.

Egyptian Medical Association 42 Kasr al Aini 354-3406 GC. Founded in 1919, this professional medical organization is open to any qualified doctor in Egypt. The association organizes discussions, meetings and conferences for further professional growth. Annual membership LE10. Monthly **Journal** in Arabic and English.

Egyptian Orthopedic Association 42 Kasr al Aini GC 354-3406. Founded in 1948 as a professional organization for orthopedic doctors. Publication: **Egyptian Orthopedic Journal.**

Egyptian School Libraries Association 35 Galaa 753001. Founded in 1968 with special focus on school libraries. Open to any library worker. Publishes **Sahifat al Maktaba** in Arabic. Offices open Sa-M 1-8 and W 5-8.

Egyptian Society for Conservation of Natural Resources Giza Zoo, Sharia Giza GI 726233. Collects information on wildlife. Holds seminars (in Arabic) to discuss current research and experiences related to conservation. Meetings irregular. Membership notified by post. Publishes annual **Egyptian Journal of Wildlife and Natural Resources** in English. For membership contact Mr. Abdel Gani 726233. Fee LE5.

Egyptian Society of Engineers 28 Ramsis 740488. Founded 1920, this professional organization is open to any qualified engineer in Egypt. It organizes weekly meetings on topics of interest. Publishes the quarterly **Journal of the Egyptian Society of Engineers** in English and Arabic. Houses a small library of books and journals in English for reference. For members only. Hours 9-1 and 5-8, closed F.

Egyptian Society of International Law 16 Ramsis 743162. Founded in 1945 to promote the study of international law and to work for the establishment of international relations based on law and justice. A small reference library in English, French and Arabic. Publication: **Revue Egyptienne de Droit International.** Hours 10-7, Th 10-1, closed F.

Egyptian Society of Political Economy, Statistics and Legislation. 16 Ramsis PO Box 732 750797. Founded in 1909, this organization holds an annual meeting open to anyone working in political economics or statistical work. Houses a small library of journals open to any post-graduate researcher. Publishes a quarterly **Journal de l'Egypte Contemporaine.** Hours 10-5, closed F.

Entomological Society of Egypt 14 Ramsis PO Box 430. Founded 1907, this society is the largest in the Middle East. Houses an old, but well-preserved, collection of birds, resident and migrant in Egypt, as well as an outstanding insect collection. Library. Publications include an annual **Bulletin** in English, an economic series and **Memoires**, a journal of special topics. 9-1 and 5-8 Th 9-3:30, closed F.

Institut d'Egypte 13 Sheikh Rihan at corner of Kasr al Aini 354-1504. Founded 1798 by Napoleon, this institute studies literary, artistic and scientific matters related to Egypt. Library of 15,000 volumes and 1,600 periodicals. Holds monthly meetings. Membership information available. Publications: **Bulletin, Memoires.** 9-12, Closed F, S.

Ophthalmological Society of Egypt Dar al Hekma 42 Kasr al Aini 354-1538. A professional organization for ophthalmological doctors in Egypt, founded in 1902. Publication: **Annual Bulletin.**

Zoological Society of Egypt Giza Zoo, Sharia Giza GI 726233. Founded in 1927, this is a local branch of the international Zoological Society. Aims to promote zoological studies, field courses and lectures. No set meetings, members are notified by post. Maintains a small library of 2,500 volumes, open to the public from 9-2 daily. Publishes a yearly bulletin **The Zoological Society of Egypt Bulletin.** For membership contact Mr. Abdel Gani at 726233. Membership fee LE5.

PUBLISHING

Egypt is the largest publisher of Arabic books in the world with distribution throughout most of the Arabic speaking countries. Modern publishing began in 1798 when Napoleon Bonaparte brought the first printing presses to Egypt.

Publishing Houses
Academic Bookshop and Publisher 121 Sharia Tahrir DO 348-5282. Publishes Arabic and English language textbooks for the Arab world. Import and Export.

Al-Ahram Sharia Galaa 758333 745666 755500. Publishes, prints and distributes Arabic and English language titles. Major foreign magazine and newspaper importer. Commercial printer.

Akhbar al-Youm 6 al Sahafa, Bulak 758899 748877. Publishes, prints and distributes two newspapers, a magazine, and trade and scholarly books in Arabic.

The American University in Cairo Press 113 Kasr al Aini 354-2964 ex6895. Publisher of English-language scholarly and trade books with Egyptian interest. Strengths in social sciences, women's studies and guide books. Commercial printing.

Anglo Egyptian Bookstore 165 Mohammed Farid 914337/391. Publishes Arabic and English language textbooks and trade books.

Boraie and Geday 34 Gamal Salem DO 348-2503. Publishes **Cairoscope**, a monthly guide to Cairo.

Dar al Bayader 35 Geziret al Arab MO 344-4330. Publishes books and works of art in English and Arabic with emphasis on the Middle East, Arab-Israeli affairs, and children's books.

Dar al Hilal 16 Mohamad Ezz al Arab off Kasr al Aini 362-3450. Publishes weekly and monthly magazines in Arabic including medical magazines and a large selection of children's magazines. Publishes Arabic-language books including contemporary Egyptian literature.

Dar al Maaref 1119 Corniche al Nil Maspero 777077. Publishes Arabic books and distributes Arabic and imported English language trade and textbooks.

Dar Nahda Misr 18 Kamel Sedki, Faggala 908895 903395. Publishes English and Arabic language textbooks and cultural books.

Dar al Shaab Printing House 92 Kasr al Aini 355-1810 354-3800. Prints books, magazines and paper products in Arabic.

Dar al Shorok 16 Gawad Husny 774814 774578. Publishes, prints and distributes Arabic-language Islamic heritage books. Distributor for all BBC English-language publications. Commercial printer.

Dar al Tahrir for Printing and Publishing 24 Zakaria Ahmed and Emad al Din 751511 754133. Publishes the three newspapers Al Gomhouria in Arabic, Le Progres Egyptien in French and The Egyptian Gazette in English.

General Egyptian Book Organization Corniche al Nil Bulak 775371 775694. The official government publishing organization. Publishes and imports books in English, French, German and Arabic in all areas of interest. Organizes the Cairo International Book Fair and regional exhibits throughout the country. Supervises the Dar al Kutub and libraries throughout the country.

Al Helal Printing and Publishing 222 al Higaz HE 245-8131/2, and for printing services 243-1455. Publishes a variety of Arabic and English-language trade and scholarly books. Commercial printer.

International House for Publishing and Distribution 19 Ahmed Rihan Tork HE 243-4908. Publishes Arabic-language titles and translations of McGraw-Hill textbooks.

Jacaranda Press A division of PBS, Osiris Building, Latin America GC 355-1913. Publishes English, French and German language tourist books and maps.

Lehnert and Landrock 44 Sherif 392-7506 394-5324. Publishes English and German language books, maps, post cards and old photos. Agent of Burda magazine.

Madbouli 6 Talaat Harb 756421. Publishes general Arabic-language books.

Middle East Books and Information Company MEBIC 3 Qassim, Taraboulsi Building DO 348-5320. Middle East agent for international publishers, wholesaler, distributor, databanks, translations.

Moharrem Press 3 Kasr al Nil 392-1588/1667, Corniche al Nil 849990, and in Alexandria, Nozha 420-8516. Produces boxes and tapes and is the only press in the Middle East to produce playing cards.

Moustafa al Babl al Halabi and Sons 2 Tarabish Factory, al Zaher, and 11 Tablita, al Azhar. Publishes, prints and distributes old religious and cultural books and Korans. Exports to Arab world.

The Palm Press 27 Hassan Assem (corner of Brazil) ZA 340-9350. English-language trade and touristic publications.

Rayan Publishing House 177 al Ahram GI 854687 852011 867780. Publishes, prints and distributes Arabic-language religious and textbooks, including Korans in French/Arabic.

Sphinx Bookshop and Publishing House 3 Sharabi 744616. Publishes Arabic-language textbooks and children's books. Distributor of Longman International titles in Egypt.

Al Wa'fa Publishing 3 Hedai'a off Gumhuria MA. Publishes and exports Arabic-language books. Distributes and imports English-language books.

Booksellers in Egypt
Foreign newspapers, magazines and periodicals may be purchased from most bookshops and kiosks downtown. Secondhand books are sold in open air bookstalls in the Ezbekia and Midan Opera area of downtown. Some rare treasures are still to be found. Other pavement vendors can be found on Talaat Harb near Groppi's. Most bookstores close on Sunday.

Academic Bookshop 121 Sharia Tahrir DO 348-5282. French, English and Arabic language general art and science, textbooks, reference, travel and children's books.

Al Ahram Bookstores Al Ahram has 11 bookstores in Cairo and an additional 8 throughout Egypt. They specialize in imported books in various languages, AUC Press titles and Al Ahram publications in English and Arabic. They carry a wide variety of imported English and French language magazines and newspapers. 165 Mohamed Farid 924499; Ain Shams University; Cairo Sheraton Hotel 988000; Cairo International Airport, Terminal I; Cairo Meridien Hotel 845444; Inter Continental Hotel 355-1717/7171; Nile Hilton Hotel 776893; Ramsis Hilton Hotel Annex 744400; Movenpick Hotel, Airport Road 664242; The Maadi Club; City of Iron and Steel Helwan; Sharia al Tayaran, MN.

Al Aila al Gedida 290-1768 and 1 Midan Roxi 258-5246 HE. English and French language and Islamic heritage books, cards and stationery.

Al Akhbar Bookshop Three locations: 6 Sahafa, Bahary Building, 2nd floor; 2 Midan Tahrir 758888/748888, and 3 Mokattam. Sells own publications plus language tapes, AUC Press publications and Arabic books.

The American University in Cairo Bookstore 113 Sharia Kasr al Aini, Main Campus 354-2964 ex5377. Complete line of AUC Press publications, general, trade, and scholarly books, and stationery.

Anglo Egyptian Bookstore 165 Mohammed Farid 914337/391. Specializes in English-language books and their own publications. Imports and distributes textbooks.

Al Arab Bookshop 28 Faggala 908025. Agent of Library of Congress in the Middle East for Arabic books. Carries import, export, out-of-print books, monographs and old magazines in English and Arabic.

Dar al Arabia lil Nashr wal Tawzia 17 Nadi al Seyd DO 718006. Arabic books on agriculture.

Dar al Bayader 35 Geziret al Arab MO 344-4330. Arab and Palestinian publications. Stationery, history, poetry and children's books in Arabic.

Dar al Kitab al Masri wal Lebnani 33 Kasr al Nil, Wahba Building 1st floor. 744657 944168. General Arabic books.

Dar al Maaref 27 Abdel Khalek Sarwat 756123. General English, Arabic, French, German and own publications; 9 Kamal Sedki, Faggala 901905, Arabic; 105 Sharia Shubra, Shubra, Arabic; Midan Sayeda Zeinab 933813, Arabic.

Dar Al Shorouk 2 Sharia Boursa, off Kasr al Nil 758071. Textbooks, English and French trade and children's books.

Dar al Sakafa al Mesihia Bookshop 51 Gumhuria 902667; 138A Teraa al Bulakia, Shoubra 770473, and 18 Cleopatra HE. Christian literature in Arabic. Old and out-of-print Arabic books.

Dar al Toras 22 Gumhuria 914223. Islamic heritage books.

Dar al Torath al Islami 12 Ismail Abaza 914223. Arabic and Islamic heritage books.

Eagle Book Shop 87 Road 9 MA 352-9450. Imported and local English and French language books, films, gifts and stationery.

Everyman's Bookshop 12 Baghdad HE 660129. English and French language books, children's books, gifts.

Garden City Bookshop next to Shepheard's Hotel on Corniche al Nil. Travel books on Egypt.

General Egyptian Book Organization Corniche al Nil Bulak 77569 775371 775694; 24 Abdel Khalek Sarwat 759612; 5 Orabi, Tawfikia 740075; 19 26th of July 748431 (English language only); 1 Murad, Midan Giza 721311 (Arabic only); 36 Sherif 759612; 22 Gumhuria 914223; Midan al Hussein 913447. Large selection of imported and domestic books in general reading.

International House for Publishing and Distribution Book Store 38 al Ahram Roxi HE 258-2887. Arabic and English language general and textbooks.

International Language Bookshop Mahmoud Azmi MO 347-4522 344-0997. English-language textbooks, GCE books, and computer books.

International Publication Ltd 95 Road 9 MA 351-6244. Importer of English, French and Arabic books. Christian literature, children's books, posters and cards. Agent for Simpkin Splendor of Egypt Publications.

Isis 88 Road 9 MA 350-6034. Trade and gifts.

Lehnert and Landrock Bookshop 44 Sherif 392-7606 393-5324. German and English language textbooks, scientific and trade books, maps, old postcards and photos, stationery. Operates the bookstore in the Egyptian Museum.

Librairie Ali Masoud 159 26th July ZA 340-1542, and 19 al Mahrousa MO. Fashion magazines, French, English and Arabic language general books.

Librairie Franco-Egyptienne Unipress formerly Hachette. 45 Champollion 757782 779275 and 14 Osman ibn Affan HE 674830. French texts and scientific books and dictionaries.

Livres de France 36 Kasr al Nil 393-5512. French literature, orientalism and lithographs. Exclusive English-language acquisitions for Library of Congress.

Madbouli 6 Talaat Harb 756421. General contemporary Arabic, English, French and German publications.

Al Mahabba Sharia Baasa, Shoubra 777448. Coptic, Christian and children's books, posters, icons and church equipment.

Mengozzi Bookshop 19 26th July 750955. Italian and English language books and magazines.

Mohammed Ali Subeih Midan al Hussein 906580. Old and out-of-print Arabic books.

Mustafa al Babi al Halabi 5 Haret Afifi, behind Wekalet al Ghuri; 2 Ittaraza and 2 Midan Masnaa Tarabish, Darrasa 929279/379. The first bookshop in Cairo. Korans in various languages including Chinese. Old and out-of-print Arabic books. Also printer and binder. Closed Friday.

Al Nahda al Masria 9 Adli 391-0994. Arabic general and textbooks, old and out-of-print Arabic and English language books.

Nile Christian Bookshop 8 Alfi 741028. English and Arabic language Christian literature.

The Orientalist 15 Kasr al Nil 926666. Old and rare western language books, prints, lithographs and postcards about Egypt.

Osor's Book Store 50 Kasr al Nil 391-1489. Scientific and children's books, Spanish books.

Oxford 5 Ibrahim al Lakkani, Roxy HE 259-6776. General books in various languages, but mostly in English.

Palace Bookshop 2 Baghdad HE 665807. English and French language novels, children's books, cards and gifts. Distributor for Tin Tin children's magazine in English and French.

Papasian 9 Adli. Music books.

Reader's Corner 33 Abdel Khalek Sarwat 748801, and Nile Hilton 750666 740777. General English-language publications. Large collection of David Roberts prints.

Romanceia corner of Ismail Mohammed and Shagaret al Dorr ZA. General English language books.

Shady 29 Abdel Khalek Sarwat 748168, and 26th July ZA. General Arabic and English language books. Large collection of secondhand books.

Shark Bookshop Talaat Harb, and Brazil, ZA. English translations of Russian classics and technical books, excellent illustrated children's books.

Sheikh Kharboush corner of Port Said and Maglis al Umma. Old and out-of-print Arabic books.

Al Shorouk Bookshop Midan Talaat Harb 393-8071. Children's and religious Arabic books, English and French textbooks and trade books.

Sphinx Bookshop and Publishing House 3 Shawarbi 3rd floor 392-4616. English-language textbooks, medical books and children's books. Distributor for Longman Group Ltd, Librairie du Liban and Ladybird.

Tash Mohi al Din Abu al Ezz MO 700210 703743. Stationery, children's books and games.

Tony Bookshop 3 Alfi 915296. Books on ancient Egypt.

Turath al Islami 14 Safia Zaghloul, off Kasr al Aini 355-3838. Arabic-language religious books.

Zamalek Bookstore 19 Shagaret al Dorr 341-9197, and Marriott Hotel 340-8888. English and French language novels, trade publications, cards and cassettes.

Manufacturing Services
Audio cassettes
Al Manar Audio Recordings 20 Adli 749777. Koranic recordings.

Bookbinders
Hassan Abdel Aziz Gamea al Ismaili, Haret al Ismaili No 4, Ard Sherif 363-3729; **Hassan Abdel Mohsen** 7 al Madbouli Abdin 933639.
Hosny Al Sayed Zahran Sheikh Mohammed Abdu, Haret Lotfi (behind al Azhar) 915313; **H. Margossian** 11 Abdel Khalek Sarwat, second floor, Apt 12, 748067; **Maison De Reliure** Wahib and Company 23 Abdel Khalek Sarwat; **Le Relieur Moderne** 5 Sherifeen.

Commercial printers
Alexandria Printing Press 8 Madina al Monawara MO 349-1117; **Al Ahram Organization** Galaa 755500; **The American University in Cairo Press** 113 Kasr al Aini 354-2964 ex6937; **Arab World Printing House** 23 Daher, Faggala, 906706; **Concorde Printing** 8 Haret al Wabour, Shoubra 948699; **Dar al Fagr for Printing, Publishing and Distribution** 2 Kady al Fadel 751139 741269; **Dar al Maaref** 1119 Corniche al Nil 777146; **Dar Noafa** 5 Wakf al Kharbutly al Daher 938797 900118; **Egyptian Modern Office Printing Press** Shubra al Kheima 955089; **Fast Printing and Typing Services** 2 Shebin, Midan Salah al Din HE 676923; **Graphic Center** 14 Salah al Din Moustafa MO 705173; **Helios Printing Company** 10 Ammar ibn Yaser HE; **Horus Center** 17 Salem, just south of Agouza Hospital, DO; **International Press** 5 Gamal al Shayhed, Sahafiyin 347-4259; **Interpack House** 167 Port Said, Zawia al Hamra 834733; **JC Center** 14 Mahmoud Hafez HE 243-7124, color separations; **Lotus Printing** 38 Kamel Sedki, Faggala, 909363; **The Master's Press** 4 Ayat al Hosan, Faggala 920189; **Nahdet Masr** Kamel Sedki, Faggala 903395; **Nubar Printing House** 6A Moalimin School, Shubra 751281 649608.

Video
Alamia for Cinema and Television 41 Gezira al Wasta, ZA 340-2117/2123, videocassette distribution of cinema productions; **Arab Company for Television** 13 Mahrany, Faggala 905624, provides technical services for video program production; **Cairo Voice for Sight and Sound** 18 Barsa, Tawfikia 754788/809, production company for radio, television and audio cassettes; **Dynavision** 52 Abdel Khalek Sarwat 910910; **Islamic Production and Advertising** 4 Addi, Midan Mesaha DO 348-6514, produces television programs, videocassettes and audio cassettes; **Radio and Television Organization** Radio and TV Building, Corniche al Nil, Maspero 757155 747120 749664; **Treasure Productions** 4 Shawarbi 347-2521 747151; **VC Video Cairo** 1 Salah Salim DO 705027. Professional video production.

AUC Press Books . . .

guide you in Egypt:

A Pocket Dictionary of the Spoken Arabic of Cairo :
English-Arabic
    compiled by Virginia Stevens and Maurice Salib
Islamic Monuments in Cairo: A Practical Guide
    by Richard B. Parker and Robin Sabin
    Third Edition, Revised and Enlarged
    by Caroline Williams
Coptic Egypt: History and Guide
    by Jill Kamil
The Fayoum: A Practical Guide
    Second Edition, Revised
    by R. Neil Hewison
Egyptian Cooking: A Practical Guide
    by Samia Abdennour
Egyptian Carpets: A Practical Guide
    by Luanne Brown and Sidna Rachid
Common Birds of Egypt
    by Bertel Bruun
    Illustrated by Sherif Baha el Din
The Street Trees of Egypt
    Revised Edition
    by M. Nabil El-Hadidi and Loutfy Boulos
    Illustrated by Magdy El-Gohary and Sami Makar

and make perfect gifts:
Egypt Revealed:
Scenes from Napoleon's Description de l'Egypte
edited by Robert Anderson and Ibrahim Fawzy
The Birds of Ancient Egypt
by Patrick F. Houlihan
The Egypt Story:
Its Art, Its Monuments, Its People, Its History
Photography by Fred J. Maroon
Text by P. H. Newby
In the Shadow of the Pyramids:
Egypt during the Old Kingdom
Text by Jaromir Malek
Photographs by Werner Forman

Available in bookstores throughout the city

The American University in Cairo Press

Foreign Publishers and Booksellers
with Middle East Interests

Abacus Press Abacus House, Speldhurst Road, Tunbridge Wells, Kent TN4 OHU, UK.

Al Saqi Books 26 Westbourne Grove London W25RH.

BBC Publications 34 Marylebone High Street, London WIM 4AA.

E. J. Brill 2300 PA Leiden, The Netherlands.

Center for Contemporary Arab Studies Georgetown University, Washington DC 20057. 202-625-3128. Publishes original research books, collections, symposium papers, special studies and lectures.

The Dumbarton Oaks Center for Byzantine Studies 1703 32nd St. NW Washington DC 20007.

East West Publications Jubilee House, Chapel Road, Hounslow, Middlesex UK

International Book Center PO Box 295 Troy, Michigan 48099. Retail and wholesale books on the Middle East.

Islam International Publication Ltd. Islamabad, Sheephatch Lane, Tilford, Surrey UK . Primarily translations of the Koran into various languages.

Islamic Text Society 5 Green St. Cambridge C22 2PN, UK.

John Murray Ltd. 50 Albemarly Street, London WIX 4BD.

Librairie du Liban Imm Esseili, Place Riad al Solk, Beirut Lebanon.

Longman Group Ltd. Burnt Mill, Harlow, Essex CM20 2GE, UK.

Lynne Rienner Publishers 948 North St. Suite 8, Boulder, Colorado 80302.

Medialink International, Inc. 191 Atlantic Avenue, Brooklyn, New York 11201. 718-852-0292. Nationwide distributors of international periodicals and books. Specializes in books on the Third World. Catalog available.

The Orleander Press 12 Stansgate Avenue, Cambridge CB2 2QZ, UK.

Oxford University Press Walton St. Oxford OX2 6DP, UK.

Princeton University Press 41 Williams St. Princeton, New Jersey 08540. 609-896-1344.

Quartet Books Ltd 27/29 Goodge St. London W1P 1FD.

Research Centre for Islamic History, Art and Culture 24 Besiktas Istanbul, Turkey.

Routledge and Kegan Paul 14 Leicester Square, London WC2H 7PH.

Simpkin Splendor of Egypt PO Box 17072 Salt Lake City, Utah.

Syracuse University Press 1600 Jamesville Avenue, Syracuse, NY 13244.

Three Continents Press 1636 Connecticut Avenue, NW Washington DC 20009. 202-332-3885.

Trade Route Enterprises 518 Fourth Street, Monessen, PA 15062. Educational material about the Middle East, and guidebooks and maps about Egypt.

University of California Press 2120 Berkeley Way, Berkeley CA 94270.

University of Chicago Press 5801 Ellis Avenue, Chicago IL 60637.

University of Texas Press Box 7819, Austin, TX 78713.

University of Utah Press Salt Lake City, UT 84112.

BUSINESS

Egypt is the largest market in the Middle East, with over 46 million consumers and over 11 million skilled and semi-skilled workers. There are over 200 major and 15,000 minor industrial companies, a growing public and private sector, a vastly improved and improving infrastructure, and a strong government commitment to business. As with any growing business atmosphere, the laws governing business in Egypt are complex. Below is an overview of the Egyptian business market. Those individuals and companies wishing to establish a business or in need of business advice should consult professional help.

Business in Egypt operates under three distinctive categories: **public sector companies,** owned and operated by the government; **private sector companies,** where individual citizens own and operate their businesses in the free market; and **joint venture projects**.

Public sector companies
The public sector companies, owned and operated by the government, were once responsible for 75% of the gross national product. In recent years, with a greater commitment to privatization, this percentage has decreased while the expertise and efficiency of public sector companies have increased.

Private sector companies
Since the onset of a strong commitment to economic development, Egyptians have been encouraged to own and operate private businesses in Egypt.

Joint venture companies
These are formed between an Egyptian partner holding a trade license and a foreign person or company. Egyptian equity participation must be negotiated on a case by case basis, except for banks dealing in local currency, in which Egyptian equity is set at 51%; construction contracting projects where the Egyptian equity is 50%; and technical consulting companies where Egyptian equity of 49% is necessary. Strict rules govern the establishment of such a company. The company must benefit the economic interests of Egypt, especially through foreign exchange earning potential. Applications and procedures are complicated and are best approached via embassy commercial sections and legal council. Costs for establishing such a company are high, but benefits are ample. There are two types of joint venture company, **inland projects** and **free zone projects.**

Inland projects are restricted to joint stock companies or limited liability companies. They may be located anywhere in Egypt. The government has created incentives for the formation of such companies. These companies are entitled to a 5-10 year exemption from corporate income tax. The number of years is determined by the type of company. Interest on foreign currency loans is exempt from all Egyptian taxes. Foreign employees are exempt from some taxes. Import duty on capital assets is assessed at the low flat rate of 5%. Projects and assets cannot be nationalised, confiscated or sequestrated. All these points have been legislated under **Law 43**, see below.

Free zone projects There are three types of Free Zone area: **public free zones, private free zones** and **city free zones.** Goods transferred into or from these zones are free of tax provided they do not enter the country. Companies within a free zone must conduct all their activities within that zone. Free zones are supervised by the Investment Authority and are considered as being outside the country and not governed by certain laws. Those eligible to operate in a free zone are companies operating as manufacturers of export items or as service companies for expediting exporting. They are eligible for all the standard benefits of Law 43, plus 100% foreign ownership, and special exemptions on tax, customs, export duty and exchange control regulations.

Investment Authority
The **General Authority for Investment and Free Zones GAFIZ** 8 Adli 390-6796/6804 oversees the implementation of Law 43. Among its divisions is the **Private Investment Encouragement Fund** to help finance joint venture projects and the **Private Sector Feasibility Studies** that identifies investment opportunities and helps finance initial visits to Egypt for feasibility studies. An **Investment Information Center** has been established to provide information and assistance to companies interested in investment projects.

Law 43
Law 43, the **Open Door Policy**, was legislated in 1974 to encourage and promote foreign investment and the transfer of technology and know-how to Egypt, and is responsible for the revitalization of business in Egypt. To encourage such investment the law, with various amendments, offers incentives by providing for 5-10 year corporate tax exemption, additional tax concessions, customs exemption or deferment on capital assets, permission to purchase foreign currencies, repatriation of profits and capital, certain labor law concessions, the right to own land, and guarantees against nationalization and confiscation. It is under these laws that most foreigners are permitted to work in Egypt.

Procedures for establishing a joint venture
The first step to establishing a joint venture company in Egypt is to prepare a feasibility study. Upon completion of the study, a detailed application form along with the feasibility study is to be submitted to the the the Investment Authority. Upon preliminary approval, the incorporation documentation must be submitted to the legal department of the Investment Authority. Once final approval is obtained the Ministerial Decree incorporating the company must be published in the official Gazette.

LAWS GOVERNING BUSINESS IN EGYPT

Companies laws
These establish the procedures under which all companies operate in Egypt. They cover such

topics as application for creation of a business, methods of accounting, documents to submit to the government, percentage of Egyptians in the corporate structure, etc.

Labor laws

Labor laws have been established to provide a healthy working environment. They cover such areas as working hours, holidays, hiring and firing, minimum wage, social insurance, unemployment, injury, retirement, pension and other topics related to labor.

Foreigners laws

The conditions under which foreigners are permitted to work in Egypt are outlined in these laws. They include information on visas, work permits, types of employment, housing, etc.

Taxation laws

Tax is imposed in Egypt on immovable property (this includes a land and constructed property tax), on revenues derived from movable capital, on commercial and industrial profits, on salaries, on inheritance, on income and on corporations. Tax laws are complex and require the assistance of expert professionals. Below is a brief overview.

Immovable property tax includes a land tax and a constructed property tax. The land tax is assessed on the annual rental value of agricultural land at the rate of 14%. Barren land, land used for buildings with annexed gardens and courtyards are not subject to the tax. The constructed property tax is assessed at 10% of annual rental value after deducting 20% for expenses. (from Arthur Andersen and Shawki)

Income tax Tax on individuals is assessed on revenues derived from movable capital at a rate of 32%. Commercial and industrial profits are assessed according to a sliding scale. Salaries are assessed according to type of employment and include exemptions. Income from noncommerical professions including doctors, accountants, lawyers, etc, is assessed at a rate of from 18% to 30% of earned income.

General income tax is levied after all the taxes listed above have been assessed. It provides for exemptions and deductions and has a sliding scale. In brief, persons earning less than LE2,000 yearly are exempt from taxation. From LE2,000 and up taxation begins at 8% and scales upward to 65% on incomes of LE200,000 and above.

Corporate tax Payable yearly, a 40% tax is levied on the net of the total profits of shareholding companies, limited liability companies, public sector companies, banks, and Egyptian branches of foreign companies. **Industrial companies** pay at the rate of 32% of profits realized through industrial activities and export operations. **Oil companies**, except national service projects of the Ministry of Defense, pay at a rate of 40.55%. **Joint venture companies** covered under Law 43 are exempt from tax for the first five to ten years. **Free zone companies** are exempt from corporate taxes.

US-Egypt Double Taxation Treaty, established in 1982 "to conclude a convention for the avoidance of double taxation of income, the prevention of fiscal evasion with respect to taxes on income, and the elimination of obstacles to international trade and investment..." includes regulations governing taxes, business profits, dividends, interest, royalties, and relief of double taxation. For a copy of this treaty consult the US Embassy.

Patents, trademark and copyright laws

Egypt is a member of the Patent Cooperation Treaty, and since 1951 has been a signatory to the 1883 Paris Convention. Application for a patent is made to the Patent Office. The process will take up to a year and official acceptance of patent is acknowledged via publication in the Journal of Patents. Patents are good for fifteen years, renewable indefinitely for additional five year periods. Fees average around LE200. Trademarks Egypt is a signatory to the 1954 Madrid Convention covering trademarks. A trademark must be submitted to the Trademark Office to be protected by Egyptian law. Trademarks are protected for 10 years from the date of application. They may be renewed indefinitely for further 10 year periods. Copyrights Egypt is a signatory of the Berne Convention and the International Copyright Convention governing all copyrights. Copyright application is made to Dar al Kutub, Corniche al Nil, c/o GEBO.

For more information

Arab Business Report N.V. Arab Group S. A. 72 Franklin Roosevelt Avenue, 1050 Brussels, Belgium; Business Directory for Egypt The US Embassy Commercial Office 4 Latin America 355-7371; The Egyptian Five Year Plan for Socio-Economic Development, 1987-92 Professional Business Services 4 Latin America, Suite 32, GC 355-1913 356-0741; Egypt Investment and Business Directory 87-88 Fiani and Partners, Tonsi Building 143 Tahrir DO 348-7353 348-5206; Investor's Guide to Egypt prepared by the Investment and Free Zone Authority and available upon request; The Middle East Library of Economic Services 6 Suliman Abdel Aziz Suliman AG 711141 is an official government organ through which all laws are announced to the public. They have a wide variety of business information available in English. Items may be purchased individually from an extensive catalog or via an annual subscription of LE250 and $500 (exclusive of Egypt) for the MELES Bulletin of economic laws, decrees and regulations. The bulletin is issued in English and Arabic, and is a translation of almost the entire official gazette in which all laws and economic decrees are published. MELES provides many other services.

BUSINESS SERVICES

Convention Center al Manassa MN. Opening June 1989 on 70 acres of land. Grounds include: an amphitheatre to seat 2,700 with facilities for simultaneous translation in 8 languages and A-V; two separate halls, each to seat 600-800 people with facilities for smaller divisions; a restaurant for 1,250 people; coffeeshop for 350; and an exhibition area of 2,500 square meters. For more information contact Maged Abaza 758300.

Accountants

Ahmed Abu El Azm 5 Rushdy Pasha, Bab al Louk 340-8388 341-9393 749073; Badawi, Samir T. 1079 Corniche al Nil GC 356-1340 355-2803 355-0427, Ernest and Whitney Representative; Farid Mansour and Co. 113 Thawra HE 291-6058, representatives of Cooper and Lybrand; Hazem Hassan & Co. 72 Mohi al Din Abu al Ezz MO 708058 714824 709559, representatives of Peat Marwick International; Mecos 4 Midan Kawakiby AG 344-1277 344-8313; Nawar & Co. Int'l 21 Talaat Harb, Apt. 12a 741615, chartered accountants; Price Waterhouse (PT) 3B Bahgat Ali, Apt. 19 ZA 340-0052 340-0352; Shawki & Co. 16 Adly 917299 917986 920780, representatives of Arthur Andersen and Company.

Advertising agencies
AMA 49 Shehab MO 346-7891 346-0662, representatives of Leo Burnett; **AP7 Aboul Fotouh Fortune Promoseven** 17 Dr Mahrouki AG 346-9245; **Americana Advertising Agency** 32H Radwan Ibn Tabib, off Sharia Giza GI 730885 730702; **Amico Advertising Marketing International** 4 Abdel Rahman al Rafai MO 348-0202; **Fiani & Partners** 143 Tahrir DO 989055 985765; **Image Advertising** 346-1525; **Look Advertising Company** 195 26th July AG 341-1965; **MECOS (Advertising & Printing)** 4 Kawakiby AG 344-1277 344-8313; **Maadi Advertising Agency** 8 Road 78 MA 351-4565 351-8626; **Publi-Graphics Cairo** 143 Tahrir DO 348-4312/5796/5164; **Shahed & Hammad** 312 Geziret al Arab MO 346-0553; **The Light Office** 3 Silehdar HE 257-1529; **Mobak** 37 Lutfi Hassuna AG 717760 717796; **Shiro International** 28 Murad GI 732949 731776; **Time/Space** 39 Higaz MO 346-5953; **Video Cairo** 1 Salah Salem DO 700713 705027.

Attorneys
Abou al Naga Law Office Masry Towers, Tower A Apt 8, 1 Gezira al Wasta ZA 342-0857 341-0515 consultants, legal advisors and patent attorneys; **Hassouna & Hosny & Saad** 12 Midan Sheikh Youssef GC 354-0608 356-0852, representatives of Sidney and Austin; **Helmy and Hamza Law Offices** 56 Gamat al Dowal al Arabiya MO 360-0071-2, representatives of Baker and McKenzie; **Kamel, Elias, Bley & Campbell** 41 Abdel Khalek Sarwat 91 0360 913854; **Kamel Law Office** 4 Shahid Ahmed Yehia Ibrahim MO 347- 4102 347-9453 347-3597 international business law; **Shaban al Sayed Younes** 37 Road 104 MA 350-3325, business law; **Yehia, Abdel Wadoud** 1b Messaha DO 348-4476, business law.

Office equipment and supplies
AT&T International Sharia al Nil, Nasr Building GI 726998; **Continental** 43 Kasr al Nil 391-7756 91 7756; **Commercial Equipment Co Ltd** 10 Road 274, New Maadi 353-1039 352-3546; **Eagles Office Supply** 49 Road 206, Digla 352-9450; **Egypto German Office Supply** 2 Sherif 750734 776855 770708; **Farid Tobugi** 21 Sherif 758722; **Galal Engineering Co. (Typewritiers & Office Equipment)** 2 & 6 Amin Sami, off Kasr al Aini 354-4539/5528/9198; **International Office Equipment Center** 8 Marquil ZA 341-5456; **ITT Africa and the Middle East** 3 Abu al Feda ZA 341-4472; **MECOS (Middle East Computer & Office Support)** 4 Midan Kawakiby AG 344-1277/8313; **Marcou** 24 Abdel Khalek Sarwat 749801 749700; **Office Supplies Industries & Trading Corp** 8 Mahmoud Azmi ZA 340-0597; **Office Support Services** 3 Abul Azm, Apt. 10, ZA 341-3768; **Olivetti** Kasr al Nil 744021 744233; **Samir & Aly** 21 & 25 Sherif 746062; **Sha'ell** 34 Talaat Harb 741722; **S.O.S.** 15 Nables, off Shehab MO 346-5376; **Toshiba** 832110 829301; **Trans-Continental** 29 Abdel Khalek Sarwat 746209 756013; **Vahe Stationary** 14 Adli 917016; **Xerox** 4 Libnan MO 346-1059/0671, service 19 Higaz MO 340-3259; **Yasinko** 81 Higaz MO 347-6711.

Office services
Bureau for University Services 21 Abdel Moneim Sanad, MN 601789, translation, typing, copying; **Central Service** 15 Ahmed Abdel Aziz MO 347-1303/3232 and 9 Mohi al Din Abu al Ezz MO 344-2004/5; **Continental** 43 Kasr al Nil 391-7756; **EARTH (Egyptian-American Recruitment Trng. & Habilit.)** 22 Omar Khattab DO 713704 349-6575; **Eurasia Business Centre** 7 Salah al Din Moustafa DO 717371 710439 and 38 al Ahram HE 258-0445; **EBS Executive Business Services** Marriott Hotel ZA 340-8888 ex8216, 8217; **International Business Associates** 31 Golf MA 350-7172, 24 Syria MO 349-0986; **International Busines Services** 27 Nasr, New Maadi 352-3538/7779 353-0450; **International Central Service** 15 Batal Ahmad Abdel Aziz MO 344-2004/5; **ISS International Service Systems** 16 Mohammed Mahdi HE 673637 671399 672399; **Kahlil Business Support Services** 9 Mohammed Mahmoud, Bab al Louk 354-7100; **PBS Professional Business Services**, Osiris Building, 4 Latin America GC 355-1913 356-0741; **Rainbow Business Services** 2 Malek al Afdal ZA 340-0065 341-0605/8606; **VIP Business Center** 46 Geziret al Arab MO 346-0940 344-4429.

Business Services Available from the US Embassy
The **US Foreign Commercial Service** USFCS offers the following services in Egypt. **TOP,**

Trade Opportunities Program, a computerized system for matching Egyptian businessmen with US suppliers of American products or services. **Investment Opportunity Program** which helps Egyptian businessmen find US partners for investment. **Import/Export Marketing Center**, a library of reference materials, product catalogs, books and journals. **Business Directory for Egypt**, a comprehensive and regularly updated manual for doing business in Egypt. **FBP,** Foreign Buyer Program helps Egyptian businessmen to facilitate travel and buying in the US. **ADS,** Agent Distributor Service helps American businessmen facilitate travel and buying in Egypt. **World Trade Date Report** provides financial and background commercial data about specific firms. The USFCS also offers Trade and Investment counseling. In addition the US Department of Commerce sponsors several thematic trade missions to Egypt every year. The consular office will notorize, help with application for social security and witness your signature for power of attorney.

BANKS AND CURRENCY

Unlike the US dollar and pound Sterling, both hard or internationally accepted currencies, the Egyptian pound is a soft currency, usable only within Egypt. Egyptian currency and exchange regulations are designed to protect the value of the Egyptian pound within Egypt, and to prevent unauthorized outflow of hard currency from Egypt.

Only Egyptian currency may be used within Egypt, except in certain officially approved circumstances. Payment in hard currency for an automobile in the duty-free zone is one such exception. Another is the requirement that foreigners pay for hotel rooms in Egypt in hard currency. Apart from these types of exceptions, within Egypt one normally may use dollar currency, travelers' checks, or personal checks only to exchange dollars for Egyptian pounds at a local bank. Exchange made by illegal means is a criminal offense.

Egyptian currency works on the decimal system. Pound notes include 100, 20, 10, 5 and 1, while piaster notes include 50, 25, 10, and 5. The denominations under one pound are smaller in size. Most pound notes are the size of the American dollar, but some extra-large notes are still in circulation. Coins include 10 and 5 piasters in white metal and 5, 2, and 1 piasters, smaller and in brown metal. Although the millim (one-tenth of a piaster) is no longer used as a unit of currency, figures are often written in millims. On receipts etc. four pounds may appear as LE4.000 or LE4 or 400p. It's all the same. Forty piasters may be written LE0.400 or 40p.

Foreign currency accounts come in two forms: **free accounts**, which require information concerning the source of funds and are fully accessable and transferrable; and **regular accounts**, where the source is not requested, but money cannot be withdrawn for a year after deposit. The use of foreign currency is restricted in Egypt to repayment of loans which were in foreign currency in existence prior to September 1981.

Corporate accounts under Law 43 for joint venture and free zone projects must be established with a Egyptian bank prior to the formation of the concern as a prerequisite to the formation. These accounts are blocked accounts in foreign or Egyptian currency. They are unblocked once the company is formed. Foreign accounts receive and disburse via export and import sales, short-term foreign currency loans, transfers from abroad, foreign currency purchases, loans, joint venture expenses, and profits transferred abroad. Profit transfer must be approved by the Investment Authority as per joint venture agreement.

Business hours: **Banks** are open 8:30-1:30 daily except Friday, Sunday and most holidays, with foreign exchange branches open daily. **Business offices** from 8 to 2 in winter and 9 to 1 and 5 to 7 in summer. They are closed Friday and most holidays. **Government offices** are open 8 to 2 daily except Friday and Saturday and most holidays. Cashiers usually close by 12:30. **Stores** are open from 10 to 5 in winter and 9 to 1 and 5 to 7 in summer. Closed Sunday and most holidays. Shops in the **Khan al Khalili** are open from 10 to 7/8 daily and closed on Sunday. They are often open on holidays.

BUSINESS CLUBS AND ORGANIZATIONS

Foreign Chambers of Commerce: **American Chamber of Commerce in Egypt**, Suite 1541, Marriott Hotel, ZA 340-8888 ex514; **French Chamber of Commerce in Egypt**, 4 Midan Falaki, Bab al Louk 354-2898/2897/8491; **Japanese Chamber of Commerce** 31 26th July 740942 740659; **German-Arab Chamber of Commerce**, 2 Sherif Pasha 769237 741754. **Greek-Arab Chamber of Commerce** 10 Suliman al Halabi 741190; **Italian-Arab Chamber of Commerce** 33 Abdel Khalek Sarwat 760275.

Cairo Chamber of Commerce Covering both the public and private sector, this is the largest chamber in Egypt. 354-8491.

Egypt-US Business Council Nil Tower Building, 21 Giza Gl. Consists of senior business executives meeting annually to discuss, develop and promote bilateral Egyptian-American investment and commercial issues. US address c/o US Chamber of Commerce 1615 H Street NW Washington DC 20062. 202-659-6000.

Egyptian Businessmen's Association EBA 737285 Senior executives from all areas of private and public sector businesses. Promotes private sector investment.

European Communities Delegation EEC 4 Gezira, eighth floor, ZA 340-8388.

The Federation of Egyptian Industries Coordinates the activities of 12 chambers of industry, representing the interests of public companies and authorities. 7,000 members. 748945.

The Federation of Egyptian Chambers of Commerce Coordinates activities of 26 regional chambers located in the major cities of Egypt. 987103.

German Agency for Technical Cooperation GIZ c/o German Embassy 8 Hasan Sabri ZA 341-2445.

International Executive Service Corps Nile Hilton Center 776771 ex22-23. Non-profit private American corporation consisting of volunteer retired businessmen to aid in short term (1-3mo) projects in Egypt. Services include Joint Venture Services, which help companies interested in entering into joint ventures and American Business Linkage which connects the Egyptian market with US suppliers.

Netherlands Development Corporation DGIS 13 Giza 723054.

Rotary Clubs in Egypt 21 clubs exist in Egypt, with 8 in Cairo. Cairo Main meets Tuesday at 2pm at the Nile Hilton. Cairo North meets Wednesday at 2pm at the Nile Hilton. Cairo South meets Sunday at 8pm at the Maadi Yacht Club. Cairo West meets Monday at 2pm at the Meridien Hotel. Heliopolis meets Monday at 2:30pm at the Heliopolis Sheraton Hotel. Zamalek meets Monday at 8:30pm at the Nile Hilton. Giza meets Wednesday at 2:15pm at the Sheraton Giza. Giza Pyramids meets Monday at 2:30pm at the Sheraton Giza.

US Investment Promotion Office Nile Tower Building 21 Giza GI 723020. Established to increase and facilitate US investment in Egypt and promote joint venture investments.

ORGANIZATIONS OUTSIDE EGYPT
WITH MIDDLE EAST INTERESTS

Egyptian American Chamber of Commerce 1 World Trade Center, Suite 8741 New York 10048. 212-466-1866. A non-profit, non-political organization holding seminars and luncheons to promote and develop economic ties between the US and Egypt.

Overseas Private Investment Corporation OPIC 1615 M Street NW Washington DC 20527. 202-457-7200. Supports US investment in developing nations via insurance, loan guarantees, direct loans and investment encouragement.

United States Agency for International Development USAID Cairo Center 106 Kasr al Aini 354-8211 ex3247/8/9. Aid in development through private sector investment.

USDOC Export Development Office, Room H1510 Washington DC 20230. Assists trade missions.

USDOC Office of the Near East, Egypt Desk, Washington DC 20230 offers counseling to businessmen planning to visit Egypt.

INTRODUCING
The best tasting diet

diet
7UP

diet
7UP

YEARLY EVENTS

The events listed below are either annual or biannual events held regularly in Egypt, or international events scheduled in Egypt during 1989. If the event is sponsored by a sporting club or federation, you will find the phone numbers in the Leisure section of this guide. In other instances we have listed the contact person whenever possible. Watch for announcements in **Cairoscope** or the **Egyptian Gazette.**

December 1988
The Artificial Intelligence Computer Conference This conference will be attended by computer experts from 20 countries including Japan, China and the United States.

(For all annual December events, see December 89 at the end of this section.)

January 1989
Akhmim Community Center Exhibition and Sale Sponsored by Christian Association of Upper Egypt at Mere de Dieu Church GC. Features naturally dyed cotton cloth and embroideries.
Cross Country Marathon December and January. Sponsored by the Track and Field Federation. 740722.
Egyptian Bridge Federation Open Pairs Championship Sponsored by the federation. 758950.
Galaa Club Tennis Championships Sponsored by the Galaa Club. 753235.
Gezira Sporting Club Golf Championships Cairo Open Foursomes, Hang's Cup, Argentina Cup. Sponsored by the Gezira Sporting   Club. 340-6000.
Heliopolis Sporting Club Tennis Championships for men, ladies and juniors. Sponsored by the Heliopolis Sporting Club. 671414.
International Omnisports Tennis, ping-pong, squash, backgammon, bridge, chess, billiards. January 15-30. Sponsored by Nicha Sports at different hotels and clubs. 346-5233/0144.
International Book Fair (21st) January 24-February 6. Sponsored by the General Egyptian Book Organization at the Madinet Nasr Exhibition Grounds. Opening day by special invitation. Next three days limited entrance requiring passes. Passes can be obtained at GEBO. Tickets at gate.
International Documentary and Short Film Festival Held for the first time in Cairo in 1989. Sponsored by the Ministry of Culture.
Open National Wrestling Championship January 26-27. Championship
between governorates. Location to be announced. Sponsored by the Wrestling Federation. 753296.
Open Tennis Championship of Cairo At Tewfikia Tennis Club. 348-1930.
Tayaran Club Tennis Championship Sponsored by the Tayaran Club. 243-2265.

Weightlifting club competitions for first category competitors at various sporting clubs. 753269.

February

Abu Simbel biannual celebration of sun penetrating into the innermost temple on February 22. Date of ascension of Ramses II.

Compuexpo Exhibition and Conference Five day seminar and computer exhibition at the Semiramis Intercontinental, organized by American Express. Seminars are open to the public by reservation except for three seminars by entrance fee (LE5). The last three seminars will raise business issues and exhibit hands-on automation. Contact Engi Haddad 750444 ext 138.

Gezira Sporting Club Golf Championships Cairo Open Greensomes, Chevky-Yousry-Shawarby Cup, Ladies. 340-6000.

Gezira Sporting Club National Tennis Championships for men and ladies. 340-6000.

Egyptian Bridge Federation Juniors Championship Sponsored by the Bridge Federation. 758950.

Egyptian Bridge Federation Team of Four Open Championships Sponsored by the Bridge Federation. 758950.

Fifth International Bridge Tournament sponsored by the Egyptian Bridge Federation during the first two weeks of February at the Ramses Hilton. 758950.

International Fishing Tournament Hurghada. Organized by Egyptian Union for Fishing, the Red Sea Governorate and the Egyptian General Authority for the Promotion of Tourism.

National Track and Field Tournament February and March. To be held in Cairo, Alexandria or Zagazig. All clubs participating must be members of the federation. 740722.

Skypak Tennis Nation's Cup sponsored by Nicha Sports at the Sakkara Country Club from February 3-24. Contact 348-8204/7228.

Weightlifting competition for the police at the Police Academy. 753269.

March

Annual Plastic Arts Exhibition, Gezira Exhibition Ground.

Annual Spring Flower Show at Andalusa Gardens opposite Al Borg Hotel and at the Orman Gardens Sharia Giza GI. Some are for sale.

Cairo International Trade Fair (22nd) sponsored by the General Organization for International Exhibitions and Fairs at the Madinet Nasr Exhibition Grounds March 11-March 24. The fair includes latest national and international products. First week closed to the public.

Darts Tournament at B's Corner, Taha Hussein ZA from March 6-17.

Documentary Film Festival This is a local festival of short and documentary films. Sponsored by the Ministry of Culture.

Egyptian Bridge Federation Marathon Sponsored by the Bridge Federation. 758950.

Egyptian Bridge Federation Mixed Pairs Championship Sponsored by the Bridge Federation. 758950.

Gezira Sporting Club Golf Championships The Cairo Amateur Golf Championship, The Treaty Challenge Cup for Men, The Treaty Challenge Cup for Women. 340-6000.

International Children's Film Festival First time in Cairo in 1989. Sponsored by the Ministry of Culture. 341-2918.

Weightlifting competition for the armed forces. 753269.

YMCA International Bazaar at the Nile Hilton. International stands, clothes, bedsheets. Proceeds finance summer holiday camp in Alexandria.

April

Gezira Sporting Club Golf Championships Lyster Cup. 340-6000.

Maadi Club Tennis Tournament Contact 350-5455.

Ramadan Chess Tournament Month long competition held at various sporting clubs with teams organized from different professional groups: Engineers, Doctors, Businessmen, etc.

Ramadan Festivities April 11-May 11 1989. May vary by a day or two. Book exhibitions, evening festivities at Hussein and al Azhar areas. Folkloric troupes perform in main squares and open public areas of the city.

Tahseen al Seha Annual Charity Bazaar at the Nile Hilton.

May

DHL Corporate Games May 5-June 10. Golf, tennis, squash, ping-pong, chess, darts, backgammon, bridge and a rally. Contact 348-5796/5164.

Food Processing and Packaging Equipment Trade Mission Four day visit to public and private factories and Egyptian government officials, in Cairo and in Alexandria. Mission headed by an official from the U.S. Department of Commerce in Washington and sponsored by the U.S Foreign Commercial Service in Cairo. Contact Mr. Hatem El Dali, senior Commercial Specialist, U.S. Embassy. 355-7371.

Marketing Information Day Open to businessmen and sponsored by the US Embassy. 355-7371.

June

Cairo Rugby Raft Races Home made crafts compete in a race from the Good Shot to the Seahorse on the Nile near Maadi. Craft must be sponsored by a company, have a crew of six dressed in a theme and be an original creation that will float. Contact Dave Jenkins 353-0301, Robert Jones 350-3340, and Andy Heath 346-7962.

Chess Tournaments June-July in Alexandria. Include Alexandria Open and Closed, Men's Only and Youth Only. Contact the Chess Federation 340-6000.

Maadi Club Chess Tournaments Open Club for any age group or sex; Second Class Tournament; Ladies Chess Tournament and Under 17 Tournament. Contact the Maadi Club 350-5455.

Maadi Club Swimming Tournaments Contact 350-5450.

Sports for Companies Annual sporting events for all companies that are members of the Sports Federation for Companies. Venues include clubs all over Egypt with finals in June.

July

American Fourth of July Celebrations sponsored by the American Embassy at Cairo American College. Full day of activities including Hot Dogs and BBQ. Free to US Citizens.

National Fishing Tournament Hurghada.

Track and Field Cup Championships July through September. Sponsored by the Track and Field Federation. 740722.

August
Chess Tournaments Local competitions. Contact the Chess Federation 340-6000.

September
FOCUS Underwater Photography Competition at Hurghada. Featuring 4 days of competition, seminars, etc. For 1989 details contact American Express. 750444.

Interbanks Omnisports September 5-20. Tennis, squash, ping-pong, bridge, backgammon, chess, billiards, basketball and football. Contact Nicha Sports c/o 346-5233/0144.

International Theatre Festival Newly established in September 1988, this festival, sponsored by the Ministry of Culture and featuring theater companies from all over the world, will be a biennial event. 341-2918/5495.

Maadi Club Swimming Tournaments Contact 350-5450.

October
Abu Simbel Biannual celebration of sun's rays reaching into the innermost chamber of the Abu Simbel monuments. October 22, anniversary of birth of Ramses II.

Alexandria Mediterranean Biennale (17th) running for three months beginning in October. An international competition open to all artists from Mediterranean countries. Sponsored by the Biennale High Committee of the Ministry of Culture. 341-2918/5495/5568.

The American University in Cairo Alumni Homecoming Approximately third Friday of October. Booths, displays, handicrafts, etc. Main campus 10-5. Contact AUC Alumni Office 354-2964.

Asian Bazaar Held at a different Asian embassy each year and featuring Asian items for sale. Contact Afro-Asian Society, Emma 351-6286.

Battle of Al Alamein Commemoration October 24 at the Al Alamein memorial between Alexandria and Mersa Matruh. Contact British War Graves Commission. 669351.

Cairo American College 24hr Marathon 352-9393/9244.

Expo Export (2nd) Importers and businessmen worldwide attend display of Egyptian products for export. Madinet Nasr Exhibition Grounds.

Gezira Sporting Club Golf Championships entries open for Club Cup, Army Cup, Mixed Foursomes, Men's Foursomes, Ladies Club Cup, Ladies Foursomes. Also Cameroon Cup, Soliman Cup, Signa Cup. 340-6000.

Horseback Riding Championships Sponsored by the International Federation for Horseback Riding 753296. Held at Gezira, Sakkara Country Club, and Maadi Sporting Clubs in Cairo and also in Alexandria.

International Folk Festival Fourth annual. Ismailia. International folk troupes from all over the world. Opening day parade.

International Pharaoh's Rally Eleven-day 4,700 kilometer world class racing in the deserts of Egypt. Entries for participants are accepted until the end of July. Considered one of the most important rallies in the world. International representation. Categories include cars, motorcycles, and trucks. Contact Rami Siag 285-6022.

Islamic Trade Fair October 10-19 at Madinet Nasr Exhibition Grounds.

Maadi Club Tennis Tournament Contact 350-5455.

Nile Hilton Playhouse Annual series of plays by different British drama troupes. October or November. Reservation necessary. Tickets available at the Nile Hilton Reservation Desk, in the Lobby. Ticket includes dinner. Contact Food and Beverages Manager, Allan Borgers, 750666 740777 ext 270/1.

November

St Andrew's Day Ball Sponsored by the Scottish Country Dance Group at one of the five-star hotels. Traditional dinner and dance in Scottish dress. Contact the British Community Association 349-8870.

The Egyptian Arabian Horse Event Sponsored by Mena Tours, the Egyptian Agricultural Organization, and the Egyptian Arab Horse Breeders Association. International representation 776951 768382.

Gezira Sporting Club Golf Competition The Open Championship, Isman Cup, The Amateur Championship of Egypt. Senior's Championship. 340-6000.

International Children's Book Fair International display of children's books, teaching aids and games. Nasr City Exhibition Grounds.

Marine Ball Tickets limited to U.S citizens and embassy affiliates and their guests. Contact the Marine Security Guide Detachment at the U.S. Embassy 355-7371, ext. 2355.

Thanksgiving Dinner Sponsored by the Maadi Women's Guild at the Maadi House. Fourth Thursday.

Weightlifting club competitions for 16-18 year old at sporting clubs. 753269.

Wrestling Ibrahim Mostafa Memorial Cup November 9-10 in Alexandria Stadium, Alexandria. Participants include Greece, Italy, Rumania, Turkey, Yugoslavia, Bulgaria, USSR and some Arab countries. 753296.

December

Ahly Club Tennis Championships for men, ladies and juniors. 753235.

Al Azhar Medical Conference Second half of December. Sponsored by the Hussein Hospital, al Azhar. Contact 921025 or 908702.

Cricket Tournament, Gezira Sporting Club, sponsored by the British Embassy 354-0850/2.

Gezira Sporting Club Golf Competition Blazek Cup, The Cairo Open Championship, Christmas Scramble. 340-6000.

International Film Festival Two weeks of films from all over the world shown at various cinemas and one of the five-star hotels. Advertised in the local newspapers.

Maadi Women's Guild Charity Bazaar Held on the first Friday in December at The Cairo American College from 11am-3pm. Tickets on sale at various locations. Look for announcements. I.D required to enter. 351-2755.

Weightlifting club competitions for youths under 20 years of age at sporting clubs. 753269.

VOCABULARY

Transcription

Vowels		Nearest English	Arabic
Short:	a	back	maktab
	i	pick	hina
	u	put	mumkin
Long:	aa	care/car	midaan, fiTaar
	ee	fate	feen
	ii	clean	yimiin
	oo	coal	koosa
	uu	cool	fuul

Consonants

D,S,T.Z the so-called emphatics; these letters are pronounced with more emphasis than the usual d, s, t, z. Get your mouth ready to say oo as in 'cool,' then without moving your tongue pronounce d, s, t, z. Your tongue should be bunched up in the back of your mouth.

H the strong h; pushed very heavily from the back of the mouth. Note that H and h are completely different sounds in Arabic. Both must always be pronounced, even before another consonant or at the end of a word.

kh like Scottish **loch**, or German **echt**

gh same articulation as 'kh' but with the vocal chords vibrating

' (apostrophe): glottal stop, like 'tt' in American **Manhattan** or cockney **matter**

' (reversed apostrophe): the **'ain**, a forcing of the air through a constriction in the throat, a kind of backward gulp. If you find it impossible, substitute 'a' as in 'cat.'

q a 'k' sound pronounced far back in the mouth

j like French 'je'

sh as in 'sheep'

g always as in 'go,' never as in 'gym'

227

NB Doubling of a consonant symbol indicates that a consonant is long, and must be articulated for twice the normal time, like the 'k' sound in English 'book-case.' The distinction is important: note for example the difference between 'Hamaam' (pigeon) and 'Hammaam' (bathroom).

Emergency

It should be noted that all doctors in Cairo speak English, or at least can communicate in English, so there is no need for an extensive Arabic vocabulary with a doctor. Here are a few words and phrases to help you in case of an emergency.

ambulance is'aaf; **accident** Hadsa; **bandage** rubaaT; **blanket** baTTaniyya; **blood** damm; **bone** 'aDm; **broken** maksuur; **burn** (n) Har'; **call** (to f) iTlubi, (to m) iTlub; **cough** kuHHa; **cramps** takaluSaat; **doctor** duktoor; **don't move her** mat-Harak-haash; **don't move him** mat-harak-huush; **drugstore** agzakhaana, Saydaliyya; **embassy** sifaara; **emergency** Haala mista'gila; **emergency police** buliis innagda; **fever** Haraara; **first aid** is'afaat awaliyya; **fire!** Harii'a!; **fire brigade** maTaafi; **get. bring** haat; **gauze** shaash; **headache** Sudaa'; **help!** ilHa'uuni; **here!** hina!; **hospital** mustashfa; **injection** Hu'na; **ill, sick** mariiD; **injured** muSaab; **medicine** dawa; **nurse** mumarriDa; **ointment** marham; **over there!** hinaak!; **pain** waga'; **patient** mariiD; **pharmacy** agzakhaana, Saydaliyya; **please** (to f) min faDlik, (to m) min faDlak; **poison** simm; **police** buliis; **prescription** rushitta; **thief!** Haraami!; **water!** mayya!

Basic Vocabulary

General expressions
again taani; **fine, thanks** il hamdulillaa; **goodbye** ma'assalaama; **good afternoon/evening** masaa' il-kheer; **good morning** SabaaH il-kheer; **good night** tiSbaH (i/u) 'ala kheer; **how are you?** izzayyak/ik/ukum; **left** shamaal; **never mind** ma'lish; **OK** Tayyib, maashi; **no** la', la'a; **perhaps** yimkin; **please** min faDlak/ik/ukum; **right** yimiin; **sorry** (f) mut'assifa, asfa; **sorry** (m) mut'assif, aasif; **straight ahead** 'alaTuul; **thank you** shukran; **yes** aywa.

Pronouns
I ana; **you** (m) inta; **you** (f) inti; **we** iHna; **you** (pl) intu; **they** humma.

Prepositions
about Hawaali; **above** foo'; **across** fi-g-ganb it-taani; **after** ba'd; **almost** ta'riiban; **among** been; **at** fi, 'and; **before** 'abl; **behind** wara; **between** been; **down** taHt; **far away** b'iid; **in** fi; **inside** guwwa; **on** 'ala; **on top of** foo'; **outside** barra; **to** li; **up** foo'; **with** ma'a; **without** mingheer.

Questions
where? feen?; **where is/are...?** feen?; **when?** imta?; **what?** eeh?; **how** izzaay?; **how much?** bikaam?; **how many?** kaam?; **who?** miin?; **why?** leeh?; **which?** anhi?; **what is this?** eeh da/di?; **do you speak English?** bititkallim/i/u ingliizi?

Numerals

0 Sifr; 1 waaHid; 2 itneen; 3 talaata; 4 arba'a; 5 khamsa; 6 sitta; 7 sab'a; 8 tamanya; 9 tis'a; 10 'ashra; 11 Hidaashar; 12 itnaashar; 13 talattaashar, 14 arba'tashar; 15 khamastaashar; 16 sittaashar; 17 saba'taashar; 18 tamantaashar; 19 tisa'taashar; 20 'ishriin; 21 waHid wi'ishriin; 22 itneen wi 'ishriin; 30 talatiin; 40 arbi'iin; 50 khamsiin; 60 sittiin; 90 tis'iin; 100 miyya; 101 miyya wi waaHid; 1,000 alf; 1,000,000 milyoon; 1,001 alf wi waaHid.

the first il-awwil; the second it-taani; the third it-taalit; the fourth ir-raabi'; the fifth il-khaamis; the sixth is-saadis; the seventh is-saabi'; the eighth it-taamin; the ninth it-taasi'; the tenth il-'aashir; the eleventh il-Hidaashar; the twentieth il-'ishriin.

Money

all kull; change (small) fakka; change (from a transaction) baa'i; currency 'umla; half nuss; money filuus; no change mafiish fakka; piaster 'irsh; pound gineeh; how much? bikaam?.

Do you have change for a pound? 'andak (m) 'andik (f) fakkit ginee?; five piasters khamsa Saagh, shilin; ten piasters 'ashra Saagh, bariiza; fifteen piasters khamastaashar 'irsh; twenty piasters 'ishriin 'irsh, riyaal; twenty five piasters khamsa wi'ishriin 'irsh, rub' ginee; fifty piasters khamsiin 'irsh, nuss ginee.

Days of the week

Sunday il-Hadd; Monday il-itneen; Tuesday it-talaat; Wednesday il-arba'; Thursday il-khamiis; Friday il-gum'a; Saturday is-sabt.

Months of the year

January yanaayir; February fibraayir; March maaris; April abriil, May maayu; June yunyu; July yulyu; August aghusTus; September sibtambar; October uktuubar; November nufambar; December disambar.

Seasons

Spring rabii'; summer Seef; fall khariif; winter shita.

Time

it is one o'clock is-saa'a waHda; it is 1:15 is-saa'a waHda wi rub'; it is 1:30 is-saa' waHda wi nuss; it is 1:45 is-saa'a itneen illa rub'; in the morning iS-Subh; in the afternoon ba'd iD-Duhr; in the evening billeel; today innaharda; tomorrow bukra.

Household

Colors

beige beej; black iswid; blue azra'; brown bunni; cream kreem; dark ghaami'; dark blue kuHli; gold dahabi; green akhDar; grey rumaadi, ruSaaSi; light faatiH; light blue labani; mauve moov; orange burtu'aani; pink rooz, wardi; purple banafsigi; red aHmar; silver faDDi; white abyaD; yellow aSfar.

Fabrics

brushed cotton kastoor; canvas kheesh; cloth 'umaash; cotton 'utn; linen tiil, kittaan; nylon nayloon; polyester bulyistir; plain saada; print man'uush; silk Hariir; tweed twiid; wool Suuf.

Household items

alarm clock minabbih; alcohol kuHuul; ashtray ta'tuu'a, Taffaaya; bath banyu; bathroom Hammaam; battery baTTariyya, Hagar; bed siriir; bell garas; blanket baTTaniyya; bottle izaaza; bottle opener fattaaHa; bowl sulTaniyya; box sanduu'; broom maknasa; brush fursha; bulb lamba; candle sham'a; carpet siggaada; cat 'uTTa; ceiling sa'f; chain silsila (small), ganziir (big); chair kursi; clock saa'a; comb mishT; cork filla; corkscrew barriima; cup fingaan; cupboard dulaab, namliyya; curtain sitaara; cushion mikhadda; dish Taba'; dog kalb; door baab; drain ballaa'a; drawer durg; faucet Hanafiyya; flat sha"a; flashlight baTTariyya; floor arDiyya; fluorescent light lamba niyoon; flowers zuhuur, ward; food akl; furniture farsh, 'afsh; garbage zibaala; glass (drink) kubbaaya; glass 'izaaz; handle ukra; home beet; house beet; iron makwa; kettle barraad; key muftaaH; knife sikkiina; ladder sillim; lamp abajuura; laundry ghasiil; light nuur; lock 'ifl; mattress martaba; medicine dawa; mirror miraaya; needle ibra; ointment marham; oven furn; paint buuya; photo Suura; pill Habba; pillow mikhadda; plate Taba'; plug fiisha; quilt liHaaf; refrigerator tallaaga; roof suTuuH; rubbish zibaala; scissors ma'aSS; shaving cream kreem Hilaa'a; sheet milaaya; shoe polish warniish; shutter shiish; sink HooD; sofa kanaba; spoon ma'la'a; stairs sillim; stove furn; suitcase shanTit safar; switch muftaaH nuur; table Tarabeeza, sufra; tablecloth mafrash; tap Hanafiyya; thread fatla; toilet twalitt; toothpaste ma'guun asnaan; toothpick khilla; torch baTTariyya; towel fuuTa, bashkiir; wardrobe dulaab; washbasin HooD; water heater sakhkhaan; window shibbaak; wire silk.

Lodging

accommodation sakan; apartment sha"a; balcony balakoona; bedroom oodit noom; building mabna; damage talaf; damp riTb; dark muzlim, Dalma; dining room oodit sufra; elevator asanseer; flat sha"a; furnished mafruusha; garden gineena; gate-keeper bawwab; grass Hashiish; grow (v) yizra'; height irtifaa'; high 'aali; kitchen maTbakh; land arD; landlady saHbit il-beet; landlord saHb il-beet; large kibiir; lift asanseer; live (lodge) yiskun; long Tawiil; move yi'azzil; new gidiid; noise dawsha; old 'adiim; open maftuuH; opposite 'uddaam; permission 'izn; place makaan; price taman; property amlaak; precious ghaali, samiin; quiet haadi; receipt waSl; rent (n) 'igaar; rent (v) yi'aggar; repair yiSallaH; return yiragga'; robbery sir'a; room ooda; rotten faasid; size ma'aas; smell riiHa; smoke dukhkhaan; solid gaamid; sound Soot; stain bo"a; steal yisra'; steam bukhaar; suburb DaHya; thing Haaga; unfurnished mish mafruusha; visit yizuur; wash yighsil.

Materials and metals

aluminum alamunyum; brass naHaas aSfar; ceramic siramiik; chrome kroom; copper naHaas aHmar; glass izaaz; gold dahab; iron Hadiid; leather gild; pottery khazaf fukhaar; porcelain bursileen, Siini; rosewood khashab il ward; rubber (synthetic) kawitsh (Sinaa'i); silver faDDa; suede shamwaa; varnish warniish; wax (dark, light) sham' (ghaami', faatiH); wood khashab.

Tools

glue Samgh (paper) ghira (wood); hammer shakuush; hoe faas; hose kharTuum; ladder (tall/ small) sillim (kibiir/Sughayyar); nail muSmaar; paint brush (small/large) fursha (Sughayyara/ kibiira); pliers kammaasha; pointed pliers zarradiyya; plunger sallaaka; rake shooka; rope Habl; scissors ma'aSS; screwdriver mufakk; screw muSmaar 'alawooz; tape (electrical) shiriiT (kahraba); turpentine tarabantiina; washer gilda.

Travel

airplane Tayyaara; airport maTaar; arrival wuSuul; automobile 'arabiyya; baggage 'afsh; bus utubiis; cargo biDaa'a; currency 'umla; customs gumruk; departure safar; domestic (flight) daakhili; distance masaafa; drive yisuu'; driving license; rukhsit siwaa'a; duty rusuum gumrukiyya; entrance madkhal; exchange (v) yibaddil; exit khuruug; first class daraga uula; flight riHlit Tayaraan; foreign agnabi; freight shaHn; hire yi'aggar; journey riHla; inspector mufattish; lost Daayi', maf'uud; luggage 'afsh; motorcycle mutusikl; nationality ginsiyya; passenger raakib; passport basboor, gawaaz safar;   photo Suura; port miina; porter shayyaal; railway station miHaTTit il 'aTr; residence (visa) iqaama; sleeper 'arabiit noom; taxi taks; ticket tazkara;   train 'aTr; tram turummaay; travel (v) yisaafir; travel agency shirkit siyaaHa; tour gawla; vaccination taT'iim; visa viza, ta'shiira.

Auto parts

accelerator baddaal il-banziin; air filter filtir il-hawa; battery baTTariyya; battery water mayyit baTTariyya; belt Hizaam; bonnet kabbuut; boot shanTa; brakes faraamil; brake lining tiil faraamil; brake fluid zeet faraamil; contact kuntakt; doors bibaan; fan belt Hizaam il-marwaHa; gear tirs; gear box sanduu' il-tiruus; gasoline banziin; hood kabbuut; hubcap ghaTa il jant; horn kalaks; headlights kashshafaat; inner tube shanbar; jack kureek; lights nuur; lubrication tashHiim; oil zeet; petrol banziin; shock absorbers musa'diin; spare tire istibn; spare parts qita' ghiyaar; spark plugs bujihaat; steering wheel diriksyoon; tire kawitsh; tire pump munfaakh; transmission fitees; trunk shanTa; trubeless tire kawitsh tuublis; water mayya; wheels 'agal; windshield barbiriiz; windshield wipers massaHaat.

Shopping

At the grocer's

aluminum foil wara' alamunyum; biscuits baskuut; bread 'eesh (local baladi, European ifrangi); butter zibda; charcoal faHm; cheese gibna; chocolate shukulaata; coffee bunn; cocoa kakaaw; coal faHm; cream 'ishTa, kreema; eggs beeD; honey 'asal; hulled grain firiik; jam mirabba; juice 'aSiir; macaroni makaroona; marmalade mirabbit laring; milk laban; mineral water mayya ma'daniyya; mushrooms 'ish il-ghuraab; noodles shi'riyya; oil zeet; olives zatuun; pepper filfil; rice ruzz; salt malH; soup shurba; sugar sukkar; tea shaay; vinegar khall; yogurt zabaadi.

Clothes

bag shanTa; bathrobe burnus; belt Hizaam; blouse bluuza; bra sutyaan; bracelet ghuweesha; button zuraar; chain silsila; clothes malaabis, huduum; coat balTu; collar yaa'a; cuffs asaawir; diaper kafuula; dress fustaan; earring Hala'; eyeglasses naDDaara; fur coat balTu farw; gloves gawanti; handbag shanTa, shanTit yad; handkerchief mandiil; heel ka'b; jacket jakitta, jaakit; lining biTaana; nappy kafuula; necktie karafatta; nightgown 'amiiS noom; pajamas bijaama; pants banTaloon; panty kilutt; pocket giib; purse kiis; purse (Am) shanTa; raincoat balTu maTar; scarf (lady's) isharb; scarf (man's) kufiyya; shawl shaal; shirt 'amiiS; shoes gazma; shoelaces rubaaT gazma; shorts shurt; skirt gunilla, jiiba; sleeve kumm; slip 'amiiS taHtaani; slippers shibshib; socks shuraab; stockings shuraab; tie karafatta; trousers banTaloon; sunglasses naDDarit shams; undershorts kilutt; underwear malaabis dakhliyya; umbrella shamsiyya; wallet maHfaZa; wristwatch saa'it iid; zip susta.

Fruit

almonds looz; apples tuffaaH; apricots mishmish; bananas mooz; cantaloupe kantalub; cape gooseberry Harankash; cherries kreez; coconut gooz hind; dates balaH; figs tiin; grapes 'inab; grapefruit greebfruut; guavas gawaafa; limes lamuun; mangos manga; oranges burtu'aan; peaches khookh; pears kummitra; persimmon kaaka; pineapples ananaas; pinenuts sineebar; plums bar'uu'; prickly pears tiin shooki; raisins zibiib; sweet melons shammaam; strawberries; farawla; tangerines yustafandi; watermelons baTTiikh.

Herbs and spices

allspice buharaat; aniseed yansuun; bayleef wara' lawra; basil riHaan; capers abu khangar; cardamom Habbahaan; caraway karawya; cayenne shaTTa; celery seed bizr karafs; chard sal'; chervil (leaves) kuzbara (wara'); chicory shikurya; chili filfil aHmar amrikaani; cinnamon 'irfa; cloves 'urunfil; coriander (seeds) kuzbara (bizr); corn cockle, (black cumin) Habbit il baraka; cumin kammuun; curry kaari; dill shabat; fennel shamar; fenugreek Hilba; ginger ganzabiil; ground matHuun; herbs a'shaab; hibiscus karkadee; horseradish figl baladi; leaves wara'; licorice 'ir'isuus; mastic mistika; mustard mustarda; mint ni'naa'; nutmeg guzt il-tiib; oregano za'tar; paprika filfil aHmar ruumi; parsley ba'duunis; pepper (white) filfil abyaD; pepper (black) filfil iswid; pepper (hot) shaTTa; peppercorns 'arn filfil; rosebuds ziir il-ward; rosemary HaSSa libaan; safflower 'usfur; saffron za'faraan; salt malH; savory stoorya; seeds bizr; sesame simsim; spices buharaat; turmeric kurkum; thyme za'tar; vanilla vanilya; whole SiHiiH.

Meat and poultry

bacon beekan; beef kanduuz; brain mukhkh; breaded veal iskalub banee; chicken firaakh; chitterlings mumbaar; duck baTT; goose wizz; gizzards 'awaanis; ham jamboon; heart 'alb; kidney kalaawi; lamb 'uuzi; liver kibda; meatballs kufta; mutton Daani; pigeon Hamaam; poultry Tuyuur, dawaagin; rabbit arnab; rissoles kufta, niifa; roast beef rusbiif; shanks kawaari'; shin of veal mooza; steak; bufteek; sausage sugu'; shish kebab kabaab; tongue lisaan; tripe kirsha; turkey diik ruumi; veal bitillu.

Vegetables

artichoke kharshuuf; aubergine bidingaan; beetroot bangar; cabbage krumb; cauliflower 'arnabiiT; carrots gazar; celery karafs; chickpeas Hummus; chives kurraat; corn (maize) dura; courgettes koosa; cucumber khiyaar; eggplant bidingaan; garlic toom; grape leaves wara' 'inab; **green beans** faSuulya khaDra; **green pepper;** filfil ruumi; **Jew's mallow** mu-lukhiyya; **leeks** kurraat; **lentils (yellow)** 'ads aSfar; **lentils (brown)** 'ads bigibba; **okra** bamya; **onions** baSal; **parsley** ba'duunis; **potatoes** baTaaTis; **pumpkin** 'ar"asali; **radish** figl; **scallions** baSal akhDar; **spinach** sabaanikh; **sweet potatoes** baTaaTa; **tomatoes** TamaaTim, 'uuTa; **taro** 'ul'aas; **zucchini** koosa.

DIRECTORY

AIRLINES

Aeroflot Soviet Airlines 8 Kasr al Nil -- 753386 743132
Air Algerie 13 Kasr al Nil ------------------------------------- 740688 750688 747398
Air Canada 26 Mahmoud Bassiouni --- 758939
Air Djibouti c/o Bon Voyage 16 Adli------------------------------------- 391-1950/8874
Air France 2 Midan Talaat Harb -- 743300/494
    Ahram HE --- 664441 743300
Air India 1 Talaat Harb -- 392-4976 393-4864/73
Air Malta c/o EMECO, 2 Talaat Harb --------------------------------- 747399 747302
Air Sinai Nile Hilton --- 760948
ALIA (Royal Jordanian) 6 Kasr al Nil ---------------------------- 750905 750875
    Zamalek Club Gate MO-- 344-3114 346-7540
Alitalia Nile Hilton -- 743488 753449
Al Yemda (Democratic Yemen Airlines) Nile Hilton --------------------- 742755 752699
Arab Wings Nasr Building, Nil GI --- 727243/618
Austrian Airlines Nile Hilton --------------------------------- 742755/0228 752699
Balkan Bulgarian Airlines 17 Kasr al Nil --------------------------------- 393-1152/1211
British Airways 1 Abdel Salam Aref, Midan Tahrir ------------ 759977 772981 762914
    Misr Helwan Road MA --- 350-2264
Canadian Airlines 26 Mahmoud Bassiouni --- 758939
Cyprus Airways c/o Bon Voyage, 16 Adli ----------------------------- 391-1950/8874/2345
--- 395-7669 390-8099
Czechoslovak Airlines 9 Talaat Harb --------------------------------------- 393-0395/0416
Eastern Airlines 26 Mahmoud Bassiouni ------------------------------------ 758939 761769
Egypt Air 22 Ibrahim al Lakkani HE -- 664305
    Nile Hilton -- 765200 759703
    Sheraton GI --- 985408/849460
    9 Talaat Harb --- 393-2836 392-2835
El Al Israeli Airlines 5 Maqrizi ZA-----------------------------341-1795/1620/1429
Emirates Airlines Marriott Hotel ZA ----------------------------340-6492/6568/1102/1142
--- 346-6568
Ethiopian Airlines Nile Hilton -- 740603/852/911
Finnair 15 Midan Tahrir -- 769571 776895
Garuda Indonesia 17 Ismail Mohammed ZA -------------- 342-0861 341-9409 340-1948
Gramco Airways 93 Road 9 MA ---350-0756/4970

Gulf Air 21 Mahmoud Bassiouni -- 743336 758391

  64 Gamat al Dowal al Arabiya MO ---------------------------------- 348-7781/2/3

Hungarian Airlines 12 Talaat Harb -------------------------------- 753111 744959

Iberia 15 Midan Tahrir --- 749955/716

  78 Higaz HE -- 245-6993/7299

  al Nil, al Nasr Building, GI ------------------------------------ 729618 727243

  62 Nasr MA --- 352-5871

Interflug 6 Adli -- 919705 933828 754200/149

Iraq Airways 22 Kasr al Nil -- 754200/149

Japan Airlines (JAL) Nile Hilton ---------------------------------- 740621/999 740809

Kenya Airways Nile Hilton Annex -------------------------------- 762494 776771 ext. 1524

KLM Royal Dutch Airlines 11 Kasr al Nil ------------------------ 751306 764264 740999

  ---747747 740717

Korean Airlines 32 Mabka Dina MA -- 350-2818

Kuwait Airlines 24 Ibrahim al Lakkani HE ------------------------- 660006 291-4909/6495

  4 Talaat Harb--- 759866 747944/7482

LOT Polish Airlines 1 Kasr al Nil ----------------------------------- 747312 757403

Lufthansa 9 Talaat Harb--393-0343/66/0425/0534

  6 Sheikh al Mersafi ZA -- 342-0471

Malev Hungarian Airlines 12 Talaat Harb ---------------------- 753111 744959 753898

Middle East Airlines 12 Kasr al Nil- ---------------------- 743151 743422 750984 743100

Nile Delta Air Service 1 Talaat Harb -------------------------------- 746191 740935

Olympic Airlines 23 Kasr al Nil --------------------- 393-1318/1459/1277 392-6367/0919

Pakistan International Airlines 22 Kasr al Nil------------------------392-4055/4213/2134

Pan American Airlines c/o EMECO, 2 Talaat Harb------------------------- 747399/02

Philippine Airlines 17 Ismail Mohammed ZA---------------------- 340-1948 341-9409

  ---342-0861

Royal Air Maroc 9 Talaat Harb ---------------------------------- 393-0561 392-2956/0378

Sabena Belgian World Airlines 2 Mariette Pasha

  Midan Tahrir --- 743984 753694 777125 751194

Scandinavian Airlines (SAS) 2 Champollion --------------------------------- 753955 753546

Singapore Airlines Nile Hilton --------------------------------------- 769681 762702/492

Somali Airways 14 Champollion --- 743537 741770

Sudan Airways 1 Bustan --- 747145 747398

Swissair 22 Kasr al Nil -- 393-7955 392-1522

  9 Baghdad HE -- 664760 291-7966

Syrian Arab Airlines 45 Talaat Harb--- 757900

Thai Air c/o Bon Voyage 16 Adli ------------------------- 391-1950/8874/2345 395-7669

  --- 390-8099

  2 Mustafa Kamel MA -- 350-1240/1

  25 Ibrahim al Lakkani HE--- 259-1954/1311

Trans World Airlines (TWA) 1 Kasr al Nil ---------------------------------- 749900

Turkish Airlines 26 Mahmoud Bassiouni ----------------------------------- 758939

Uganda Airlines 1 Abdel Hamid Badawi HE -------------------------- 245-3779/6535/8110

United Airlines c/o Bon Voyage, 16 Adli --------------------- 350-1240/1 391-1950/2345

Varig Brazilian Airlines 37 Abdel Khalek Sarwat ------------------------------391-3937
Yemen Airways 15 Mahmoud Bassiouni -----------------------344-6965 743313 740711
--346-6799
Yugoslav JAT Nile Hilton ---742166/054/185
20 Ahmed Tayseer HE ---668374
ZAS Novotel, Cairo Airport Road ---------------------------------------291-8032

BANKS

Alexandria Kuwait International Bank 110 Kasr al Aini -------------------------355-4754
Alwatany Bank of Egypt 50 Abdel Khalek Sarwat -------------------------------392-4477
    Telex: 94132 WETNY UN Cable: ALWATANY
Bank Misr, H.O. 151 Mohammed Farid --912711/150
    Telex:92242 BANSR UN Cable: BANISR
Bank Nasser al Egtemai 35 Kasr al Nil --------------------------------392-4536/4625
Bank of Alexandria 49 Kasr al Nil---391-6796
    Telex: 92069 BNALX UN Cable: BANALEX
Bank of Commerce and Development (Al Tegaryoon)
    30 Ramsis--755915/4748
    13 26th July MO --340-9208 819502
    Telex 94330 BCD UN or 21607 BCD UN
    Cable ALTEGARYOON CAIRO
Bank of Credit and Commerce (Misr) S.A.E.
    106 Kasr al Aini Cairo Center Building GC --------------775321/3/7 355-7328/3/7/1
    Telex 94330 BCCKA UN, Cable BCCMISR
Banque du Caire 22 Adli--392-6966
Banque du Caire et de Paris S.A.E.
    14 Saray al Kobra GC or 3 Latin America GC -----------------------------354-8323/4
    Telex 93722 BACAP UN, Cable BACAIPAR
Cairo Far East Bank S.A.E. 104 al Nil DO---------------------------------710280 713554
    Telex 93977 CASOL UN, Cable CAIFABANK
Central Bank of Egypt 31 Kasr al Nil --751667/738
    Hesseen Rashad DO ---348-0241
    Telex 92237 CBECR UN, Cable MARKAZI
Commercial International Bank (formerly Chase National Bank)
    21-23 Giza GI--726132
Delta International Bank 1113 Corniche al Nil ----------------------------753484 743456
    Telex 93319 DIB UN, Cable BNKDELTA
    Corner of Rd 79 and 10, MA------------------------------------351-2602 350-9715
Egyptian American Bank 4 Hasan Sabri ZA --------------------------------341-6150/7/8
    Telex 92683 EGAMB UN, Cable EGAMBK BANK

Egyptian Gulf Bank 2 Abdel Kader Hamza GC ----------------------355-1603/2124/2970
　Kalifa al Mamun HE --291-4801/2
　Telex 93545 EGUB UN
Egyptian Worker's Bank 10 Mohammed Helmi Ibrahim ------------------------------760481
Faisal Islamic Bank of Egypt 1113 Corniche al Nil------------------------------753109/65
　15 Higaz HE ---258-1256
　1 Midan al Azhar --911208
　Telex 792131 FBANK UN, Cable FAISAL ISLAMIC BANK CAIRO.
Giza National Bank for Development 114 Tahrir DO ------------------------------712393
Hong Kong Egyptian Bank 3 Abu al Feda ZA -----------------------340-9186/8930/4849
　Telex 20471 HKEB UN.
Misr America International Bank (Bank of America)
　8 Ibrahim Naguib GC ---355-7071
　1 Behlar --393-4159
　5 Saray al Kobra GC --355-4359/4360/1
　6 Botros Ghali HE---258-0730
　Telex 23050 MAIBG UN
Misr International Bank/First National Bank of Chicago
　14 Alfi --912409
　7 Merghani HE --665876
　79 Road 9 MA ---350-9097/0992
　31 Ahmed Heshmat ZA ---341-3798
　Telex 92165 MIBCAI, UN Cable MIBANKCAI
Misr Rumanian Bank 15 Abu al Feda ZA --------------------------819275 341-4081/2795
　Telex 93653 MRB UN, Cable ROMISBANK ----------------------------/8045 340-3292
　Higaz HE --259-2030
Mohandes Bank 30 Ramsis --748659 750972
　Gawhar al Kaed, Darassa ---932070
　Telex 93950 MB UN, Cable HANDESBANK
National Bank for Development
　48-50 Abdel Khalek Sarwat --933331/559
　Telex 94089 NBD UN, Cable TANMIA
National Bank of Egypt 24 Sherif --744143/75
　Telex 92911 NBEFX UN or 92238 NBE UN, Cable NATIONAL
Nile Bank 35 Ramsis --743502
　87 Road 9 MA ---350-4480/5740
　24 Ibrahim HE --258-0859
　32A Morad GI--723350
　Gamat al Dowal al Arabiya MO --346-9492
　Telex 344 BANIL UN
Pyramids Bank 12 Ittihad al Muhamiyin al Arab GC ------------------------------354-7112
　Telex 92228 AHRBK UN, Cable AL AHRAM BANK -------------------------355-4865
Suez Canal Bank Ltd. 11 Mohammed Sabri Abu Alam -------------------------751033/66
　Telex 93852 SCB UN, Cable BANCANAL CAIRO

Non-Commercial Banks

Arab African International Bank
5 Midan Saray al Kobra GC --391-6701/7747/6744
Telex 93531 AAIB UN, Cable ARABAFRO

Arab-Land Bank 33 Abdel Khalek Sarwat ----------------------------------748506 759937
Cable ARACARI CAIRO

Cairo Barclays International Bank
12 Midan Sheikh Yusef GC --354-2195/9415
Telex 92343 CABAR UN or 93734 CABAR UN

Credit Foncier Egyptien 11 Mashhadi--------------------------------------911977 910197
Telex 93863 CFEBK UN

Credit International d'Egypte 2 Talaat Harb --------------------------------757441 759738
Telex 93680 CIE UN, Cable CREDEGYPT

Egypt Arab African Bank 5 Midan Saray al Kobra GC ----------------------354-5094/5/6
44 Abdel Khalek Sarwat --391-6701/6744
21 Ramsis HE --667413
Telex 93531 AAIB UN

Export Development Bank 10 Talaat Harb -----------------------------------769964/8190
Telex 20850 EDBE UN

Housing and Development Bank
14 Talaat Harb --750880
26 Batal Ahmed Abdel Aziz DO--717170 703695
12 Sorya MO ---349-2013
Telex 94075 HDB UN, Cable HOUSEBANK EGYPT

Industrial Development Bank 110 Galaa -----------------------------------779247/188
Telex 92643 DIBAK UN, Cable DEVBANK

Islamic International Bank for Investment and Development
4 Addi DO ---348-9974/5/6/80 843298/926
Telex 94248 IBID UN, Cable ISLAM ASRF CAIRO

Misr Iran Development Bank 8 Adli--------------------------------------939049 727273
Telex 92389 MIDB UN, Cable MIRBANK
21 Giza GI --727371/142
Telex 22407 MIDB UN

National Societe Generale Bank 10 Talaat Harb -------------------------747396 770291
Telex 22307 NASOG UN, Cable NASGEBCA

Principal Bank for Development and Agricultural Credit
110 Kasr al Aini GC ---355-3148
Telex 93045 PBDAC, Cable TASLIF CAIRO

Societe Arabe Internationale de Banque (S.A.I.B.)
10 Abdel Salam Aref ---747266 759736
Telex 92693 SOBANK UN, Cable SOAR INBANK CAIRO

Union Arab Bank for Development and Investment
(Arab Investment Bank) 1113 Corniche al Nil ---------------------------753302/150
Telex 93625, 93792 INVBK UN, Cable INVESBANK CAIRO

Branches of Foreign Banks

American Express International Banking Corporation
4 Ibn Zanki ZA --- 340-1236 341-2287
Telex 93610 AMBNK UN, Cable AMEXBANK

Arab Bank Limited 28 Talaat Harb -- 746026
Telex 92716 92781 ARBNK UN, Cable BANKARABI

Banca Commerciale Italiana 3 Ahmed Nessim GI ----------------------- 726109 727742
Telex 92669 BCICAI UN, Cable COMITBANXA CAIRO
2 Wadi al Nil MO--- 346-1823/36/64 92275
Telex BCIFX UN

Bank Melli Iran 6 Gezira al Wasta --- 340-0053/5
Telex 92633 CMELI UN, Cable BANK MELLI

Bank of America 106 Kasr al Aini GC --- 355-2747
Telex 92425 BOFA UN, Cable BANKAMERICA

Bank of Credit and Commerce International O/S Ltd.
106 Kasr al Aini
44 Mohammed Mazhar ZA -- 341-5693/1179
Telex 93806 BCCAR UN, Cable ZAMRE COM
48 Giza GI --- 848877 982509
Telex 92929 BCCGA UN

Bank of Nova Scotia 3 Ahmed Nessim GI--------------------------------- 726055/146
Telex 92187 BNSCUN, Cable SCOTIACARE

Bank of Oman Ltd. 21 Darih Saad off Kasr al Aini------------ 355-0366/7430 354-7876
Telex 93819 OMANCA UN, Cable BANOMNTD
Nile Tower Building GI -- 730732/5270

Bank Saderat Iran 28 Sherif--- 770147
Telex 92611 SADBK UN, Cable SADERBANK CAIRO

Banque Paribas 5 Birgas, Arab African International
Building, GC --- 354-0391/7323 355-7278
Telex 22332 BPBE UN

Citibank N. A. 4 Ahmed Pasha GC --- 355-1843-7
Telex 92832 CITAR UN, Cable CITIBANK

Credit Lyonnais 3 Abu al Feda -- 340-3712/43/61
Telex 92577 CRELYO UN, Cable CRELYOREP

Credit Suisse 6 Oqba DO --- 348-6618/4666/4333
Telex 92427 CSCA UN, Cable CREDSWISS

Jammal Trust Bank S.A.L. 4 Ahmed Pasha GC ---------------- 354-8260/5585 355-7651
Telex 22508 JAMBK UN, Cable TRUST JAMI
15A Ahram HE --- 291-6854/6830

Lloyds Bank International Ltd.
44 Mohammed Mazhar ZA -------------------------------------- 341-8366 340-6578
Telex 92344 LLOYD UN, Cable INTER LOYD
48 Abdel Khalek Sarwat --- 933384

Middle East Bank Ltd. 30 Abdel Khalek Sarwat ---------------------------- 776345 769302
 Telex 93591 MIBNK UN
National Bank of Abu Dhabi 21 Murad GI ------------------------------------- 722-989/768
 Telex 92310 BNZAB UN, Cable BNZABIE
 22 Kasr al Nil --- 393-4220
National Bank of Greece 2 Aziz Osman ZA ---------------------------- 341-1772 340-6610
 Telex 92825 NATCA UN, Cable ETHNOBANK CAIRO
National Bank of Oman Ltd. 26 Kasr al Nil ------------------------------------- 355-7430
 Telex 93309 NBO UN, Cable NATOMBANK CAIRO
National Bank of Pakistan 1113 Corniche al Nil GC ---------------------------- 349-8955/9
 Telex 92527 MILLAT UN, Cable MILLATBANK CAIRO.
National Bank of Sudan Nile Hilton, Midan Tahrir --------------------------------- 392-1691
Rafidain Bank 114 Tahrir DO--- 349-6851

Free Zone Banks

Manufacturers Hanover Trust Co. 3 Ahmed Nessim GI ---------------------- 726703/644
 Telex 92660 MHTCO UN, Cable MANTRUST

Representative Offices

Banque Indosuez 12 Midan Sheikh Yusef GC ------------------------------- 356-0915/2329
 Telex 21175 INDOS UN
IT Commerciale de France 26 Mahmoud Bassiouni ------------------------- 740441 752980
 Telex 92687 CCF UN
Chase Manhattan Overseas Corp. 21-23 Giza GI ------------------------- 728485/419/502
 Telex 23215 CMOC UN
Chemical Bank 14 Talaat Harb -------------------------------- 762357 750727 740707/652
 Telex 23423, 92066 CHMBK UN, Cable CHEMSAM
Commerzbank A. G. 2 Ali Labib Gabr -------------------------------------- 751661 766203
 or 2 Behlar Passage off Kasr al Nil, Telex 92194 CBK UN
Credito Italiano 3 Abu al Feda ZA -- 341-8656
Den Norske Credit Bank 3 Ahmed Nessim GI ------------------------------ 727825 729499
 Telex 93750 USSI UN
Deutsche Bank A.G. 23 Kasr al Nil --- 762341 741373
 Telex 92306 DEUCAI UN
Development Industrial Bank Galaa -- 779087/247
 Telex 92643 DIBAK UN
Dresdner Bank A. G. 33 Kasr al Nil -- 773841
 Telex 92603 DRESAG UN
Midland Bank 3 Ahmed Nessim GI --- 726934 728332
 Telex 92439 MIDBK UN
Monte Dei Paschi Banking Group Nile Hilton Annex ----------------------- 764441 770505
 Telex 22108 PASCH UN
Morgan Grenfell and Co. Ltd. 1 Latin America GC ----------------------- 354-8018/6720
 Telex 92390 MORGN UN

Royal Bank of Canada 3 Abu al Feda ZA -- 340-8115/5972
    Telex 92725 ROCAR UN
State Bank of India 15 Kamel Shinnawi GC ---------------------------------- 354-3504/2522
    Telex 93068 SBICA UN
Societe Generale 9 Talaat Harb -- 393-7957/2347
    Telex 92512 SGCAI UN
Sumitomo Bank Ltd. 16 Sherif --- 772609
    Telex 92470 SUNBK
Swiss Bank Corp. 3 Ahmed Nessim GI ---------------------------------- 727005 729384
    Telex 92469 SBCET UN
Union de Banque Arabes et Francaise (UBAF)
    4 Behlar Passage off Kasr al Nil --- 744654
    Telex 93277 UBAFC UN
United Bank Ltd. 8 Sadd al Aali DO --- 709935
    Telex 21260 UBL UN

Other Banks

Arab International Bank 35 Abdel Khalek Sarwat ------------------------ 918794 916726
    Telex 92079 AIB UN or 92081 AIBEX UN
Arab Investment Bank 1113 Corniche al Nil ------------------------ 753116/301/302/380
    Telex 93025, 93792 INUBNK UN
Banco do Brazil 48 Abdel Khalek Sarwat -- 924309
    Telex 93581 BBSAE UN
Bank fur Handel und Effekten 2 Midan Messaha DO --------------------------- 349-0140
    Telex 92096, 93644 ALKAN UN
Bank of Tokyo Ltd. Nile Hilton Business Center --------------------------- 766318 755460
    Telex 92392 TOHGIN UN
Bankers Trust Co. 17 Kasr al Nil -- 743427/898
    Telex 93514, 93826 BTCRO UN
Banque de l'Union Europeene 3 Ahmed Nessim GI --------------------- 727504 729508
    Telex 92450 AMIN UN
Banque Francaise du Commerce Exterieur
    50 Abdel Khalek Sarwat -- 904667 905173
    Telex 21780 BSCE UN
Banque National du Paris 14 Saray al Kobra GC -------------------- 355-7080 354-1534
    Telex 92419 NATPAR UN
Misr Exterior Bank Cairo Plaza, Corniche --------------------------------- 778380/619/701
    Telex 21616 XTMSR UN
Nasser Social Bank 35 Kasr al Nil --------------------------------------- 393-2113 763292
    Telex 92754 NSRBNK UN
National Investment Bank
    18 Abdel Meguid al Remali Bab al Louk---------------------------------- 354-1336/4903

CHURCHES

Catholic Churches

Church of the Annunciation 36 Mohammed Sabri Abu Alam, near Midan Talaat Harb 393-8429. Armenian Rite. Holy Liturgy Sunday 8:15 am (in Coptic with Arabic readings); 9:30am, 10:30am and 6:30pm (in Armenian with French readings).

Our Lady of Peace Melkite (Greek Catholic) 4 Midan al Sheikh Yusef, 96 Kasr al Aini 354-5826. Byzantine Rite in Arabic. Holy Liturgy Sunday at 8:30am, 10:30am, and 6:00pm, weekdays at 7:30am. English, French, German, Spanish, Italian, and Dutch translations of the Holy Liturgy are available on the porch.

Cathedral of St. Anthony the Great 7 Yusef Soliman, off 55 Kamel Sidki, Faggala 905593. Coptic Rite, in Coptic and Arabic. Holy Liturgy Sunday at 7, 8, and 9am and 6pm.

St. Marun Church (Kanisat al Mawarna) 15 Beirut HE 743916. Maronite Rite in Syriac and Arabic. Holy Liturgy Sunday 8am, 11am, and 7pm. Feast Days at 8am, 11am, and 7:30pm.

St. Joseph's Cathedral 24 Hamdi, al Daher 923327. Maronite Rite in Syriac and Arabic. Holy Liturgy Sunday at 7am, 8am, 9am, 10am, and 6pm; every day at 7am.

Basilica of Our Lady Midan al Ahram HE 669037 662769. Latin Rite in French and Arabic. Monsignor Genaro De Martino. Service Sunday 9am; 10:30am; 8pm in French; 7pm in Arabic.

The Chapel of Sisters of St. Charles Borromeo (German Sisters) 8 Mohammed Mahmoud, Bab al Louk 354-2226. Latin Rite. Holy Mass Sunday 9:15 am in German; every third Sunday at 6pm.

Holy Family Catholic Church 55 Road 15 MA 350-2004. Latin Rite. Father Damien Dougherty. Daily Mass in French 8am Friday. Family Mass 10am Saturday in English. Saturday Mass 6pm in German, 7pm in French. Sunday Mass 9:30am in French 10:30am and 6pm in English. Confessions Saturday 4:30-6pm.

Cordi Jesu Church of the Fathers of Verona (Combonian Friars) 3 Abdel Khalek Sarwat at 47 Ramses 758272. Latin Rite. Holy Mass Sunday 8am in Arabic; 9am in French. In summer, extra service Sunday 6:30am in French.

St. Clare's College and Convent Isna between Thawra and Beirut HE 665701. Latin Rite. Holy Mass Sunday 10:30am and Friday 6pm in English.

St. Joseph's Church (Italian and Egyptian Franciscan Friars) 2 Bank Misr at corner of Mohammed Farid 393-6677. Latin Rite. Holy Mass Sunday 7:30am in French; 8:30am in Arabic; 10am in Italian; 12:30pm in French; 5:30pm in English; 6:30pm in French. Weekdays 7:30am and 6:30pm in French.

St. Joseph's Roman Catholic Church 4 Ahmed Sabri ZA 340-8902/9348. Latin Rite. Holy Mass Sunday 8:30am in Arabic; 11am in English; 6pm in French. Weekdays 6pm in French. Saturday 6pm in Italian (sometimes Spanish).

St. Theresa of the Child Jesus (Carmelite Friars) 163 Shubra, Shubra 943490. Latin Rite. Holy Mass Sunday 7:30 am, 9am, 10am, 6pm in Arabic (Father Prior is Spanish).

Orthodox Churches

Armenian Orthodox Cathedral of St. Gregory the Illuminator 179 Ramses near Coptic Hospital 901385. Armenian Rite in Armenian. Holy Liturgy Sunday 9-11am.

Greek Orthodox Cathedral of St. Nicholas 85 al Azhar 903516 900013. Byzantine Rite in Greek. Holy Liturgy Sunday 8am. Vespers weekdays 4:30pm.
Abu Sarga Church Old Cairo 987887. Coptic Rite in Coptic and Arabic. Holy Liturgy Sunday 8am-12pm; Ash Wednesday service 7am in English. Visiting hours for the church daily from 9am-5pm; the church building is of historic interest.
St. Mark's Cathedral 222 Ramses Abbassia 820681 831822. Coptic Rite in Coptic and Arabic. Holy Liturgy Sunday 6-8am; Solemn Liturgy 8-11am. Fridays 8-10am. Pastors speak English, French.
Church of Saints Peter and Paul, (al Botrosia) 222 Ramses Abbassia 281-2274 282-5358. Coptic Rite in Coptic and Arabic. Holy Liturgy Sunday 7-8:45am and 8:45-11:30am.
Church of the Virgin (the "Hanging Church," al Muallaqa), Old Cairo, facing the Mari Girgis station on the Cairo-Helwan Metro line, 989081. Holy Liturgy Sunday 7-9am and 9-11am; Fridays 7-10am. The church building is of historic interest.
Church of the Virgin Mary 6 Mohammed Marashli ZA 340-5153. Coptic Rite in Coptic and Arabic. Holy Liturgy Sunday 7:30-9:30am and 9:30-11am.

Protestant Churches

All Saints' Cathedral 5 Michel Lutfallah ZA, behind the Marriott Hotel 345-9391 340-2074. Episcopal/Anglican. Services in **English**: S 8am Holy Communion (Chapel); S 10:30am (1st, 3rd, 5th S:) Holy Communion, (2nd, 4th S:) Morning Prayer (Main Auditorium); S 7:15pm Evening Prayers, except 4th S: Holy Communion (Main Auditorium); T, Th 7:30am Morning Prayer (Chapel); W 7:30am Holy Communion (Chapel); F 7:30am, 9am Holy Communion (Chapel); F 6pm Fellowship meeting. Services in **Arabic**: S 6pm Evening Service (Main Auditorium). Provost, the Very Reverend Philip Cousins; Assistant Chaplain Robin Lee; Reverend Doctor Bill Musk; Minister to the Arabic-speaking congregation, Reverend Canon Aziz Wasif; Pastoral Assistant, Miss Daphne Goodwin.
Assemblies of God 7 Road 6 MA, Lillian Trasher Orphanage 350-7818. Pastor, Reverend Dwight R. Dobson.
Christian Science Society 3 Midan Mustafa Kamel, P.O. Box 1363 Ataba 350-6194 351-7850. Service and Sunday School, Sunday 7:30pm. Testimony Meeting Wednesday 7:30pm. Reading Room with Bible references and Christian Science literature open Wednesday and Sunday 6-7:20pm and Friday 11am-2pm.
Church of Christ 14A Road 206, Apt. 4, Digla 354-8211 350-4055 (Joe Cormack).
Church of God 15 Emad al Din, Apt. 45, Rev. Russel Skaggs. Home 350-5708, office 912198. 18 Road 6 MA, Rev. James Albrecht. Home 350-4676, office 912198. Sunday service 10:30am, Rev. Mounir Riskallah at 8 Youssef Beynoud, Shoubra, in Arabic.
Church of God Cairo Christian Fellowship St. Andrew's Church, corner of Galaa and 26 July 350-5708. Study and fellowship service 6pm Sunday in English. Sunday service 6pm in English.
Church of Jesus Christ of Latter-Day Saints (Mormon) 44 Road 20 MA 350-4721. Weekly sacrament service Friday at 9:30am.
Coptic Evangelical Church 7 Sheikh Rihan, behind Mugamma 354-6161. Sunday Service in Arabic at 8:30am, 11:15am and 7pm. The Coptic Evangelical Church was established by the United Presbyterian Church of North America in 1854. It is now self-governing and self-supporting. It has an extensive educational service. There are some 20 congregations in Cairo, 300 in the country.

First Baptist Church corner of 50 Khalafawi and Sherif, Shubra 948481 (pastor's home: 271 Shubra, Apt. 4 Shubra). Worship Sunday at 10am and 3pm, Thursday at 7pm.
German Evangelical Church 32 Galaa, Bulak (opposite telephone exchange) 347-8549. Pastor: Reverend H. Seifert, speaks English. Services in German 5:30 first and third Sundays.
Heliopolis Community Church (St. Michael's Church) 10 Seti, off Baghdad HE 668476. Worship Service Sunday 6:30pm, Friday 9:30am. Bible School Friday 10:45. Holy Communion first Sunday of month. Prayer meeting Wednesday 7am. International and interdenominational congregation. Pastor, Rev. Louis Prontnicki.
Korean Congregation Maadi Community Church, corner of Port Said and Road 17 MA. Sunday Worship Service 3pm. Pastor: Rev. Joon Kyo Lee, 350-4620.
Maadi Community Church (The Church of St. John the Baptist) Corner of Port Said and Road 17 MA 351-2755. Services in English Friday 8:30am and 11am, with nursery; Sunday 7pm, no nursery. Church School 9:45am Friday. Communion first Sunday and Friday. Bible Studies: contact Sally Wilkie, 352-8433. International and interdenominational. Pastor, Harold H. Chapman, 353-2118. Youth Director, David Ginter, home/youth center 352-8394. Church office open 9am-3pm or by appointment.
Presbyterian Church 8 Seka al Beida, Abbassia 282-2162 820574. John Lorimer.
Saint Andrew's United Church 38, 26 July and Ramsis 759451. Service in English Sunday 9:30am. Holy Communion Vespers Thursday at 6:30pm. Pastor, Reverend Dr. Michael Shelley.
Saint John the Baptist Church see Maadi Community Church. 350-1486.
Saint Michael's Community Church see Heliopolis Community Church.
Seventh Day Adventist Church 16 Kubba, Roxi HE 258-0292/0785.
Swiss Evangelical Church 39, 26 July at corner of al Galaa, 748199 (home). Service in French Sunday 10:30am at the Swiss Pastor's home, 30 Sherif, fifth floor, Apt. 18.

Religious Community Organizations
Cairo Evangelical Theological Seminary 8 Seka al Beida, Abbassia 820574. Offers B.A. in Theology to graduate and secondary school students. Arabic instruction with some English. Accepts students from other denominations.
Social Services Center/ Episcopal Church in Egypt Services center at 36 Galaa 766655. Episcopal church next to the Marriott Hotel ZA. Services in social work, health education, and religious instruction Sunday 10am.
Society of Friends (Quakers) Ron Wolfe 355-1913.

COMPUTER COMPANIES

This list is provided courtesy of Sheira & Sheira, Management, Computer and Publishing Consultants, publishers of Computer Review and Desktop magazines, 24A Abul Mahasin al Shazli MO 344-8169.

Add-on Boards
Computek Electric & Electronic House
    29 Tahrir DO -- 712765 348-5328

CompuWorld 5 Geziret al Arab and
19 Batal Ahmed Abdel Aziz MO -- 349-8930/9536
Egyptian Advanced Technologies-Balsam
3 Osman Ibn Affan MO --- 344-3001/3002
Brand: Acer, Wang
Systems Research Egypt 55 Merghani HE -- 666282
Brand: AST
Technologia 44 Dokki DO -- 708374

Computer Systems Apple Macintosh
CITE Cairo Information Technology and Engineering
68 Kasr al Aini Flat 76,77 GC ---------------------------- 356-0531 354-5626 355-1661
MicroLand 38 Road 6, Apt. 14 MA --- 350-4941
NGC Computers 22 Mahmoud Hasan 4th District HE ------------------- 667266 291-8026
Pan Arab Computer Center-Egypt (PACC-Egypt)
70 Gamat al Dowal al Arabiya MO -- 348-1381
United Systems 1 Sadd al Ali DO--- 713462

Computer Systems Home Computers
Cat Computers Mahmoud Badr al Din MO ------------------------------------- 346-0705
Brand: Sakhr
CompuWorld 5 Geziret al Arab
19 Batal Ahmed Abdel Aziz MO---------------------------- 349-8930/9536 347-9014
Brand: Atari
Kinow Electronics 8 Samir Said Ahmed
Midan Pasha, Manial --- 842623
Brand: MicroCat
Matsico Zamalek Club Shopping Center MO -------------------------------- 347-5504
Brand: Sinclair
Pan Trade Associates 32 Mosaddaq DO ------------------------------------- 706611
Brand: Atari
PICO 6 Dar al Shifa GC ------------------------------ 354-3175 355-6543/5440 356-1782
1 Latin America--- 354-8190/4565
Zamalek Club Wall Special Passage MO------------------------------------- 345-0418
off Saray al Gezira ZA -- 342-0021
3 Mamalik Roxi HE --- 258-4279
Radwan El Ogeil & Company
4 Gamat al Dowal al Arabiya MO --- 347-0723
Brand: Commodore

Computer Systems Other
Giza Systems Engineering 2 Midan Misaha DO --------------------------- 349-8696/9098
Brand: Digital, Tektronix
Emeco Accounting 26 Ahmed Taysir Flat 502
Madinet al Marwa Kulliet al Banat HE -- 679138

18B, Marashli ZA -- 340-3308
Brand: Prime
IBM World Trade Corp. Egypt Branch
56 Gamat al Dowal al Arabiya MO -- 349-2533
ICL 3 Abul Mahasin al Shazli MO ------------------------------ 346-0899/0748 347-0016
Kolali For Engineering Projects
33 Abdel Khalek Sarwat --- 748787/8 755927
Brand: Cromenco

Computer Systems PC Compatibles

Adel Wissa and Company 18 Shagaret al Dorr ZA ------------------------------ 340-9393
Al Alamia Computers 66 Tayaran MN--- 260-6373
Al Anwar International Computer Co.
31 Suliman Abaza MO --- 702665
Alexandria Computer Systems Technology (ACT)
38 Abdel Hamid Lotfi MO --- 717211 348-1214
Brand: ICL
Alpha Information Management (AIM)
34 Gul Gamal AG --- 346-6967 344-5149
Brand: Cordata, Telex
Al Safa Computers 40 Ansar DO -- 349-8745
Brand: Mandrax
Applied Microsystems Technology (AMT)
98 Mohi al Din Abu al Ezz MO--- 348-0005
Brand: AMT
APTEC Egypt 3 Mahmoud Nashid HE ------------------------------- 245-5634 247-5255
Brand: Epson
Arabia Computer Systems 14 Dimishk MO -------------------------------------- 344-8232
Brand: Circle
AT&T Al Nasr Building Nile GI -- 728872/934
Brand: ATT
Balsam (see listing under Egyptian Advanced Technologies)
BIT Business Information Technology
12 Rashdan Midan Misaha DO ------------------------------------- 348-0599/4941
Brand: IBM PS/2
Building Effective Decision (BED)
22 Geziret al Arab MO--- 346-0229
Brand: Televideo
Cairo Trading 4 Iraq MO --- 348-7741/7517
Brand: Casio, Mandrax, SVI
Cat Computers Mahmoud Badr al Din MO ------------------------------------ 346-0705
Brand: MicroCat
Channel Communications Flat 7,
27 Gezira al Wasta ZA --- 341-3438
Brand: Micronet

CompuLand Data Processing Company
    51 A, Misr Helwan MA --- 350-8210/8060 351-5208
    Brand: Commodore
Computek Electric & Electronic House
    29 Tahrir DO---712-765 348-5328
    Brand: Micronet
ComputerLand 3A Nabatat GC -- 355-3067 354-1810
Continental Assad Najjar & Co.
    43A Kasr al Nil -- 914655/7756 346-0515
    Brand: Continental, Toshiba
Data Care Ltd. 58 Lebanon MO --- 347-4619 346-2161
    Brand: Unitron
Data Computers 48 Sheikh Ahmed Ibrahim HE ----------------------------------- 234-7759
Data Egypt 11 Doctor Mahrouki
    4th Floor HE -- 668907 670947/1689
Datel Systems 6 Shahed Mohammed Abdel Hadi
    Golf Area HE --667927 679539
    Brand: Datel
Egyptian Advanced Technologies-Balsam
    3 Osman Ibn Affan MO---344-3001/2
    Brand: Acer, Balsam, Wang
Egyptian Automated Equipment
    El Nahda Tower 21 Ahmed Orabi MO ----------------------------- 346-0321 347-3868
    Brand: ATT, Olivetti
Egyptian Computer Systems (ECS)
    56 Gamat al Dowal al Arabiya ------------------------------------ 704-553 348-7007
    Brand: IBM PS/2
Egypto German Office Supply (EGOS)
    2 Sherif Lewa Building -- 750734
    Brand: Micronet, Olympia
Egyptian Technology Center 1 Okasha Midan Misaha DO --------------------348-0184
Electrum 5 Makrizi ZA--340-8913 341-1795
    Brand: Samsung
Electronics Consulting Office 31- 33 Private Passage
    2nd floor Zamalek Club Shop. Cntr. MO ----------------------------------- 347-6730
    Brand: Zenith
Elgeil El Gedid 8 Ibrahim Naguib GC --------------------------------------- 355-0861/4331
El Nakhil for Trading & Construction 161 Sudan MO----------------------------346-5266
    Brand: Cordata
Engineering Data Systems 78 Gumhuria Flat 23 --------------------------914035 904668
    Brand: Leo
Engineering Office for Integrated Services
    4 Road 268 New Maadi ---352-4523/1727
General Micro Computer Systems & Services
    19A Khalifa al Mamun HE --- 291-2937

Giza Systems Engineering 2 Midan Misaha DO --------------------------- 349-8696/9098
    Brand: Digital
Informatic for Managerial & Electronic Systems
    13 Kasr al Nil --- 740822/0631
InfoTek Management Consultants
    18 Darih Saad Apt 7 Kasr al Aini -- 355-0362
International Company for Computing Machinery (ICCM)
    34 Mohammed Youssef al Kadi, Kulliet al Banat HE ----------------------------- 669331
International Computers 66 Tayaran MN -- 260-6373
Kafco 21 Ahmed Orabi MO ------------------------------------- 346-0321 347-4823 616762
Khalifa Engineering (KECCA) 3rd floor, Building 7
    Madinet Faisal GI --- 861794
    Brand: Universe
Kemet Corporation 39 Beirut HE --- 291-7529
Kinow Electronics 8 Samir Said Ahmed
    Midan Pasha, Manial --- 842623
    Brand: MicroCat
MAS 1 Al-Abour Building, Salah Salem Road HE --------------------------------- 616059
Matsico Zamalek Club Shopping Center MO -------------------------------------- 347-5504
    Brand: Amstrad
Metra Computer 21 26th July MO ------------------------------------ 344-3133 345-2538
    Brand: Tandy
MicroWare Services 16 Madinet al Tewfik MN ----------------------------------- 616762
Middle East Scientific Agencies (MSA)
    58 Nabawi al Mohandis AG -- 346-8925/1898
Misr Computer and Systems 18 Mansour Mohammed ZA ---------------------- 341-3906
Misr Computer 3 Road 73 MA --- 350-3870
Misr International Systems 4 Abaza Midan Mahkama HE ------------------------ 742744
Misr Micro Computers 1A Sayed al Bakri ZA ---------------------------------- 340-2827
    Brand: Kaypro
Modern Computer Services 16 Abdel Rahman Rushdi HE --------------------- 246-0777
Modern Management Methods
    6 Gezira al Wasta ZA -- 340-3642/3674
Mokash Advanced Systems
    46 Shahed Abdel Meneim, Almaza HE -- 663973
NCR Egypt Ltd. 21 Giza GI --- 729866/9664 738425
NGC Computers 22 Mahmoud Hasan 4th District HE ------------------ 667266 291-8026
    Brand: PC Net
Orascom Onsi Sawiris and Co. 160 26th July AG --------------------- 344-1962 347-8262
    346-5674 345-1135
Perfect Data Systems 42 Al Zahraa DO -------------------------------------- 349-4441/0442
Pharaoh's Computer Center 19 Khalifa al Mamun
    Suite 511 Roxi HE -- 291-0367
Pheonix Systems 4 Gamal al Din Abul Mahasin GC-------------------------------- 354-6833
Pyramids Computers 46 Syria Flat 5 MO -- 712031

Sakrko International 70 Mosadaq DO ---702963
Salsabeel 14 Amin al Rafai DO ---348-5308
  Brand: AMT
Sigma Co. for Eng. & Trading
  29 al Makrizi 5th floor, Flat 12 HE ---259-4644
Systems Engineering of Egypt 45 Dr. Hasan Aflaton
  Golf Grounds HE ---665948
Systems Research Egypt 55 Merghani HE ---666282
  Brand: AST
Technico Misr 8 Yusef Abbas MN ---260-5277/4161
Technologia 44 Dokki DO ---708374
TIT Engineering 25 Sheikh Ali Abdel Razek HE ---244-8594
United Electronics & Trade Co. 55 Giza Flat 6 GI ---733095
United Projects 64 Higaz HE ---247-1102
Xerox 2 Libnan MO ---346-1059 346-1221 344-8138
  Brand: Xerox

Modems
Channel Communications Flat 7 27 Gezira al Wasta ZA ---341-3438
Racal Melgo 24 Abaza HE ---243-0777
Systems Research Egypt 55 Merghani HE ---666282

Plotters
CompuWorld 5 Geziret al Arab
  19 Batal Ahmed Abdel Aziz MO ---349-8930/9536 347-9014
  Brand: Graphtec
Kemet Corporation 39 Beirut HE ---291-7529

Power Protection/UPS
Egyptian Advanced Technologies-Balsam
  3 Osman Ibn Affan MO ---344-3001/3002
Immunelec Middle East
  87A Abdel Aziz al Saud Manial ---989785 356-8777
Mega Systems
  25 Sheikh Ali Abdel Razek HE ---244-8594
Orabi 36 Gamat al Dowal al Arabiya MO ---347-3845

Printers
Computek Electric & Electronic House 29 Tahrir DO ---712765 348-5328
  Brand: Hewlett Packard, Super Five
CompuWorld 5 Geziret al Arab
  19 Batal Ahmed Abdel Aziz MO ---349-9536 347-9014
  Brand: Star
Continental Assad Najjar & Co.
  43A Kasr al Nil ---914655/7756 346-0515
  Brand: Continental, Toshiba

Egyptian Advanced Technologies-Balsam
3 Osman Ibn Affan MO -- 344-3001/3002
Brand: Acer, Balsam, Wang
Salsabeel 14 Amin al Rafai DO -- 348-5308
Xerox 2 Libnan MO --- 346-1059/1221 344-8138

Computer Software

Advanced Computer Applications (ACA)
8 Talaat Harb -- 747441 712765
Advanced Computer Engineering Solutions (ACES)
189 Higaz HE --- 247-4235
Al Alamia Computers 66 Tayaran MN -- 260-6373
Al Anwar International Computer Company
31 Suliman Abaza MO -- 702665
27 Road 9 MA -- 351-3583
Alpha Misr Computer Consultant 7 Okasha DO -------------------------------- 348-4742
APTEC Egypt 3 Mahmoud Nashid HE ------------------------------- 245-5634 247-5255
Arabic Micro Systems (AMS) 12 al Baidak Ataba ----------------------------- 390-3323
Automatic System Services (A.S.)
5 al Gamaa Midan Giza GI --- 723017
Automation 24 Abdel Rahman Rushdi HE ------------------------------------- 244-3943
CITE Cairo Information Technology and Engineering
68 Kasr al Aini Flat 76,77 GC --------------------------- 354-5626 356-0531 355-1661
Compact Computer Systems
8 al Abour Building, Salah Salem MN -- 610694
Computer Consulting and Supplies Co.
33B Mohammed Mazhar ZA --------------------------------- 340-2558/2557 341-5424
CompuLand Data Processing Company
51A Misr Helwan MA --------------------------------------- 350-8210/8060 351-5208
Computek Electric & Electronic House
29 Tahrir DO -- 712765 348-5328
Data Care 58 Libnan MO --- 346-2161 347-4619
Datacom Int. Co. For Systems & Computer
5 Zahraa DO -- 717957 707011
Data Management Systems
6 Dr. Mohammed Mamun HE --------------------------------------- 243-8800 244-9373
Delta Computer Center 5 Abdulla Ibn al Zubair HE ---------- 244-4997/0375 246-7338
DPS 87 Road 9 MA -- 351-2078 350-7475
Egyptian Advanced Technologies-Balsam
3 Osman Ibn Affan MO --- 344-3001/3002
Electro George 33 Ahmed Hishmat ZA --------------------------- 341-1797/7969 340-2504
Engineering Data Systems (EDS)
78 Gumhuria Apt #23 --- 914035 904668
Environmental Quality International
18 Mansur Mohammed ZA -- 340-1924 341-3296

Fancy Soft 162 Higaz HE ---247-3171
GaMed Computer Consultants and Engineers
   7 al Saad Flat 62 Roxi --257-8942
IBI Software 82 Mohi al Din Abu al Ezz MO ---------------------------------------702780
InfoArab Arabic Information Systems
   4 Midan Ibn al Walid off Shooting Club DO--700287
ISM Consulting Group 24 Anas Ibn Malek MO --------------------------713172 349-0208
Kemet Corporation 39 Beirut HE ---291-7529
Khalifa for Engineering and Computer P.O. Box 339 Imbaba---861794
Metra Computer Show Room: Computer Center
   21 26th July MO --- 344-3133 345-2538
MicroTech 5 Gul Gamal AG ---347-8218
PICO 6 Dar al Shifa GC ------------------------------354-3175 355-6543/5440 356-1782
Rai Company 62 Libnan Floor 2 MO -----------------------------------347-3837 350-3765
Ram Computer Services 63 al Nadi Golf District MA -----------------------------350-5561
Sarhank & Washi Group 56 Gamat al Dowal al Arabiya MO ----------------------704553
   Brand: MicroSoft ---348-7007
Score Consultants 40 Kambez MO ---349-1645 704881
Sigma Eng. & Trading Co. 29 al Makrizi
   Manshiet al Bakri HE--259-4644
Standard Data 7 al Nadi Roxi-- 670039 291-7333
   13 Ahmed Orabi MO ---346-9164

Services and Consulting
Al Ahram Management and Computer Center
   28 Murad GI --745666 755500/8333
Al Alamia Computers 66 Tayaran MN--260-6373
Al Anwar Computers 31 Suliman Abaza MO --------------------------------------702665
Alexandria Computer Systems Technology (ACT)
   38 Abdel Hamid Lotfi MO ---717211 348-1214
Al Fath for Training and Preparation
   181 Sudan MO --346-5266
APTEC EGYPT 3 Mahmoud Nashid HE -------------------------------245-5634 247-5255
Arabian Data Systems (ADS)
   24A, Abul Mahasin al Shazli MO ---344-8299/9738
Automation 24 Abdel Rahman Rushdi HE---244-3943
Balco 43 Abdel Khalek Sarwat ---390-8450
Channel Communications Flat 7, 27 Gezira al Wasta ZA -----------------------341-3438
CompuLand 51A Misr Helwan MA --------------------------------350-8210/8060 351-5208
Computer Consulting and Supplies Co.
   33B Mohammed Mazhar ZA ------------------------------340-2558 340-2557 341-5424
Computer Technical Company 15 Hasan DO --------------------------715784 349-3279
ComSys The British Institute Building
   Sahafiyin MO--346-2505

Digital Systems 1st May District MN
   10 Building Apt. #111 --607027
Egyptian Advanced Technologies (Balsam)
   3 Osman Ibn Affan MO --344-3001/3002
Egyptian Computer Systems Training Center (ECS)
in Association With Sarhank & Washi Group
   56 Gamat al Dowal al Arabiya MO ------------------------------------ 704553 348-7007
Egyptian Center for Computers and Education
   17 Mohammed Hafez DO ---715486
Electronics Consulting Office 21 al Sahaba DO ---------------------------713287 705121
   31 & 33 Private Passage, Zamalek Club
   Shopping Center MO ---347-6730
El Mohandes National Company for Information
   48 al Kods al Sherif MO ---347-2723
El Shark Computer Center 44 Brazil ZA --- 341-5958
Emeco Accounting
   502 Madinet al Marwa, Kulliet al Banat HE --------------------------------------- 679138
   18B Marashli ZA --340-3308
Engineering Data Systems (EDS)
   78 Gumhuria Apt 23 --914035 904668
Engineering Offices for Integrated Services
   4 Road 286 New Maadi ---352-4523 352-1727
Environmental Quality International
   18 Al Mansour Mohammed ZA ---------------------------------------340-1924 341-3296
Ericsson 9 Orabi MO --753633/3601/3582
High Tech 28 Mohi al Din Abu al Ezz MO -------------------------------------349-1051
ICL 3 Abul Mahasin al Shazli MO ---346-0899/
InfoTek Management Consultants
   18 Darih Saad Apt. 7 ---355-0365
Internatiaonal Advanced Business Sheraton Complex
   Misr Lil Tamer Area 2, Bldg. 18, first floor HE --------------------291-8522 290-2714
International Center For Systems
   4 Gama Nashaat ZA ---340-8897
I.S.M. Consulting Group 24 Anas Ibn Malek MO -----------------------------713172 349-0208
ICS 4 Gama Nashaat ZA --340-8897
KECCA 3rd Floor, Building 7 Madinet Faisal, Faisal GI------------------------------ 861794
Management Information Systems Services 36 Higaz MO --------------------346-7774
Mohamed Abdel Wahab 7 al Yemen MO ---------------------------------346-4843 707079
NCR 186 Nile AG ---738425 729866/9664
Nile-Net International 8 Wissa Wassef
   Opposite Kobri al Gamaa GI-- 735415
NGC Computers 22 Mahmoud Hasan HE -------------------------------667266 2918026
Omar Seif El Din & Sons 5 Mahmoud Azmi ZA ---------------340-3416/7125 341-4934
Score Consultants 40 Kambez MO -------------------------------------349-1645 704881
SC Systems 80 Khalifa al Mamun Roxi ---258-5583

Shawki & Company Member firm of Arthur Andersen & Co.
  16 Adli --- 920780 917299/9986
Sheira and Sheira Computer, Management and
    Publishing Consultants 24A, Abul Mahasin al Shazli MO ------------------ 344-8196
System 96 Mohi al Din Abu al Ezz MO -- 702386
TEAM Miisr 2 Shahed Ismail Fahmi HE -------------------------------- 668017 6340-7125
Technologia 44 Dokki DO -- 708374
TRT Telecommunications Corp. 14 Gawad Hosni Kasr al Nil -------------------- 762461

Supplies
Computer Consulting and Supplies Co.
  33B Mohammed Mazhar ZA -- 340-2558 340-2557
  -- 341-5424 341-8529
Elgeil El Gedid 8 Ibrahim Naguib GC --- 355-0861/4331
M.E.S. Computer Systems 87 Abdel Aziz al Saud Manial ------------------------ 989785
Modern Office Automation 7 Iraq MO-- 248-0023
    Dysan Diskettes
Mona Trading Co. 16 Huda Shaarawi Bab El Louk------------------------ 769704   758956
    TDK Diskettes
Pharaoh's Computer Company 19 Khalifa al Mamun
    Roxi HE --- 291-0367
United Electronics & Trade Co 55 Giza 6th Floor, Flat 6 --------------------------- 733095

Maintenance
CompuServe Mohamed Abboud 1 Ahmed Shawki GI -------------------------------- 673259
Computer Island 13 Abdel Hamid Lotfi MO--------------------------------------- no phone

Computer Furniture
Dimension 17A Higaz MO --- 346-1237 347-0737
IDEA Zamalek Club Shopping Center MO --- 346-2430

Training
Al Fath for Training and Preparation 181 Sudan MO ---------------------------- 346-5266
American Training Center 3A Nabatat GC ---------------------------- 355-3067 354-1810
American University In Cairo
    Division of Commercial and Industrial Training CIT
    28 Falaki Bab el Louk-- 354-2964/69
American University In Cairo
    Division of Public Service (DPS) Computer Education Dept.
    28 Falaki Bab el Louk-- 354-2964/69
Egyptian Advanced Technologies (Balsam)
    3 Osman Ibn Affan MO --- 344-3001/3002
Egyptian Computer Systems Training Center (ECS)
    in Association With Sarhank & Washi Group
    56 Gamat al Dowal al Arabiya MO ----------------------------------- 704553 348-7007

Egyptian Center for Computers and Education
 17 Mohammed Hafez DO --715486
Professional Business Services (PBS)
 4 Latin America Suite 32 Osiris Building GC ----------------------355-1913   356-0741
Sadat Academy for Management Science
 Corniche El Nil Entrance to Maadi MA --350-5673
Scientific Computing Center Ain Shams University Abbassia --------------------822326
Shawki & Company Member firm of Arthur Andersen & Co.
 16 Adli P.O. Box 2095 --- 920780 917299 917986
TEAM Misr
 2 Shahed Ismail Fahmi HE --668017/5825 697734

EMBASSIES

Names, titles, and home addresses of all diplomatic officers in Cairo are published in the **Liste Diplomatique**, available from the Department of the Ministry of Foreign Affairs, Giza Building, just north of the western end of the Giza Bridge. Most embassies also compile similar information for their own staffs.

What your embassy can do for you

There are many ways in which your embassy can help you. An embassy's consular section can assist in handling student letters, Egyptian visa difficulties, financial problems, emergency medical problems, deaths, or arrests; as well as with birth certificates in certain cases, passports, marriage certificates, and notarizations. Some of these services carry nominal fees. Most embassies close Fridays and Saturdays or Sundays; some close Saturdays and Sundays.

Afghanistan Embassy of India Interests
 Section of Afghanistan 59 Oruba HE ------------------------------------666653 664104
Albania 29 Ismail Mohammed ZA --341-5651
Algeria Embassy of India Interests
 Section of Algeria 14 Brazil ZA --340-2466
Angola Fuad Mohi al Din MO --- 707602 340-8259
Apostolic Internuncio 5 Mohammed Mazhar ZA --------------------------------340-6152
Argentina 8 Salah al Din ZA ------------------------------------- 340-1501/5234 341-7765
 Economic Office: 17 Brazil ZA --340-9241
Australia Cairo Plaza, Corniche al Nil, Bulak------------------------------- 777900/994
Austria al Nil and Wissa Wassef GI------------------------------------- 737640/658/602
Bahrain 8 Gamaiyet al Nisr MO -------------------------------- 706202 705413 709291/217
Bangladesh 40 Syria MO -------------------------------- 349-0646 709811 707486 708294
Belgium 20 Kamel al Shinnawi GC--354-7494/5/6
Bolivia 19 Gamal al Din Abul Mahasin GC ------------------------------------354-6878

Bourkina Fasso 40 Thawra, Madinet al Zobbat DO ------------------------------- 709754
Brazil 1125 Corniche al Nil, Maspero ------------------------------------ 756938 773013
Bulgaria Embassy of Democratic Germany
Bulgarian Interests Section Malek al Afdal ZA ------------------------------- 341-3025/6077
Burma 24 Mohammed Mazhar ZA -- 341-2644/6793
Burundi 13 Israa MO -- 346-2173/9940
Cameroon 42 Babel DO-- 704843/622/954
Canada 6 Mohammed Fahmi al Sayed GC ----------------------------------- 354-3110/9
Central Africa 13 Shehab MO ------------------------------- 350-2337 713291/152
Chad 31 Adnan Omar Sidki DO ------------------------------------ 704726 703232
Chile 5 Shagaret al Dorr ZA -- 340-8711/8446
China 14 Bahgat Ali ZA------------------------------------ 341-7691/1219 340-9459
Colombia 20a Gamal al Din Abul Mahasin GC ----------------------------- 355-9226
Cuba 6 Fawakeh MO/DO ----------------------------------- 704044 710525/390
Cyprus 23a Ismail Mohammed ZA----------------------------------- 341-1288/0327
Czechoslovakia 4 Dokki DO------------------------------------- 348-5531/5469/6550
Democratic Republic of Germany 13 Hussein Wassef DO --------------------- 348-4525
-- 844236/092/306/435
Denmark 12 Hasan Sabri ZA ------------------------------------ 340-7411/2502/8673
Djibouti 157 Sudan MO-- 349-0611/5
Ecuador 8 Abdel Rahman Fahmi GC ----------------------------------- 354-06113/6372
El Salvador 20 al Sadd al Aali DO ------------------------------------ 700834
Ethiopia 59 Evan DO -- 705372/133
Federal Republic of Germany 8A Hasan Sabri ZA ------------------------------- 358-4540
----------------------------------- 340-6017/3687 341-0015/8227/8153/2445
Finland 10 Kamel Mohammed ZA -- 341-1487/3722
France 29 Morad GI-- 393-4316/4645
Gabon 17 Makka al Mokarama DO------------------------------------ 348-1395 709699
Ghana 24 al Batal Ahmed Abdel Aziz DO ----------------------------------- 704154/275
Great Britain 7 Ahmed Ragheb GC ------------------------------------ 354-0850-9
Greece 18 Aisha al Taymuria GC ------------------------------------ 355-1074/0443
Guatemala 29 Mohammed Mandour MN---------------------------------- 608094 600371
Guinea 46 Mohammed Mazhar ZA ----------------------------------- 340-8109 341-0201
Hungary 36 Mohammed Mazhar ZA ------------------------------------ 346-2215/2240
India 5 Aziz Abaza ZA -- 340-6053 341-0052
Indonesia 15 Aisha al Taymuria GC ----------------------------------- 354-7356/7200/9
Iran Embassy of Switzerland Iran
    Interests Section 12 Rifa'a DO ----------------------------------- 348-7641/7237
Iraq 9 Mohammed Mazhar ZA ----------------------------------- 340-9815/2633/7941
Ireland 3 Abu al Feda Tower ZA----------------------------------- 340-8264/8547
Israel 6 Ibn Malek GI ------------------------------------ 729329 728264 726000
Italy 15 Abdel Rahman Fahmi GC ------------------------------------ 354-6578/3194/5
Ivory Coast 39 Kods al Sherif MO---------------------------------- 346-0233
Japan 14 Ibrahim Naguib GC ------------------------------------ 354-9283/4
    106 Kasr al Aini, Cairo Central Building ------------------------------- 354-4518

Jordan Embassy of Pakistan Interests
Section of Jordan 6 Gohaini DO --------------------------------- 348-5566/6169/7543
Kampuchea 2 Tahawia GI --- 348-9436/8934
Kenya 20 Boulos Hanna DO --- 704546/455
Korea (North) 6 Salah al Din ZA -------------------------------- 340-5009 640970
--- 355-7087 354-3402
Korea (South) 6 Hesn GI --- 847101 841101
Kuwait 12 Nabil al Wakkad DO ------------------------------- 716091/706331 340-0970
Lebanon 5 Ahmed Nessim GI --- 728315/454
Liberia 11 Brazil ZA --- 341-9864/5/6
Malaysia 7 Wadi al Nil MO -- 346-0988
Mali 3 Kawsar Madinet al Ataba DO -------------------------------------- 701641/895
Mauritania 31 Syria MO --- 349-0671/1048
Mauritius 72 Abdel Meneim Riad AG --------------------------- 347-0929 346-7642
Mexico 5 Dar al Shifa GC --- 354-8622/3931
Mongolia 3 Midan al Nasr DO --- 346-0670
Morocco 10 Salah al Din ZA --------------------------------------- 340-9677/4718
Nepal 9 Tiba Madinet al Kodah DO -------------------------------------- 704447/541
Netherlands 18 Hasan Sabri ZA ------------------------------ 340-8744/6872/6434
Niger 1010 Pyramids GI --- 856617/607
Nigeria 13 Gabalaya ZA --- 341-7879/3573
North Yemen 4 Ahmed Shawki GI -------------------------------- 737398 727537
Norway 8 Gezira ZA --------------------------------- 340 8046 341-3955 640955
Oman 30 Montaza ZA ------------------------------- 340-7811/7942 341-9073
Pakistan 8 Saluli DO --- 348-7806/7677
Panama 97A Merghani, 4th floor, Apt. 9 HE --------------------------- 666163 662547
Peru 11 Brazil, Apt. 5 ZA -- 341-1754 340-1971
Philippines 5 Ibn Walid DO -- 348-0398/6
Poland 5 Aziz Osman ZA -- 340-5416/9583
Portugal 15A Mansour Mohammed ZA ------------------------------------- 340-5583
Qatar 10 Themar MO -- 702176
Rumania 6 Kamel Mohammed ZA ----------------------------- 340-9546 341-0107
Rwanda 9 Ibrahim Aswan MO --------------------------------- 346-2587/1126/1079
Saudi Arabia 2 Ahmed Nessim GI ------------------------------------- 729805/727237
Senegal 46 Abdel Meneim Riad MO ----------------------------- 346-1039/0946/0896
Singapore 40 Babel DO ------------------------------------ 703772 349-0468/5045
Somalia 38 Abdel Meneim Riad MO -------------------------------------- 704577/038
Spain 9 Hod al Laban GC --------------------------------------- 354-7069/7359/7648
Sri Lanka 8 Sri Lanka ZA ------------------------------------ 341-7138 340-4966/0047
Sudan 3 Ibrahim GC -- 354-5034/9661/5658
Sweden 13 Mohammed Mazhar ZA ---------------------- 341-4132/9169/0259/8374
Switzerland 10 Abdel Khalek Sarwat ----------------------------------- 758133 770545
Tanzania 9 Abdel Hamid Lotfi DO ---------------------------------- 704286 704155
Thailand 2 Malek al Afdal ZA --- 340-8356/0340
Tunisia 26 Gezira ZA --- 340-4940 341-2479

Turkey 25 Falaki, Bab al Louk --354-8364 730249
Uganda 9 Midan al Misaha DO ---981945 980329
United Arab Emirates 4 Ibn Sina GI -------------------------------------729107/226
Union of Soviet Socialist Republics 95 Giza GI -------------------- 348-9638/9355
United States 5 Latin America GC ---------------------------------------355-7371 354-8211
Uruguay 6 Lutfallah ZA ---340-3589 341-5137
Venezuela 15A Mansour Mohammed ZA -------------------------------341-3517/4332
Vietnam 47 Ahmed Hishmat ZA---340-2401
Yugoslavia 33 Mansour Mohammed -------------------------------------340-9876
Zaire 5 Mansour Mohammed ZA --------------------------------341-1069/7954 340-3662
Zambia 22 Nakhil DO ---709620/67

FOREIGN PRESS

The Foreign Press Association is located at room 2037, Cairo Marriott Hotel ZA 340-8888 ex2037.

ABC News 18 Sahel al Ghelal, Maspero --------------------------- 762825 769718 767958
ADN News Agency 17 Brazil ZA --340-2182/4006
The Age, Melbourne 19 Gabalaya, Apt. 41, ZA ---------------------------341-8548/9
Agence France Presse 33 Kasr al Nil ------------------------- 751896 779089 776096
Al Ahram-MAYO Galaa, Al Ahram Building ------------------------------728377 729388
Al Tadamon 28 Higaz MO --754451
Anatolian Agency 17 Huda Shaarawi --778726
Ansa 19 Abdel Khalek Sarwat ---------------------------------------770403 749821
ARD-German TV 18 Sahel al Ghelal, Maspero --------------------------759593 767470
Asahi Shimbun 17 Huda Shaarawi--778628
Asahi TV 3 Mohammed Ibrahim, AG--346-0693
   18 Abu al Feda, Apt. 29 ZA ---341-5274/8868
Associated Press 33 Kasr al Nil---------------------------------------751896 779089
BBC 19 Gabalaya, Apt. 41, ZA --341-8546/7
Bulgarian News Agency 25 Ahmed Hishmat ZA ------------------------------340-1348
Business Monthly Suite 1541,
   Cairo Marriott Hotel, ZA --340-8888 x1541
Business Week 29 Abu al Feda ZA---341-6925
Cairo Today 24 Suria MO --349-0986
CBS News 18 Sahel Ghelal, Maspero -------------------------- 757016 769651 759310
Christian Science Monitor c/o Reuters
   P.O.Box 2040, Sherif St --340-5436
CNN 1127 Corniche al Nil, Maspero----------------------------------776558 746868
CPV (Tokyo) 11 Saray al Ezbekia ---910415
De Volkskrant 26 Mahmoud Bassiouni, Apt. 19, ZA ---------------- 758961 748904
Der Spiegel 18 Fawakeh MO --704015

Deutsche Rundfunk c/o DPA, 33 Kasr al Nil --------------------- 774637 744327 767019
DPA 33 Kasr al Nil, 13th floor -- 774637 767019
Economic Daily of China 3 Mousseline ZA ----------------------------------- 341-4805
The Economist 29 Abu al Feda ZA -- 341-6925
Ente Nazional Idrocarburi 2 Wadi al Nil MO -------------------------- 346-0936/0137
Financial Times 19 Gabalaya, Apt. 41, ZA ------------------------------------ 341-8548/9
Frankisher Volksball 27 Aden MO --------------------------- 346-2959/8487 706730
Fuji Television 1 Kamel Mohammed, Apt. 6, ZA ----------------------------- 340-1140
Gamma 22 Zemzem, Apt. 7, MO --- 348-3742
GDR Radio 87a Abdel Aziz al Saad, Manial --------------------------------- 845330
GDR Television 87a Abdel Aziz al Saad, Manial ------------------------------- 845149
Guangming Daily 3 Mousseline, Apt. 10, ZA --------------------------------- 341-2585
The Guardian 19 Gabalaya, Apt. 41, ZA ------------------------------------ 341-9725
Hungarian News Agency 12a Marashli ZA ----------------------------------- 341-0648
International Journal de Geneve 17 Hadayek MA -------------------------- 351-6915
Izvestia 28b Mohammed Mazhar, Apt. 8, ZA -------------------------------- 340-5924
Japan Broadcasting Corporation 12a Hasan Sabri ZA --------------------- 340-7912
Japan Economic Journal 18 Saray al Gezira ZA --------------------------- 342-1209
Kyodo News Service 9 Kamel Mohammed ZA ----------------------- 340-6105 341-1571
La Libre Belgique c/o ANSA, 19 Abdel Khalek Sarwat-------------------- 749821 770403
Le Monde c/o ANSA, 19 Abdel Khalek Sarwat ------------------------ 770403 749821
Los Angeles Times 29 Abu al Feda ZA ------------------------------------ 341-6925
Maclean's c/o DPA, 33 Kasr al Nil --- 767019 774638
Maghreb Arab Press 5 Gamat al Dowal
   al Arabiya MO-------------------------------------- 344-0807 345-2336 346-0351
Main Post 27 Aden MO --- 346-2959/8487 706730
Mainichi Newspapers 159 26th July, Apt. 9, ZA --------------------------- 341-1124
Majalla 31 Gezira al Arab MO --- 346-1143/8
McGraw Hill c/o UPI, 4 Alfi --- 340-1528
Meed c/o DPA, 33 Kasr al Nil --- 767019 774637
Middle East News Agency 18 Huda Shaarawi --------------------------- 741102 778726
Middle East Times 39 Higaz MO -- 346-5953
Milliyet Daily 110A 26 July, Apt. 53, ZA ---------------------------------- 341-9113
Monitor Radio 6 Road 2 MA --- 350-3810
NBC News 1129 Corniche al Nil, Maspero --------------------------------- 779916/894
NBC Radio Network News TV News Training Center,
   American University in Cairo, 113 Kasr al Aini --------------------------- 354-2964-9
Neues Deutschland 6 Abdel Hamid Lotfi MO -------------------------------- 707001
New York Times 19 Gabalaya ZA --- 341-8560/8002
News Agency of Nigeria 30 Road 11 MA ------------------------------------ 350-8541
Newsday 19 Gabalaya, Apt. 81, ZA -- 340-0877
Newsweek 1079 Corniche al Nil --- 355-4802
Novosti 5a Aziz Abaza, ZA --- 341-9566/9929

Oslobodjenje 20 Mansour Mohammed ZA ------------------------------ 341-3746 340-9507
The People's Daily 28 Iraq, Apt. 8, MO --- 349-7971
Pfizer Egypt 47 Ramsis -- 741474
Philadelphia Inquirer 4 Salah al Din ZA -------------------------------- 341-3746 340-9507
Phileleftheros (Cyprus) 32 Talaat Harb -- 912765
Picture Group Photo Agency 23b Ismail Mohammed ZA ----------------------- 340-1604
Polish Press Agency 11 Kamel Mohammed ZA -------------------------------------- 744000
Pravda 11 Shagarat al Dorr ZA --- 341-4778
Qatar News Agency 17 Huda Shaarawi --- 777429
Radio France International c/o ANSA,
    19 Abdel Khalek Sarwat --- 770403 749821
Radio Peking 2 Hadid wal Solb MO --- 346-9016
Reuters 26 Sherif, Immobilia Building ------------------------------- 745667 770358 762795
Sankei Shimbun 17a Mohammed Mazhar ZA -------------------------------------- 341-5674
Saudi Journals' Group 26B al Mahrousa, Sahafiyin ---------------------- 347-6045/2257
Septimus International 160 26th July ZA --------------------------------- 340-0803 341-9784
Soviet TV 14 Gezira al Wasta ZA --- 340-1584 341-4922
Spanish News Agency 33b Mohammed Mazhar ZA ---------------------------- 340-1580
St. Petersburg Times 29 Abu al Feda ZA --- 341-6925
Sueddeutsche Zeitung 33 Kasr al Nil --------------------------------------- 767019 744327
Sunday Times c/o DPA, 33 Kasr al Nil --------------------------------------- 767019 744327
Swiss Radio 17 Hadayek MA --- 351-6915
Sygma c/o Press Syndicate,
    4 Abdel Khalek Sarwat -- 763314 770552/331
T.I. 19 Abu Kuda, Abbassia --- 830628
Tanjug 9 Kamel Mohammed ZA --- 340-2683
Tass 30 Mohammed Mazhar ZA --- 341-9784 340-0803
Time Magazine 19 Gabalaya ZA --- 341-8400 340-8508
Tokyo Broadcasting System 23 Gezira al Wasta ZA ------------------ 340-1631 951481
Trud 17a Mohammed Mazhar ZA -- 340-6560
Ummah Press 24 Digla, Flat 9, MO --- 708556
United Press International 4 Elwi -- 744000 769106
Video Cairo News Services
    1129 Corniche al Nil, Maspero ------------------------------------ 759310/7016 700713
Video Press Agency 18 Shagarat al Dorr ZA --------------------------------------- 340-2601
VISNEWS 1127 Corniche al Nil, Maspero ----------------------------------- 750583 767052
Voice of America 5 Midan Hay'at al Tadris DO --------------------------------- 704970/986
Voice of Greece Radio 32 Talaat Harb -- 912765
Wall Street Journal 9 Gabalaya ZA --- 340-7908
Washington Post 6 Gezira ZA --- 341-2290 340-5436
Worldwide Television News 18 Sahel al Ghelal, Maspero -------------------------- 775744
Xinhua News Agency 2 Midan Musa Galal MO -------------------------------- 344-8950/1
Yomiuri Shimbun 5 Mahmoud Azmi ZA --- 340-1026
ZDF-German TV 1127 Corniche al Nil, Maspero -------------------------------------- 755016

GOVERNMENT

Presidency

Oruba Palace HE ------917019
Kubra Palace HE ------243-1915/1916
Abdin Palace ------910420 910288

Prime Minister and Cabinet

Maglis al Shaab, GC ------354-7376/5000/3116
------355-1608 /3192/8024

Ministries

Agriculture and Land Reclamation Wizaret al Ziraa DO ------702677/566 /3388
Awqaf (Islamic Endowments) 5 Sabri Abu Allam, Bab al Louk ------746305
------/6022/6163/8403 758699
Cabinet Affairs 1 Maglis al Shaab, Midan Lazoghli GC ------354-3484
------913027 355-0164
Civil Aviation Airport Ave HE ------245-0933/3955 244-0933
Communications 26 Ramses ------355-5516/63/64
Culture 2 Shagarat al Dorr ZA ------341-2918/5495/5568
------340-2195/6449/6469
Defense and Military Production
   Khalifa al Mamun, Kubri al Kubba ------834345/8351
------257-8697/2915 822921
Economy and Foreign Trade 8 Adli, 5th floor ------919278/661 907344
Education 12 Falaki, Sayeda Zeinab ------354-3454/1591
   Higher Education 4 Ibrahim Naguib GC ------355-6962/2155
Electricity and Energy Abbassia ------829565 823699 834351/574
Finance Maglis al Shaab GC ------354-1543/1055/6508 355-7136
Foreign Affairs 4 al Nil GI ------721688 720851
   Midan Tahrir ------354-1414/466
Health 3 Maglis al Shaab GC ------354-3462/8318/1507
Housing and Public Utilities 1 Ismail Abaza ------355-3468/7978/7013
------/3320 354-0110/0419/9920/0291
Immigration 1 Maglis al Shaab, Midan Lazoghli ------354-8415/2366/6044
Industry 2 Latin America GC ------354-1126/9372/3600
------355-1855/8306/4826
Information Radio and Television Building,
   Corniche al Nil, Maspero ------760518 749349 759570
Interior Sheikh Rihan ------354-5897/4095/2275
------355-3029/2300/7500

International Cooperation Kasr al Aini GC --------------------------------910008/913145
Justice Justice Building, Maglis al Shaab GC ------------------------------355-1176/8103
Manpower and Training Yusef Abbas, Madinet Nasr -------------------------260-9362/4
Maritime Transport 7 Abdel Khalek Sarwat -------------------------------------755614/735
Parliamentary Affairs Maglis al Shaab GC--355-7101
Petroleum and Mineral Resources 2 Latin America GC----------------------354-5022/3
--354-4224 355-7425
Planning Oruba and Tayaran, MN ---601-524/416/199
Scientific Research 101 Kasr al Aini ------------------------------------354-6039 355-7952
Social Affairs Sheikh Rihan ---354-2900 355-7007
Social Insurance 3 Alfi --917799 934747
Supply and Home Trade 99 Kasr al Aini --------------------------------355-0961 354-5238
Tourism Burg Masr al Siaha, Abbassia -------------------------------------282-8439/430
Transport 105 Kasr al Aini GC ----------------------------355-3566/5568 985203 775544
Water Works and Resources Kasr al Aini --------------------354-5777/4527/7960/6439

GOVERNORATES

Alexandria --903)482-5800/1/2
Assiut --(088)324000 323058; direct 747809
Aswan --(097)322000/326/489/222
Behira Damanhur --(045)323848/675
Beni Suef Corniche Beni Suef --------------------(082)323000/333/014/438 2000, 2813
Cairo Midan Abdin --------------------------------------(02)937050 914369 906673 906710
Dakahlia Mansura ---(050)325504 324437 325740
Damietta Saad Zaghloul--(057)25788 25799
Fayoum Batal al Salam------------------------------------(084) 22586 23044 22899 22079
Gharbia Tanta--(040) 335272 333111
Giza Pyramids Road---850171/011 855000
Ismailia --(064)21071/2/3 21121
Kafr al Sheikh ---(047) 323040 322629
Kaliubia Benha --(013) 324328 325502/90
Kena ---(096)322233/444
Marsa Matrouh --(094)943151/333 945055
Menufia Shebin al Kom --(048)20189 320344
Minia ---(086)322191/2
North Sinai Al Arish---(064)341245/7 340232
Port Said --(066) 24656 21885 25821 23634
Red Sea Hurghada --------------------------(062)40000 40337 762060 40990 755494
Sharkia Zagazig --(055)322440 324040 743224
Sohag ---(093)322044/023
South Sinai --Gabal al Tur (062)71222/733/111/777

Suez -- (062) 24950 25450 21971/2/3
Wadi al Gedid Kharga --- (088)900301/450

HOTELS

The lists of classified hotels here were compiled from the Egyptian Hotel Guide 1987-88 published by the Egyptian Hotel Association. The classification by stars rates hotels according to their facilities. The unclassfied hotels offer a wide variety of facilities but tend to be inexpensive.

Price ranges for double rooms with bath are **5 star**, $60-100; **4 star,** $35-60; **3 star**, $20-40; **2 star**, $10-30; **1 star**, $6-20.

In three, four and five star hotels, payment must be made in foreign currency, by credit card, or in Egyptian currency with a bank exchange receipt. Egyptians and foreign five-year residents are exempt from this rule.

Five Stars

Cairo Concorde Cairo International Airport -- 664242
Cairo Marriott Saray al Gezira ZA --- 340-8888
Cairo Sheraton Midan al Galaa DO ------------------------------------ 348-8600/8700
Gezirah Sheraton Gezira Island ZA ---------------------------- 341-3442/1333/1555
Heliopolis Movenpick Hurria HE -------------------------- 664242 247-0077 679799
Heliopolis Sheraton Airport Road HE ----------------------------- 667700 665500
Holiday Pyramids Cairo/Alexandria Desert Road GI ----------------------------- 856477
Hyatt Al Salam 61 Abdel Hamid Badawi HE ----------------------------- 245-5155/2155
Mena House Oberoi al Haram GI ----------------------- 855444 857999 855174
Meridien Corniche al Nil GC --- 845444
Meridien Heliopolis 51 Oruba HE -- 290-5055/1819
Nile Hilton Corniche al Nil, Midan Tahrir ---------------------------- 750666 740777
Ramada Renaissance Cairo/Alexandria Desert Road ---------------------------- 538995/6
Ramses Hilton 1115 Corniche al Nil Maspero -------------------- 777444 758000 744400
Safir Hotel 4 Midan Misaha DO ---------------------------------- 348-2424/2828/2626
Semiramis Intercontinental Corniche al Nil GC ---------------------------- 355-3900/3800
Shepheard's Hotel Corniche al Nil GC ---------------------------------- 355-3804/3814
Siag Pyramids 59 Mariutia Sakkara Road ---------------------------- 856022/623 857399
Sonesta 4 Tayaran, MN --- 611066 609444

Four Stars

Atlas Zamalek 20 Gamat al Dowal al Arabiya MO ------------------- 346-4175/5782/6569
Baron Hotel Heliopolis off Oruba HE ---------------------------------- 291-2468/7/5757
Bel Air Cairo Hotel Mokattam -- 922685/816/884

Green Pyramids 13 Helmiet al Ahram GI ----------------------------------856786/778/887
Holiday Sphinx Cairo/Alexandria Desert Road ----------------------------854700/930/485
Under renovation
Jolieville Movenpick Cairo/Alexandria Desert Road ----------------------855118/539/612
Under renovation
Maadi Hotel Maadi Entrance MA ---350-5050/6555
Manial Palace Hotel Village Kasr Mohammed Ali, Manial----------844083 846014/315
Nile Savoy 9 Saray al Gezira ZA --341-0430/0509/0308
Novotel Cairo Airport HE---671715 679080 661330
Oasis Hotel Cairo/Alexandria Desert Road --------------------------856988 866477/406
Transit Airport Cairo International Airport ---666074

Three Stars

Alnabila Cairo Hotel 4 Gamat al Dowal al Arabiya MO ------346-1131/7016 347-3384
Aman Hotel 58 Giza DO--348-4446/4348
Atlas Mohammed Rushdi, Midan Opera --------------------------------918183/311 911022
Beirut 56 Beirut HE --662347 671061 291-1092
Caesar's Palace 45 Abdel Aziz Fahmi HE ------------------------------------ 245-7241/0
Cairo Inn 26 Syria MO--349-0661/2/3
Carlton 21, 26th July --755181/022/232
Cleopatra 2 Bustan, Midan Tahrir --------------------------------708751 701873 710768
Concord 146 Tahrir DO --708751
Continental Savoy 10 Midan Opera --911322
Cosmopolitan 1 Ibn Taalab, Kasr al Nil --------------------------------753531 743956/845
Crillon 19 Montasser AG--347-7570/6729 346-0097
Dreamers 5 Gadah DO--709526/540
Egyptel 93 Merghani HE ---661716 662304/258
El Borg Saray al Gezira --341-7655/6827/4746
El Hurria 14 Hurria HE---290-3472/2496/0070
El Kanater Chalets Kanater Gardens, Kaliubia --------------------------958328/130/975
El Manar 19 Abdel Hamid Lotfi --------------------------------------- MO 709299/903 708299
El Nil 12 Ahmed Ragheb GC --354-2808/7/0
El Tonsi 143 Tahrir DO ---348-4600/7231/6355
Fontana 10a Seif al Din al Mohrani, Midan Ramsis ------------------------------922145/321
Heliopark 100 Higaz HE ---245-1346/9789 244-4617
Horris 5, 26th July, Ezbekia --910855/478/389
Horus House 21 Ismail Mohammed ZA ------------------------------------340-3977/3182/3634
Indiana 16 Saray MO--349-3774 714422/503
Kanzy 9 Abu Bakr al Siddik MO --------------------------------------709461/443 711576
Kemet Hotel Midan Abbassia, Abbassia ---------------------------825447 824018 826016
Khan al Khalili 7 Bosta, Ataba --900271/230
Lido Hotel 465 Ahram, GI-- 727-373/960 735-317/327
Longchamps 21 Ismail Mohammed ZA --------------------------------340-9644/2311/8445
Lo Lo Et El Maady (Pearl) Roads 6 and 82 MA ----------------------350-4153/5313/5385

Marwa Palace 11 Khatib DO---348-8830/25/27
New Star 34b Yehia Ibrahim ZA------------------------------------340-1865/0928 341-1321
Odeon Palace 6 Abdel Hamid Said ---776637 767971
Pharaos Hotel 12 Lotfi Hassouna DO------------------------------------712314/233 717807
President 22 Dr. Taha Hussein ZA------------------------------------341-6751/3195 340-0718
Pyramids Hotel 198 al Haram GI-----------------------------------857555 539322 538400
Raja 34 Mohi al Din Abu al Ezz DO ---702240 708521
Rehab 4 Fawakeh MO ---707664 703112/559
Residence 11 Road 18 MA---350-7189/7276 351-0825
Salma 12 Mohammed Kamel Morsi MO ----------------------------700901 701482 706232
Sand 103 Kom al Akhdar, al Ahram --------------------------------852494 855479 856549
Sheherazad 182 al Nil AG---346-1326/0634
Sphinx 8 Maglis al Umma, Abdin -------------------------------------355-7439/1641 354-8258
Sweet Hotel 39 Road 13 MA---350-4544/61
Vendome 287 al Haram GI --850977/818/339
Victoria 66 Gumhuria, Midan Ramsis -------------------------------------918766/038/869
Windsor 19 Alfi --915277/810 921621

Two Stars

Abu al Hol Palace 161 al Haram GI ------------------------------------856043/938/926
Amoun Midan Sphinx AG--346-1434
Aviation Hotel P.O. Box 2688 HE --345-0393
Cairo Commodore 10 Fawzi Ramah DO--346-0592
Capsis Palace 117 Ramsis, Midan Ramsis --------------------------------754219/188/029
Caroline Crillon 49 Sayria MO --346-5101/4101/0219
El Hussein Midan Hussein, al Azhar---918664/089
El Nil Garden 131 Abdel Aziz al Saoud, Manial -----------------------------985767 983931
El Nil Zamalek 21 Maahad al Swissri ZA --------------------------------340-1846/0220
Grand Hotel 17, 26th July, Ezbekia ------------------------------------757509/628/700
Green Valley 33 Abdel Khalek Sarwat --756317/188
Hamburg 18 Bursa, Tawfikia ---744799/447
Happy Joe facing 10 Corniche al Nil GI--------------------------------------721252 720946
Helio Cairo 95 Abdel Hamid Badawi HE --------------------------------------245-0682/0563
Holiday Home 63 Higaz HE --693354
International 3 Abdel Azim Rashid DO--------------------------------------712154/9 710243
Kasr al Nil 33 Kasr al Nil ---754523 758437
King 20 Abdel Rahim Sabri DO --710939/869 719455
Kino 383 al Haram GI--859260
Lotus 12 Talaat Harb --750627/966
New Hotel 12 Adli ---747033/124/176
New Riche 47 Abdel Aziz, Midan Ataba --------------------------------------900145 925380
Noran 13 Mohammed Khalaf DO --------------------------------707086 709696 703958
Ommayad 22, 26th July --755044 759675
Piccadilly 19 Midan 26th July AG --------------------------------347-3819/3708 346-7723
Rose 6 Iran DO ---707059 708464/525

Safa Inn Abbas al Akkad, MN --606917 604326
Scarabee 16, 26th July, Ezbekia --759434/675/366
St. George 7 Radwan Ibn al Tabib GI ------------------------------721580 734656 724649
Taher Touristic 12 Yaman MO --651876
Tiab House 24 Mahmoud Khalaf DO ---709812/170
Tulip 3 Talaat Harb --766884 762704 758433
Viennoise 11 Mahmoud Bassiouni ---751949 743153
Zayed 42 Abul Mahasin al Shazli AG -------------------------------346-3318/9 347-4571

One Star

Amin 38 Midan Falaki, Bab al Louk ---779813
Big Ben 33 Emad al Din --908881
Blue Nile 4 Hokama, Manshiet al Bakri ---664516
Cairo Palace beginning of Gumhuria, Midan Ramsis ------------------------906327/387
Central 7a Bosta, Ataba --907563 909914/899
Champs Elysees 19a Osman Ibn Affan HE --------------------------------661769 670514
Des Roses 33 Talaat Harb ---758022
Ebeid House 179 Gisr al Suweis HE ---------------------------245-4079/1219 242-4538
Garden City 23 Kamel al Din Salah GC --------------------------------354-4969/8400/4126
Happy Day Chalet Abdel Aziz, Helwan ---782437
Hotel Des Princes 16 Dr. Mustafa Safwat, Helwan -------------------------------781373
Montana 25 Sherif ---748608 746264 756025
Nitocrisse 171 Mohammed Farid--915166/738
Radwan 83 Gawhar al Kaed, Midan Azhar----------------------------------901311 900427
Tary 12 Bab al Bahr, Midan Ramsis --------------------------------------931535 912285
Tourist Palace 12 Baidak, Muski ---915126

Unclassified

Al Aman 58 Giza GI --348-4475
Anglo-Swiss Pensione 14 Champollion ---751479
Chateau des Pyramides 10 Sadat, Pyramids Garden ------------------851342 538236/5
Dokki House 42 Madina al Munawara DO -----------------------------------705611/713
Everest Midan Ramsis--742707/688
Al Faraana 12 Lotfi Hassouna DO ---712233
Garden Palace 11 Mudiria GC
Gabali Hotel 221 Higaz HE--245-5224
General 28 Shagaret al Dorr ZA--340-3490
Golden Hotel 13 Talaat Harb--392-2659/9916
Hotel Beau Site 27 Talaat Harb --749877
Hotel of Youth & Sports Masaken Madinet Nasr ---------------------------260-6991/2
Luna Park 65 Gumhuria --904592
Lotus Tourist Village Tiraat Mariutia GI--------------------------------------735197/125
Mena Palace 5 Gumhuria ---390-2945
National 30 Talaat Harb--745516
New Helwan 29 Sherif, Gamat Helwan ---784508

Oxford Pensione 32 Talaat Harb --- 758172/3
Pensione Roma 169 Mohammed Farid --- 391-1088
Pensione de Famille Abdel Khalek Sarwat -------------------------------------- 745630
Safir Zamalek 21 Mohammed Mazhar ZA --------------------------- 342-0055 341-8447/8

RESTAURANTS

Fine dining to suit everyone's palate is available in abundance in Cairo. In fact, there are so many choices that it is impossible to list all of them. Many hotel restaurants feature weeklong food fests from various countries with special chef's and imported items brought in for the occasion. Watch for the announcements in **Cairoscope, Cairo Today** and **The Egyptian Gazette**. This list tries to provide a good cross section of what is available in the city. **Cheap** means less than LE5; **Inexpensive** is LE5-10; **Average** is LE10-25; and **Expensive** is LE25 and above. Credit cards are listed where applicable. **TA** means Take Away.

Central Cairo
Hotel Dining
Inter Continental Hotel Corniche al Nil 355-7171.
Feluka Brasserie Expensive. All major cards. Cater. 7am-1am. Middle Eastern and continental open buffets.
Far East Expensive. All major cards. Open only on Friday, 7am-1am. Friday Brunch 9am-12noon. Oriental foods.
Night and Day coffeeshop. Average. All major cards. 24hrs. Continental food a la carte.
Semiramis Grill Expensive. All major cards. 7pm-1am. French cuisine.
Sultana's Disco Average. All major cards. 10-closing. Teen matinees Thursdays 5pm-9pm. International live shows, talent and theme nights.

Meridien Hotel Corniche al Nil 845444.
Fontana Average. All major cards. 24hr. Coffee shop offering a variety of fare including International and Middle Eastern meals and snacks.
Kasr al Rashid Expensive. All major cards. 7:30pm-11:30pm. Middle Eastern atmosphere and cuisine amid oriental entertainment.
La Belle Epoque Expensive. All major cards. 10pm-3am. Nightclub and restaurant. Reservations and formal dress required.
La Palme D'Or Expensive. All major cards. 12:30-3:30 and 7:30-10:30. French dining to live music. Reservations and formal dress required.
Nafoura Average. All major cards. 7pm-1:30am. Summer restaurant offering Middle Eastern specialities.

Nile Hilton Corniche al Nil 740777 750666
Abu Ali's Cafe Average. 11am-11pm in summer; 11am-5pm in winter. sheesha and green tea on the terrace.

Belvedere Expensive. 9:30pm-2:30am. Winter night club. Roof top dinner a la carte. International and oriental shows.

Ibis Cafe Average. TA. 24hrs. Continental cuisine.

Jackie's Disco Average. All major cards. No membership necessary. 9pm-3am. Teen matinees 4-8 Thurs and Sat.

La Pizzeria Average. All major cards. 12-2am. Italian pizzas, open buffets, dinner a la carte.

Le Gateau Average. TA. 9am-9pm. Pastry corner.

Lobby Lounge Average. 3:30pm-7:30pm. Viennese pastries, coffee, English afternoon tea and sandwiches.

Rotisserie Average. All major cards. 12:30-3:30 7:30-10:30. International and Egyptian cuisine. Business lunch buffet and dinner a la carte.

Safari Bar Average. All major cards. 11am-1am.

Taverne du Champ de Mars Average. Bar/Restaurant. 11am-1am. Drinks, snacks and daily buffet.

Tropicana Bar Average. 10pm-2:30am. Summer night club at the pool area.

Ramsis Hilton 1115 Corniche al Nil 758000 777444 744400

Citadel Grill Expensive. All major cards. 12:30-3:30 and 5-10:30. Elegant dining offering seafood and grills. Reservations advised. Formal dress required.

Club 36 All major cards. 12-1am. Drinks and sandwiches only. Piano entertainment.

Garden Cote Bar 12-1am. Drinks and snacks only. Live band.

Falafel Expensive. All major cards. 7:30am-midnight. Egyptian foods and snacks.

La Patisserie Average. All major cards. 11:30am-10pm. Coffeeshop including cakes and ice cream specialities. Excellent hamburgers.

Terrace Cafe Average. All major cards. 6:30am-11pm. Coffeeshop with International and Middle Eastern meals and snacks. Buffet breakfast.

Shepheard's Hotel Corniche al Nil 355-3900/3800.

Caravan Average. Ax, V. 24hr. Minimum charge after 7pm LE6. International and Middle Eastern meals and snacks.

Steak Corner Average. 7am-10:30pm. Continental grills a la carte.

Continental Food

Ariston 40 Talaat Harb, in the passage next to Cinema Miami. Inexpensive. 12-4 and 7-1. Colorful atmosphere with excellent mezzas and Greek salads. Casual.

Caroll 12 Kasr al Nil 746434. Average. All major cards. 11:30-3:30 and 7-11. Excellent dining amid a vintage Cairo atmosphere.

Estoril 12 Talaat Harb (in passage) 743102. Average. 12-3:30 and 7-10:30. Excellent dining in a pleasant vintage Cairo atmosphere.

Lux 26th July 392-9596. Cheap. Meals and vintage Cairo.

Paprika 1129 Corniche, next to the Radio and TV building, 749447. Average. 12-12. Excellent dining. Haunt of radio and TV personalities. Try the mezzas.

Rex 33 Abdel Khalek Sarwat, just off Midan Talaat Harb, 745763. Inexpensive. 12:30-4 and 6:30-10:30. Good food in a small old-fashioned atmosphere.

268 DIRECTORY

Middle Eastern Food
Abu Shakra 69 Kasr al Aini 848811/602. Average. 1-5 and 7-11. No alcohol. One of the best kebab and kufta restaurants in Cairo. Casual atmosphere.
Aladin 26 Sherif 755694. Inexpensive. All major cards. No alcohol. 1-4 and 8-12. Serves traditional Egyptian food from mezza to Um Ali.
Alfi Bey 3 Alfi 771888 774999. TA. Noon-1am. Kebab and kufta.
Arabesque 6 Kasr al Nil 759896. Average. All major cards. 12:30-3:30 and 7:30-11:30. Excellent Egyptian cuisine in an elegant atmosphere. Try the Um Ali. Also has an art gallery.
Al Chimi 45 Talaat Harb 393-5145. Cheap. TA. Delivery nearby. 10am-2am.
Felfela 15 Huda Shaarawi 392-2751. Cheap. TA. 7am-1am. Offers a wide variety of a la carte Egyptian cuisine in an exotic, casual atmosphere. Try the fatta, kebab, and fuul in all varieties.
Hag Mohamed al Sammak Abdel Aziz, across from Omar Effendi, 9013376. Specializes in grilled and fried fish, including shrimp and perch.
Al Hati 8 Midan Halim, behind Cicurel on 26th July, 918829. Average. 12noon-midnight. Specializes in moza, roast lamb. Casual, old world vintage Cairo decor.
New Aton 15 Talaat Harb 392-2753. Cheap. TA. 8am-1am. Egyptian cuisine.
Sofar 21 Adli 393-9360. Inexpensive. Serves beer. Lebanese type Middle Eastern food.
Taverna 3 Alfi. Inexpensive. 12-4 and 7-1. Mediterranean cooking specializing in shrimp.

Oriental Food
Fu Ching 28 Talaat Harb 393-6184. Inexpensive. TA. 12:30-10:30. Located in passageway off Talaat Harb. Offers good Chinese food in a modest setting.
Naniwa Ramses Annex of Ramsis Hilton, 752399. Expensive. 12-3 and 7-11. Shisha, Teppanyaki and Sukiyaki in a pleasant atmosphere.

Fast Food
American Fried Chicken 8 Huda Shaarawi 742238. Cheap. TA. till 1pm. Specializes in chicken, hamburgers and pizza.
Bambo Cafeteria 39 Talaat Harb 392-5179. Cheap. 7am-12pm.
Casa Blanca 46 Talaat Harb. Cheap. TA. Delivery nearby. 9am-12pm. Egyptian fast food and pizza.
Fatattri al Tahrir 166 Tahrir. Cheap. TA. Sells only fitiir, an Egyptian pancake with a variety of mixes both sweet and savory.
Kentucky Fried Chicken Abdel Khalek Sarwat, 392-9658. Cheap. TA. 10am-12:30pm.
El Tabi 31 Orabi 754211. Cheap. TA. 7am-11pm. Fuul and taamiyya.
Take Away 1 Latin America 355-4341. Inexpensive. 8am-12pm. Hamburgers and other fast foods.
Wimpy Immobilia, off Sherif; Talaat Harb; and Huda Shaarawi. Cheap. 9am-12pm.
Zeina 32 Talaat Harb 745758. Cheap. 7am-1pm. Egyptian fast foods. Try the shawarma and the juice bar. You'll meet lots of budget travelers.
Z Midan Tahrir 354-4230. Cheap. TA. Egyptian juice bar.

Coffee, Tea and Ice Cream
A l'Americaine 44 Talaat Harb 393-7731. Cheap. TA. Delivers. 7am-11pm. Offers fast foods at a stand up counter and a coffeeshop famous for good ice cream. Vintage Cairo. Haunt of

lawyers and judges.
Brazilian Coffee Shop 38 Talaat Harb 755722 and 12 26th July. Cheap. TA. Caters. 6am-12pm. Counter service downstairs. Cafeteria upstairs. Makes its own freshly ground coffee. Specialities include expresso, cappuccino and iced coffee.
Cafe Riche 17 Talaat Harb 392-9793. Cheap. 11:30am-10pm. Vintage Cairo with tea, coffee, ouzo and beer in an outside cafe. Dining inside. Former haunt of Free Officers and literary personalities.
Excelsior 35 Talaat Harb 392-5002. Inexpensive. 7am-12pm. Restaurant, bar and coffeeshop. Pre-revolution vintage Cairo atmosphere, haunt of Egyptian artists and writers. Try the ice cream and shawarma sandwiches.
Groppi Midan Talaat Harb 743244. Average. TA. Caters. 7:30am-10pm. Famous Groppi's confections for sale, special seasonal sweets and savories, coffeeshop once a must for every visitor to Egypt. Vintage Cairo. Dining room with linen tablecloths.
Groppi's Garden 2 Abdel Khalek Sarwat 391-6619 392-3473. Average. TA. Caters. No alcohol. 7:30am-9pm. Serves snacks and pastries in a nostalgic setting made famous by British soldiers during WWII. Excellent take away featuring pastries, meats, home-made noodles and savories.
Indian Tea Center 23 Talaat Harb, in the passage 393-3396. Inexpensive. Afternoon tea and snacks.
Victoria Coffeeshop 66 Gumhuria, in Victoria Hotel, 918869. Cheap. 8am-12pm. True vintage Cairo over a cup of coffee.

Lounges and Bars
After Eight 6 Kasr al Nil, in the passage. Average. 8-closing. Popular bar.

Dokki and Agouza
Hotel Dining
   Safir Midan Misaha 348-2828/2424.
Diar El Andalos Average. 5pm-midnight. Lebanese and Middle Eastern cuisine with sheesha.
Filaka Average. All major cards. 24hr. Coffeeshop featuring excellent daily buffet.
Gazirat al Dahab. Expensive. All major cards. 12:30-3 and 8-11. French and Middle Eastern food.

Continental Food
Flying Fish 166 Nil AG 349-3234. Average. AX,V,Gold. 12-12. Specializing in seafood.
Pizzeria La Casetta 32 Kambis 348-0659. Average. Pizzas and Italian foods. Excellent Ramadan sohour (pre-dawn meal). Casual.
The Silver Fish 39 Mohi al Din Abu al Ezz 349-2272. Average. All major cards. 12pm-1am. In addition to seafoods also serves continental and oriental cuisine.
Steak Corner 8 Midan Aman 349-7326. Average. All major cards. 12pm-1am. Specializes in steaks of all kinds.

Middle Eastern Food
Bawadi 10 Hasan Wassef, Midan Misaha 348-4878. Average. All major cards. TA. 12:30pm-11:30pm. Lebanese food.

El Takkeba 42 Abdel Meneim Riad 348-2686. Inexpensive. Golden Card. TA. 9am-1am. Middle Eastern specialities including kobeiba.

Oriental Food

Okamoto 7 Ahmed Orabi AG 349-5774. Average. Ax, visa. TA. Cater 12-4pm 6pm-11pm. Closed monday. Excellent Japanese food.

Taj Mahal 15 Midan Ibn Affan 348-4881. Average. All major cards. TA. 12-midnight. Indian food.

Fast Food

Al Mastaba 65 Mohi al Din Abu al Ezz 249-1157. Cheap. TA. Delivers. 9am-2am. Kebab, kufta and other Middle Eastern dishes.

Free Time 75 Mosaddaq 348-0006. Cheap. Golden card, Egypt card, Visa. TA. 11am-2am. North American food including submarines, hamburgers and torpedos. Also Middle Eastern specialities.

Indiana Cafeteria 45 Dokki 349-1879. Cheap.

McBurger 16 Nil 348-0288 AG. Inexpensive. TA. 10am-2am. Burgers, pies and onion rings.

El Takea 12 Mohamed Ibn al Walid 711470. Cheap. Ax, Visa. TA. Delivery. Cater. 12-3am. Closed Wed. Excellent Middle Eastern dishes including fatta and grape leaves.

Coffee, Tea and Ice Cream

Cafe Saint Germain 41 Babel 704519. Inexpensive. TA. 7:30am-midnight. European bakery and coffeeshop.

Dairy King 46 Nadi al Seyd 348-3000. 9am-1am. Ice cream parlor.

Farghaly Fruits 45 Midan Dokki 348-2341. Inexpensive. Fruit juices freshly squeezed. Considered by some the best juice shop in Cairo.

Giza

Hotel Dining

Cairo Sheraton Sharia Giza 348-8600/8700.

Aladin Expensive. All major cards. 8pm-1am. Middle Eastern cuisine with Middle Eastern entertainment.

Alhambra Expensive. All major cards. 10pm-2:30am. Rooftop nightclub with one of the best Middle Eastern floor shows in Cairo.

Arousa al Nil Expensive. All major cards. 24hr. Ground floor restaurant offering a variety of Continental and Middle Eastern cuisine.

La Mamma Expensive. All major cards. 12-12. Excellent Italian foods in a festive atmosphere. Strolling musicians.

Mashrabia Bar Average. All major cards. 11am-2am.

Oasis Bar Average. All major cards. 11am-2am.

Gezirah Sheraton Tahrir Gardens, Gezira 341-1333/1555/1336.

Andalus Cafe Average. All major cards. 24hr. Coffeeshop offering meals and snacks.

Cleopatra's Pool Average. 10am-7pm. Drinks and snacks.

La Fontana Seafood Expensive. All major cards. 7pm-1am. Seafood varieties in an outdoor setting on the Nile.

Layalina Average. 10:30pm-3am. Outdoor summer nightclub with belly dancing and Middle Eastern shows.
Le Gandool Bar Average. All major cards. 11am-2am. Cocktail lounge.
Paradise Island 11am-2am. Floating restaurant on the Nile. Barbecues, mezzas and drinks.
The Grill Expensive. All major cards. 12-3 and 8-2. Nile view and international cuisine. Reservations required.
Kebabgy al Gezirah Average. All major cards. 12-12. Oriental food with an oriental view.
El Samar Winter Nightclub Expensive. All major cards. 10pm-3am. Continental cuisine with live entertainment, all overlooking the Nile. Formal attire.

Green Pyramids Hotel Helmiet al Ahram, off Pyramid Road 856778/887/786 852600.
Al Basha Average. All major cards. 12pm-11pm. Continental and Middle Eastern cuisine.
Al Boddega Average. All major cards. 24hr. Coffeeshop with continental meals and snacks.
Coffeeshop 24hr continental food and snacks.
Pyramid Sweet TA. 10am-10pm. Patisserie.

Mena House Oberoi, Pyramids Road 855444 857999
Abu Nawas Nightclub Expensive. All major cards. 10pm-3am. October-May. Continental and Middle Eastern menu accompanied by Middle Eastern entertainment. Formal attire.
The Greenery Coffeeshop Average. All major cards. 24hrs. Buffet in the garden.
Khan il Khalili Average. All major cards. Coffeeshop with international and Middle Eastern meals and snacks overlooking the pyramids.
Mameluke Bar Average. All major cards. 7:30-12pm.
The Mogul Room Expensive. All major cards. 12:30-2:30 and 7:30-11. Reservations necessary. Excellent Indian food, elegantly presented amid strains of live Indian music.
Oasis Summer Nightclub Expensive. All major cards. 10pm-3am. Continental and Middle Eastern meals with live entertainment.
The Rubayyat Expensive. All major cards. 12:30-2:30 and 7:30-11pm. Main dining room with continental and Middle Eastern meals and live entertainment. Reservations necessary.
The Saddle Disco 10pm-3am. Couples only. No minimum charge.
El Sultan Lounge Average. All major cards. 9am-3am. Lounge with drinks and classical music.

Ramada Renaissance Hotel Alexandria Desert Road 538111.
Garden Restaurant Moderate. All major cards. 24hr. Coffeeshop featuring continental meals and snacks.
Golden Club Average. All major cards. 9am-3am. Disco and fast foods.
Habiba Nightclub Average. All major cards. 9pm-3am. Continental cuisine and live entertainment.
Les Fontaines Average. All major cards. 7pm-midnight. Continental food.
Sultan Average. All major cards. 7pm-midnight. Middle Eastern meals.

Continental Food
Il Camino 5 Wissa Wassef, off Sharia Nil, Riyad Tower 722786. Average. AX. No alcohol. 1-5:30 7:30-midnight. Italian restaurant specializing in pizzas.

Swissair Le Chalet 31 Sharia Nil, Nasr Building 728488. Average. All major cards. TA. 10am-12pm. Authentic Swiss foods. Try the ice cream.
Swissair Le Chateau 31 Sharia Nil, Nasr Building, 729487. Expensive. All major cards. 1-4 and 8-12. Reservations recommended. Continental dining in an elegant atmosphere.

Middle Eastern Food
Amonit 138 Bahr al Aazam 727119. Ax. TA. Cater. Delivery. 12-1am. Egyptian folklore and Lebanese cuisine.
Andrea's 60 Mariutia Canal 851133. Inexpensive. 1-5 and 7-11. Chicken on the spit, pigeon and excellent mezzas in outdoor dining. Casual. In winter, dine by the open fire.
Andreana Fish Restaurant 60 Mariutia Canal 851133. Inexpensive. 1-5 and 7-11. Fish shrimp and calamari served in a garden. Excellent dining. Casual.
Bonito Mariutia Canal, next to The Farm, 851870. Indoor and outdoor seafood restaurant with Turkish accent. Try the grilled fish. The premise has a children's playground area 11am-8pm.
Casino des Pigeons 153 Bahr al Aazam, south of Abbas Bridge on the Nile, 721299. TA. Cater. 10am-2am. Mezzas and pigeons in a variety of ways: stuffed, grilled and roasted.
Christo's 10 Pyramid Road, across from the Mena House, 853852. Average. Specializes in fish, shrimps, shish kebab, and chicken.
El Dar Sakkara Road 852289. Lunch and dinner. Average. Middle Eastern foods and grills.
Al Fanous 5 Wissa Wassef, off Sharia Nil, Riyad Tower 737592. Expensive. AX. No alcohol. 1-4:30 and 7:30-12. Excellent Moroccan food.
The Farm 23 Mariutia Canal 851870. Average. Follow the signs to good eating. Try the roast lamb.
Felfela Village 95 Mariutia Canal 861950. Average. 10-7. Good home-spun Egyptian food served up with dancing horses, bellydancers and other entertainment. Live shows on F and Sa only.
Lebanese Restaurant 287 Pyramids Road, in Vendome Hotel 850977. Average. AX,V. 24hrs.
Mashrabia Restaurant 4 Ahmed Nessim 725059. Expensive. All major cards. TA. Delivery. No alcohol. 11am-1am.
Sakkara Nest Sakkara Road, off Pyramids road, Shubramant 534109. Average. Grilled chicken and steaks.

Oriental Food
Chandani 5 Wissa Wassef, off Sharia Nil, Riyad Tower 737592. Expensive. AX. No alcohol. 7:30pm-12pm and Fridays 1-4. Jacket required. Good Indian food served in an elegant atmosphere.
Golden Dragon, Vendome Hotel, 287 Pyramids Road 850818/339/977. Average. TA. 12-11. Cantonese food.
Sakura 5 Wissa Wassef, off Sharia Nil, Riyad Tower 737592. Expensive. AX. No alcohol. 6:30pm to 12. Jacket required. Teppan-Yaki table cooking.

Fast Food
Kentucky Fried Chicken Pyramid Road. Cheap. 10am-12pm.
Rarian 445 Pyramid Road 859334. Cheap. Golden Card. TA. 12-12. Seafood take away.

Swiss Chalet Bar B Q 3 Ahmed Nessim. Noon-2am. Inexpensive. Charcoal broiled chicken.
Wimpy Pyramid Road; Sharia Manial; Sharia Murad. Cheap. TA. 9am-12pm.

Coffee, Tea and Ice Cream
Cafe Cairo 5 Wissa Wassef, off Sharia Nil, Riyad Tower 737592. Average. AX. No Alcohol.
10am-1am. Home made Italian pastas.

Heliopolis/Madinet Nasr
Hotel Dining
Le Baron Hotel Maahad al Sahara 291-5757/2467.
Le Baron Coffeeshop Average. All major cards. 24hr. International and Middle Eastern meals and snacks.
Pasha Bar Average. All major cards. 9am-2am. Cocktail lounge.
Pastry Shop Moderate. All major cards. TA. 9am-11pm. Pastries and beverages.
Le Jardin Average. All major cards. Daily buffet created along an Italian, Lebanese, Indian, Middle Eastern or BBQ theme.

Egyptel Hotel 93 Merghani 662258/304.
El Tarboush Restaurant Average. All major cards. 9am-11pm. Middle Eastern dining and grills.
Lord Average. All major cards. 24hr. Pizza specialties and continental cuisine.

Hyatt Al Salam Hotel Abdel Hamid Badawi 245-2155.
Cafe Jardin Average. All major cards. 24hr. Coffeeshop with nightly buffet.
Marquis Moderate. All major cards. TA. 9am-midnight. Lobby outlet with pastries, teas and beverages. Try the turnovers.
Ya Salam Nightclub Expensive. All major cards. 10pm-3am. Reservations and formal dress required.
Vito's Average. All major cards. 5pm-3am. Disco 11pm-closing. Italian specialties and disco. Minimum charge for the disco LE10.
Whispers All major cards. 11am-1am. Happy hour. Cocktail lounge and bar.

Movenpick Hotel Hurria, Cairo Airport   247-0077.
Il Giardino Moderate. All major cards. 11am-1am. Taverna with Italian snacks and live entertainment.
Gourmet Shop Moderate to Average. All major cards. TA. 7am-10:30pm. Pastry shop offering a wide variety of Swiss sweets.
Karawan 6pm-1am. Middle Eastern and oriental cuisine and barbecues in the garden.
Movenpick Average. All major cards. 24hr. International and Middle Eastern meals and snacks with a Swiss twist and special ice cream menu.
Papillon Disco 9pm-3am. Minimum charge weekdays LE10; Thurs LE15.
Al Sarraya Average. All major cards. 7pm-1am. Continental dining both a la carte and buffet.
St Germain Bar Average. All major cards. 11am-1am. Happy hour. Full range cocktails, pastries, and soups.

Novotel Hotel Cairo Airport 2914794 2455674.
Gazebo 10am-1am. Poolside snack bar with international buffets and live entertainment. 50% discount for children.
Gelateria 9am-1am. Ice cream parlor. Try the Coupe Hawaii.
Le Comptoir Average. All major cards. TA. 9am-midnight. Pastry shop.
Le Jardin d'Heliopolis Average. All major cards. 24hr. French dining.
Le Rendezvous Average. All major cards. 10am-1am. Cocktail lounge.

Sheraton Heliopolis Sharia Oruba (Airport Road) 667700 665500.
Alfredo's Expensive. All major cards. 6-11:30pm. Good Italian food.
Le Baron Expensive. All major cards. 9pm-closing. Disco
Bierstube Average. All major cards. Noon-3am. German cuisine and special food fests.
Al Halaka Expensive. All major cards. 7pm-11:30pm. Seafood with fresh fish.
King Tut Expensive. All major cards. 7:30pm-11:30pm. Elegant formal dining with good food and excellent service.
Oriental Tent Expensive. All major cards. 12noon-3am. Egyptian village atmosphere, with dancing and Egyptian buffet.
Al Sakia Average. All major cards. Minimum charge. 11am-1am. Bar with drinks and entertainment in a tropical setting.
Swan Pub Average. All major cards. 11:30am-2am. Victorian pub featuring English snacks and a buffet.
Vienna Cafe Moderate. TA. All major cards. 7am-11pm. Pastry in a sidewalk cafe.
Al Zahraa Average. All major cards. 24hrs. Coffeeshop offering a variety of cuisines via a daily buffet: Lebanese, Italian, International and Chinese.

Sonesta Hotel 4 Tayaran, MN 609444 611066.
Arabic Lounge Average. All major cards. 11am-2am. Cocktails.
Le Cafe Moderate. TA. All major cards. 10am-11pm. Pastries and breads.
The Garden Grill Expensive. All major cards. 8pm-12:30am. Summers only. Open air summer restaurant featuring grills.
Gondola Average. All major cards. 12-3 and 7-12. Italian dining.
Greenhouse Average. All major cards. 24hr. Coffeeshop with international meals and snacks.
Rib Room Expensive. All major cards. 7-12pm. Reservations recommended.
Sindbad 9:30pm-3am. Disco. Weekdays minimum charge LE10; Thurs and Sat LE15. Couples only. Reservations necessary for groups. Full attire.
Speke's Bar Average. All major cards. 11am-2am. Cocktail lounge.

Continental Food
La Terrine 105 Higaz, near Heliopolis Hospital HE 257-8634. Average. Excellent French cuisine.
Swissair Le Chantilly 11 Baghdad 669026. Average. All major cards. TA. 8am-12pm. Excellent continental cuisine.

Middle Eastern Food
Amphitrion al Ahram 258-1379. Inexpensive. TA. 7:30am-1am. Western and oriental dishes,

tea, coffee, etc. Ready made lunch boxes.
Andalusia Oriental Restaurant 8 Granada, Roxi 2581292. 1pm-midnight. Western and Egyptian food; outdoor cafe.
Five Stars 50 Khalifa al Mamun 2577563. TA and restaurant. Continental and Middle Eastern food and sweet specialties.
Karakeesh 126 Osman Ibn Affan 246-2727. Average. TA. Caters. 12-midnight. Egyptian food and deserts. Try the tawagen.
Om al Kora 30 Baghdad 662821. 11am-midnight. Closed Tuesday. TA. Caters. Delivery. Middle Eastern foods.

Oriental Food
Han's Baghdad, near Beirut Hotel. Average. Chinese, Korean.
Seoul House 4 Said Abdel Wahed, Roxi 258-1515. Average. 11-11. Korean food.

Fast Food
McBurger Midan Ismailia 661712. Cheap. TA. 10am-2am. McBurgers, McPies, McOnion rings and Mcmore.
Cafeteria Abu Heidar 13 Ibrahim al Lakkani, Roxi 257-0871. Cheap. TA. 8am-2pm. No alcohol. Take away with cafeteria offering Middle Eastern and American fast foods.
Chicken Tikka 5 Said Abdel Wahed, Roxi. Inexpensive. TA. 12-12. Pakistani takeaway.
New Kamal 22 Baghdad 663325. Cheap. TA. 8am-midnight. Pizzas, hamburgers and Middle Eastern fast foods.
Buset 1 Midan Roxi 257-1369. Inexpensive. TA. Deliver if nearby. 24hr. Middle Eastern food.
Wimpy 102 Merryland; 7 Sayed Abdel Wahed; and Khalifa al Mamun. Inexpensive. 9am-midnight.

Coffee, Tea and Ice Cream
Cafe Saint Germain 97 Higaz 245-5300. Average.TA. Deliver if nearby. 9am-midnight.

Khan al Khalili
Arafa Seif 14 Dubabia. Sweet fitiir.
Cafeteria Khan al Khalili 5 Badestan, next to the old gate, 903788. Managed by the Oberoi for Misr Travel this new restaurant offering western and oriental foods is scheduled to open in the fall of 1988.
Egyptian Pancakes 7 Khan al Khalili south of Sharia Muski 908623. Cheap. 12-12. Made to order fitiir with a wide selection of ingredients including jam and raisins, coconut, cream and raisins, honey, egg and cheese, butter and sugar, oil, and any combination of the above. Quick service sidewalk tables.
El Dahan, Chicken Home 82 Gawad el Kaed (Muski) near Midan Hussein 939278. Chicken Tikka.
Fishawi Khan al Khalili 906755. Inexpensive. 24hr. Considered the oldest coffeehouse in Cairo. Founded in 1773, five generations of the same family have managed this famous teahouse. Motto: Never been closed or shut down for over 200 years. Frequented by artists and famous people. Mint tea, coffee, sheesha with tobacco from India.

Hagg Sai'd il Zorbi corner of Muski and Midan Hussein, on the square. 11am to 2-3am. Kebab and kufta.
El Hussein Midan Hussein, Khan al Khalili. Inexpensive. 8am-midnight. Rooftop outdoor dining overlooking Midan Hussein.
Mustafa Yusef il Gahaer on Midan Hussein. Newly opened vegetarian restaurant featuring Egyptian salads, oven dishes and pastas. 11am-2am.
Salem Ahmed Salem Midan Hussein 910844. Candy stand.

Maadi

Hotel Dining
Maadi Hotel Misr Helwan Road. 350-5050.
Regency Restaurant Average. Ax, Visa. 11-4 and 6-12. French and Middle Eastern dining.
Coffeeshop All major cards. 24hr. Middle Eastern and continental food.
Bar Average. 9am-1am. Cocktail lounge.
Takeaway Average. TA. 12:30-1:30. French and Middle Eastern pastries.

Pearle Hotel Road 82, off Road 6. 350-5313.
Restaurant Average. TA. 24hr. Full service restaurant offering French cuisine.

Residence Hotel 11 Road 18 351-0825 350-7189.
Flash 8pm-1am. Disco
Palma Restaurant Average. All major cards. Noon-11:30pm. French and Middle Eastern specialities.
Terrace Average. All major cards. 11am-1am. American style bar.

Continental Food
Aberdeen Steak House 67 Road 9 350-8730. Average. Catering. 12-12. Charcoal grilled steak in a friendly atmosphere.
Fouquets Nasr, New Maadi 352-3450. Expensive. TA. 11:30am-12:30pm. Italian, grills and seafood.
Lola Grill House 15 Road 9b 351-5587. Expensive. Ax, Visa. TA. Cater. 6pm-1am French menu. 12-midnight, Italian menu.
Lolita's 15 Road 9b 351-5587. Average. TA. Caters. 12am-1pm. Italian pastas and pizza. Seafood. Thursday evening BBQ. Pleasant atmosphere and good eating.
Mama Lola's 15 Road 9b 351-5587. Expensive. TA. Caters. 12am-1pm. French and Italian meals with an emphasis on seafood. Occasional entertainment. Try the mocha cheesecake.
Mermaid 77 Road 9 350-3964. Average. TA. 9am-11:30pm. Alcohol. Small restaurant with good Italian food. Try the pizzas.
Mermaid Steak House 77 Road 9 350-3964. Average. 11-midnight. 11 kinds of steak a la carte.
Nile Garden Corniche 350-5121. Average. 9am-3pm. Offers full services, nightclub, children's playground and good food, including Mexican, in an open air atmosphere along the Nile.
Petit Swiss Chalet 9 Road 151 351-8328. Average. TA. 9am-12pm. Good family place featuring Italian pastas and pizzas.
Pub 13 Road 13 350-4544. Average. 10am-12pm. Variety of foods and entertainment.

Middle Eastern Food
Abu Shakra New Club Road, next to Cinema Fontana, New Maadi 352-1145. Average. TA. Caters. 10am-11pm. Branch of the famous restaurant on Kasr al Aini.
Andrea's 47 Road 7 351-139. Average. TA. Caters. Branch of the famous restaurant along the Kerdassa road.
Good Shot Corniche, at Maadi fountain, 350-3327. Average. TA. 8am-12pm. Oriental food served up open-air along the Nile. Occasional entertainment and skeet shooting.
Seahorse Corniche, at the Nile Badawi Hospital exit, 988499. 12:30-5 and 7-11. Average. Excellent seafood in an open air restaurant along the Nile. In winter, cozy room with fireplace.

Oriental Food
Cho's 7A Road 252 Digla 352-6118. Average. TA. 11am-11pm. Korean and Chinese food.
Four Seasons 12 Mustafa Kamel 351-6218. Expensive. 12-12. Korean and Chinese food.
Walima Good Shot Corniche al Nil, 350-3327. Expensive. TA. Cater. Deliver when nearby. 10am-midnight. Korean and Chinese food.

Fast Food
Astra 90 Road 9 350-2473. Cheap. TA. 10am-11pm. Egyptian food. Deliver when nearby.
Happy Joe's 67 Road 9 350-1526. Inexpensive. TA. Delivery. 10am-12pm. Family restaurant with pizza and ice cream. Will cater parties on premises.
Kentucky Fried Chicken Road 9. Inexpensive.

Coffee, Tea and Ice Cream
Dairy King 5 Road 204, Digla. Ice cream parlor.
La Dolce Vita Ice Cream Parlor 21 Misr Helwan Road, next to the Maadi Hotel. Inexpensive. Excellent home-made ice cream and cones in a variety of flavors including butterscotch, mocha and mint.
Meringo 100 Corniche 350-4337. Inexpensive. TA. 8am-11pm. Bakery with small coffeeshop on premises.
Al Tounsia 9 Road 151 351-8328. Inexpensive. Bakery with small coffeeshop on premise.

Mohandiseen
Hotel Dining
Atlas Zamalek 20 Gamat al Dowal al Arabiya. 346-4175/6569.
Chez Zanouba Average. All major cards. 10am-11pm. Middle Eastern dining.
Kahraman Average. All major cards. French dining.
Tamango Disco Average. All major cards. 10pm-3am. Reservations advised. Disco mania in the hottest dance spot in Cairo.

Cairo Inn 26 Syria 346-0661/0662.
Eagle Arms English Pub. Average. All major cards. 24hrs. Pub atmosphere and continental food.
Espana Average. All major cards. 24hr. Spanish food and entertainment.
Taberna Espanola Average. All major cards. 24hrs with Spanish entertainment in the evening. Excellent Spanish foods.

Continental Food

Bon Appetit 21 Wadi al Nil 346-4937. TA. Ax, Visa. Deliver when nearby. 7am-2am.

Da Baffo 15 Batal Ahmed Abdel Aziz 346-7490 344-8468. 9am-2am. Italian and Swiss cuisine.

La Casetta 32 Kambis 348-7970. Average. TA. Deliver when nearby. 1pm-3am. Closed Monday. Italian food and pizza.

Kahraman 20 Gamat al Dowal al Arabiya 346-4175. Average. All major cards. 12-12. Classic French restaurant.

Prestige 43 Geziret al Arab 347-0383. Average. All major cards. TA. Deliver when nearby. 12pm-2am. Sidewalk cafe.

Swiss Chalet al Nakhil 10 Nakhil 707799. Inexpensive. All major cards. 12 noon to 2am. A variety of fares including pizza.

Tia Maria 32 Jeddah 713273. Average. 11am-11pm. Home-made pastas and Italian dishes in a friendly atmosphere.

Tirol 38 Geziret al Arab 344-9725. Inexpensive. Noon-1am. Austrian food in a casual atmosphere.

El Yotti 44 Mohi al Din Abu al Ezz 349-4944. Average. 12:30pm-2am.

Middle Eastern Food

Baba's 164 26th July, Agouza 347-1194. Inexpensive. TA. Caters. 9am-2am.

Bent al Sultan Behind the Shooting Club, Midan al Thawra 360-1213. Restaurant. Expensive. Turkish and Lebanese menu. Sweet shop of Arabic/Turkish sweets. Inexpensive. TA.

Kahila 22 Abd al Hamid Lotfi 704558 348-0289. Average. TA. 8am-1am. Restaurant 12:30pm-2am.

El Khedawi 35 Syria 347-6636. Inexpensive. TA. Noon-1am. Middle Eastern foods.

Petra 3 Surnadi 347-1367. Average. TA. 11-11. Jordanian food.

Sphinx 162 26th July 346-3215. Average. TA. Caters. 9am-1pm. Egyptian entrees with emphasis on seafoods.

Oriental Food

Paxy 26th July at Midan Sphinx 346-1434. Average. TA. Caters. 11-11. Japanese, Chinese and Korean cuisine.

Naniwa 3 Libnan 346-5943. Average. AX. TA. Caters. 1-4 and 7-11. Excellent Japanese food.

Tandoori 11 Shehab 348-6301. Average. All major cards. TA. 12-12. No alcohol. Indian curries and grills in a casual atmosphere.

Fast Food

Fast Foods 64 Libnan 346-5350. Cheap. TA. 10am-12am. Pizzas and Egyptian specialities.

Kentucky Fried Chicken 47 Batal Ahmed Abdel Aziz 344-8673. TA. 10am-1am. The Colonel's best.

McBurger 16 Gamat al Dowal al Arabiya 344-2410. Cheap. TA. 9am-2am. It's all here. Burgers, pies, onion rings, the works.

Queen 12 Wadi al Nil 346-7921. 7am-midnight. Hamburgers, chicken burgers and Egyptian sandwiches.

Show In 11 Abbas al Akkad 260-9189. Cheap. TA. Chicken burgers and assorted sandwiches.

Tikka 47 Batal Ahmed Abdel Aziz 346-0393. Inexpensive. TA. Delivery. 10am-12pm. No

alcohol. Egyptian and Indian dishes.
Wienerwald Batal Ahmed Abdel Aziz 346-6940. Inexpensive. TA. 12-12. Egypt's division of the famous Bavarian chain of fast dining. German and Austrian dishes served up in fast order.
Wimpy 49 Batal Ahmed Abdel Aziz. Inexpensive. TA. 8am-1am.

Coffee, Tea and Ice Cream
Cafe Saint Germain 59 Zahraa 717867. Inexpensive. TA. 7:30am-Midnight. Bakery with coffeeshop on the premises.
Cookie Man 21 Aden, off Shehab. Inexpensive. TA. 9am-10pm.
Cookies like Mamma used to make. Chocolate chip, coffee walnut and many more.
Dairy King 46 Nadi al Seid 348-3000. Ice cream parlor.
Le Glacier 74 Gamat al Dowal al Arabiya 349-3884. Inexpensive. TA. Deliver when nearby. 9am-11pm. Sorbets, biscuits and sweets.
Pharaoh's Coffee Shop 12 Lotfi Hassouna 712314. Inexpensive. All major cards. 24hr. Serves a buffet daily.
Samadi Batal Ahmed Abdel Aziz 344-8671. Middle East sweets and ice cream parlor.

Lounges and Bars
Kutcher Bar 15 Batal Ahmed Abdel Aziz 344-8468. Expensive. All major cards. Cocktail lounge and dinner. Swiss cuisine .

Zamalek
Hotel Dining
  Horus House Hotel 21 Ismail Mohammed 340-3977/3182/3634.
Restaurant Average. TA. Small. British atmosphere.

  Cairo Marriott Saray al Gezira 340-8888.
Almaz Nightclub Expensive. All major cards. 10pm-3am. Summer nightclub.
Empress Nightclub Expensive. All major cards. 10pm-3am. Reservations required. Winter nightclub.
Eugenie's Lounge   Average. All major cards. 11am - 2am. Happy Hour from 5-9pm. Elegant atmosphere.
Garden Promenade Cafe Moderate. All major cards. 10am-midnight Open air cafe in the Khedive Ismail's garden.
Gezira Grill Expensive. All major cards. 1-4 and 7-11. French cuisine elegantly served in the former billiard rooms of the Gezira Palace.
Omar's Cafe Average. All major cards. 24hr. Coffeeshop with good snacks and dining.
Roy Rogers Moderate. All major cards. TA. 12-12. Mexican salad bar, hamburgers and other fast foods.
The View Average. All major cards. 11am-2pm. Elegant atmosphere with a panorama of the city.

  El Nil Zamalek Hotel 21 Maahad al Swissri 340-1846/0220.
Restaurant Inexpensive. TA. Students and year-abroads' hang out. Video.

President Hotel 22 Taha Hussein 341-6751/3195 340-0718.
B'S Corner Average. All major cards. 11am-closing. Bar and Restautant.
Le Bec Sucre Average. All major cards. TA. 10am-midnight. French pastries and snacks.
Cairo Cellar Average. All major cards. 12am-2am. Excellent food. Mezzas a speciality.
La Terrace Average. All major cards. Noon-1am. Rooftop restaurant with International and Middle Eastern cuisine.

Safir 21 Mohammed Mazhar 342-0055.
Abu Nawas Bar 5pm-2am. Cocktail lounge.
Afandina Average. 7am-2am. Continental and Middle Eastern buffets.
Grill Garden Average. 8pm-midnight. A variety of meat and chicken grills served in the garden, under a tent.
Salmeya Coffeeshop 24hr.

Continental Food
Angus Brasserie 34 Yehia Ibrahim 341-1321. Average. Most major cards. TA. Caters. 12-12. Charcoal grill specialties. Can be rented for a party.
Il Capo 22 Taha Hussein 341-3870. Inexpensive. TA. 12-4 and 7-12. Specialized in pastas, pizzas and antipastos.
La Cloche D'Or 3 Abu al Feda 340-2314/2268. Expensive. TA. 12-midnight. Excellent decor and excellent French cuisine.
Don Quichotte 9A Ahmed Hishmat 340-6415. Expensive. 12:30-3:30 and 7:30-11:30. European cuisine with some Middle Eastern specialities.
Five Bells 9 Adel Abu Bakr 340-8980/8635. Average. AX. TA. Caters. 12:30pm-1am. Choice of garden dining.
Justine's 4 Hasan Sabri 341-2961. Expensive. All major cards. 12:30-3 and 7:30-11. Elegant formal dining at Four Corners.
La Mediterranee 13A Mohammed Marashli. Average. 12:30-5 and 7-12. Specializes in seafood.
El Patio 5 Sayed al Bakry 340-2645. Average. AX,V. TA. Caters. 9am-1pm. Excellent Argentinian food in a casual atmosphere.
La Piazza 4 Hasan Sabri 340-4385. Average. All major cards. 12:30-12. Featuring Italian food in a pleasant atmosphere at Four Corners. Casual.
Pub 28 28 Shagaret al Dorr 340-0972. Average. TA. 12am-1pm. Mezzas and dinners. Good dining. Bar.
Romantica 23 Ismail Mohammed 341-9991. Average. TA. Catering. Happy Hour. Private parties. Dancing.

Middle Eastern Food
Omar Khayyam Saray al Gezira 340-8553. Average. 12-4pm; 8pm-1am. Dining and entertainment on a boat moored along the Nile.

Oriental Food
Balmoral Hotel Chinese Restaurant 157 26th July 340-6761. Average. TA. 12am-10pm. Cantonese food in a casual atmosphere.

Hana Korean Restaurant 21 Maahad al Swissri. Average. TA. 12am-10pm. Korean and Japanese food.
Japanese Restaurant 2 Sayed al Bakri 341-0502. Average. TA. Caters. 10-3 and 6-12. Closed Saturday.
Tokyo 4 Maahad al Swissri. Average. TA. Delivery nearby. 12-3 and 6-11. Authentic Japanese food in a casual atmosphere.

Fast Food
Big Bite 2 Taha Hussein 340-7601. Average. TA. 10am-2am. Lunchtime delivery. Sandwiches, submarines and grills.
Cafeteria Friends 1A Sayed al Bakri 340-3891. Inexpensive. TA. 9am-12pm. Burgers, kebab.
Flamenco Pastries 11 Abu al Feda 340-0815/6/8/9. Average. Breads, croissants, and cakes.
Ghranim 130 26th July. Cheap. TA. Chicken, kebab and kufta.
El Gumhuria 132 26th July 341-7981. Broiled chicken, kebab and kufta to take out.

Coffee, Tea and Ice Cream
Queen Grill House Midan Sedqi 340-1846. Moderate. TA. AX,V. 10am-12pm. French, American and Oriental foods in a casual atmosphere.
Simonds 112 26th July 340-9436. Inexpensive. TA. 8am-9pm. Closed on Shamm al Nasim. Small coffee shop with pastries and excellent expresso and cappuccino.

Lounges and Bars
Matchpoint 4 Hasan Sabri 341-2961. Expensive. All major cards. 1pm-2:30am. Snacks amid a pub-like atmosphere of fun and games. Minimum charge 1pm-9pm LE6; 9pm-1:30am LE8.

Floating Restaurants
Nile Pharaoh Docks at 31 Nil, Gi 726713. Average. All major cards. Lunch cruise 2:30-4. Summer early dinner cruise 7:15-9. Dinner cruise 9:30-12. Simulates a Pharaonic boat complete with lotus decor.
Scarabee Docks across from Shepheard's Hotel 984967. Lunch at 2:30 and dinner at 9:30.

SPORTS FEDERATIONS

By consulting the Sporting Clubs or the Sports Federations listed below a sports enthusiast can find all the information available on facilities, lessons, competitions, tournaments, etc.

General Federations
Armed Forces Sports Federation Kubri al Kubba HE --------------------823126 836051
Police Sports Federation Dar Sak al Nokoud, Darrasa ------------------------------826505
Sports Federation for Companies 9 Sherifein ----------------------------- 741568 751842
Sports Federation for Universities 14 Harun al Rashid DO --------------------348-1130

African Federations

Basketball Federation 10 26th July -- 930292
Billiards Federation 83 Ramsis --- 744934
Football Federation 5 Um Kalthoum, Gezira------------------------------------- 341-6730
Karate Federation 13 Dar al Shifa GC --- no phone
Long Distance Swimming Federation
   Egyptian Federation Houseboat
   Corniche al Nil GC --- 354-7128
Table Tennis Federation 2 Mustafa Abu Heif,
   Bab al Louk-- 740108
Volleyball Federation 2 26th July-- 930567
Weightlifting Federation 13 Kasr al Nil --- 753296

Olympic Federations

Basketball Federation 10 26th July -- 918575
Boxing Federation 5 Talaat Harb --- 742732
Cycling Federation Education Ministry Pool (temporary)------------------------- 805988
Fencing Federation Ezbekia Gardens
   Fencing Club Building --- 920120 912513
Football Federation 5 Um Kalthoum, Gezira -------------------------- 340-1793 341-3730
Gymnastics Federation 32 Sabri Abu Alam --- 743026
Handball Federation 13 Kasr al Nil--- 753296
Hockey Federation 44 Kasr al Aini -- 354-0491
Horseback Riding Federation 13 Kasr al Nil--------------------------------------- 753296
Judo Federation 50 Gumhuria-- 900361
Rowing Federation 3 Shawarbi, Kasr al Nil -- 754350
Shooting Federation 37 Abdel Khalek Sarwat ------------------------------------- 916955
Swimming Federation 16 26th July
   Midan Sphinx Apt 13 MO --- 347-1725
Table Tennis Federation 2 Mustafa Abu Heif,
   Bab al Louk-- 740108
Tennis Federation 13 Kasr al Nil--- 753235
Track and Field Federation 13 Kasr al Nil -- 740722
Volleyball Federation 2 26th July-- 930567
Weightlifting Federation 13 Kasr al Nil --- 753269
Wrestling Federation 13 Kasr al Nil-- 753296
Yachting and Water Skiing Federation
   Federation Houseboat, Sharia al Nil,
   near University Bridge, Manial --------------------------------- 901852 936745

Non-Olympic Federations

Ball Federation 28 Sherif, Apt 9 --- 750748
Billiards Federation (see African above).
Body-Building Federation al Shahid Abdel Ghani Mansour,
   behind Ahmed Maher Hospital -- 912272

Chess Federation Gezira Sporting Club --- 340-6000
Croquet Federation Gezira Sporting Club --- 340-6000
Diving and Swimming Federation Gabalaya,
    in front of National Sporting Club -- no phone
Fishing Federation --- no phone
Handicapped, General Federation for the
    Higher Council for Youth and Sports -- no phone
Karate Federation Leadership and Youth Institute
    Madinet Nasr --- 837753
Long Distance Swimming Federation Federation Houseboat
    Corniche al Nil, GC -- 354-7128
Parachuting Federation Galaa,
    Al Ahram Newspaper --- 755000 745666
Polo Federation 13 Kasr al Nil -- 753296
Squash Federation Heliopolis Sporting Club HE ------------------------------------ 604585
Tae Kwan Do Federation Police Sports Federation ------------------------------- 340-7687

SYNDICATES

Acting 1 26th July --- 391-2174
Administrative & Social 3B Mohammed Haggag ------------------------------------ 742134
Agriculture 21 Mansour, Bab al Louk -- 354-1419/1387
Agriculture Vocations Shann, Off Galaa ----------------------------- 766305/8968 779192
Air Transport 62 Osman Ibn Affan HE --- 243-6149
Applied Arts 70 Gumhuria --- 913504 931122
Banks 5 Kasr al Nil --- 710149
Building and Timber 9 Emad al Din --- 932207/2251
Cartel 30 Ramses -- 750411/7763
Cinema Careers 20 Adli --- 756687
Dentists 6 al Hadika, GC --- 356-1098
Educational Services 91 Maglis al Shaab -- 340-1302
Engineering Metallic and Electrical
Industries 90 Galaa --- 742519/859
Engineers 30 Ramses -- 750494/2675
Food Industries 3 Hosni, Hadayek al Kubba --------------------------- 834181/080 824176
Health Services Galaa, 7th floor --- 835376
Instructors GI --- 801302 808333
Lawyers 2 Abd al Khalek Sarwat --- 741055/1227
Military Production 90 Galaa -- no phone
Mines and Salines 5 Ali Shaarawi, Hadayek al Kubba ---------------------- 820887/2129
Musicians 1 Sabri Abu Alam -- 742563
Nursing 5 al Saray, Manial --- 987627

Petroleum and Chemicals 90 Galaa --- no phone
Pharmacists Kasr al Aini,
Dar al Hekma Bldg. GC --- no phone
Physicians 42 Kasr al Aini --- 354-0738/3166
Press 4 Abd al Khalek Sarwat --- 770522/331
Press Printing and Information 90 Galaa ------------------------------------- 742836/0556
Public Utilities 30 Sherif --- 758293
Railway 15 Emad al Din --- 930305
Scientific Professions 8 Bustan al Dikka ------------------------------------- 901265/05/16
Spinning & Weaving 327 Taher, Shubra --------------------------------------- 940519 941599
Teachers ZA --- 340-8333/1302
Tourism & Hotels 66 Galaa, 6th floor --- no phone
Transport 90 Galaa --- 754919/2955
Trade 70 Gumhuria -- 936904 902780

INDEX TO MAPS

See note on transliteration page xv